D0984479

SACRA DOCTRINA

SACRA DOCTRINA

REASON AND REVELATION IN AQUINAS

by Per Erik Persson

Translated by
ROSS MACKENZIE

BASIL BLACKWELL
OXFORD

A translation of
SACRA DOCTRINA
En studie till förhållandet mellan ratio
och revelatio i Thomas' av Aquino teologi
(Studia Theologica Lundensia, No. 15)
published by
C. W. K. GLEERUP,
Lund, Sweden
1957

631 11860 8

Library of Congress Catalog Card No.:
69–14383

Printed in Great Britain by
Western Printing Services Ltd, Bristol
Bound by Kemp Hall Bindery, Oxford

PREFACE TO THE ENGLISH EDITION

Twelve years have passed since this book was published in its Swedish edition. During that time, research on Thomas Aquinas has gone on further. It is a great pleasure for me that the English translation now makes my work available also for students outside the Scandinavian language barrier, but I regret that it has not been possible for me to update my discussion with regard to the publications in this field during the last ten years. There was, however, no time for the rewriting that would have been necessary. As my primary intention with this study was not to debate with Thomists but to give an introduction to the thought-world of Thomas Aquinas himself, I hope that the book may still be a useful tool for those interested in this exciting period of the history of Christian theology.

In this connection I would also like to express my sincere thanks to the translator, Dr Ross Mackenzie, and to the editors. Without their interest and laborious efforts, this book would never have come to the reader.

Lund, February 1969   PER ERIK PERSSON

CONTENTS

CONTENTS

SUMMA THEOLOGIAE

Latin text and English translations,
Introductions, Notes, Appendices
and Glossaries

Blackfriars in conjunction with Eyre & Spottiswoode, London
and McGraw-Hill Book Co. Inc., New York

General Editor: Thomas Gilby, O.P.

The following list gives the division of the SUMMA into volumes (some
of the titles being provisional). Those volumes not yet published are
marked with an asterisk.

PRIMA PARS

PRIMA SECUNDÆ

SECUNDA SECUNDÆ

TERTIA PARS

ABBREVIATIONS

Abbreviations for the works of Thomas are as follows:

Summa theologiae, without title: 1a = Pars Prima: 1a2ae = Pars Prima Secundae; 2a2ae = Pars Secunda Secundae; 3a = Pars Tertia; Suppl. = Supplementum. Part, question, article and reply are given as follows: e.g. 1a, 3, 2, ad 3 = Pars Prima, question 3, article 2, reply 3.

CG = *Summa contra gentiles*. Book, chapter; e.g. *CG* II, 12.

Sent. = *Scriptum super libros sententiarum Magistri Petri Lombardi*. Book, distinction, question, article, solution and reply; e.g. III *Sent*. 25, 2, 3, ii, ad 3.

Compend. Theol. = *Compendium Theologiae*.

De Ver. = *Quaestiones disputatae de veritate*. Question, article; e.g. *De Ver*. 14, 11.

De Pot. = *Quaestiones disputatae de potentia*. Question, article; e.g. *De Pot*. 7, 3.

In De Trin. = *In librum Boethii de Trinitate*. Question, article; e.g. *In De Trin*. 2, 3.

Quodl. = *Quaestiones quodlibetales*. *Quodlibetum septimum*, article; e.g. *Quodl*. 7, 14.

In symb. Apost. = *In symbolum Apostolorum expositio*. Article; e.g. *In symb. Apost*. 9.

In De div. nom. = *In librum Dionysii De divinis nominibus*.

Contra Graec., Arm. et Sarac. = *Declaratio quorundam articulorum contra Graecos, Armenos et Saracenos*.

Commentaries on scripture are given as follows: e.g. *In Joan.* = Commentary on John; Epistles of Paul, e.g. *In ad Rom.* = Commentary on the Epistle of Paul to the Romans. Chapter, verse, paragraph as required; e.g. *In 2 ad Cor*. 2, 1 (455).

Other frequently used abbreviations are as follows:

p. = page, pages

col. = column, columns

INTRODUCTION

1

THOMAS AS MAGISTER IN SACRA PAGINA

The period known as high scholasticism has traditionally been associated with the revival of philosophy which followed the rediscovery of Aristotle, whose work was mediated to the Middle Ages through Arabic and Jewish philosophy. The importance which the Roman Catholic Church in particular attaches to the study of scholasticism is demonstrated from the end of the nineteenth century onwards in what is called neo-scholasticism and more especially in neo-Thomism. This study has given us a great many scholarly works by which our knowledge of the scholastic period has been enriched. It has also given us a wholly new insight into the crucial disputes of a period in the history of thought which has not hitherto received sufficient attention. Above all, of course, it has brought Thomas Aquinas into the centre of scholarly research.[1]

This renaissance of scholastic thought among Roman Catholic theologians is to some extent paralleled among Protestant theologians, for instance in the corresponding revival of Luther studies. While, however, Luther studies have moved in a recognisably *theological* direction, neo-scholasticism has been markedly preoccupied with *philosophical questions.*[2] Thus the concepts of Thomas have very often been expressed in neo-Thomism as an alternative position in a continuing philosophical debate. But this has meant that the historical study of Thomas has often been determined by

---

[1] For a summary of neo-Thomist literature see P. Mandonnet and J. Destrez, *Bibliographie thomiste* (Bibliothèque thomiste 1), Kain 1921; V. J. Bourke, *Thomistic Bibliography 1920–1940*, St. Louis 1945; P. Wyser, *Thomas von Aquin* (Bibliographische Einführungen in das Studium der Philosophie 13/14), Bern 1950, and the same author's *Der Thomismus* (Bibliographische Einführungen in das Studium der Philosophie 15/16), Bern 1951.

[2] While neo-Scholasticism has concentrated on questions of philosophy and the philosophy of religion, in modern Roman Catholic theology historical research has had a purely *theological* character and has focussed rather on patristic studies, biblical theology and the history of liturgy. On the significance of this return to pre-Scholastic sources see R. Aubert, *La théologie catholique au milieu du XXe siècle*, Tournai-Paris 1954.

modern questions which are unrelated to the content of his philosophy, and this at times has impeded the purely historical study of his world of thought.

The assumption that his basic philosophical concepts represent a *philosophia perennis* valid for all time has obscured the fact that Thomas, like all major thinkers of high scholasticism, was primarily a *theologian* and must therefore be understood as such. Any study of Thomas will become one-sided, and in the last resort misleading, if we simply take our point of departure in the characteristic interest shown by the high Middle Ages in Greek philosophy and above all in Aristotelianism. Thomas did indeed write commentaries on the writings of Aristotle, but he never thought of this as his primary task. It is significant that he himself never provided the kind of comprehensive discussion of his 'philosophy' which we can find in the writings of the neo-Thomists.

The explanation of this is that within the thought of high scholasticism, and therefore of Thomas as well, two movements are to be discerned—first a re-orientation in philosophy, and also (a frequently neglected factor) a renewal of the study of the *Bible*. Recent studies have focussed our attention still more closely on the 'return to the gospel'[3] which is to be found throughout the whole church from the middle of the twelfth century onwards. H. Grundmann has given us a lively and well-documented picture of the religious movements of the period in the church in the West, and indeed has shown us precisely how the study of the Bible inspired these differing attempts to reform the life of the church and to restore the 'evangelical' pattern of life.[4] This is true in particular of the mendicant preachers who are found throughout the church, and of the disciple bands who gathered around them in an attempt to realise the ideal of 'apostolic' poverty. We know from a study of church history how these biblically inspired movements were at first misunderstood and rejected by the leaders of the church, and to begin with were totally excluded from the fellowship of the church as were, for instance, the Waldensians. Later the need for renewal was recognised, however, and the newly constituted mendicant orders, adopted the aims and fulfilled the purposes of the 'revival movements' *within* the church.

[3] The term is from M.-D. Chenu, *Toward Understanding Saint Thomas*, Chicago 1964, p. 44.
[4] H. Grundmann, *Religiöse Bewegungen im Mittelalter* (Historische Studien 267), Berlin 1935.

In this connection, the name of the order of the Dominicans, *Ordo praedicatorum*, is significant. B. Smalley has shown us in her remarkable study *The Bible in the Middle Ages* how this renewal also had its effect on the work of theologians, both in the seclusion of the cloister and in the universities also.[5] Hence we find in this period not only an intensified study of the Latin Bible in order to produce a more accurate text,[6] and the appearance of translations into the vernacular for the purposes of evangelism,[7] but a deepened and productive study also of the content of the Bible.[8] The study of the holy scriptures which was previously undertaken in the solitude of the cloister or in the closed circle of the monastic community became part of the open and public *studium generale* of the university, with its teeming intellectual life.[9] The object of this study was no longer private edification but the acquisition of knowledge, as in the case of every other subject studied. As a consequence theological study began to move in a wholly new direction along the lines laid down by the religious movements and mendicant orders referred to above. It is no accident that these are the orders which took the lead in the theological faculties and supplied the teachers who drew around themselves throngs of students. This is particularly true of the University of Paris,[10] where in the middle of the thirteenth century the leading figures are a Dominican, Thomas, and a Franciscan, Bonaventure. It was in this way, as M.-D. Chenu has shown, that a direct connection was established between those earlier, biblically inspired attempts to renew the church and theological studies at the university.[11] One particular example of this is the dominant place

[5] B. Smalley, *The Study of the Bible in the Middle Ages*, Oxford 1941.
[6] See in this connection H. Denifle, 'Die Handschriften der Bibel-Correctorien des 13. Jahrhunderts', in *Archiv für Literatur- und Kirchengeschichte des Mittelalters* (=*ALKMA*) 4 (1888), p. 263ff. and C. Spicq, *Esquisse d'une historie de l'exégèse latine au moyen âge* (Bibliothèque thomiste 26), Paris 1944, p. 165ff.
[7] Chenu, *Saint Thomas*, p. 241.
[8] See Smalley's conclusion in her work cited above; 'The twelfth century rediscovered biblical scholarship; the thirteenth rediscovered exegesis', *Study*, p. 266f.
[9] H. Denifle, *Die Entstehung der Universitäten des Mittelalters bis 1400*, vol. I, Berlin 1885, has a good introduction to the problems connected with the growth of the universities. On the term *studium generale* see especially p. 1ff.
[10] See also especially F. X. Seppelt, *Der Kampf der Bettelorden an der Universität Paris in der Mitte des 13. Jahrhunderts* (Kirchengeschichtliche Abhandlungen 3), Breslau 1905, p. 199ff.
[11] Chenu, *Saint Thomas*, p. 44ff. and 234ff. See especially p. 242: 'It is the reawakening to the Gospel, however, that comes first in theology's development. . . It is no chance happening if the XIIIth century leaders of the theological enterprise are recruited from among the sons of the evangelicals of the beginning of the

B

given to the Bible in the teaching of the university. The significance of this will become clearer if we study briefly Thomas's own work as a teacher.

In 1252, having completed his basic study of philosophy and theology first at Paris and afterwards at Cologne under the direction of Albertus Magnus, Thomas Aquinas returned to Paris to prepare for his examination as *magister*. His first responsibility as *baccalaureus biblicus* was to work through the books of the Bible *secundum modum parisiensem* (according to the manner of Paris). This was a pedagogical method which spread from Paris to other universities and consisted in a brief but detailed survey of the books of the Bible with the help of glosses and parallel texts.[12] For the students of divinity this was their first experience of theological instruction and it attempted to provide an elementary but basic knowledge both of the biblical text itself and of its subject-matter. The whole of the Bible was surveyed in this way in daily lectures over a period of three years. After working as a *biblicus* for two years Thomas was promoted to *baccalaureus sententiarum* in 1254, which meant that he had now to expound the four books of Peter Lombard's *Sentences*. This collection of dogmatic teachings had slowly grown in popularity after being explicitly recommended by the Lateran Council in 1215, and from about 1230 it was universally accepted as the official text-book for theological instruction—a position which it retained throughout the Middle Ages. Thomas spent two years working through the text, and to this period is to be dated the greater part of his *Commentary on the Sentences* (some of it was clearly revised later by Thomas himself). This, the most notable of his early writings to survive, proved that Thomas at 30 was a theologian of more than ordinary capabilities.[13]

century—the Minors and the Preachers—and not in the old corporations'. See the same author's 'Évangélisme et théologie au XIIIe siècle', in *Mélanges offerts au R. P. Ferdinand Cavallera* (=*MFC*), Toulouse 1948, p. 339ff.

[12] Nothing of Thomas's teaching survived from this period except the inaugural course rediscovered at the beginning of the twentieth century; see Chenu, *Saint Thomas*, p. 243. For a detailed treatment of this and his other theological courses see especially, in addition to Chenu, the discussion in P. Mandonnet, 'Chronologie des écrits scripturaires de saint Thomas d'Aquin' in *Revue thomiste* (=*RT*) 33 (1928) and 34 (1929), an essay which contains much more than the title seems to indicate. There is a good summary in J. van der Ploeg, 'The place of Holy Scripture in the theology of St. Thomas' in *The Thomist*, 10 (1947), p. 404ff.

[13] See also Chenu, *Saint Thomas*, p. 264ff. The *Commentary on the Sentences* provided Thomas's companion and amanuensis, Reginald of Piperno, with the text of the *Supplementum* with which he completed the *Summa theologiae* after his master's death.

In 1256 Thomas was promoted to *magister*, which means that once again he concentrated in his teaching on the exposition of the Bible. While he would assign the more elementary instruction in the Bible and the exposition of Lombard to his two assistant instructors, the *baccalaureus biblicus* and *baccalaureus sententiarum*, the latter having the higher position, still the special responsibility of the professor was to study the books of the Bible at a deeper level. According to the Parisian system of instruction, which all other centres of learning were quick to follow, the teaching of the *magister* ordinarily consisted in required lectures on selected books of the Bible.[14] The central position accorded to the Bible as a text-book for higher theological instruction is also expressed in the official title conferred on the professor of divinity at his promotion—*doctor* or *magister in sacra pagina*, i.e. teacher of holy scripture.[15] The first hours of the morning were set aside for this biblical exegesis, from the point of view of

[14] Mandonnet in *RT* 33 (1928), p. 35: 'Au XIIe siècle et pendant les deux siècles suivants . . . dans toutes les écoles de théologie, grandes ou petites, celui qui en a a la direction, sous le nom de maître, docteur, régent ou lecteur, a pour mission première et essentielle de lire et interpreter le texte de la sainte Écriture'.

[15] On the term *magister in sacra pagina* see J. de Ghellinck, ' "Pagina" et "Sacra Pagina". Histoire d'un mot et transformation de l'objet primitivement désigné', in *Melanges Auguste Pelzer*, (=*MAP*) (Université de Louvain. Recueil de travaux d'histoire et de philologie, Sér. 3:26, Louvain 1947) p. 23ff. This title was preserved longest in conservative England but elsewhere had usually been replaced in the thirteenth century by what was regarded as a synonymous term, *magister in theologia*. This in no way altered the fact, however, that the main task of the *magister* was and continued to be biblical exegesis; see particularly the discussion in H. Denifle which he documents with printed and manuscript material. 'Quel livre servait de base à l'enseignement des maîtres en théologie dans l'université de Paris?' in *RT* 2 (1894), p. 149ff. See also H. Felder, *Geschichte der wissenschaftlichen Studien im Franziskanerorden bis um die Mitte des 13. Jahrhunderts*, Freiberg im Breisgau 1904, p. 495, and Chenu, *Saint Thomas*, p. 47, 'The *magister in theologia* . . . still remained a *magister in sacra pagina*'. It may be of interest to note in this connection that the order of studies followed at Paris was essentially that followed in Germany, and that therefore Martin Luther in his own theological education and teaching at the beginning of the sixteenth century followed the same course as Thomas in the thirteenth. Cf. O. Scheel, *Martin Luther. Vom Katholizismus zur Reformation* vol. II, Tübingen 1917, p. 71: 'Die Pariser Fakultät war das Vorbild. Dort hatte das theologische Studium mit den kursorischen Vorlesungen über die Schrift begonnen, war zu den Vorlesungen über das dogmatische Lehrbuch des Lombarden, des 'Meisters der Sentenzen', fortgeschritten und hatte mit den den Doktoren der Theologie vorbehaltenen ausführlichen exegetischen Vorlesungen über die Schrift geendigt. Die deutschen Universitäten übernahmen diese Ordnung'. After his early education at Erfurt Luther became *biblicus* at Wittenberg in 1509 and immediately afterwards *sententiarius* in Erfurt, after which he was promoted to *magister* in Wittenberg in 1512 with the duty of lecturing on the Bible, a responsibility which he exercised for more than thirty years as *Doctor der Heiligen Schrift*. See, e.g., Scheel, *Luther*, vol. II, p. 59ff., 210ff. and 309ff.

study the best period of the day.[16] Books of the New and Old Testaments by turns were studied in detail, and commentaries (*Expositiones*) on Isaiah, Jeremiah, Lamentations, Job, Romans, and I Corinthians 1–7 and 14, still survive in his own handwriting from the required course of lectures offered by Thomas. His lectures (*Lecturae*) on the Psalter (Ps. 1–54), the Gospels of Matthew and John, I Corinthians, 11–16, the remaining Pauline epistles and Hebrews, survive in the faithful transcript of his own secretary or of those who attended his course.[17] There are hardly any noticeable differences between an *expositio* and a *lectura*, which indicates that the *Lecturae* also faithfully reproduce what Thomas actually said.[18]

This study of the biblical text gave rise to what is perhaps the most characteristic form of instruction in the Middle Ages, and the form preferred by Thomas himself, namely, the disputation.[19] In expounding a difficult or disputed passage the master could take up a special problem for fuller and deeper examination and so pose a *quaestio* within the course of his commentary, often indicating it with a formula like, *Hic oritur quaestio. . . , Potest aliquis quaerere. . .* (the question arises here. . . , the question may be raised . . .) etc.[20] But such a *quaestio* could also be separated from the ordinary *lectio* and be discussed at a special time in the presence of all or the larger part of the faculty. This is the disputation proper.[21] The preference

[16] See Mandonnet, *RT* 33 (1928), p. 35, van der Ploeg, *Thomist* 10 (1947), p. 405.

[17] Cf. C. Spicq's article on 'Saint Thomas d'Aquin exégète', in *Dictionnaire de théologie catholique* (=*DTC*) 15:1, Paris 1946, col. 694–738: 'La plupart des grands commentaires bibliques du XIIe siècle, en effet, ne sont pas autre chose que la rédaction des cours officiels des maîtres en théologie durant leur carrière universitaire'. See also the same author's *Esquisse*, p. 142. On Thomas' biblical commentaries see especially Mandonnet, *RT* 34 (1928), and 35 (1929), where the chronological problem is discussed in detail. There is a general survey in Spicq, *Esquisse*, p. 298ff. and Chenu, *Saint Thomas*, p. 233ff.

[18] Van der Ploeg, *Thomist* 10 (1947), p. 401, concludes from this that Thomas must have read his lectures slowly and clearly or simply dictated them.

[19] While it was normal at an earlier period for a *magister* at the University of Paris to lead disputations only a few times a year, Thomas departed from this custom by holding as many as two disputations a week, see Chenu, *Saint Thomas*, p. 281.

[20] See e.g. *In Joan.* 1, 14 (5); 3, 1 (4); 6, 4 (7); 6, 5 (3).

[21] Two days were generally required for a disputation. On the first the master's *baccalaureus* or assistant lecturer acted as 'respondent'. The *magister* himself then discussed the objections which had been raised on his next lecture day and answered them in a *determinatio magistralis*. See P. Mandonnet, 'Chronologie des questions disputées de saint Thomas d'Aquin', in *RT* 23 (1918), p. 266ff. and Chenu, *Saint Thomas*, p. 88ff. and 280ff. Cf. also van der Ploeg, *Thomist* 10 (1947), p. 403: 'The disputations arose from the questions or difficulties put to a master on the occasion of a lecture on a special text of Scripture'.

shown by Thomas for this form of teaching is indicated in the series of *Quaestiones disputatae*, which by reason of their full discussion of the problem are often of considerable value in determining Thomas's meaning in other places where he expresses himself in a more concise manner.[22] These disputations are of especial interest to us since they provided Thomas with a model when he came to plan his major work of systematic theology, the *Summa theologiae*.[23] In this, just as in the *Quaestiones disputatae*, a series of *articuli* are appended to *quaestiones*. These articles are all set down in essentially the same way: a series of objections is raised against a proposition, after which the proposition is clearly stated and then each objection taken up in turn and shown to have no real basis. Thomas began his *Summa*[24] about the year 1267 to take the place of a projected and partially completed revision of the earlier *Commentary on the Sentences*. It was intended to take the place of Lombard's *Sentences* as an elementary introduction to dogmatics for divinity students. The work, however, was cut short by Thomas's death in 1274 before he succeeded in finishing.[25] The *Summa* stands by itself in scholastic literature by reason of its strictly developed concepts and clarity of exposition, and consequently it is still the primary source of all research in the thought of Thomas both as regards his theology and his philosophical views. It was not intended—any more than the Sentences were—to take the place of the Bible as the basic text-book of theological study. It was not an end in itself but was designed, as we hope to show later, to be used in elucidating the meaning of the biblical writings. M.-D. Chenu seems to have understood Thomas's own intention correctly when he says of the *Summa*: 'Its most perfect rational structures are never an end, but a means to arrive at a better knowledge of the Word of God'.[26]

[22] Proof of Thomas's energetic activity in the conduct of disputations is provided by the fact that there are 510 of them extant, collected under the titles, *De veritate*, *De potentia*, *De malo*, *De spiritualibus creaturis*, *De anima*, *De virtutibus*, and *De unione Verbi incarnati*. Each *articulus* in these collections represents the concluding summary of a disputation.

[23] We prefer this title to the frequently used *Summa theologica*, since the latter appears to be a comparatively modern form without any historical basis. See P. A. Walz, '*De genuino titulo "Summa theologiae"* ', in *Angelicum* 18 (1941), p. 142ff.

[24] On the term *summa* see the historical surveys in M. Grabmann, *Die Geschichte der scholastischen Methode*, Freiburg im Breisgau 1911, vol. II p, 23ff., and Chenu, *Saint Thomas*, p. 298ff.

[25] Thomas's work was ended by his death at the point where he came to deal with the sacrament of penance, 3a, 90, 4. On the *Supplementum* which followed the *Summa* in all later editions, see footnote 13 above.

[26] Chenu, *Saint Thomas*, p. 322. Cf. van der Ploeg, *Thomist* 10 (1947), p. 404, on

This brief survey has perhaps shown that scholastic theology, at its apex in the middle of the thirteenth century, is to be seen from a purely historical standpoint as a theology of scripture. The teacher of theology was a *magister in sacra pagina*, and his assigned responsibility as such can be summarised in the three verbs *legere*, *disputare* and *praedicare*.[27] His official duty was, firstly, to expound the text and content of the Bible, and this he did primarily in the regular, required *lectio* or lecture. His task, however, was not only to expound the revealed truth but also to defend it against attack and mis-interpretation and to explain its difficulties and obscurities. This was done principally in the disputation. The disputations, however, were held only occasionally and at irregular intervals, while the normal form of instruction was the exposition of the Bible. The teacher had in addition the responsibility of unfolding the meaning of the biblical writings in preaching, primarily for his students but also for ordinary church members. This was a duty on which as a preaching friar Thomas particularly seems to have laid much stress.[28] In each of these three types of instruction used by the teacher of theology holy scripture was clearly understood to be the point of departure and the central matter of his study.[29] For the scholastics not only was scripture to be held in the highest esteem but, as H. Felder puts it, 'all theological study centres solely and exclusively on holy scripture.'[30]

For the scholastic theologian, and therefore for Thomas also, the primary task is to elucidate and set forth the divine revelation communicated in scripture. Philosophical speculation is a matter of

the study of Lombard: 'Its purpose was only to help the student to a better under-standing of the richness of Holy Writ'; and Mandonnet, *RT* 33 (1928), p. 507: 'Le livre inspiré l'emportait sur tout et la théologie elle-même ne se considérait que comme un moyen de mettre en ordre la doctrine scripturaire et d'en approfondir l'intelligence'.

---

[27] Cf. Chenu, *Saint Thomas*, p. 237f.
[28] During his stay in Naples in 1273 Thomas preached daily during Lent to the students and inhabitants of the city, see Mandonnet, *RT* (1928), p. 214. On the preaching duties of the *magister* of theology and the form this preaching took, see Spicq, *Esquisse*, p. 349ff.
[29] Cf. Peter the Chanter, *Verbum abbreviatum*, 1 in Migne, *Patrologiae cursus completus . . . series Latina* (=*MPL*), 205, 20: *In tribus igitur consistit exercitium sacrae Scripturae: circa lectionem, disputationem et praedicationem.* The passage continues with an interesting statement concerning the relation between academic teaching and preaching itself: *Post lectionem igitur sacrae Scripturae, et dubitabilium, per disputationem, inquisitionem, et non prius, praedicandum est.*
[30] Felder, *Geschichte*, p. 491. The account given by Felder of the Franciscan theological tradition on p. 490ff. corresponds in all essential points with the picture which we have given of Thomas. In this regard scholasticism is uniform.

secondary importance. But this does not mean that the latter is to be disregarded: on the contrary, the study of philosophy comes to its height in high scholasticism. It is not, however, undertaken for its own sake, but is subordinated to the stated aim of theology, and any discussion of Thomas's thought which fails to take this approach to his subject-matter into account will be dangerously one-sided and misleading in its interpretation.

With these preliminary observations we have defined the nature of the problem which underlies our present inquiry and gives it its starting-point. On the one hand Thomas's function as *magister in sacra pagina*, which was to expound the holy scriptures, determines the formulation of all his thought. On the other hand, however, though this may seem difficult to reconcile with the statement just made, it is also true that in Thomas concepts derived from Greek philosophy, and particularly from Aristotelianism, are brought to a peak of development earlier unknown. He thought of himself as a theologian, but it is as a philosopher that he is best known among scholars. The problem lies ultimately, it is clear, in the manner in which Thomas did his work as a theologian, and it is the work of theology which he himself conceived to be the primary one.

Accordingly, we take our point of departure in the fact that Thomas is to be understood primarily as a theologian, and as a theologian for whom the interpretation and comprehension of the meaning of scripture is central. For this reason our interest is focussed on Thomas's *sacra doctrina*, which is the term he habitually uses for what we would call 'theology'. We do not therefore regard the question of whether Thomas is to be regarded primarily as an Aristotelian or a neo-Platonist in his philosophical outlook as vitally important for the present study.

Our aim is to explain the relationship which exists between reason and revelation in *sacra doctrina*. What does Thomas have in mind when he speaks about *revelatio* and how does he regard the relationship between revelation and the biblical writings? Again, within this special interpretation of the meaning of scripture what is the relationship between what is given in scripture and those elements which are unmistakably derived from Greek philosophy? How does Thomas himself interpret this relationship, and how is it actually expressed when he employs it in his *sacra doctrina*? Is it possible to see how ideas drawn from *revelatio* influence and eventually correct thoughts and motifs derived from *ratio*? What effect does Greek philosophy have in the formulation of *sacra doctrina*, the purpose of which is to reproduce the central meaning of the biblical writings? Where do we find the systematic principle in the structural framework which indicates the view of Christianity held by Thomas—in revelation or reason, or possibly in a synthesis of elements from both? It is our hope that this study will allow us not perhaps to give a final answer to these and similar questions but at least to bring them closer to solution.

This means that *ratio* and *revelatio* are not to be understood as permanent or static elements which remain constant throughout Church history and whose relationship to one another can be quantitatively measured. Both are included—though it is difficult to indicate how—in the unity created by the hermeneutical method of a particular theologian who attempts to *interpret* what is given in revelation. They are not, therefore, neutral in their signification; on the contrary, both scripture and the tradition of thought of which the interpreting theologian is part have a definite content, and the essence of the problem is to indicate the clash between thoughts and motifs which come from different sources. It is this clash which is of particular interest to us, and the purpose of our study is to try to show what form it takes at a particular point in the Christian tradition, viz. in Thomas Aquinas.

The choice of Thomas as the focus of our study surely needs no further justification. Few theologians have had so decisive a significance as he, not only in his own time but also and particularly for subsequent theology. This is made plain not only in the almost unbelievably extensive material written about him but especially by the fact that the Roman Catholic Church has declared in a series of authoritative decrees that Thomas is the *Doctor communis*, in whose philosophy and theology this church sees the most genuine expression of its doctrine.[1] Hence a study of Thomas's theology has not only

---

[1] On the relation between Roman Catholic theology and Thomas and also pronouncements and declarations of the Church on this matter, see e.g. K. E. Skydsgaard, *Metafysik og Tro. En dogmatisk Studie i nyere Thomisme*, Copenhagen 1937, p. 18ff., G. M. Manser, *Das Wesen des Thomismus* (Thomistische Studien 5), 3rd ed., Freiburg in der Schweiz 1949, p. 67ff., or F. Diekamp, *Katholische Dogmatik nach den Grundsätzen des heiligen Thomas*, vol. 1, 10th and 11th eds., Münster in Westfalen 1949, p. 55ff. The regulation of the *Codex iuris canonici*, canon 1366, sect. 2, is here of crucial importance: *Philosophiae rationalis ac theologiae studia et alumnorum in his disciplinis institutionem professores omnino pertractent ad Angelici Doctoris rationem, doctrinam et principia, eaque sancte teneant.* Cf. also canon 589, sect. 1.

historic interest but to a certain extent also brings us into confrontation with patterns of thought which are still theologically relevant.

Amongst the voluminous writings of Thomas we are interested primarily in those which are of greatest theological significance.[2] Thus our material is drawn in the main from the *Summa theologiae*, the purpose of which, according to Thomas's own intention, was to set down in ideal form all that belonged to *sacra doctrina*. It may be added that parts of the *Summa* are to be supplemented and interpreted by parallel passages from other theological works, notably the *Commentary on the Sentences*, the *Summa contra gentiles*, *Quaestiones disputatae*, *Compendium theologiae*, and his commentaries on Boethius's work on the Trinity and Pseudo-Dionysius's *De divinis nominibus*. Particularly to be noted too are the biblical commentaries mentioned above, viz. the transcript of his lectures as *magister*, and among these chiefly the commentaries on John's Gospel and the epistles of Paul. Our purpose in studying these writings is to use as widely representative sources as possible to elucidate the characteristics of Thomas's general theological viewpoint. Questions of change or development within the subject-matter itself will therefore be treated as peripheral. So far as we can find, there is no such development of any particular significance, at least in regard to what we take to be the primary questions. We therefore assume that in this respect Thomas has a uniform and clearly defined viewpoint. In doubtful matters we shall regard the *Summa* as conclusive, since it represents the mature and definitive formulation of his thought.

The amount of material which deals with the thought of Thomas is almost too vast to measure, and for this reason it is not possible to deal with it exhaustively in the present study. Nor does there seem to be any value in citing all the literature which we have consulted at various stages in preparing this work. Our principle of selection has been to refer primarily to those works which we have found to be of value in discussing the disputed points or which bear directly upon them. In certain cases supplementary references are also given in footnotes where it has been necessary to deal summarily with a

---

[2] A survey of Thomas' writings and an introduction to the frequently intricate problems of textual criticism and chronology is to be found in P. Mandonnet, *Des écrits authentiques de saint Thomas d'Aquin*, 2nd ed. Fribourg 1910; and M. Grabmann, *Die Werke des hl. Thomas von Aquin*, 3rd ed. Münster 1949. See also the general surveys in P.-A. Walz, 'Écrits de saint Thomas', in *DTC* 15:1, col. 635ff. and Manser, *Thomismus*, p. 13ff.

matter or where some knowledge has been assumed, and in these instances it may perhaps be helpful for the reader to have further references.

The method which we propose to follow in this volume is indicated in the title of the work itself.[3] It is, as we have already stated, the theology of Thomas—his *sacra doctrina*—which is of central importance to us. Consequently, we are interested both in his methodological principles and in the concrete expression of these principles at crucial points in his theology. We shall therefore concentrate particularly on elucidating the decisive problem of the relationship between *revelation* and *reason* in Thomas.

Thus in chapter 1, '*Revelatio* and *sacra doctrina*', we shall attempt first to define what Thomas means by the term *revelatio*. Two lines of inquiry will here be developed: first, What is the nature of the event denoted by the term *revelatio*?, and second, What is the knowledge given with revelation and what is its relationship to the biblical writings? We shall also discuss the question of the communication of revelation and Thomas's view of the function of theology and its relation to scripture.

In chapter 2, '*Ratio* and *revelatio* in *sacra doctrina*', which forms the central part of our study, we shall try to see what function the relationship between *ratio* and *revelatio* plays at crucial points in Thomas's theology. Our first task will therefore be to examine what he holds to be the causal relationship between God and the world. In this connection we shall also deal briefly with his doctrine of the Trinity. Finally, we shall attempt to deepen the discussion by tracing the development of the central idea of God as immediately present and at work in all that happens in the world of his creation. This will then bring us to a discussion of the central question of the meaning of grace and incarnation.

---

[3] Since there is another work with the same title—G. F. van Ackeren, *Sacra doctrina. The Subject of the First Question of the Summa Theologica of St. Thomas Aquinas*, Rome 1952—we should say something about the difference between that work and this study. As its sub-title indicates, van Ackeren's book is limited to a linguistic study of the meaning of the term *sacra doctrina* which occurs particularly in *quaestio* 1 of the *Summa*. This limitation means that the author does not anywhere discuss the content and formulation of *sacra doctrina*—for us this is the central matter—and therefore he does not deal with the whole problem of the relationship between *ratio* and *revelatio*. We have chosen this title since the term *sacra doctrina* includes at one time both the inseparable relationship of theology to *revelatio* (it is SACRA *doctrina*) and the decisive part played by *ratio* in the cognitive aspect of theology (as *sacra* DOCTRINA).

The general outline presented in the earlier chapters will enable us to deal fruitfully in chapter 3, '*Ratio* and *sacra doctrina*', with the main problem. The aim of this chapter is twofold: first, to examine what Thomas himself says about the relationship between *ratio* and *revelatio*, for this is obviously important for our study; and second, to recapitulate and emphasise the main aspects of this relationship, basing our conclusions on the material discussed in the first two chapters. While our interest in chapter 1 is directed primarily to *revelatio* and the part which it plays in *sacra doctrina*, our attention in the last chapter will be focussed on *ratio* and its significance for both the formulation and the content of theology. We shall finally try to summarise what we take to be the conclusions of our study.

I

REVELATIO AND *SACRA DOCTRINA*

1

THOMAS'S CONCEPT OF REVELATION
KNOWLEDGE AND SALVATION

When we turn from the study of theology in general to deal with the problems which are to be found at a particular point in the history of Christian thought, our first task is to define the concepts which are central to our study. Over the centuries certain meanings have been associated with terms which have retained their verbal similarities, while the meanings themselves have changed. Our task is, therefore, to clarify both the meaning and the function of the terms as they are found in the material before us. First, then, we must try to define the meaning of *revelatio* in Thomas. What, that is to say, is the nature of the event to which he refers when he speaks of 'revelation', and what is the content of this revelation? We shall concentrate on the first of these questions, preferring to leave the discussion of the latter to the following section.

We search the writings of Thomas in vain for the kind of discussion of revelation which characterises more recent works of doctrine. But we must not conclude from this that revelation has no decisive part to play in his theology. A closer investigation will soon disclose that on the contrary revelation is the basic presupposition of all his writing. In the first article of the *Summa* Thomas defines theology as *doctrina quaedam secundum revelationem divinam* (schooling in what God has revealed).[1] He also indicates in the same passage that *revelatio* not only constitutes the essential presupposition for theology but is of crucial consequence for man's salvation. The *salus hominis* means that man attains the goal which has been set for him by God and which is nothing less than God himself—the beatific vision of God. Without revelation this goal would be unattainable by man, for it far transcends what it is possible for him to reach with the aid of his natural endowments. Apart from it he cannot even begin to perceive his high destiny. Everything turns on the revelation of this destiny, on his gaining knowledge about it. Only when this revelation has come

[1] 1a, 1, 1.

19

can he set about attaining his goal, and so revelation is the primary and indispensable presupposition on which everything in man's salvation depends.[2]

Even though, as we have already noted, Thomas nowhere provides an explicit definition of the concept of revelation in general, it is not difficult to see what he means by it. There is a useful starting-point in certain passages in the *De veritate* and *Summa theologiae*[3] in particular, where he deals directly and in some detail with a special form of revelation, viz. *prophecy*, which is defined more closely as *sicut quiddam imperfectum in genere divinae revelationis* (something imperfect in the genus of divine revelation).[4] What is true in the particular case of this lower degree of perfection is true of the nature and structure of the event iself, and also on a larger scale of revelation. Any exhaustive treatment of Thomas's views, however, is ruled out at this point, and we shall limit ourselves to noting some of the main features of his argument which are relevant to what follows.

When we turn to the passages in which Thomas discusses the nature of prophecy, we notice at once his strong emphasis on revelation as *knowledge*. In the preface to his discussion of prophecy in the *Summa* he states that *prophetia primo et principaliter consistit in cognitione* (prophecy first and chiefly consists in knowledge).[5] For Thomas a prophet is not primarily a man who *says* or *does* anything,

---

[2] 1a, 1, 1: *Finem autem oportet esse praecognitum hominibus, qui suas intentiones et actiones debent ordinare in finem. Unde necessarium fuit homini ad salutem, quod ei nota fierent quaedam per revelationem divinam, quae rationem humanam excedunt;* cf. *CG* I, 5: *Nullus enim desiderio et studio in aliquid tendit nisi sit ei praecognitum.* See also *De Ver.* 14, 10.

[3] *De Ver.* 12 and 2a2ae, 171–174. The question is also dealt with, though not in anything like the same detail, in *CG* III, 154 and *In 1 ad Cor.* 14, 1. There is a good introduction to Thomas's view of prophecy in P. Synave and P. Benoit, *La prophétie*, 1947, p. 269ff. In any discussion of Thomas's concept of revelation we can hardly avoid reference to the 'classical' works on Thomism, R. Garrigou-Lagrange, *De revelatione per Ecclesiam catholicam proposita*, vols. I and II, 3rd ed. Rome 1929–31 and A. Gardeil, *Le donné révélé et la théologie*, 2nd ed. Juvisy 1932. These works, however, come out of a more recent school of Thomistic interpretation and are apologetic in their orientation, and so have relatively little to offer those who are not interested in the validity of the Thomistic concept of revelation in a situation determined by the thought of the turn of the century, but who do want to know what 'revelation' means to *Thomas* himself. A very helpful exception is V. White, 'Le concept de la révélation chez saint Thomas', in *L'année théologique* (=*AT*) 11 (1950), an essay which deals primarily with the historical analysis of the actual writings. This author's starting-point leads him, as we might expect, to an interesting criticism of the works of Garrigou-Lagrange and Gardeil, see p. 1ff.

[4] 2a2ae, 171, 4, ad 2.

[5] 2a2ae, 171, 1.

but one who has *knowledge* of something which is concealed from other men. This knowledge may be expressed in a statement or *locutio* and confirmed by works, *operatio miraculorum*, but these are to be regarded as secondary and consequent.[6] Prophecy, and therefore also revelation, are thus defined in Thomas primarily as a cognitive act, 'un évènement psychologique cognitif', or a metaphysical transaction in the minds of certain chosen individuals.[7]

But what relationship does this revealed knowledge have to ordinary, human knowledge? As a creature endowed with reason, *ratio*, man also possesses in his soul a light, given in and with this reason, whereby he 'sees' and comprehends both himself and the things around him. This *lumen naturale rationis* (natural light of reason) is a *participatio* or participation on the human level in the light in which God sees and knows all things.[8] According to Thomas, the attainment of knowledge or *cognitio* is contingent on two things which he defines as *phantasmata ex sensibilibus accepta* (images derived from the sensible world) and the *lumen naturale intelligibile, cuius virtute intelligibiles conceptiones ab eis abstrahimus* (natural intellectual light by which we make abstract intelligible concepts from these images).[9] As *intellectus possibilis* the intellect is receptive and can acquire knowledge. But this knowledge is not derived from within the intellect itself, which from the first is a *tabula rasa*. The starting-point of knowledge is found rather in sense perception, *naturalis nostra cognitio a sensu principium sumit* (the knowledge that is natural to us has its source in the senses),[10] and through it we receive impulses which produce 'impressions' or *phantasmata* in the soul. As *intellectus agens* the

[6] See the whole passage in 2a2ae, 171, 1. Cf. also 2a2ae, 174, 3: *Magis autem est proprium prophetiae cognitio quam operatio; De Ver.* 12, 13: *denuntiatio . . . non principaliter, sed consequenter se habet in prophetia.*

[7] See White, *AT* 11 (1950), p. 14: 'Principalement et essentiellement, la prophétie n'est pas une certaine espèce de discours, mais une certaine espèce de conscience ou de connaissance: une évènement psychologique cognitif que le langage prophétique présuppose et exprime extérieurement'. This primary emphasis on the cognitive aspect of revelation is indirectly to be seen in Gardeil, *Le donné*, where the specific treatment of 'La Révélation' (p. 41ff.) is preceded by a purely philosophical discussion of the conditions of human knowledge, 'L'affirmation humaine' (p. 1ff.). On the principles involved in this procedure, see ib. p. xxivf.

[8] 1a, 12, 11, ad 3: *ipsum lumen naturale rationis participatio quaedam est divini luminis;* 1a2ae, 91, 2: *lumen rationis naturalis . . . nihil aliud sit quam impressio divini luminis in nobis.*

[9] 1a, 12, 13.

[10] 1a, 12, 12; cf. 1a, 1, 9: *Est autem naturale homini ut per sensibilia ad intelligibilia veniat: quia omnis nostra cognitio a sensu initium habet,* see also 1a, 18, 2; 1a, 84. 6–7; 2a2ae, 8, 1; *CG* I, 3; *CG* I, 12 and other passages.

C

reason, proceeding from this starting-point and the light given in and with the intellect, forms the first principles or rules of thought.[11] In compliance with these it continues similarly to build up a knowledge of existence and its order and context by abstracting the intelligible forms of things from the impressions given by the senses, and through these *species intelligibiles* (intelligible species) the intellect attains true knowledge of the world around it.[12]

The structure of revealed knowledge is conceived in an analogous way. Since we are dealing here with a type of knowledge which transcends what human reason can ordinarily attain, the assumption is that the soul of the recipient of revelation is given a higher light than is conferred by natural reason, *ad prophetiam requiratur quoddam lumen intelligibile excedens lumen naturalis rationis* (prophecy requires an intellectual light surpassing the light of natural reason),[13] and it is the communication of this higher light which constitutes prophecy as such.[14] Revelation consists of many varying forms, and it can be expressed in different ways, but it is this divinely bestowed *lumen* which gives it its formal unity and makes prophecy a special form of knowledge.[15]

But just as in the case of naturally acquired knowledge the light which is given in and with natural reason is not by itself sufficient, so too, in regard to revealed knowledge something above and beyond the new and higher light is needed. At this point Thomas discusses

[11] *De Ver.* 11, 1: *primae conceptiones intellectus, quae statim lumine intellectus agentis cognoscuntur per species a sensibilibus abstractas.*
[12] On this theory of the building up of human knowledge see especially 1a, 84–88. We cannot at this point discuss these general questions of the theory of knowledge in any greater detail, but refer simply to some recent introductions for a treatment of these questions. There is a lucid general introduction in E. Gilson, *The Philosophy of St Thomas Aquinas* (authorised translation from the 3rd revised and enlarged ed. of *Le Thomisme*), 2nd revised and enlarged ed. Cambridge and St Louis 1929, p. 260ff. In our citations, however, we shall usually quote from the later edition, *Le thomisme. Introduction à la philosophie de saint Thomas d'Aquin* (Études de philosophie médiévale 1), 5th ed. Paris 1948.
[13] 2a2ae, 171, 2.
[14] *De Ver.* 12, 1: *Cum autem omne quod manifestatur, sub lumine quodam manifestetur . . . oportet ut ea quae manifestantur homini supra communem cognitionem, quodam altiori lumine manifestentur, quod lumen propheticum dicitur, ex cuius receptione aliquis propheta constituitur;* 2a2ae, 176, 2: *donum prophetiae consistit in ipsa illuminatione mentis ad cognoscendum intelligibilem veritatem;* see also 2a2ae, 173, 2; *CG* III, 154: *revelatio fit quodam interiori et intelligibili lumine mentem elevante ad percipiendum ea ad quae per lumen naturale intellectus pertingere non potest.*
[15] 2a2ae, 171, 3, ad 3: *formale in cognitione prophetica est lumen divinum, a cuius unitate prophetia habet unitatem speciei, licet sint diversa quae per lumen divinum prophetice manifestantur.*

two possibilities.[16] On the one hand this additional element may be given in such a way that simultaneously with the new light God imparts some wholly new knowledge. This he may do *mediante sensu exterius* (externally by means of the senses) (as when Daniel saw a hand writing on the wall), but also *per formas imaginarias* (by forms of the imagination) or by *species intelligibiles* (intelligible species) directly infused into the soul, i.e. without passing indirectly through sense perception.[17] As a purely intellectual act the latter is the highest form of revelation, since it *magis . . . appropinquet ad visionem patriae* (approaches nearer to the heavenly vision)[18] In other words, for Thomas the culminating point of revelation is not something which happens or is given *in via* but occurs with the beatific vision of God: *perfectio autem divinae revelationis erit in patria* (the divine revelation will be brought to its perfection in heaven).[19] On the other hand Thomas also raises the possibility that there is no impartation of new knowledge but only new light, in the strength of which something already present, given either naturally or supernaturally, is judged and so given a new signification. This is what we find, for example, in the case of the apostles when they see and interpret in the light of the revelation given to them the writings of the old covenant, whose meaning is given to them supernaturally. But the same thing applies to what is given through the natural power of cognition, *ea quae cursu naturali homo apprehendit* (the things which a man apprehends in the ordinary course of nature).[20]

---

[16] On what follows see especially the comments in Synave and Benoit, *Prophétie*, p. 243ff. and 272ff.

[17] See especially *De Ver.* 12, 7 and 2a2ae, 173, 2, but also *CG* III, 154 and *In 1 ad Cor.* 14, 1 (812).

[18] 2a2ae, 174, 2.

[19] 2a2ae, 171, 4, ad 2; 2a2ae, 173, 1: *manifestum est quod cognitio prophetica alia est a cognitione perfecta, quae erit in patria. Unde et distinguitur ab ea sicut imperfectum a perfecto, et ea adveniente evacuatur.*

[20] 2a2ae, 173, 2: *Lumen autem intelligibile quandoque quidem imprimitur menti humanae divinitus ad diiudicandum ea quae ab aliis visa sunt: sicut dictum est de Ioseph; et sicut patet de Apostolis, quibus Dominus aperuit sensum ut intelligerent Scripturas. . . Sive etiam ad diiudicandum secundum divinam veritatem ea quae cursu naturali homo apprehendit. . . Sic igitur patet quod prophetica revelatio quandoque quidem fit per solem luminis influentiam: quandoque autem per species de novo impressas vel aliter ordinatas; In ad Rom.* 12, 2 (978): *Dicuntur etiam prophetae in Novo Testamento, qui prophetica dicta exponunt, quia sacra scriptura eodem spiritu interpretatur quod est condita.* In Thomas's view, however, a higher form of revelation is involved when both the judgment and the knowledge imparted are supernaturally given, cf. 2a2ae, 174, 2, ad 3: *Si vero lumen intellectuale alicui divinitus infundatur non ad cognoscendum aliqua supernaturalia, sed ad iudicandum secundum certitudinem veritatis divinae ea quae humana ratione cognosci possunt; sic talis*

Hence, according to Thomas, there are two essential elements in revelation, as in any other act of cognition, if we are to speak of a real knowledge: first, *acceptio cognitorum*, or the receiving of the content of knowledge, and second, *iudicium de acceptis*, the judgment and interpretation of that content.[21] Both are necessary, but the latter is of greater consequence: *iudicium, per influxum intellectualis luminis . . . principalius est in prophetia: quia iudicium est completivum cognitionis* (judgment by the inflow of intellectual light . . . holds the chief place in prophecy, since judgment is the complement of knowledge).[22] There is a parallel relationship in the structure of natural knowledge; only as the intellect *iudicat rem ita se habere sicut est forma quam de re apprehendit* (judges that the thing corresponds to the form of the thing which it apprehends) can we speak of knowledge in the proper sense, *tunc primo cognoscit et dicit verum* (then for the first time it knows and affirms truth).[23] At this point we are to note the decisive importance which Thomas attaches to *lumen propheticum* (prophetic light) as the constitutive element of revelation, for this 'light' is in fact nothing other than a divine strengthening of the power of reason to interpret and judge knowledge.[24] An event occurring at a given time and place is not revelation as such, nor is the observation or perception of that event, any more than the observation of some other thing which may be an object of knowledge. This is so even in the case of what is directly and supernaturally infused into reason. It becomes *revelatio* only when the observing or perceiving subject can classify and interpret it in an intelligible way, *quando cum visione habetur significatio intellectus eorum quae videntur,*

prophetia intellectualis est infra illam quae est cum imaginaria visione ducente in supernaturalem veritatem. On this basis Thomas draws a distinction in the Old Testament between the writers of the prophetic books and the writers of the hagiographa: the former have received both *lumen* and a new *species*, while the latter, on the basis of a supernaturally given *lumen*, are in most cases simply passing judgment on a knowledge given by reason as such. See also *De Ver.* 12, 12 and ad 10.

---

[21] *De Ver.* 12, 7: *Ad cognitionem autem duo requiruntur; scilicet acceptio cognitorum, et iudicium de acceptis;* 2a2ae, 173, 2: *Per donum autem prophetiae confertur aliquid humanae menti supra id quod pertinet ad naturalem facultatem, quantum ad utrumque; scilicet et quantum ad iudicium, per influxum intellectualis luminis; et quantum ad acceptionem seu repraesentationem rerum, quae fit per aliquas species.*

[22] 2a2ae, 173, 2. This strong emphasis on *iudicium* in Thomas is correctly underscored by White, *AT* 11 (1950), p. 119f.: 'Ce qui, en fait, est essentiel et même fondamental, c'est l'importance première du jugement lui-même'.

[23] 1a, 16, 2.

[24] *De Ver.* 12, 7: *Iudicium igitur supernaturale prophetae datur secundum lumen et infusum, ex quo intellectus roboratur ad iudicandum.*

tunc est revelatio (revelation occurs when the seeing of a thing is accompanied by the understanding of it).[25] External events may be the material for the judgment of the illuminated reason, and consequently there is a relationship between the two, but these events are not in themselves revelation. Revelation, therefore, according to Thomas, can not consist, for example, in events recorded in the Gospels,—the birth, death or resurrection of Christ, and the like. We may not even regard the incarnation as a divine revelation. Only *knowledge* of the incarnation can be revelation, and this is always something internal to man. In the phrase of V. White, who closely reproduces the line of thought which we find in Thomas, it is 'a vision . . . in the inspired mind of the apostle and the Evangelist, a vision indeed and above all in the prophetic and human mind of Jesus Christ himself.'[26] If it is possible to speak of 'a revelation of God in Christ' in Thomas—an expression which he himself never uses—this must refer to a knowledge brought about by God in the human soul of Christ, on the ground of which he can be said to be *primus et principalis Doctor*.[27] The incarnation may indeed be the presupposition of revelation, but because the cognitive viewpoint is all-decisive, the event of the incarnation itself cannot be understood as a *revelatio*. Supernaturally communicated knowledge does not *point to* revelation but as *cognitio* it is itself *the same as* revelation.[28]

For a fuller explanation of the peculiar nature and structure of knowledge given by revelation in relation to other supernatural acts of cognition it may be illuminating to compare it with what Thomas calls *scientia beatorum* (knowledge of the saints) on the one hand and the act of faith or *fides* on the other.

As we have already indicated, Thomas regards the beatific vision as the highest point of revelation. In the vision of God which is given to the saints in heaven the human intellect is given a knowledge of God's being through the *lumen gloriae* (light of glory), and this knowledge is as perfect as it is possible for created beings to

---

[25] *In 2 ad Cor.* 12, 1 (442); cf. *De Ver.* 12, 7: *Quandoque igitur cognitio est supernaturalis secundum acceptionem tantum, quandoque secundum iudicium tantum, quandoque secundum utrumque. Si autem sit secundum acceptionem tantum supernaturalis, non dicetur ex hoc aliquis propheta. . . Si vero habeat supernaturale iudicium, vel simul iudicium et acceptionem, ex hoc dicitur esse propheta.* See also *De Ver.* 12, 12 and *CG* III, 154. Cf. White *AT* 11 (1950), p. 123ff.
[26] White, *AT* 11 (1950), p. 129.
[27] 3a, 7, 7.
[28] Cf. K. E. Skydsgaard, 'Idealisme og Realisme i Thomismens Gudserkendelse', in *Festskrift til Jens Nørregaard 1947*, Copenhagen 1947, p. 283.

possess.[29] In regard to content, however, there is a difference of degree between this knowledge and that which is given in earthly revelation— the former is more perfect than the latter.[30] Thus Thomas can say that what is revealed to us is only *quaedam pauca* (a few mysteries) in comparison with what is seen by the saints.[31] But in addition a clear distinction can be made in regard to *mode* between this perfect act of cognition and the *revelatio* which is given to us under earthly conditions. The *lumen gloriae* which constitutes blessedness represents a *lumen intellectuale . . . per modum formae permanentis et perfectae* (intellectual light . . . by way of an abiding and complete form),[32] and the knowledge given with it is therefore something which remains permanently in the intellect of the blessed in heaven. The experience of rapture described by Paul in II Corinthians 12 and fully discussed by Thomas represents an intermediate form between the beatific vision and earthly revelation.[33] There is, of course, no intrinsic difference between Paul's transitory experience and the enduring vision of the saints in heaven, but it is precisely the momentary form of the experience[34] which leads Thomas to classify rapture as a special type of prophecy.[35] Revelation does not normally involve an immediate vision of God himself but a *visio . . . in quibusdam similitudinibus* (vision . . . in certain images),[36] for what is seen by the prophet or apostle is not the eternal itself but its reflection in what is created, which thus may be said to be the *speculum aeternitatis* (mirror of eternity).[37] Furthermore, the knowledge here referred to is not a

[29] On the meaning of this beatific condition see 1a, 12, 1–10 and 1a2ae, 3, 1–8.
[30] Cf. the passages referred to in footnote 19.
[31] *CG* IV, 1: *non omnia mysteria quae in Prima Veritate visa angeli et alii beati cognoscunt, sed quaedam pauca nobis revelantur.*
[32] 2a2ae, 171, 2.
[33] 2a2ae, 175, 3, ad 2: *lumen gloriae . . . dupliciter participari potest. Uno modo, per modum formae immanentis: et sic beatos facit sanctos in patria. Alio modo, per modum cuiusdam passionis transeuntis: sicut dictum est de lumine prophetiae. Et hoc modo lumen illud fuit in Paulo, quando raptus fuit. . . . Et ideo talis raptus aliquo modo ad prophetiam pertinet.* See also *De Ver.* 13, 2; *In 2 ad Cor.* 2, 1 (455); *In ad Gal.* 1, 3 (34).
[34] See *De Ver.* 13, 1–5 and 2a2ae, 171, 2.
[35] Cf. 2a2ae, 171, introd.: *primo occurrit considerandum de prophetia; et de raptu, qui est quidam prophetiae gradus.*
[36] 2a2ae, 173, 1: *visio prophetica non est visio ipsius divinae essentiae: nec in ipsa divina essentia vident ea quae vident, sed in quibusdam similitudinibus, secundum illustrationem divini luminis.*
[37] *De Ver.* 12, 6: *Quod autem a magistris dicitur, prophetas in speculo aeternitatis videre, non sic intelligendum est quasi ipsum Deum aeternum videant prout est speculum rerum; sed quia aliquid creatum intuentur, in quo ipsa aeternitas Dei repraesentatur: ut sic speculum aeternitatis intelligatur non quod est aeternum, sed quod est aeternitatem repraesentans.*

permanent or abiding possession of the recipient of revelation, any more than it was in Paul's case, but is given only through an occasional glimpse of light in the soul. The prophet can not bring the revelation about by himself. Whenever revelation comes, there must be a new illumination of the intellect from without,[38] hence the insight given in and with this illumination may have a different degree of perfection on different occasions in the same person.[39] Thomas summarises his argument by saying that neither prophecy nor revelation can be regarded as a *habitus*—it is rather to be characterised as a *passio vel impressio transiens*, an impermanent or transitory experience in the intellect of a particular individual.[40]

But these are also the characteristics, according to Thomas, by which revelation is to be distinguished from the third type of supernatural cognitive acts mentioned earlier, viz. *fides*, faith. For Thomas even faith is an intellectual phenomenon, and he defines it as an *actus intellectus assentientis veritati divinae ex imperio voluntatis a Deo motae per gratiam* (an act of the intellect assenting to the divine truth at the command of the will moved by God through grace).[41] This emphasis on the cognitive intention of the act of faith is connected with the fact that its object is the truth given in and with the revelation,[42] but even if it is said that the content of faith and revelation are identical in this way, yet there is also at this point a clear distinction in regard to the *modus* of the cognitive act. *Fides*, that is to say, does not itself constitute a *cognitio* in the proper sense, for even if

---

[38] 2a2ae, 171, 2: *sicut aer semper indiget nova illuminatione, ita etiam mens prophetae semper indiget nova revelatione; CG* III, 154: *impressiones quaedam fiunt a Deo quae cessant actu cessante, et eas oportet iterari cum actus iterari fuerit opportunum: sicut prophetae mens in qualibet revelatione novo lumine illustratur.*

[39] *De Ver.* 12, 13, ad 3: *cum lumen propheticum non sit aliquid immanens prophetae, sed sit quasi quaedam passio transiens, non oportet ut propheta semper sit in eodem gradu prophetiae; immo quandoque fit ei revelatio secundum unum gradum, quandoque secundum alium.*

[40] See *De Ver.* 12, 1; 2a2ae, 171, 2; 2a2ae, 176, 2, ad 3.

[41] 2a2ae, 2, 9; cf. 2a2ae, 4, 2: *Credere autem est immediate actus intellectus: quia obiectum huius actus est verum, quod proprie pertinet ad intellectum.* There is a good treatment of Thomas' concept of faith in Skydsgaard, *Metafysik*, p. 230ff.

[42] 2a2ae, 1, 1: *in fide, si consideremus formalem rationem obiecti, nihil est aliud quam veritas prima: non enim fides de qua loquimur assentit alicui nisi quia est a Deo revelatum.* On the term *obiectum formale* see the analyses in Skydsgaard, *Metafysik*, p. 80ff. and 237ff. On the connection between faith and revelation see also the same author in *FJN* p. 283: 'Revelation is an intellectual concept, the communication of a supernatural truth, of mysteries, therefore faith is also clearly defined in intellectual terms as the supernatural appropriation and acknowledgment of these truths'.

faith is a firm *assensus* in the intellect, determined by the will, this assent implies a knowledge which is possessed not by the believer himself but by *some other*.[43] In this respect a man finds himself in the same situation as the pupil who must believe the word of his teacher, *oportet addiscentem credere*, before he attains any knowledge of his own.[44] Faith in this regard is less perfect than prophecy, which also finds expression in being bound to the conditions of hearing, *auditus fidei*, while the knowledge of the prophet or apostle, which is directly given through divine intervention in his intellect, may be classified as a *visio*, though even this is quite imperfect in comparison with the final *visio beatifica*.[45] Nevertheless, there is an affinity between the latter and faith, for in each instance we are dealing with something of a lasting nature, while the *visio prophetica*, as a *passio transiens*, is something occasional, something which belongs to *certis temporibus et locis* (definite times and places).[46] Faith must remain a habitual perfection in the soul, for without it no man can reach the goal of salvation; indeed, *fides* is not only an indispensable condition of eternal life but, despite its incompleteness as an act of cognition, is an anticipation of this life and can therefore be defined by Thomas as a *habitus mentis, qua inchoatur vita aeterna in nobis* (a habit of the mind whereby eternal life is begun in us).[47]

The insight which is given to us *in via* in and with revelation may be, as we have defined it above, relative and imperfect, yet as a word of God it is an impression of God's own knowledge in the soul of the apostle and prophet, and therefore unalterably true. Here too Thomas employs the metaphor of the relationship between teacher and pupil. Just as there must be a direct affinity between the teacher's own

[43] Thomas expresses this relation by saying that the assent of faith to any given knowledge does not come *propter proprium testimonium* but *propter testimonium alienum, De Ver.* 14, 9.

[44] 2a2ae, 2, 3.

[45] 2a2ae, 171, 3, ad 2: *Fides autem etsi sit de invisibilibus homini, tamen ad ipsam non pertinet eorum cognitio quae creduntur: sed quod homo per certitudinem assentiat his quae sunt ab aliis cognita;* cf. also 1a, 12, 13, ad 3; *De Ver.* 12, 1, ad 4: *fides assimilatur auditui; sed prophetia visioni; CG* IV, 1: *quia revelata veritas de divinis non videnda, sed credenda proponitur, recte dicit, 'audiverimus'.* On *visio* as a characteristic of revelation, see also *De Ver.* 12, 7 and 12; and 2a2ae, 173, 1 and 2.

[46] *CG* III, 154.

[47] 2a2ae, 4, 1; the same definition is given in *De Ver.* 14, 2. It is the light itself, given to the soul in and through faith, which constitutes the *habitus fidei*, see *In De Trin.* 3, 1, ad 4. Cf. *In symbolum Apostolorum,* 1: *per fidem inchoatur in nobis vita aeterna: nam vita aeterna nihil aliud est quam cognoscere Deum. . . Haec autem cognitio Dei incipit hic per fidem, sed perficitur in vita futura. . . Nullus ergo potest pervenire ad beatitudinem, quae est vera cognitio Dei, nisi primo cognoscat per fidem.*

knowledge and that which his pupil derives from his teaching, so also the *cognitio* of the recipient of revelation is on its level a direct expression of the eternal truth which is found in its perfection only in God and indeed is God's own proper nature as *veritas prima* (original truth).[48] The whole authority of revelation rests on this direct affinity between the two. Knowledge of God may indeed be given through human mediation, but for Thomas the assurance of faith rests in the last resort neither on reason nor on any other human authority, nor even on the apostles themselves, but solely on the fact that the content of revelation is a truth bestowed by God himself.[49] According to Thomas, therefore, we are not to regard *revelatio* as the antithesis of autonomy on man's part. As a creature endowed with intellect man is directed to the truth, *intelligere enim est simpliciter veritatem intelligibilem apprehendere* (to understand is the simple apprehension of intelligible truth),[50] and since the truth itself is given to him, it cannot in any way come into conflict with his nature. On the contrary, this communication of truth implies his own perfection as man, since through it he fulfils his destiny as a reasonable being. Thus, according to Thomas, revelation does not come to man as an imperious authority or as something imposed from without which he has to accept against his will. Its authority is that of the truth itself—in other words, it is God's own authority, for God is Truth itself, *veritas prima*.[51]

Thus far we have concentrated on the concept of revelation as a cognitive act. For Thomas this is central. There is another broad approach, however, which we can take in summarising what he has

---

[48] 2a2ae, 171, 6: *prophetia est quaedam cognitio intellectui prophetae impressa ex revelatione divina per modum cuiusdam doctrinae. Veritas autem eadem est cognitionis in discipulo et in docente: quia cognitio addiscentis est similitudo cognitionis docentis. . . . Oportet igitur eandem esse veritatem propheticae cognitionis et enuntiationis quae est cognitionis divinae, cui impossible est subesse falsum.* On God as *prima veritas* see 1a, 16, 5 and *CG* I, 60.

[49] Cf. *In Joan.* 4, 5 (2): *Recta quidem est fides, cum veritati non propter aliquod aliud, sed ei propter seipsam obeditur. . . Indicunt autem nos ad fidem Christi tria. Primo quidem ratio naturalis. . . Secundo testimonia Legis et Prophetarum. . . Tertio praedicatio Apostolorum, et aliorum. . . Sed quando per hoc homo manuductus credit, tunc potest dicere, quod propter nullum istorum credit: nec propter rationem naturalem, nec propter testimonia legis, nec propter praedicationem aliorum, sed propter ipsam veritatem tantum.*

[50] 1a, 79, 8.

[51] Thomas never speaks of the church in this context as a guaranteeing authority standing between God and man. Faith is solely a faith in the authority of God. Skydsgaard, *Metafysik*, p. 282ff. throws light on Thomas's interpretation of authority by comparing it with other concepts of authority.

to say about *revelatio*, and which we need to take in order to understand correctly even the meaning of the cognitive line of thought
which we have followed so far. When Thomas speaks of *prophetia*
and *revelatio*, it is not any kind of knowledge that he has in mind but
—as we have already indicated in our introductory remarks—a knowledge on which man's salvation wholly depends. Before we go more
deeply into the meaning of this primary soteriological conception, we
shall discuss more fully some matters which have not yet been dealt
with, since it is easier to explain what they mean from the point of
view of relationship which exists between revelation and man's *salus*.

The question now to be discussed is the extent to which *revelatio*
is a part of knowledge, and its relationship to the sphere which is
controlled by natural reason. At first glance it might seem as though
the revealed knowledge which is given to us in holy scripture extends
to the whole of human experience, *tam divina quam humana, tum
spiritualia quam corporalia* (things both divine and human, both
spiritual and bodily).[52] There is also a naturally given knowledge of
these things—thus for Thomas there is a *cognitio naturalis* of God
given independently of revelation, and in his frequent discussion of
this point Thomas refers to Rom. 1:19, *invisibilia Dei per ea quae
facta sunt, intellecta, conspiciuntur*.[53] Further, revelation seems to
include also those things which *a doctis per demonstrationem sciuntur*
(the educated know by demonstration),[54] and which did not require
to be divinely revealed. Even though there is a large area of human
knowledge about which revelation has nothing at all to say to us, in
this respect *revelatio* seems in part at least to coincide with *ratio*.
Nevertheless, revelation does impart a knowledge which transcends
what is accessible to human reason, even the most highly developed
reason, e.g., God's triune nature or *futura contingentia* (contingent
events in our future). For Thomas the unifying concept which holds
together those many varieties of revelation is *salus*, for what is revealed can be defined as a knowledge of *omnia illa quorum cognitio
potest esse utilis ad salutem* (all those things the knowledge of which
can be useful for salvation).[55] Thus *revelatio* gives two things: first, an
understanding of truths which would otherwise have been inaccessible

---

[52] 2a2ae, 171, 3.
[53] Few biblical passages are cited by Thomas more frequently (and then always in
the form stated above), see, e.g., 1a, 2, 2; 1a, 13, 5; 1a, 56, 3; 1a, 65, 1, ad 3; 1a, 79
9, etc.
[54] *De Ver.* 12, 2.
[55] *De Ver.* 12, 2; cf. Gilson, *Philosophy of St Thomas*, p. 42ff.

to *ratio* because of the utter inadequacy of human reason, and second, an understanding of that which, though it lies within the sphere of reason, would have remained unknown had it not been revealed to those who for one reason or another cannot devote themselves to study.

Since salvation is intended to be open and available to all, that which is in itself accessible to reason must be made known to all through revelation.[56] The substance of revelation can therefore be expressed so that it includes *omnia quae . . . non sunt ab homine cognoscibilia nisi per revelationem divinam* (all those things that are . . . unknowable to man except by divine revelation),[57] whether this refers to what is otherwise unknown to the majority of men or to what would have in the main been hidden apart from revelation. The prophets are thus described by Thomas as men who *cognoscunt . . . quae sunt procul remota ab hominum cognitione* (know . . . what is far removed from human knowledge)[58]—they see what is concealed from others and therefore have a knowledge which transcends that possessed by others.[59]

Among different men and in different periods this knowledge may vary in its degree of perfection, hence, according to Thomas, there is also a difference of degree between the various classes of those who receive revelation. He usually makes a distinction in this regard

[56] 1a, 1, 1: *Ad ea etiam quae de Deo ratione humana investigari possunt, necessarium fuit hominem instrui revelatione divina. Quia veritas de Deo, per rationem investigata, a paucis, et per longum tempus, et cum admixtione multorum errorum, homini proveniret: a cuius tamen veritatis cognitione dependet tota hominis salus, quae in Deo est. Ut igitur salus hominibus et convenientius et certius proveniat, necessarium fuit quod de divinis per divinam revelationem instruantur.* Cf. *De Ver.* 12, 2 and 14, 10; *CG* I, 4 and 5.

[57] 2a2ae, 171, 3, ad 2.

[58] 2a2ae, 171, 1.

[59] This concealment may depend in part on the things about which knowledge is given, as in the case of *futura contingentia*, but it may also be due to the *debilitas* of human reason, e.g. in regard to God's triune nature which is otherwise in itself *maxime cognoscibilis. In ad Rom.* 12, 2 (978): *Sunt autem procul a cognitione nostra secundum se quidem futura contigentia, quae propter defectum sui esse cognoscibilia non sunt; sed res divinae sunt procul a nostra cognitione, non secundum se, cum sint maxime cognoscibiles . . . sed propter defectum intellectus nostri, qui se habet ad ea, quae sunt in seipsis manifestissima, sicut oculus noctuae ad lucem solis.* See also *De Ver.* 12, 2 and 2a2ae, 171, 3. It is to be noted that for Thomas *prophetia* cannot by any means be limited to predictions of the future, but refers to any supernaturally given knowledge of what is otherwise concealed. Cf. *In ad Rom.* 12, 2 (978): *Dicitur tamen prophetia communiter etiam revelatio quorumcumque occultorum; In 1 ad Cor.* 14, 1 (812): *visio eorum quae sunt procul, sive sint futura contingentia, sive supra rationem nostram, dicitur prophetia.*

between patriarchs and prophets on the one hand and the apostles on the other, the former lacking the clearer understanding of the latter. The knowledge of the fathers and prophets of the Old Testament is a presupposition of and is included within that possessed by the apostles, but the difference between the two is that the apostles have been given a *manifestior revelatio* (clearer revelation).[60] While the former had a knowledge of the hidden things of salvation *in generali*, the latter possess in addition a knowledge of *singulares et determinatas circumstantias* (individual and definite circumstances).[61] This larger measure of knowledge is explained at times by Thomas by reference to the fact that the apostles were taught directly by Christ himself, who is *fidei primus et principalis Doctor* (the first and chief teacher of faith),[62] while the prophets and fathers of the old covenant received their revelation through the mediation of angels.[63] Christ himself as man possessed the gift of prophecy in fullest measure, for as *perfectus homo* he must have possessed in the most perfect manner possible all gifts of grace, amongst which the *donum prophetiae* (gift of prophecy) is also included.[64] Hence the apex of revelation on earth

---

[60] *De Ver*. 12, 14, ad 5: *In novo tamen testamento facta est manifestior revelatio: unde dicitur II Corinth. III, 18: Nos autem revelata facie; ubi expresse Apostolus se et alios apostolos Moysi praefert.*

[61] *In ad Eph*. 3, 1 (139): *Licet enim mysteria Christi prophetis et patriarchis fuerint revelata, non tamen ita clare sicut Apostolis. Nam prophetis et patriarchis fuerunt revelata in quadam generalitate; sed Apostolis manifestata sunt quantum ad singulares et determinatas circumstantias;* 1a, 57, 5, ad 3: *Et licet prophetis ea quae Deus facturus erat circa salutem humani generis, in generali revelaverit; quaedam tamen specialia Apostoli circa hoc cognoverunt, quae prophetae non cognoverant.*

[62] 3a, 7, 7.

[63] *In ad Eph*. 3, 1 (141): *ipsi Apostoli habuerunt revelationem immediate a Filio Dei. . . . Prophetae vero et patres Veteris Testamenti, ipsi edocti sunt per angelos, vel per aliquas similitudines. . . Et ideo isti Apostoli clarius acceperunt.* Thus, as Thomas conceives it, the *lumen propheticum* is brought about by God directly in the soul of the prophet, while the *formatio specierum* is due to the influence of the angels, see *De Ver*. 12, 8 and 1a, 111, 1. Cf. also *CG* III, 154; 2a2ae, 172, 2; 3a, 55, 2 and the extensive discussion in White, *AT* 11 (1950), p. 116ff.

[64] 3a, 7, 7: *Oportet autem eum qui docet, habere ea per quae sua doctrina manifestetur: aliter sua doctrina esset inutilis. Spiritualis autem doctrinae et fidei primus et principalis Doctor est Christus. . . Unde manifestum est quod in Christo fuerunt excellentissime omnes gratiae gratis datae, sicut in primo et principali Doctore fidei;* see also 3a, 7, 8 which deals directly with the question, *Utrum in Christo fuerit prophetia*, 3a, 11, 1, and also *In Joan*. 4, 6 (2) and 6, 2 (1). Scripture bears witness to Christ as prophet, which means that Thomas had to include Christ in his psychology of revelation, but this raises many difficulties for him, since as *beatus* Christ cannot have the knowledge that is found in the prophet in the form of a *passio transiens*. This whole problem is dealt with in detail by Ch.-V. Héris, *Le verbe incarné*, vol. II, 2nd ed. 1927, p. 346ff.

is the teaching which Christ gave to the apostles, and which was after-wards completed when the Spirit descended upon them.[65]

We have now shown how Thomas interprets revelation from the standpoint of salvation. The knowledge communicated in revelation is to be understood in categories of *grace*. More exactly, he defines the *donum prophetiae* as one of the gifts of grace or charisms described by Paul in I Corinthians 12:4ff. These Thomas summarises as *gratiae gratis datae* (graces gratuitously given).[66] We shall discuss his doctrine of grace more fully later.[67] At present all that we need to do is to show more clearly what he means by *revelatio*.

The gift of grace, as Thomas defines it, is something which *supra facultatem naturae, et super meritum personae, homini conceditur* (is bestowed on a man beyond the capability of nature and beyond the merit of a person).[68] To speak of grace as *gratis data* is to rule out any idea of a rightful claim on the part of the one who receives the gift. This claim, Thomas states, can be understood in two ways: it may mean, first that on the basis of his merit, a man could claim that he was worthy of receiving grace, or, second, that human nature needs the addition of grace for its perfection as nature. According to this latter interpretation the endowments conferred on man at his creation, e.g. his reason, *ratio*, can be claimed by man on the basis of his nature—for without them he would no longer be a man—even though that which is given in creation *excludit rationem debiti* (excludes the notion of debt), in the sense that it is given without any preceding merit of any kind. It is a mark of the gifts of grace, however, that they are given in a way that excludes the possibility of any such claim being made to them. It is quite clear where Thomas himself lays the empha-sis. In all his discussion the crucial question is the relationship between 'grace' and 'nature', not grace as opposed to merit. The gifts of grace are primarily to be seen as *supra facultatem naturae* and are

---

[65] Cf. *De Ver.* 14, 11, ad 6: *veritatis cognitio ad suum complementum pervenerat, quod proecipue factum est in adventu Spiritu sancti;* 1a2ae, 106, 4, ad 2: *Docuit autem Spiritus Sanctus Apostolos omnem veritatem de his quae pertinent ad necessitatem salutis: scilicet de credendis et agendis.* On this special position of the apostles see also p. 81f.

[66] On the distinction between *gratia gratum faciens* and *gratia gratis data* see 1a2ae, 111, 1 and 5. A good summary of what Thomas understands by *gratia gratis data* is to be found in 1a2ae, 111, 4: *Et ideo gratia gratis data illa sub se continet quibus homo indiget ad hoc quod alterum instruat in rebus divinis, quae sunt supra rationem.* On prophecy as a gift of grace see *CG* III, 154 and 2a2ae, 171, introd.

[67] See p. 170ff.

[68] 1a2ae, 111, 1.

therefore also designated *dona supernaturalia*.[69] This definition of grace with primary reference to the concept of nature is thoroughly typical of Thomas's theology.[70] Like grace in its entirety, the gift of prophecy and revelation are also *super naturam*. It is grace in the first instance because it transcends man's natural endowments. The question here is primarily that of a knowledge which cannot be obtained by man's own *ratio*. Those who have devoted their lives to study can indeed acquire at least in a partial way through such study the revealed knowledge which belongs to the sphere of reason, though this is not true of the majority. What remains undisclosed is beyond the reach of any man, whatever his situation may be. The same is true also of the *modus* of revelation, its particular cognitive form, which no human being has the power to create by himself. A phrase constantly found in the writings of Thomas, though he does not use it in this particular context, may provide some clarification: revelation is always *aliquid supernaturale quoad modum* (supernatural in regard to its mode), though it is not always so in regard to its content, *quoad substantiam*.[71] It is striking to note that Thomas nowhere connects the necessity of revelation with the fact of sin. In accordance with the medieval tradition he includes among the wounds inflicted by sin on human nature the *vulnus ignorantiae* (wound of ignorance),[72] but he never relates the supernatural knowledge of God to a lack of knowledge caused by sin. It is characteristic of Thomas that he can answer the question, *utrum homo sine gratia aliquod verum cognoscere possit* (whether without grace men can know any truth), without reference to sin or its effects. He answers the question simply by examining the relationship between the natural *lumen intelligibile* and the *lumen gratiae*, the latter being understood primarily as a completion of the former.[73] It is clear that Thomas does not deduce the necessity of

---

[69] 1a2ae, 111, 1, ad 2: *gratia, secundum quod gratis datur, excludit rationem debiti. Potest autem intelligi duplex debitum. Unum quidem ex merito proveniens, quod refertur ad personam, cuius est agere meritoria opera. . . . Aliud est debitum ex conditione naturae: puta si dicamus debitum esse homini quod habeat rationem et alia quae ad humanam pertinent naturam. . . Dona igitur naturalia carent primo debito, non autem carent secundo debito. Sed dona supernaturalia utroque debito carent: et ideo specialius sibi nomen gratiae vindicant.*

[70] Skydsgaard, *Metafysik*, p. 109ff. We shall return to this problem later, see p. 173ff.

[71] See e.g. Synave and Benoit, *Prophétie*, p. 272: 'Ainsi les vérités manifestées dans la révélation prophétique peuvent être surnaturelles ou naturelles selon leur formalité intrinsèque (*quoad substantiam*), mais elles sont surnaturelles quant à leur mode d'acquisition (*quoad modum*).'

[72] See 1a2ae, 85, 3.

[73] 1a2ae, 109, 1: *Sic igitur intellectus humanus habet aliquam formam, scilicet ipsum*

revelation from any sinful reduction or corruption in the natural knowledge of God. This as far as it goes is a true knowledge, but it is imperfect, and through grace man is given a far fuller knowledge of God than he can find through *ratio naturalis*.[74] What makes revelation what it is and renders it essential is simply that this knowledge, on which his salvation depends, far transcends man's natural capabilities, and would have been beyond his reach had it not been revealed through divine intervention.

The decisive importance which Thomas attaches to the cognitive character of revelation is best explained from the standpoint of the connection which he establishes between revelation and redemption. We have already seen how he explicitly classifies prophecy among man's intellectual functions—*prophetia pertinet ad intellectum* (prophecy has reference to the intellect).[75] Prophecy may be described as a perfecting of the intellect of the recipient of revelation, and constitutes a *perfectio intellectus*.[76] The *lumen naturale intellectus* (natural intellectual light) is reinforced by the new light given in and with revelation, and over and above the *phantasmata* (images) given to the soul by external knowledge *revelatio* bestows new insights which

intelligibile lumen, quod est de se sufficiens ad quaedam intelligibilia cognoscenda: ad ea scilicet in quorum notitiam per sensibilia possumus devenire. Altiora vero intelligibilia intellectus humanus cognoscere non potest nisi fortiori lumine perficiatur, sicut lumine fidei vel prophetiae; quod dicitur lumen gratiae, inquantum est naturae superadditum. The lack of any interest in sin in this passage may be related to the fact that for Thomas sin has nothing to do primarily with the intellect as such but resides in the will, cf. 1a2ae, 74, 1: *peccatum sit in voluntate sicut in subiecto*, see also 1a2ae, 83, 3. The destructive effect of sin does not penetrate as deeply into the intellect, he holds, as it does into the will, cf. 1a2ae, 109, 2, and 3: *magis est natura humana corrupta per peccatum quantum ad appetitum boni, quam quantum ad cognitionem veri.* Hence ignorance, *ignorantia*, cannot be regarded as a sin even in the case of something which a man *potest et debet scire*, see 1a2ae, 74, 5. If Thomas were consistent, however, this would mean that not even *unbelief* could properly be regarded as sin, since there is no place for any knowledge which should or could be naturally acquired in the faith that is directed toward revealed truth. Thomas gets around this difficulty by showing how the rejection of supernaturally revealed knowledge by unbelief may in one way be said to be contrary to nature, since man as a creature endowed with reason is directed towards the truth as such: 2a2ae, 10, 1, ad 1: *habere fidem non est in natura humana: sed in natura humana est ut mens hominis non repugnet interiori instinctui et exteriori veritatis praedicationi. Unde infidelitas secundum hoc est contra naturam.*

---

[74] 1a, 12, 13: *per gratiam perfectior cognitio de Deo habetur a nobis, quam per rationem naturalem.*
[75] 2a2ae, 172, 4.
[76] 2a2ae, 172, 2, ad 1.

express divine realities in a more perfect way.[77] As a creature endowed with reason man's primary object is the acquisition of knowledge; whenever, therefore, his understanding is deepened, his nature is brought correspondingly nearer to its perfection. It follows that where knowledge of God has been fully attained, the *perfectio hominis* is complete. Thus in Thomas the *salus hominis* (salvation of man) and *perfectio hominis* become quite simply synonymous and interchangeable terms.[78] Man's salvation and his perfection as an intellectual being are one and the same: *ultima autem salus hominis est ut secundum intellectivam partem perficiatur contemplatione Veritatis Primae* (the ultimate salvation of man is to be perfected in his intellective part by the contemplation of the First Truth).[79] Since revelation *in via* is a momentary foretaste of the final *perfectio* of this blessedness within the conditions of earthly life, it is natural to find *revelatio* also described by Thomas as an intellectual act, or, more accurately, as a *perfectio intellectus*.

The same is true, *mutatis mutandis*, of faith. Like revelation, faith is also something brought about in man by grace alone. The act of faith, whether it is a *fides formata* or merely *informis*, has as its basis and starting-point a *habitus* which is *per lumen fidei divinitus infusus* (bestowed on him by God through the light of faith).[80] No man can attain a saving faith in God by his own strength or by his reason alone. But as in the case of revelation, this is contingent on the fact that the truth, which is given through revelation and is the object of faith,

---

[77] 1a, 12, 13: *Cognitio enim quam per naturalem rationem habemus, duo requirit: scilicet, phantasmata ex sensibilibus accepta, et lumen naturale intelligibile, cuius virtute intelligibiles conceptiones ab eis abstrahimus. Et quantum ad utrumque, iuvatur humana cognitio per revelationem gratiae. Nam et lumen naturale intellectus confortatur per infusionem luminis gratuiti. Et interdum etiam phantasmata in imaginatione hominis formantur divinitus, magis exprimentia res divinas, quam ea quae naturaliter a sensibilibus accipimus; sicut apparet in visionibus prophetalibus.*

[78] *Salus* and *perfectio* are synonymous in Thomas's thinking, as we see strikingly expressed in 2a2ae, 2, 3. He asks *utrum credere aliquid supra rationem naturalem sit necessarium* AD SALUTEM, and answers the question by speaking of the PERFECTIO *rationalis creaturae.* Cf. also *De Ver.* 14, 10: *Ultima autem perfectio ad quam homo ordinatur, consistit in perfecta Dei cognitione: ad quam quidem pervenire non potest nisi operatione et instructione Dei, qui est sui perfectus cognitor; Compend. Theol. 1: Consistit enim humana salus in veritatis cognitione.*

[79] *CG* IV, 42.

[80] 2a2ae, 2, 3, ad 2; *De Ver.* 14, 7: *fides formata et informis non distinguuntur sicut duo diversi habitus, sed sicut habitus perfectus et imperfectus,* see also 2a2ae, 4, 4. On the other hand only *fides formata* is to be regarded as a *virtus theologica,* 2a2ae, 4, 5; 1a2ae, 62, 1 and 3. We should note that the idea of *a fides naturaliter acquisita* is not found in Thomas.

infinitely transcends man's natural gifts. The goal of salvation is super-natural in the sense that it far surpasses the possibilities of nature. As a cognitive act faith is perhaps inferior to natural knowledge in this re-spect, that its object is not immediately perceived by the believer but must be believed on another's testimony.[81] But at the same time the ob-ject of faith is so sublime and its understanding of the being of God so profound that Thomas can hold that no philosopher for all his pains can attain the knowledge of God possessed by the simple believer through faith.[82] On the natural plane, however, this truth is concealed from believer and philosopher alike—there is no *proportio* between human nature as such and this higher knowledge, which is its supernatural goal appointed by God. Since, according to Thomas, *nihil autem potest ordinari in aliquem finem nisi praeexistat in ipso quaedam proportio ad finem* (nothing can be directed to any end unless there pre-exists in it a certain proportion to the end),[83] such a relationship must be brought about in man's soul, and this is the work of grace. When the habit of faith is infused into his soul, it is illuminated and raised to a level where it becomes possible for man to acquire the truth which is supernaturally given in revelation. Here all is grace, but in regard to both revelation and faith itself the meaning of grace is wholly determined by cognitive and theoretical reflection on man's being as a *creatura rationalis*.[84]

This idea of revelation and of faith as a perfection of man's natural condition is vividly expressed in Thomas's definition of grace as an elevation or raising of human nature to a higher plane. The same is true of all the gifts of grace: *omne donum gratiae hominem elevat ad aliquid quod est supra naturam humanam* (every gift of grace raises man to something above human nature).[85] Since revelation is by definition a gift of grace, its meaning is to be defined in terms of this *elevatio* or raising, which is significant for the whole of Thomas's thought.[86]

[81] Cf. 1a, 12, 13, ad 3: *fides cognitio quaedam est, inquantum intellectus determinatur per fidem ad aliquod cognoscibile. Sed haec determinatio ad unum non procedit ex visione credentis, sed a visione eius cui creditur. Et sic, inquantum deest visio, deficit a ratione cognitionis quae est in scientia.*

[82] *In symb. Apost.*, 1: *nullus philosophorum ante adventum Christi cum toto conatu suo potuit tantum scire de Deo et de necessariis ad vitam aeternam, quantum post adventum Christi scit una vetula per fidem.*

[83] *De Ver.* 14, 2.

[84] Cf. K. E. Skydsgaard, 'La signification luthérienne du Credo', in *Positions luthériennes* 4 (1956), p. 26: 'En dernière analyse, la question des rapports entre grâce et foi chez Thomas d'Aquin est une question d'épistémologie surnaturelle'.

[85] 2a2ae, 171, 2, ad 3.

[86] Cf. Skydsgaard, *Metafysik*, p. 279: 'Thomas' basic view of the Christian faith is therefore that of raising up, the perfection of human nature'.

D

This is expressed with particular clarity in a passage in the *Summa contra gentiles* where Thomas defines the meaning of the revelation event in the following terms : *revelatio fit quodam interiori et intelligibili lumine mentem elevante ad percipiendum ea ad quae per lumen naturale intellectus pertingere non potest* (revelation is accomplished by means of a certain interior and intelligible light, elevating the mind to the perception of things that the understanding cannot reach by its natural light).[87] Prophecy, like revelation in general, is a work of God, a divine *actio*. But this divine action does not mean that God 'comes down' to man from a remote and unknown place. As we shall see in the discussion following, the idea of God as distant or far away from the world of his creation is quite alien to Thomas—*nihil est distans ab eo*.[88] The distance to which he refers is 'une distance de connaissance',[89] man's lack of knowledge of the God who is already present and active in the created world *sicut agens adest ei in quod agit* (as an agent is present to that in which its action is taking place).[90] The object of knowledge is not in itself obscure or indistinct; the obscurity is in the knowing subject. The new condition brought about in revelation is therefore a change in the soul of man in which the veil, *obscuritatis et ignorantiae velamen*,[91] which conceals from his view the works of God, is removed by a divine act of enlightenment. Behind Thomas's description of this enlightenment as an 'elevation' lies the idea of God himself as the absolute light in relation to which the natural light in man's reason is a distant reflection. Imperfect though it is, the resemblance between man and God given by this light is increased by *elevatio*, just as an object becomes 'lighter' the nearer it is brought to the source of light.

The revelation event referred to above is sometimes described by Thomas as a divine inspiration. In Thomas's vocabulary the term *inspiratio* does not refer to the writing of the scriptures but is used to describe an event in the soul which is brought about not by any principle inherent within it—e.g. man's reason—but by an impulse from without.[92] In discussing the meaning of revelation Thomas uses

---

[87] *CG* III, 154; cf. *De Ver.* 12, 3: *Per prophetiam . . . elevatur mens hominis, ut quodammodo conformiter substantiis separatis intelligat*, and also 27, 3: *Gratia . . . est quaedam perfectio elevans animam ad quoddam esse supernaturale.*

[88] 1a, 8, 1, ad 3.

[89] White, *AT* 11 (1950), p. 17.

[90] 1a, 8, 1.

[91] 2a2ae, 171, 1, ad 4.

[92] Cf. 1a2ae, 68, 1: *Inspiratio autem significat quandam motionem ab exteriori. Est enim considerandum quod in homine est duplex principium movens: unum quidem*

the term *inspiratio* to indicate that the raising of the intellect, whereby it becomes possible for the recipient of revelation to *percipere divina* (perceive the things of God), is not an achievement of human reason but is a work of God.[93] No man can raise himself by his own reason or powers to the level of the prophet or apostle. This is wholly a work of grace. At the same time this work of grace is an activity which takes place wholly within the recipient of revelation, since the divinely given light confirms the *lumen naturale* which is given with human nature. Through *inspiratio* human reason is brought to a new and higher viewpoint from which it sees far more than it did before, just as a climber sees far more from the mountain top than he could from the valley below. The divine act of raising creates the conditions for the *perceptio divinorum* which, according to Thomas, is *revelatio* in the truest sense and consists in the perception and comprehension by the enlightened intellect of that which can be seen from the higher viewpoint.[94] This means that in the last resort *revelatio* is man's own cognitive act, although it is dependent on the enlightenment given by God which confirms the natural power of the intellect to interpret and evaluate the content of knowledge.[95] The new light comes from God, but at the same time it is a *lumen interior* within the recipient of revelation. On the one hand the higher knowledge given in revelation is wholly grace and therefore a work of God; on the other hand this activity of grace is wholly a human act, since it comes about in a man as a perfection of his rational nature. Revelation is primarily an event which happens to and takes place in a human being—one particular expression of this, as Thomas puts it, is that the supernatural destiny or *beatitudo* of man is at one and the same time the highest point of revelation, *perfectio revelationis*, and man's own

interius, quod est ratio; aliud autem exterius, quod est Deus. On Thomas's view of inspiration see also 2a2ae, 171, 1, ad 4 and *De Ver.* 12, 1, and also the instructive account in Synave and Benoit, *Prophétie*, p. 277ff.

---

[93] 2a2ae, 171, 1, ad 4: *ad prophetiam requiritur inspiratio quantum ad mentis elevationem.*

[94] The passage referred to in the previous footnote continues: *revelatio autem, quantum ad ipsam perceptionem divinorum, in quo perficitur prophetia; per ipsam removetur obscuritatis et ignorantiae velamen.*

[95] Cf. p. 24f. above and Synave and Benoit, *Prophétie*, p. 280: 'L'inspiration est la motion préalable qui élève l'esprit au-dessus de son niveau ordinaire, en lui conférant une vigueur intellectuelle accrue; la révélation en résulte, dans le jugement que porte l'esprit ainsi surélevé et par lequel il perçoit les choses divines'; see also p. 227.

perfection as an intellectual being, *perfectio hominis*,[96] Revelation does not originate in reason, though it does take place within reason and in accordance with it. This brings us to the problem which will be constantly before us in the section following and which we must try to state in order to elucidate its meaning and its implications for Thomas's theology.

In stating that revelation is a gift of grace Thomas gives us a further important qualification of its relation to man's salvation. It is the peculiar mark of all the charisms or gifts of grace, *gratiae gratis datae*, as opposed to saving and sanctifying grace, *gratia gratum faciens*, that they are given not for the benefit of the recipient but for the profit of the church, *ad utilitatem ecclesiae*.[97] Revelation is primarily a *cognitio*, and therefore a perfection of the intellect of the recipient of revelation, but it has also a 'social' or outward-directed function in the fellowship of the church.[98] The prophet and apostle are not given a revelation only for their own personal salvation, but rather in order that others too may share in the saving knowledge, *ad hoc enim Deus revelat, ut aliis denuntientur*.[99] Of necessity, there-fore, revelation is expressed in being communicated also to others in a *denuntiatio* or *locutio*, and it is from this perspective that we have to see what Thomas says about the communication of revealed knowledge to each new generation. This will be the object of our study in the following section.

[96] Cf. p. 22f. and 36 above.
[97] 2a2ae, 172, 4: *datur enim prophetia ad utilitatem Ecclesiae, sicut et aliae gratiae gratis datae;* cf. also 1a2ae, 111, 1 and 4.
[98] Gardeil, *Le donné*, emphasises this point of view, e.g. p. 74: 'La Révélation chrétienne est une grâce intérieure sans doute, mais *sociale* et non individuelle'; see also p. 43 and 70.
[99] *In 1 ad Cor. 14*, 1 (812).

2

THE COMMUNICATION OF REVELATION

In the previous section we have seen how Thomas describes revelation: it is, he holds, a knowledge essential for salvation but inaccessible to man, and therefore communicated through a divine act. This *cognitio*, which conveys within the soul of the recipient of revelation an impression of God's own knowledge of himself and the context of existence, is given moreover in order to be communicated to others. The outward-directedness of revelation is consequent upon the fact that revelation is one of the gifts of grace, all of which have been given, says Thomas, for instruction and the communication of knowledge—*gratia gratis data illa sub se continet quibus homo indiget ad hoc quod alterum instruat in rebus divinis, quae sunt supra rationem* (gratuitous grace embraces whatever a man needs in order to instruct another in divine things which are above reason).[1] Amongst the *gratiae gratis datae* Thomas includes not only the primary assumption in all instruction, viz. that the teacher himself possesses the knowledge which is to be transmitted, but also his ability to communicate it to others in such a way that it is received and understood.[2]

Instruction itself is a necessary consequence of the fact that revealed truth far surpasses in its content man's natural capacities. Since he cannot attain it through his own reason, this truth must come to him from without and be transmitted by someone who already knows it. Thus Thomas can even at times speak of the revelation event as instruction given by God, e.g. when he says that *mens prophetae . . . a Deo instruitur* (the prophet's mind is instructed by God)[3] or that *revelatio* is given *per modum cuiusdam doctrinae* (by means of teaching).[4] From God, who as *prima veritas*, is the source of all truth, there comes the supernatural knowledge which is given to the angels in the highest rank, and these in turn transmit it to those of lower orders. Here, as in the case of the beatific vision of the saints in

[1] 1a2ae, 111, 4.
[2] See 1a2ae, 111, 4 and *CG* III, 154 and also the fuller discussion in 2a2ae, 176, 1–2 (*gratia linguarum*) and 2a2ae, 177, 1–2 (*gratia gratis data quae consistit in sermone*).
[3] 2a2ae, 171, 5.
[4] 2a2ae, 171, 6; the passage is quoted in full on p. 29 above, footnote 48.

heaven, Thomas is speaking of a clear and unimpeded view of truth, an *aperta visio*, though of different degrees according to the ontological perfection of the various angels. But even here revelation is a work of grace. No created intellect has the power to see God as he is, *videre Deum per essentiam*, even though it may have the perfection of the immaterial form of angelic existence. Even here grace is required, because blessedness always surpasses the *facultas naturae*.[5] From angels, then, supernatural truth is transmitted to prophets and apostles in the form of a momentary and passing experience, *passio transiens*, the result of which in them is a firm and abiding faith.[6] Revealed knowledge is thus transmitted in a hierarchical order along a scale of declining perfection, *quidam a Deo reciperent, alii vero ab his, et sic per ordinem usque ad ultimos* (some received them from God, then others from them, and so on in an orderly way down to the humblest).[7] This hierarchical order is then continued and fulfilled in the church, descending from the perfect vision of divine reality granted to the apostle (perfect, at least, with regard to earthly circumstances) down to the simplest believer, and in this way divine truth comes down to men, *non tamen quasi demonstrata ad videndum, sed quasi sermone prolata ad credendum* (not, however, as though proved, but to be believed as heard).[8]

Revelation is primarily a cognitive act, a *cognitio*, but since it involves a knowledge on which the salvation of all men wholly depends, it must also have a secondary expression in the communication of this knowledge, in a *locutio*.[9] All teaching—or *doctrina*, to use the term preferred by Thomas—consists in the communication of knowledge by use of words.[10] What is com-

---

[5] See 1a, 62, 1–7.

[6] *CG* III, 154: *In quibuscumque autem est aliquis ordo, oportet quod, quanto aliquid est propinquius primo principio, tanto virtuosius inveniatur. Quod in hoc ordine manifestationis divinae apparet. Invisibilia enim, quorum visio beatos facit, de quibus fides est, primo a Deo revelantur angelis beatis per apertam visionem . . . .Deinde, angelorum interveniente officio, manifestantur quibusdam hominibus, non quidem per apertam visionem, sed per quandam certitudinem provenientem ex revelatione divina;* cf. Gilson, *Thomisme*, p. 21.

[7] *CG* III, 154.

[8] *CG* IV, 1.

[9] 2a2ae, 171, 1: *prophetia secundario consistit in locutione, prout prophetae ea quae divinitus edocti cognoscunt, ad aedificationem aliorum annuntiant;* 2a2ae, 177, 1: *Cognitio autem quam aliquis a Deo accipit, in utilitatem alterius converti non posset nisi mediante locutione.*

[10] 2a2ae, 16, 2: *Acceptio quidem scientiae vel intellectus fit per doctrinam et disciplinam;* 2a2ae, 181, 3: *fit enim doctrina per locutionem.*

municated in this process is not the objects about which the teacher speaks. Rather, he imparts his knowledge by addressing to the pupil words and concepts which signify these objects. At times, therefore, Thomas uses this analogy when he refers to the work of God in infusing into the soul of the recipient of salvation a supernatural light, which, in relation to his previous knowledge, is a new *species*. This infusion he refers to as a divine 'address' or *locutio Dei*, since God does not allow himself to be seen when he reveals, but merely gives *aliqua spiritualis similitudo suae sapientiae* (some spiritual likeness of his wisdom).[11]

The knowledge given to certain chosen individuals through this *locutio interior*[12] is passed on to others through a *locutio exterior*, by which Thomas clearly means oral rather than, say, written teaching. He regards this form of teaching, indeed, as more perfect than the written form, which explains why Christ—whose teachings may be said to represent the highest revelation of the knowledge of God *in via*—did not leave any writings behind him. The same is true of other great teachers—Pythagoras and Socrates, for example.[13] The truth given through revelation is to be transmitted in speech or writing both to the contemporaries of those who receive the revelation and to coming generations through the *locutio exterior*, *qua Deus nobis per praedicatores loquitur* (external speaking, by which God speaks to us through preachers).[14] There is for Thomas no fundamental difference at this point between preaching and teaching, preaching being essentially instruction in revealed truth; hence he can use both words as synonyms and speak of *praedicatio vel doctrina*.[15] We should note that in Thomas *doctrina* does not have the more precise meaning which it has for us of a fixed and formal system of teaching,

---

[11] *De Ver*. 18, 3: *Est etiam quaedam locutio . . . interior, qua loquitur* (*Deus*) *nobis per inspirationem internam. Dicitur autem ipsa interior inspiratio locutio quaedam ad similitudinem exterioris locutionis: sicut enim in exteriori locutione proferimus ad ipsum audientem non ipsam rem quam notificare cupimus, sed signum illius rei, scilicet vocem significativam; ita Deus interius inspirando non exhibit essentiam suam ad videndum, sed aliquod suae essentiae signum, quod est aliqua spiritualis similitudo suae sapientiae*. Yet Thomas does not speak here of 'the Word of God'. *Verbum Dei* is for him a trinitarian concept which does not belong to the theology of revelation; cf. Skydsgaard, *Metafysik*, p. 284.

[12] 2a2ae, 3, 1: *exterior enim locutio ordinatur ad significandum id quod in corde concipitur*.

[13] See 3a, 42, 4.

[14] *De Ver*. 18, 3.

[15] *In 2 ad Cor*. 11, 2 (382); cf. 1a2ae, 106, 4, ad 4; 2a2ae, 187, 1; 2a2ae, 188, 6 and especially 3a, 42, 1–4, where the preaching of Christ is discussed under the heading *De doctrina Christi*.

or 'doctrine'. As used by Thomas it has an *active* meaning which corresponds most closely to what we mean by 'teaching', hence it denotes at the same time both the act of teaching and the knowledge communicated in teaching.[16]

Like revelation itself, which was once given to men *per modum cuiusdam doctrinae* (after the fashion of a certain teaching),[17] the teaching first given by prophets and apostles and by those who came after them in the church is a continuation of this original *doctrina* given by God. The commission given to the apostles when they were first sent out by Jesus, 'Go, teach', has passed in the first instance to their successors, the bishops, whose task is to preach and expound the same gospel, *docere, id est exponere evangelium, pertinet proprie ad episcopum* (to teach, i.e., to expound the gospel, is the proper office of a bishop).[18] But others, too, share in this apostolic and episcopal office—e.g. those who have received a revelation, or 'prophets' as they are designated in the New Testament, as well as the teachers or *doctores* whose work is to teach what others have been given through revelation.[19] As we hope to show in the present section, it is from this perspective of a continuing tradition of teaching within the church that Thomas views his own work as a theologian.

How, then, in Thomas's view does this tradition of teaching mediate the content of revelation?—According to his interpretation, Christ, who as God is Truth itself, and as man possessed all supernaturally given knowledge[20] in the highest degree, is *fidei primus et principalis Doctor* (the first and chief teacher of the faith).[21] He himself taught the apostles, and through them this teaching was handed on in both oral and written form.[22] Accordingly, the teaching de-

---

[16] See particularly in this connection the review by Y. M. -J. Congar in *Bulletin thomiste* (=*BT*) 5 (1938), p. 496, footnote 1, and the same author's Letter of Introduction in van Ackeren's *Sacra doctrina*, p. 13.

[17] 2a2ae, 171, 6.

[18] 3a, 67, 1, ad 1; cf. also *In ad Eph.* 4, 4(212): *Et sub eodem addit et Doctores, ad ostendendum quod proprium officium pastorum ecclesiae est docere ea quae pertinent ad fidem et bonos mores.*

[19] *In 1 ad Cor.* 12, 3 (755): *Et quamvis ad apostolos praecipue pertineat doctrinae officium, quibus dictum est Matth. ult.: 'Euntes docete omnes gentes', tamen alii in communionem huius officii assumuntur, quorum quidam per seipsos revelationes a Deo accipiunt, qui dicuntur prophetae; quidam vero de his, quae sunt aliis revelata, populum instruunt, qui dicuntur doctores.*

[20] Cf. p. 205ff. below.

[21] 3a, 7, 7; *In 1 ad Tim.* 6, 1(237): *Nam Dominus Iesus venit, ut testimonium perhibeat veritati. . . Et ideo missus est a Patre sicut doctor et magister.*

[22] 3a, 42, 4: *ipse scilicet discipulos suos immediate docuit, qui postmodum alios verbo et scripto docuerunt;* cf. 3a, 25, 3, ad 4 and *In 2 ad Thess.* 2, 3(60).

livered to those who received revelation is now found in the canonical scriptures. These are their *locutio* in written form, and through them knowledge of the supernatural truth which is necessary for salvation is transmitted in the church to each new generation. For this reason Thomas holds that the written word serves the spoken word, for *scripta . . . ordinantur ad impressionem doctrinae in cordibus* AUDI-TORUM *sicut ad finem* (writings . . . are ordained for the purpose of imprinting teaching on the hearts of the hearers).[23] It may be further noted that Thomas includes scripture in his concept of tradition, hence he frequently speaks of *traditio sacrae scripturae*[24] or *traditiones scripturae*.[25] The tradition here specified goes back in the last resort to God himself, and therefore the biblical writings may be designated *scripturae . . . divinae a Spiritu sancto traditae* (divine scriptures transmitted by the Holy Spirit).[26] Following biblical usage Thomas can at times contrast a *traditio quae est a Deo* with a *traditio hominum*, concerning which he says that it is *eradicanda, si sit contra Deum* (to be uprooted, if it is against God). This human tradition with its laws and regulations is further exemplified in connection with *jejunare* (fasting) and *canones* (regulations).[27]

When it is said in II Thessalonians 2:15 that the apostles taught by word, *per sermonem*, and epistle, *per epistolam*, this means that in addition to the apostolic writings there is also in the church a *traditio apostolorum*. If we try to define more closely what is meant by this term, we shall find that it hardly ever refers to the substance of revealed faith. Tradition which is specifically scriptural is always related to ideas like *faith* and *truth*,[28] and so may be designated a *traditio credenda* (tradition to be believed); the oral tradition of the apostles, on the other hand, is best defined as a *traditio servanda* (tradition to be preserved), which traces to the apostles in the first instance those

---

[23] 3a, 42, 4.
[24] 2a2ae, 140, 1, sed contra and 2, sed contra.
[25] *CG* IV, 34.
[26] *De Pot.* 4, 1; cf. *In ad Gal.* 1, 2(25): *Quaedam vero doctrina tradita est a Deo immediate, sicut doctrina evangelii.*
[27] See *In Matt.* 15(1): *Ex hoc habemus quod homo majus debeat sibi conscientiam facere de transgressione mandati, quam de transgressione ecclesiasticae constitutionis.* Cf. *In 2 ad Thess.* 2, 3(60): *documenta quae traduntur a minoribus, quandoque non sunt servanda, quando scilicet contrariantur documentis fidei. Documenta fidei* is here a synonym of *doctrina fidei*, cf. *De unitate intellectus* and 1a, 79, 4.
[28] See e.g. 2a2ae, 5, 3, ad 2: *veritatem primam propositam nobis in Scripturis:* 2a2ae, 110, 3, ad 1: *fidei certitudo, quae auctoritati sacrae Scripturae innititur; CG* IV, 29: *fide nostra . . . quae Sacris Scripturis innititur.*

practices which are to be retained and observed in the church.[29] The only exceptions to this rule are to be found, first, in the statement appended to the New Testament account that at the Supper the Lord lifted up his eyes to heaven[30]—which may hardly, however, be said to belong to the substance of the faith in the narrower sense—and, second, in the institution of the sacrament of confirmation, which is not mentioned in scripture, but according to Thomas goes back to Christ himself.[31] Though he frequently associates the term *traditio* in this way with the apostles, nowhere, it appears, does Thomas refer the word to the fathers or doctors of the church and their teachings. On the other hand, he can at times speak of a *traditio Ecclesiae*—as when he refers to the doctrine of original sin[32]—or he can state that the two natures of Christ are in accordance with *catholicae fidei traditio*,[33] and here it is quite clear that the traditions to which he refers are *traditiones credendae* and relate to what belongs to the very substance of the faith.

Only when we have examined what Thomas says about the specifically scriptural tradition and its function as a whole will we be in a position to seek a final answer to the question of what the concept of tradition means. Nevertheless, the survey which we have already provided may prompt some preliminary reflections. If we examine Thomas's use of the term to see what it means, it will be seen that his actual use of the word—though it appears too infrequently to let us form any conclusions with confidence—indicates that whereas the

---

[29] See e.g. 3a, 25, 3, ad 4: *Apostoli, familiari instinctu Spiritus Sancti, quaedam ecclesiis tradiderunt servanda quae non reliquerunt in scriptis, sed in observatione Ecclesiae per successionem fidelium sunt ordinata. . . Et inter huiusmodi traditiones est imaginum Christi adoratio; In 1 ad Cor.* 11, 7 (708): *Ex quo patet quod Ecclesia multa habet ex dispositione Apostolorum, quae in Sacra Scriptura non continentur; In 2 ad Thess.* 2, 3(60): *Et has traditiones dupliciter ediderunt, quasdam verbis unde dicit 'per sermonem', quasdam in scripturis ideo addit 'sive per epistolam'. Unde patet, quod multa in ecclesia non scripta, sunt ab Apostolis docta, et ideo servanda.* Cf. also 2a2ae, 10, 12, where Thomas speaks about *Ecclesiae consuetudo* or *Ecclesiae usus.*
[30] 3a, 83, 4, ad 2.
[31] 3a, 64, 2, ad 1: *Ea vero quae sunt de necessitate sacramenti, sunt ab ipso Christo instituta, qui est Deus et homo. Et licet non omnia sint tradita in Scripturis, habet tamen ea Ecclesia e familiari Apostolorum traditione.* In the parallel passage in IV *Sent.* 7, 1, 3, what was said above to be *de necessitate sacramenti* seems to be identical with the *forma* of confirmation, i.e. the formula used at the ceremony to constitute the sacrament. (Cf. also IV *Sent.* 23, 1, 1, 3, 3, ad 1.)
[32] *CG* IV, 54, *Ex traditione Ecclesiae docemur totum humanum genus peccato esse infectum.*
[33] *CG* IV, 39; cf. also 1a, 32, 1, obi. 3, where the doctrine of the Trinity is stated to be a *traditio divina.*

specifically scriptural tradition has a primary reference to the substance of the faith, oral traditions which stand side by side with scripture belong primarily to the sphere of the activity and outward ordering of the church and are therefore to be regarded as *traditiones servandae.* If, on the other hand, we examine the more formal meaning of the concept, we find that it can be used by Thomas of every form of the communication of knowledge within the church. It is apparent from this that tradition in Thomas includes scripture, but it is also striking that he applies the word *tradere* both to his own work as a theologian and to that of others. Thus, he states in the prologue to the *Summa theologiae* that his purpose is to *ea quae ad Christianam religionem pertinent, eo modo* TRADERE, *secundum quod congruit ad eruditionem incipientium* (to convey the things which belong to the Christian religion in a style serviceable for the training of beginners).[34] Here the term *traditio* is almost synonymous with *doctrina,* and denotes the teaching which is perennially necessary in the church, and through which revealed truth is transmitted from generation to generation.

The impressive use of the word in the most widely varied contexts and the fact also that its appearance in his writings is correspondingly infrequent,[35] alike indicate that at this point in his theology of revelation Thomas is not using the term with any precise dogmatic connotation. He is aware of and presupposes an oral tradition originating with the apostles, but it is not clearly defined as a separate source of the knowledge of what is central and essential in the content of faith.

If there are certain difficulties in defining exactly what Thomas means by the term *traditio,* because there are relatively few passages in which the word occurs, there is no similar difficulty when we come to determine his view of *scripture.* The supernatural knowledge which is given in revelation and which is essential for salvation was given to certain individual men, to prophets and apostles, and is inseparable from these clearly defined groups. In so far as we are dealing with the substance of the faith, revelation is full and complete

---

[34] 1a, prol. Cf. how Thomas sometimes rejects earlier teachings which *a diversis conscripta sunt* because these other theologians *ea quae sunt necessaria . . . ad sciendum, non* TRADUNTUR *secundum ordinem disciplinae.*

[35] It is significant that the term *traditio* does not appear in the *Index materiarum seu capitum doctrinae* or the *Index elementorum* which list the contents of the *Summa theologiae* and the *Summa contra gentiles* in vol. XVI of the official Leonine edition of Thomas's writings.

in and with these individuals, and if it is transmitted after the apostolic period to those who receive the gift of prophecy, Thomas explicitly states that this happens *non quidem ad novam doctrinam fidei depromendam, sed ad humanorum actuum directionem* (not indeed for the declaration of any new doctrine of faith, but for the direction of human acts).[36] Faith, therefore, rests wholly and entirely on the revelation which has been given to the writers of the canonical scriptures, but *not* on any revelations which may have come to 'doctors' of the church at a later period: *Innititur enim fides nostra revelationi Apostolis et Prophetis factae, qui canonicos libros scripserunt: non autem revelationi, si qua fuit aliis doctoribus facta* (for our faith rests on the revelation made to the Prophets and Apostles who wrote the canonical books, not on a revelation, if such there be, made to any other teacher).[37] It is not coincidental that in this particular passage Thomas holds that revelation has been given to the authors of the biblical writings, for the crucial distinction which he makes here between these writers and later teachers within the church underlies his explanation of the origin of the scriptures which we find in a passage in the *Summa contra gentiles: Quia enim homines revelationem a Deo accipiunt non solum pro praesenti tempore, sed etiam ad instructionem omnium futurorum, necessarium fuit ut non solum ea quae ipsis revelantur, sermone narrarentur praesentibus; sed etiam scriberentur ad instructionem futurorum* (since men receive revelation from God not only for their own time, but also for the instruction of all men that are to come, it was necessary that the things revealed to them not only be recounted to their contemporaries, but also that they be written down for the instruction of men to come).[38] The revealed knowledge which has been given in a unique way to prophets and apostles was intended to be given not only to their contemporaries but to all future generations as well and therefore it was *necessary*—nowhere else does Thomas use this term of any other part of the church's tradition of teaching—that it be defined in written or *scriptural* form. This and this alone is the particular knowledge toward which the faith that anticipates the intellectual perfection of eternal life is turned, and it is this that constitutes the primary condition of man's salvation. Apart from this, Thomas has little interest in the way in which the different books of the Bible were written, and lacks any explicit doctrine of the inspira-

---

[36] 2a2ae, 174, 6, ad 3. [37] 1a, 1, 8, ad 2.
[38] *CG* III, 154.

tion of scripture. As we have seen earlier,[39] in Thomas the term *inspiratio* denotes the work of God in illuminating the intellect of the recipient of revelation, and on this process which he describes in psychological categories all his interest is focussed, while the question of the origin of the biblical writings is sometimes treated as wholly peripheral.[40] The explanation, of course, is that he conceives of revelation primarily as a *cognitio* and not as a form of *locutio*. There are thus, according to Thomas, three classes of men to be found in the course of church history—first, those who have received revelation and have passed on the knowledge which they have received in written form; second, those whose task is to expound and interpret what has been given in revelation; and finally, the great majority of believers, who *ea quae aliis sunt revelata, et per alios interpretata, fideliter credunt* (faithfully believe the things that are revealed to others, and interpreted by still others). In each case there is a work of grace. revelation itself, and the power to interpret it, and faith, all alike transcend man's natural capacities.[41]

Accordingly, for Thomas holy scripture does not coincide with revelation, since he does not understand revelation as a spoken or written word but regards it primarily as an event which takes place in the depths of the soul. Nevertheless, the Bible contains and communicates the divine truth given in and with this event.[42] If the content of revelation had not been defined in this way once and for all, it would have been wholly inaccessible to us—*ea enim quae ex sola Dei voluntate proveniunt, supra omne debitum creaturae,* NOBIS INNOTESCERE NON POSSUNT NISI QUATENUS IN SACRA SCRIPTURA TRADUNTUR, *per quam divina voluntas innotescit* (such things as spring

---

[39] See p. 38f. above.

[40] We get some idea of what Thomas thinks about the question in *Quodl.* 7, 14, ad 5 and 7, 16, where the relation between the Holy Spirit and the writer of scripture is spoken of in terms of *auctor principalis* and *auctor instrumentalis*. The interpretation found in F. Kropatschek, *Das Schriftprinzip der lutherischen Kirche*, vol. 1, *Die Vorgeschichte. Das Erbe des Mittelalters*, Leipzig 1904, is misleading, e.g. p. 428f. where Thomas's discussion of *inspiratio* is connected with 'die Entstehung der Bibel'. When Diekamp, *Dogmatik*, devotes three sections (8–10) to discussing the inspiration of scripture, he has really abandoned 'die Grundsätzen des heiligen Thomas'.

[41] *CG* III, 154: *Unde et oportuit aliquos esse qui huiusmodi scripta interpretarentur. Quod divina gratia esse oportet, sicut et ipsa revelatio per gratiam Dei fuit . . . Sequitur autem ultimus gradus: eorum scilicet qui ea quae aliis sunt revelata, et per alios interpretata, fideliter credunt. Hoc autem Dei donum esse superius* (cf. *CG* III, 152) *ostensum est.*

[42] *In De div. nom.* 1, 1: *Nullus igitur potest vere loqui de Deo vel cogitare, nisi quantum a Deo revelatur. Quae quidem divina revelatio in Scripturis sacris continetur.*

from God's will, and beyond the creature's due, can be made known to us only through being revealed in sacred scripture, in which the divine will is made known to us).[43] It is to be noted that Thomas does not appear at this point to regard oral tradition as a vehicle of revelation, but this may be due to the fact that for Thomas, as we have seen above, oral tradition is not to be thought of primarily as a *traditio credenda* but as a *traditio servanda*. Scripture is not to be identified with revelation, but presupposes it and builds upon it; hence Thomas can indicate the connection between them by speaking of a *revelatio . . . super quam fundatur sacra scriptura* (revelation . . . which is the basis of sacred scripture).[44] Since the substance of knowledge which is given through revelation is to be found primarily in scripture, *sacra scriptura* and *divina revelatio* can sometimes be used as synonyms.[45] This identification of the content of scripture and of revelation finds expression particularly in those passages where Thomas speaks of the connection between faith and the biblical writings. The object of faith is the truth which is given in and with revelation, viz. the knowledge of man's supernatural destiny and the means of attaining this goal, but this truth is to be found *in scripture*,[46] and therefore the object of faith may be said to be the same as the content of scripture. By this Thomas means in the first instance the central reality of faith, viz. that which saves a man,[47] or, more precisely defined, the *occultum divinitatis, cuius visio nos beatos facit* (the secret of the godhead, to see which is to be made blessed), and the *mysterium humanitatis Christi, per quem in gloriam filiorum Dei accessum habemus* (the mystery of Christ's humanity, by whom we have access to the glory of the sons of God),[48] but in addition to this the object of faith consists in everything else that is to be found in the Bible, for all that is there recorded *narrantur in sacra scriptura in ordine ad manifestationem divinae majestatis vel incarnationis Christi* (is related in holy scripture for the purpose of manifesting the divine majesty or incarnation of Christ).[49] Here the content

---

[43] 3a, 1, 3.
[44] 1a, 1, 2, ad 2.
[45] See e.g. 1a 1, 8 or 1a2ae, 62, 1.
[46] 2a2ae, 5, 3, ad 2: *veritatem primam propositam nobis in Scripturis.*
[47] 2a2ae, 2, 5: *id per quod homo beatus efficitur.*
[48] 2a2ae, 1, 8; cf. 2a2ae, 1, 6, ad 1: *Quia vero fides principaliter est de his quae videnda speramus in patria . . . ideo per se ad fidem pertinent illa quae directe nos ordinant ad vitam aeternam: sicut sunt tres Personae, omnipotentia Dei, mysterium incarnationis Christi, et alia huiusmodi.*
[49] 2a2ae, 1, 6, ad 1.

of the whole Bible is identified with the object of man's faith.[50] This confident assurance of faith rests on the foundation of scripture—Thomas speaks of *fidei certitudo, quae auctoritati sacrae scripturae innititur* (the certitude of faith, which rests on the authority of holy scripture),[51]—and this 'certitude' is dependent on the fact that God himself is the author of scripture, *auctor sacrae scripturae est Deus*.[52] The authority of scripture is thus none other than that of him who is Truth itself, for what we find in the Bible, written in the ordinary words of men, is in fact *veritas prima*,[53] and therefore scripture may be designated *fidei fundamentum* (the ground of faith).[54]

It will now be clear from what has just been said that the specifically scriptural tradition plays a decisive role in Thomas's theology. The significance of this will be seen even more clearly after we have examined what he says about the canon of scripture at three further points.

First, we note that for Thomas scripture has a clearly *normative* character. This, as we have seen above, is really a consequence of the fact that for Thomas the ground and object of faith is the truth which prophets and apostles have received and communicated in their writings, and not any other revelations which may subsequently have been given to others. Thomas also insists that full credence should not be given to those who expound scripture, for they may be mistaken in many respects, but the object of faith is rather SOLUM SCRIPTURA CANONICA, *quae in veteri et in novo testamento est* (only the canonical scripture which is in the Old and New Testaments).[55] As he points out

---

[50] 2a2ae, 2, 5: *paratus est credere quidquid in divina Scriptura continetur;* cf. the comments on the passages quoted in P. de Vooght, *Les sources de la doctrine chrétienne*, Paris 1954, p. 24: 'Saint Thomas enseigne en outre qu'en dehors des Livres canoniques, on ne trouve aucune révélation qui intéresse le dépôt de la foi. Des révélations faites à d'autres docteurs, remarque-t-il, si tant est que ce cas se présente, n'ont pas d'intérêt au point de vue de la doctrine catholique. Si la Révélation a été faite aux auteurs des Livres canoniques, il est évident que l'obligation de croire s'étend à tout ce que l'Écriture contient et à rien d'autre'.

[51] 2a2ae, 110, 3, ad 1; 2a2ae, 4, 8, ad 3: *(naturale lumen rationis) quod deficit a certitudine verbi Dei, cui innititur fides; CG* IV, 29: *fide nostra . . . quae Sacris Scripturis innititur.*

[52] 1a, 1, 10.

[53] 2a2ae, 5, 3: *Formale autem obiectum fidei est veritas prima secundum quod manifestatur in Scripturis sacris.*

[54] 3a, 55, 5: *per auctoritatem sacrae Scripturae, quae est fidei fundamentum.*

[55] *Quodl.* 12, 26: *Expositores autem in aliis quae non sunt fidei, multa ex suo sensu dixerunt, et ideo in his poterant errare; tamen dicta expositorum necessitatem non inducunt quod necesse sit eis credere, sed solum Scriptura canonica, quae in veteri et in novo testamento est.* When it is necessary to choose between different *expositores*

in his commentary on I Timothy 6:3, the use of the term 'canonical' to distinguish this collection of writings from all others indicates that scripture is to be a guide and rule in all teaching given in the church, and *ideo nullus aliter debet docere* (so we should be taught by none other).[56] Elsewhere Thomas maintains that the content of scripture is to be regarded as an *optima regula veritatis* (best rule of truth), to which nothing can be added, from which nothing may be subtracted, and which no false interpretation must be allowed to distort.[57] The idea of the canon as the norm by which the scriptures are distinguished from all other documents of faith is a characteristic of Thomas and may be concisely expressed in the definition which is to be found in his commentary on the Gospel of St. John: SOLA CANONICA SCRIPTURA EST REGULA FIDEI (canonical scripture alone is the rule of faith).[58]

Second, we find in Thomas explicit statements about the sufficiency (*sufficientia*) of scripture as a source if revelation. We have already touched on this idea earlier in discussing the proposition that the content of revelation is identical with that of the Bible, and also in examining what Thomas says about the need for writing the content of revelation down in scripture and in our remarks on *sola scriptura*, but further examples may be provided to illustrate his position. The idea that something new may need to be added to complete the revelation given by prophets and apostles is clearly uncongenial to Thomas. This revelation already contains all the truth that is necessary for salvation, and to it both the apostles and their successors in the church—the bishops—are bound. They are the appointed *vicarii Dei* and rulers of the church, but this does not mean that they can introduce any innovation beyond what was once given in its fulness to the apostles. They have no more authority to create a new church than they have to institute new sacraments or *tradere aliam fidem*

---

of scripture, one can be played off against the other according to their conformity to scripture; at one point, for instance, Thomas prefers Augustine to Jerome, *quia cum dictis Apostoli magis concordat, In ad Gal.* 2, 3, (88).

[56] *In 1 ad Tim.* 6, 1(237): *Doctrina enim Apostolorum et prophetarum dicitur canonica, quia est quasi regula intellectus nostri. Et ideo nullus aliter debet docere;* cf. *In ad Gal.* 1, 2(25) and (27).

[57] *In De div. nom.* 2, 1: *ea quae in sacra Scriptura sunt posita, oportet nos custodire, sicut quamdam optimam regulam veritatis; ita quod neque multiplicemus addentes, neque minoremus subtrahentes, neque pervertamus, male exponentes.*

[58] *In Joan.* 21, 6(2); cf. 2a2ae, 1, 9, obi. 1: *Sacra enim Scriptura est regula fidei, cui nec addere nec subtrahere licet,* and in footnote 55 above, the passage quoted from *Quodl.* 12, 26.

(hand on another faith).[59] The purpose of scripture is to transmit the truth which men need to know in order to be saved—*sacra scriptura ad hoc divinitus est ordinata, ut per eam nobis veritas manifestetur necessaria ad salutem* (holy scripture is appointed by God so that it may disclose to us the truth that is necessary for salvation).[60] Through the mediation of the Holy Spirit the apostles have received part of the 'whole truth' which men must have in order to attain the goal of salvation, and this truth teaches both what they are to believe and what they are to do.[61] In order to know this truth men need go no further than holy scripture, for scripture contains the *doctrina Christi et Apostolorum*, in which the *veritas fidei* is sufficiently explained (*sufficienter explicata*). It is clear from the context of the passage under discussion that when Thomas goes on to speak of apostolic doctrine and the other scriptures (*apostolicam doctrinam et ceteras Scripturas*), *doctrina* is synonymous with scripture.[62] Even within the canon of scripture Thomas gives precedence to certain writings on the grounds that they contain everything that is essential as regards doctrine. The Psalter and the Pauline epistles contain *fere tota theologiae . . . doctrina* (almost the entire teaching of theology).[63] A further illustration of this idea is found in Thomas's explanation of why there is no mention in the Gospels of the institution of confirmation or holy unction. According to Thomas, this is because these two sacraments, unlike the others, are not necessary to salvation (*de necessitate salutis*), hence there was no reason for including them within the scripturally defined tradition which contains *illa . . . quae ad salutis necessitatem et ad ordinem ecclesiasticae dispositionis pertinent* (those things which are necessary for salvation or relate to the ordering of the church).[64]

[59] 3a, 64, 2, ad 3: *Apostoli, et eorum successores, sunt vicarii Dei quantum ad regimen Ecclesiae institutae per fidem et fidei sacramenta. Unde, sicut non licet eis constituere aliam ecclesiam, ita non licet eis tradere aliam fidem, neque instituere alia sacramenta.* The apostles, therefore, do not have the right—and their successors even less right—to introduce any innovations in the church; and for this reason, Thomas holds, all the sacraments of the church must go back to Christ's own institution, cf. IV *Sent.* 7, 1, 1, 1, ad 1: *ipsi Apostoli quamvis essent bases Ecclesiae, tamen non fuerunt legislatores; unde ad eos non pertinebat sacramenta instituere.*
[60] *Quodl.* 7, 14.
[61] 1a2ae, 106, 4, ad 2: *Docuit autem Spiritus Sanctus Apostolos omnem veritatem de his quae pertinent ad necessitatem salutis: scilicet de credendis et agendis.*
[62] 2a2ae, 1, 10, ad 1.
[63] *Super epistolas S. Pauli lectura, prol.*
[64] IV *Sent.* 23, 1, 1, 3, 3, ad 1: *multa Dominus fecit et dicit quae in Evangeliis non continentur. Illa enim praecipue curaverunt Evangelistae tradere quae ad salutis*

E

A third point perhaps worth noting in this connection is the attitude which Thomas takes to the question of the *consistency* and *clarity* of scripture. In looking at this we propose to examine his view of the contemporary theory of the fourfold interpretation of scripture.[65] When we turn to the passages in which he deals with the question, we shall soon find that for Thomas scripture is to be interpreted in a twofold rather than a fourfold 'sense'. He refers constantly to a *significatio per voces* and a *significatio per res*, a distinction which corresponds in the conventional terminology to the *sensus historicus vel litteralis* on the one hand and the *sensus mysticus seu spiritualis* on the other. The other three current interpretations, *sensus allegoricus*, *sensus moralis*, and *sensus anagogicus*, are special instances of the spiritual sense. Only the biblical writings, which are unique among all other writings in having God as their author, can have a literal as well as a spiritual meaning. Men have only one way

necessiiatem et ad ordinem ecclesiasticae dispositionis pertinent; et ideo potius institutionem baptismi et poenitentiae et eucharistiae et ordinis a Christo factam narraverunt, quam extremae unctionis vel confirmationis; quae neque sunt de necessitate salutis, neque ad dispositionem sive distinctionem Ecclesiae pertinent; cf. Suppl. 29, 3, ad 1, where this passage is applied to the sacrament of extreme unction. This idea of the sufficiency of scripture is by no means peculiar to Thomas, but is to be found in all his contemporaries, as two quotations from Bonaventure will make plain. In his Commentary on St John we find the statement: Et ideo non omnia scripta sunt, sed quae sufficiunt ad fidem nostram (In Joan, 20, 61 in the Quaracchi ed. vol. VI p. 516), and in an exposition of the rule of the order this statement: Veritas enim fidei et vitae sanctitas non aliunde quam ex scripturarum fonte hauritur (Opusc. 13, Determinationes quaestionum circa regulam fratrum minorum, 1, 3, Quaracchi ed. vol. VIII, p. 339). Cf. also Kropatschek, Schriftprinzip, vol. 1, p. 434, who holds that in general to theologians of the Middle Ages, 'die Schrift ist irrtumslos, vollkommen, zureichend, deutlich'. The approach of J. Beumer, 'Das katholische Schriftprinzip in der theologischen Literatur der Scholastik bis zur Reformation', in Scholastik 16 (1941), p. 24ff. is typical of the difficulties faced by recent Roman Catholic theology in trying to do justice to these clear statements on the sufficiency of scripture in terms of the principles from which they start, principles which we do not find in medeival theologians. Beumer regards these statements as disturbing and holds that they are incidental and lacking essential significance (p. 35) or are 'eigenartig' and 'übertrieben' (p. 48f).

---

[65] Cf. the common medieval mnemonic which summarises this whole theory: *Littera gesta docet, quid credas allegoria, moralis quid agas, quid speras anagogia*, and H. de Lubac, 'Sur un vieux distique: la doctrine du "quadruple sens" ', in *MFC*, p. 347ff. On Thomas's biblical exegesis see especially Spicq, *Esquisse*, but also P. Synave, 'La doctrine de saint Thomas d'Aquin sur le sens littéral des Écritures', in *Revue biblique* (=*RB*) 35 (1926), p. 40ff. and van der Ploeg, *Thomist* 10, (1947), p. 413ff. and Chenu, *Saint Thomas*, p. 234ff. The most important passages dealing with this question besides 1a, 1, 10 are to be found in *De Pot.* 4, 1; *Quodl.* 7, 14–16; and *In ad Gal.* 4, 7 (254).

by which to express their meaning, viz. *per voces*, and therefore the only possible interpretation which is to be found in any human 'science' is the literal one, *sensus litteralis*.[66] The case is quite different with the 'science' which we find in scripture, where we also have a *significatio per res*, for the historical event, *cursus rerum*, is controlled by God himself, and it is within his power to give those persons and events described by biblical writers a meaning other than the historical one. The *sensus litteralis*, or literal meaning of the scripture, is that which is expressed *per verba* or *per voces*, while the *sensus spiritualis* also includes what God intends to be understood by those persons and events which, since both they and scripture alike are under the direct control of God, may serve as 'figures' for something else.[67]

But how are these two types of interpretation related to one another? A study of Thomas's biblical commentaries will quickly show that the literal interpretation is for him incomparably the most important.[68] His commentary on Job is perhaps the most striking example of how far Thomas diverges from the earlier, traditional exegesis with its predilection for the deeper spiritual meaning of scripture, by which was meant in particular the allegorical and moral interpretation. Holding that the moral interpretation has already received adequate and indeed unsurpassed treatment in Gregory's *Moralia in Iob*, Thomas gives his whole attention to the *sensus litteralis*.[69] This preference for the literal meaning of the Bible is also seen, however, to be based on principle. Thomas explicitly states that the true sense of the scripture, *quem auctor intendit*, is not the spiritual but the literal meaning of the passage.[70] The historical or literal 'sense' is the basis and presupposition of the spiritual interpretation, and the latter is not to be regarded as distinct from or independent of the former. Nor is the spiritual sense better or more profound than the literal, hence capable of giving a further meaning,

[66] Cf. *Quodl.* 7, 16: *in nulla scientia, humana industria inventa, proprie loquendo, potest inveniri nisi litteralis sensus.*

[67] See *In ad Gal.* 4, 7(254); cf. 1a, 1, 10 and *Quodl.* 7, 14: *Auctor autem rerum non solum potest verba accommodare ad aliquid significandum, set etiam res potest disponere in figuram alterius: et secundum hoc in sacra Scriptura manifestatur veritas dupliciter. Uno modo secundum quod res significantur per verba: et in hoc consistit sensus litteralis. Alio modo secundum quod res sunt figurae aliarum rerum; et in hoc consistit sensus spiritualis, et sic sacrae Scripturae plures sensus competunt.*

[68] Chenu, *Saint Thomas*, p. 251f.: 'The adherence to the letter of the text . . . is a characteristic trait of the commentary of Saint Thomas'.

[69] Cf. Smalley, *Study*, p. 236; Spicq, *Esquisse*, p. 310f.; Chenu, *Saint Thomas*, p. 257.

[70] 1a, 1, 10.

for *nihil sub spirituali sensu continetur fidei necessarium, quod scriptura per litteralem sensum alicubi manifeste non tradat* (nothing necessary for faith is contained under the spiritual sense that is not openly conveyed through the literal sense elsewhere).[71]

As B. Smalley has shown in her pioneering work on the study of the Bible in the middle ages, this insistence on the superiority of the literal interpretation is characteristically Aristotelian. A parallel can be found in Thomas's general doctrine of knowledge, where he takes his point of departure not in an inward 'illumination' but in knowledge attained through the senses. The relationship between 'letter' and 'spirit' in scripture is understood throughout the whole of the church's tradition by the analogy of the relationship between body and soul. 'The body is the words of the sacred text, the "letter", and the literal meaning; the soul is the spiritual sense'.[72] Just as the influence of Aristotle in the theory of knowledge put an end to the idea of the body as a hindrance or at any rate a regrettable necessity and made it instead a self-evident prerequisite for knowledge, a view which differed from earlier theories in regarding the whole man, body and soul, as a unity, so now in biblical exegesis also the 'letter' and 'spirit' of scripture begin to converge. The true meaning of scripture is no longer to be found beneath or above the literal, but precisely in the letter of the text.[73] The increasing influence of Maimonides, whose rationalistic interpretation of scripture was drawn from Arabian and Aristotelian philosophy, carried the process further in the same direction.[74]

---

[71] 1a, 1, 10, ad 1; *Quodl.* 7, 14, ad 1: *sensus spiritualis semper fundatur super litteralem, et procedit ex eo,* and also ib. ad 3: *spiritualis expositio semper debet habere fulcimentum ab aliqua litterali expositione sacrae Scripturae.* We must not disregard these facts if we want to provide a correct account of scholastic exegesis. V. Baroni, *La contre-réforme devant la bible. La question biblique,* Lausanne 1943, should be a warning against building any argument on the basis of assumptions without reference to the actual text. In an introductory discussion of the medieval background Baroni says, p. 38, that 'les grands scolastiques, qui élaborèrent la théologie catholique, citent constamment l'Écriture saint sans aucun souci de sa signification historique', and then to prove his argument cites a commentary by Thomas on the Song of Songs which scholars unanimously regard as apocryphal (cf. Spicq, *Esquisse,* p. 303f. and Manser, *Thomismus,* p. 37f. with the references quoted)!

[72] Smalley, *Study,* p. 1.

[73] Smalley, *Study,* p. 229f.

[74] Smalley, *Study,* p. 230ff., and cf. also p. 232: 'Maimonides taught them (i.e. 'the Christian commentators') to find reason and edification in the literal sense'. Just as Jewish biblical exegesis (Philo) inaugurated the dominance of the allegorical interpretation, so also Jewish exegesis was chiefly responsible for the gradual disappearance of this tradition in the high Middle Ages.

It would appear, however, that more requires to be said if we are to explain why Thomas lays such emphasis on the literal interpretation of scripture. He has profound theological reasons for this, as we shall see as soon as we note the context in which these statements appear. In the *Summa theologiae* the fourfold 'sense' of scripture is discussed in connection with an article in which he considers whether *sacra doctrina* is *argumentativa*.[75] This allows Thomas then to discuss the metaphorical language of scripture in the following section in which he maintains that this does not imply any obscuring of its truth, for *ea quae in uno loco scripturae traduntur sub metaphoris, in aliis locis expressius exponuntur* (truths expressed metaphorically in one passage of scripture are more expressly explained elsewhere).[76] The objections which are then alleged both here and in the parallel passage in the *Quaestiones quodlibetales* 7:14 against the fourfold interpretation of scripture are intended to show that there are many different meanings to be found in the words of scripture, and these make any clear understanding impossible and preclude any effective argument based on scripture. If both interpretations could be freely employed independently of one another, the result would be a *confusio* or *multiplicitas*, and so proceeding from these objections Thomas seeks to avoid such obscurity by always subordinating the spiritual sense to the literal and allowing it to be controlled by the literal.[77] No theologically valid argument can be derived from the purely spiritual or allegorical interpretation.[78] Even though the biblical writings may seem to be obscure in certain places because of their metaphorical language, it is always possible to get a clear understanding from other passages in the Bible—*nihil est quod occulte in aliquo loco sacrae scripturae tradatur quod non alibi manifeste exponatur* (nothing is recorded anywhere in scripture in a hidden way that is not explained openly elsewhere).[79] The obscurity and uncertainty do not reside in the object but in the subject, and are due to man's inability to

---

[75] 1a, 1, 8.

[76] 1a, 1, 9, ad 2.

[77] *Quodl.* 7, 14, ad 1: *varietas sensuum, quorum unus ab alio non procedit, facit multiplicitatem locutionis; sed sensus spiritualis semper fundatur super litteralem, et procedit ex eo.*

[78] 1a, 1, 10, ad 1: *omnes sensus fundentur super unum, scilicet litteralem; ex quo solo potest trahi argumentum, non autem ex his quae secundum allegoriam dicuntur;* cf. *I Sent.* prol., 1, 5: *Ad destructionem autem errorum non proceditur nisi per sensum litteralem, eo quod alii sensus sunt per similitudines accepti et ex similitudinariis locutionibus non potest sumi argumentatio.*

[79] *Quodl.* 7, 14, ad 3; cf. 1a, 1, 9, ad 2.

comprehend clearly a truth of such profundity. Nevertheless, scripture must have a clear, comprehensible and communicable meaning. Were this not so, it would bring about a *deceptio* rather than an *eruditio hominum.*[80] The fact that scripture teaches about the truth provides the basis from which we must consider the priority of the literal interpretation and in consequence the clarity of scripture. If it had a variety of meanings and lacked clarity, it would not be possible for us to find in it any *efficax argumentum,*[81] and this in the last resort would invalidate the doctrinal and scientific character of both scripture and theology.

But even though scripture is both normative and in itself clear and sufficient, it does not by any means follow from this that the truth which is revealed within it is readily accessible. The reverse is rather the case, and indeed Thomas can regard its very inaccessibility as a positive value. It prevents idleness and stimulates zeal. It also keeps the exegete from supposing that he has complete and immediate comprehension of its meaning, and Christian truth from being exposed to the reproach of unbelievers.[82] But its very difficulty also means that truth can be found in scripture only after long and painstaking study.[83] If revelation had been attainable only in this form, only the *studiosi* would have access to it,[84] while the great majority of men, who have neither the time nor the opportunity for study, would have been excluded from saving knowledge.

This according to Thomas, is the explanation of the origin of *the Apostles' Creed.* We cannot believe a truth unless it is set before us in a comprehensible way. But here the truth of which we are speaking is essential for man's salvation, and in order to make faith available to all it became necessary as early as the apostolic period to prepare a brief and convenient summary of what had been given in revela-

---

[80] *CG* IV, 29.
[81] *Quodl.* 7, 14, ad 4.
[82] See 1a, 1, 9, ad 2; *CG* I, 5 and IV, 1; *Quodl.* 7, 14, ad 2.
[83] 2a2ae, 1, 9, ad 1: *veritas fidei in sacra Scriptura diffuse continetur et variis modis, et in quibusdam obscure; ita quod ad eliciendum fidei veritatem ex sacra Scriptura requiritur longum studium et exercitium, ad quod non possunt pervenire omnes illi quibus necessarium est cognoscere fidei veritatem, quorum plerique, aliis negotiis occupati, studio vacare non possunt.*
[84] *CG* IV, 1: *Haec etiam pauca quae nobis revelantur, sub quibusdam similitudinibus et obscuritatibus verborum nobis proponuntur: ut ad ea quomodocumque capienda soli studiosi perveniant.* That this general statement refers in fact to scripture is made clear in what follows, where Thomas says that revealed truth consists in *ea quae in sermonibus Sacrae Scripturae sunt tradita.*

tion.[85] This was the origin of the Apostles' Creed, which Thomas holds to be a summary of their teaching composed by the apostles themselves, and accordingly he speaks of it as having been composed *ex diversis locis sacrae scripturae* (from different passages in holy scripture)[86] or *ex sententiis sacrae scripturae* (from the statements of holy scripture).[87] It is a confession of faith which may, therefore, be regarded as a kind of popular Bible in which the content of scripture is summarised in a way that may be plain to all.

The articles which the Apostles' Creed contains are not, therefore, to be regarded as additions to scripture. On the contrary, Thomas insists, what it contains *non est additum sacrae scripturae, sed potius ex sacra scriptura assumptum* (is no addition to holy scripture, but something taken from it).[88] The same is true in principle of the other creeds of the early church, the Nicene and the Athanasian: the church fathers who drew them up, *nihil de suo apposuerunt; sed ex sacris scripturis ea quae addiderunt, exceperunt* (added nothing of their own; but took from holy scripture what they added).[89] The idea that a creed has an authority superior to scripture itself is therefore rejected by Thomas as *omnino falsum*. What is given in the creed is a summary of what scripture means when it is correctly interpreted.[90] Since the articles of faith, *articuli fidei*, and the canonical scriptures are identical in content when they are seen in this way, anything that may be said of the one can also apply to the other—hence Thomas can state that the articles of the creed, which constitute the *principia* of theology, have been given *immediate a Deo per revelationem* (directly from God through revelation).[91] Furthermore, because of

---

[85] 2a2ae, 1, 9: *Credere autem non potest aliquis nisi ei veritas quam credat proponatur. Et ideo necessarium fuit veritatem fidei in unum colligi, ut facilius posset omnibus proponi, ne aliquis per ignorantiam a fidei veritate deficeret.* See also ib. ad 1. Thomas is referring here primarily to the Apostles' Creed, but it is clear from the context that his statements also apply to the Nicene Creed, cf. 2a2ae, 1, 8, obi. 5 and 2a2ae, 1, 9, ad 6.

[86] III Sent. 25, 1, 1, 3: *Omnes Apostoli collecti hanc regulam fidei ediderunt, unusquisque quod suum est apponens . . . ex diversis locis sacrae Scripturae colliguntur ea quae credenda sunt, ut in promptu habeantur.*

[87] 2a2ae, 1, 9, ad 1.　　　　　[88] 2a2ae, 1, 9, ad 1.

[89] III *Sent.* 25, 1, 1, 3, ad 2.

[90] *Contra errores Graecorum*, 32: *Posset enim aliquis intelligere, quod definitio dicti Concilii, auctoriate praeferatur litterae veteris, vel novi testamenti; quod est omnino falsum. Intelligendum est autem quod per dictum Concilium verus intellectus ex sacra Scriptura est acceptus quem soli Catholici habent; licet littera sacrae Scripturae sit communis Catholicis et Haereticis et Judaeis.*

[91] 1a, 1, 5, ad 2. On the question of the *articuli fidei* as the *principia* of theology see p. 74ff. below. In 2a2ae, 1, 5, ad 2 these principles appear as interchangeable

their identity of content both the articles of the creed and the scripture itself may be termed the *regula fidei*.[92] This normative function of the creed is based in the last resort upon the fact that it is derived from the truth given in the biblical writings, of which it is itself a summary. Even in the earliest creeds it is thus scripture, Thomas holds, and scripture alone, that is the *regula fidei*.

All the symbols of the faith have basically the same content, and whenever there is a new credal formulation, it is always a further clarification of the meaning of an already existing dogma. The connection between the two can be demonstrated by the relationship between the Apostles' and the Nicene Creeds—to use Thomas's phrase, *symbolum Patrum est declarativum symboli Apostolorum* (the Creed of the Fathers is an explanation of the Apostles' Creed).[93] The formulation of a new and at certain points fuller statement of faith is occasioned by heretical misinterpretations and attacks on the faith—for Thomas there is no other conceivable cause for a reformulation of dogma. The heretics are those who pick and choose at will from the inherited faith of the church and so do not hold to all that has been truly handed down by Christ, *vere a Christo tradita*.[94] Hence they no longer possess the whole truth which has been given to the church in the teaching which is propounded in scripture. Heresy is thus a violation of the unity and catholicity of the church which are manifested in the one faith which is confessed in the church.[95] False doctrine is expressed in *falsas expositiones fidei*,[96] and those who espouse it are wicked men who distort for their own

terms for *auctoritates sacrae Scripturae;* cf. also *In De div. nom.* 1, 1: *Sic igitur principia ex quibus procedit haec doctrina, sunt ea quae per revelationem Spiritus sancti sunt accepta et in sacris Scripturis habentur.*

---

[92] Cf. *In De div. nom.* 2, 1; III *Sent.* 25, 1, 1, 3; 2a2ae, 1, 9, cf. obi. 1 and 6; 2a2ae, 1, 10, ad 3.

[93] 2a2ae, 1, 9, ad 6; cf. 1a, 36, 2, ad 2 and 2a2ae, 1, 9, ad 2: *necesse fuit edere plura symbola. Quae in nullo alio differunt nisi quod in uno plenius explicantur que in alio continentur implicite, secundum quod exigebat haereticorum instantia.*

[94] 2a2ae, 11, 1. The nature of heresy is dealt with in detail from various aspects in 2a2ae, 11, 1–4.

[95] *In symb. Apost.* 9: *Causatur autem unitas Ecclesiae. . . . Primo ex unitate fidei; CG* IV 76: *Ad unitatem Ecclesiae requiritur quod omnes fideles in fide conveniant; In decretalem I expositio: Unitas autem Ecclesiae est praecipue propter fidei unitatem: nam Ecclesia nihil est aliud quam aggregatio fidelium; In ad Eph.* 4, 2(199): *quia unum et idem est quod creditur a cunctis fidelibus, unde universalis seu catholica dicitur;* cf. also 2a2ae, 1, 9, ad 3 and *De Ver.* 14, 12.

[96] 2a3ae, 11, 2, ad 2.

purposes the apostolic teaching given in scripture.[97] Hence, as Thomas puts it—and in this he follows Augustine—the church must devote itself with greater zeal than ever to the study of holy scripture.[98]

It is when he turns to discuss these new interpretations of faith which have been produced by the misunderstandings of the heretics that Thomas introduces the *pope* and the *magisterium* or teaching ministry of the church. From the standpoint of the relationship between *ratio* and *revelatio*, which constitutes the main topic of our investigation, the question of how the *datum* of revelation is related to the teaching ministry of the church is of a peripheral nature and cannot be discussed in any great detail. Nevertheless, a few general remarks on how Thomas interprets this relationship may help to show how he conceives the knowledge given in revelation to have been transmitted into his own period, and may therefore be appropriate at this point.

When the unity of the faith is threatened, the unity of the church is also at stake, for *ad unitatem Ecclesiae requiritur quod omnes fideles in fide conveniant* (the unity of the church requires that all the faithful agree as to the faith).[99] It is in this situation, according to Thomas, that the papacy comes into prominence: successor of Peter, the pope possesses the *potestas regitiva* in the church to *sententialiter determinare ea quae sunt fidei* (to decide matters of faith finally), in order that the faith transmitted within the church may be preserved inviolate.[100] The pope thus personifies the true interpretation of the meaning of the faith and revelation which should always be found within the church, and in his discussion of this claim Thomas repeatedly points both to the promise given by Christ to the disciples

---

[97] 2a2ae, 1, 10, ad 1: *in doctrina Christi et Apostolorum veritas fidei est sufficienter explicata. Sed quia perversi homines apostolicam doctrinam et ceteras Scripturas 'pervertunt ad sui ipsorum perditionem', sic dicitur II Petr. ult., ideo necessaria est, temporibus procedentibus, explanatio fidei contra insurgentes errores.*

[98] 2a2ae, 11, 3, ad 2: *ut excutiamus pigritiam, divinas Scripturas sollicitius intuentes.*

[99] *CG* IV, 76; cf. also the previous pages and passages cited in footnote 95.

[100] 2a2ae, 1, 10: *nova editio symboli necessaria est ad vitandum insurgentes errores. Ad illius ergo auctoritatem pertinet editio symboli ad cuius auctoritatem pertinet sententialiter determinare ea quae sunt fidei, ut ab omnibus inconcussa fide teneantur. Hoc autem pertinet ad auctoritatem Summi Pontificis. . . Unde et Dominus, Luc. 22, Petro dixit, quem Summum Pontificem constituit: 'Ego pro te rogavi, Petre, ut non deficiat fides tua: et tu aliquando conversus confirma fratres tuos'. Et huius ratio est quia una fides debet esse totius Ecclesiae. . . Quod servari non posset nisi quaestio fidei de fide exorta determinaretur per eum qui toti Ecclesiae praeest, ut sic eius sententia a tota Ecclesia firmiter teneatur;* see also *Quodl.* 9, 16; *Contra errores Graecorum*, 32; *De Pot.* 10, 4, ad 13; *CG* IV, 76; 2a2ae, 11, 2, ad 3; *Suppl.* 40, 6.

that he would send the Spirit of Truth and also to Christ's prayer that Peter's faith may not fail.[101] As the principal minister of the church's *magisterium*, the pope by virtue of these promises of Christ represents the inerrant faith of the Catholic church,[102] and therefore his decision is to be preferred to any past or present pronouncement in disputed questions of interpretation.[103]

It is characteristic of Thomas, however, that his interest is focussed, not on the *magisterium* as such, but on the transmitted confession of faith. In contrast with more recent Roman Catholic theology, for example, Thomas never refers to Matthew 16:18 as the primary basis of the teaching authority of the pope, but rather to Luke 22:32, which speaks of Jesus' prayer that Peter's *faith* may not fail.[104] When he does comment on Matthew 16:18 in a different context, he does not interpret the passage to refer to Peter himself or his ministry but *always* to Peter's *confession* and the content of that confession: *super revelatione facta Apostolis de fide unitatis et trinitatis fundatur tota fides Ecclesiae: secundum illud Matt. 16: 'Super hanc petram',* SCILICET CONFESSIONIS TUAE, *'aedificabo Ecclesiam meam'* (the entire faith of the church is founded on the revelation given to the apostles concerning the faith in the one God and three persons, according to Matt. 16:18, *'On this rock,* i.e. of your confession, *I will build my church'*).[105] It is not Peter nor even the apostolic ministry which constitutes for Thomas the foundation of the church, but the teaching of the prophets and the apostles, their witness to Christ. He can therefore say of the apostles that *intantum dicuntur fundamenta, inquantum eorum doctrina Christum annuntiant* (they are called foundations in so far as they make Christ known by their teaching)—

---

[101] On Luke 22:32, which for Thomas was clearly of central importance in this context, consult *CG* IV, 76; 2a2ae, 1, 10; 2a2ae, 2, 6, ad 3; *Suppl.* 25, 1 sed contra and *Suppl.* 40, 6, ad 1; on John 14:26, *Quodl.* 9, 16; and on John 16:13 2a2ae, 1, 9, sed contra.

[102] 2a2ae, 2, 6, ad 3: *universalis Ecclesiae fidem, quae non potest deficere.*

[103] *Quodl.* 9, 16: *certum est quod judicium Ecclesiae universalis errare in his quae ad fidem pertinent, impossibile est. Unde magis est standum sententiae Papae, ad quem pertinet determinare de fide, quam in judicio profert, quam quorumlibet sapientum hominum in Scripturis opinioni;* cf. 2a2ae, 11, 2, ad 3.

[104] Cf. footnote 100.

[105] 2a2ae, 174, 6; cf. how in *In Matt.* 16(2) Thomas refers to Peter as the vicar of Christ *inquantum habet confessionem Christi*; see also *Declaratio quorundam articulorum contra Graecos, Armenos et Saracenos, 1: Beatus Petrus Apostolus, qui promissionem accepit a Domino ut super eius confessione fundaretur Ecclesia; Suppl.* 25, 1, *sed contra* 2: *dixit Petro, super cuius confessione Ecclesia fundata est.*

a statement which in fact he bases in the context on Matthew 16:18.[106] The faith and teaching of the apostles is the basis of the church's faith, and the function of the teaching office is to guard this apostolic *doctrina* and keep it from being corrupted. It belongs to the teaching office to expound and define in matters of doubt the meaning of what has been revealed, but Thomas never states that the teaching office itself is the *regula fidei*, which can only be the substance of the revelation which is found in scripture and the earliest creeds.[107] Thus in one sense Thomas regards the teaching office of the church as essentially subordinate to scripture, in that its function, as he says, is to safeguard, interpret and expound its content. That which has been given once in revelation is *sufficienter* to be found in scripture and in what is derived from scripture—creeds and articles of faith—and nothing new can be added to it whether by the apostles themselves or their successors.[108] The same is true also of church councils and their decisions in matters of doctrine. As in the case of the pope, here too teaching authority is constituted by a *potestas interpretandi*. There is no question of any addition to the faith which has been received, but rather the *nova editio symboli*, or revised edition of the creed— which has been challenged by heresy at a particular point of doctrine and is therefore now interpreted by the council—represents in the light of changed circumstances simply a better explanation of what has already been given.[109]

---

[106] *In ad Eph.* 2, 6(127–31): '*superaedificati supra fundamentum Apostolorum et Prophetarum*', id est, qui sunt Apostoli et Prophetae, id est, super doctrinam eorum . . . idem est dicere Christum esse fundamentum, et doctrinam Apostolorum et Prophetarum, cum Christum tantum, non seipsos, praedicaverint; unde accipere eorum doctrinam est accipere Christum crucifixum. . . Qui (scil. Apostoli) intantum ponunt fundamenta, inquantum eorum doctrina Christum annuntiant. Matth. XVI, 18: '*Super hanc petram aedificabo ecclesiam meam*' . . . cum dicit 'in quo', scilicet fundamento, qui Christus est principaliter, et doctrina Apostolorum et Prophetarum secundario.

[107] It is typical of Diekamp's *Dogmatik* that in the sections (17–20) in which he describes the magisterial office of the church in general terms as *regula proxima fidei* all citations from Thomas are absent, see Diekamp, *Dogmatik*, p. 60ff.

[108] Cf. 3a, 64, 2, ad 3 and the references given on p. 52ff. to passages dealing with the sufficiency of scripture, and also III *Sent.* 25, 2, 2, 1, ad 5: *Et sic fides implicita explicatur in articulis fidei determinatis. Et haec explicatio completa est per Christum; unde ejus doctrinae quantum ad essentialia fidei nec diminuere nec addere licet;* 2a2ae, 1, 10, ad 1: *in doctrina Christi et Apostolorum veritas fidei est sufficienter explicata;* De Pot. 10, 4, ad 13: *doctrina catholicae fidei sufficienter tradita fuit in symbolo Nicaeno.*

[109] See e.g. *De Pot.* 10, 4, ad 13: *Sicut autem posterior Synodus potestatem habet interpretandi symbolum a priore symbolo conditum, ac ponendi aliqua ad ejus*

In discussing the criterion by which the truth of a particular doctrine of the church may be adjudged, Thomas does not point to the power of interpretation given to the teaching office. The criterion is rather, he states, conformity to the teaching of the apostles. There is an instructive passage in his *De Veritate*, where he deals with the following objection: Granted that God has revealed supernatural truth to prophets and apostles. But they in their turn have transmitted it to their successors, and in this way it has been passed on to our own time. But all those who have transmitted the content of the faith to us have shared the common human experience of error—*decipi et decipere potuerunt*—hence no one can be certain that what has been transmitted is really also a *veritas infallibilis* (infallible truth). Thomas replies to this objection by referring to Mark 16:20 and stating, first, that we believe in the witness of the prophets and the apostles, *ex hoc quod Dominus testimonium perhibuit miracula ficiendo* (because the Lord has been their witness by performing miracles), and then he adds: *Successoribus autem eorum non credimus* NISI IN QUANTUM NOBIS ANNUNTIANT EA QUAE ILLI IN SCRIPTIS RELIQUERUNT (we believe their successors only in so far as they tell us those things which they [i.e. prophets and apostles] have left in their writings).[110] We give credence to what has been passed down in the church because and to the extent that it conforms to scripture.[111]

explanationem, ut ex praedictis patet; ita etiam Romanus Pontifex hoc sua auctoritate potest, cujus auctoritate sola, Synodus congregari potest, et a quo sententia Synodi confirmatur, et ad ipsum a Synodo appellatur (Thomas is referring here to the Council of Chalcedon, A.D. 451); 2a2ae, 1, 10, ad 2: *Non enim per huiusmodi sententiam synodi generalis ablata est potestas sequenti synodo novam editionem symboli facere, non quidem aliam fidem continentem, sad eandem magis expositam.* Cf. van der Ploeg, *Thomist* 10 (1947), p. 419: 'According to St Thomas, the general Councils of the Church only explain the teaching of the Scripture to which they appeal'.

[110] *De Ver.* 14, 10, ad 11; cf. especially the formulation of obi. 11. To an objection of this kind almost all of the more recent works of Roman Catholic theology would respond by referring to the church's teaching office and its infallibility, see e.g. B. Bartmann, *Lehrbuch der Dogmatik*, vols. I and II, 8th ed. Freiburg im Breisgau 1932, vol. I p. 35, vol. II p. 152ff. or Diekamp, *Dogmatik*, p. 12f., 22, 24, 59ff. [111] Cf. also 2a2ae, 2, 6, ad 3: *minores non habent fidem implicitam in fide maiorum nisi quatenus maiores adhaerent doctrinae divinae: unde et Apostolus dicit, I ad Cor. 4:* 'Imitatores mei estote, sicut et ego Christi'. *Unde humana cognitio non fit regula fidei, sed veritas divina,* and *In 1 ad Tim.* 6, 1(237), where, in answering the question, *Si vis scire, quae doctrina sit erronea,* Thomas refers to the correspondence between Jesus' own teaching and that of the apostles. See also 2a2ae, 11, 2, ad 2: *ille dicitur aliter exponere sacram Scripturam quam Spiritus Sanctus efflagitat qui ad hoc expositionem sacrae Scripturae intorquet quod contrariatur ei quod est per Spiritum Sanctum revelatum.*

At the same time, however, Thomas does in fact hold that the interpretation of scripture taught in the church and sanctioned by papal pronouncements substantially conforms and indeed is identical to revelation. Hence this *doctrina Ecclesiae, quae procedit ex veritate prima in scripturis manifestata* (teaching of the church which proceeds from the first truth manifested in holy scripture) may also be designated a *regula infallibilis et divina* (infallible and divine rule).[112] The teaching of the church is infallible, but it is so, Thomas holds, because it is derived from scripture and represents a true interpretation of what it contains, the truth being guaranteed by Christ's promise to his church. Scripture and the teaching of the church thus constitute a unity.

Though we have digressed in order to see more clearly what Thomas means by the transmission of revelation, we may now return to our discussion of the content of tradition and try also to identify his various lines of thought. There is a clear distinction between Thomas and post-Tridentine Catholic theology in the treatment of these questions, though this distinction is seldom discussed in works on Thomas. A brief comparison between his point of view and the later theological tradition may therefore now be in order, particularly since such a comparison will show more clearly what is distinctive in his thought.

If we turn to Thomas after a study of early twentieth century Roman Catholic scholars, we soon discover that the proofs from tradition, which are so prominent a feature in these writers, are almost wholly absent in Thomas. He does indeed frequently cite the church fathers, especially Augustine and Pseudo-Dionysius, but it is quite clear that the purpose of their citation is not to point to a *unanimis consensus Patrum* in order to prove the truth of a doctrine.[113]

[112] 2a2ae, 5, 3; cf. ib. ad 2: *Sed omnibus articulis fidei inhaeret fides propter unum medium, scilicet propter veritatem primam propositam nobis in Scripturis secundum doctrinam Ecclesiae intellectis sane.*

[113] Cf. van der Ploeg, *Thomist* 10 (1947), p. 419: 'The idea and the term "unanimous opinion of the Fathers' (*unanimis consensus Patrum*), which occurs so often in the Catholic theology since the Council of Trent, is not met with in the works of St. Thomas'; see also A. Deneffe, *Der Traditionsbegriff* (Münsterische Beiträge zur Theologie 18), Münster in Westfalen 1931, p. 76. The only clear exception to this rule is found in a few passages in which Thomas discusses questions related to *filioque*, and in his argument against the Greeks seeks to base his argument on the statements of their own *doctores*, cf. *CG* IV, 24: *Ad hoc etiam induci possunt auctoritates doctorum Ecclesiae, etiam Graecorum;* see also *De Pot.* 10, 4, ad 13 and *Contra errores Graecorum.* The argument from tradition thus arises only in connection with a point of controversy in theology and is limited to that part of

Ordinarily Thomas uses statements of the fathers purely as illustrations of the general drift of his argument, which sometimes means that they are introduced in a context which bears little relation to the idea which they were originally designed to express. Thus they have obviously a different function in his writings from what they have in the scholasticism of the Roman Catholic Church which was formulated during and after the events of the Reformation.[114] This is connected with the fact that for Thomas *auctoritates doctorum*[115] do not in the last resort represent the revelation which is the ground and object of faith, and therefore no proof can be sought in them which is theologically conclusive. Such proof can be found only in the *auctoritates canonici scripturae.*[116] The crucial distinction which

the tradition which is also accepted by the other party involved in the discussion, but it plays hardly any part in his normal dogmatic interpretation. Perhaps, therefore, the use at every point of theological discussion of the argument from tradition which we find in post-Tridentine Catholic theology may be seen as an expression of a tendency which can be noted frequently elsewhere, viz. that modern Roman Catholic theology has been negatively influenced at almost every point by its conflict with Protestantism, both in regard to the questions which it raises and its selection of the questions for theological discussion.

---

[114] Cf. G. Geenen, 'L'usage des "auctoritates" dans la doctrine du baptême chez S. Thomas d'Aquin, in *Ephemerides theologicae lovanienses* (=*ETL*) 15 (1938) p. 299: 'Il est donc évident qu'il ne peut être question ici de véritable preuve, au sens que nous donnons à ce mot aujourd'hui. Il faut se défaire de la mentalité et des théories actuelles sur les sources de la foi et se garder de les prêter aux médiévaux', and Chenu, *Saint Thomas*, p. 133: 'We cannot see in them (sc. the 'authorities') the exact medieval equivalent of what we call, since the XVIth century, the argument of tradition, that is, the argument established through a consensus of witnesses unanimously testifying throughout the centuries in favor of a doctrine of faith. . . . The medieval *auctoritas* is much more supple in its application than the modern argument based on tradition, and it is not required to fulfil the same scientific objective'. See also J. de Ghellinck, 'Patristique et argument de tradition au bas moyen âge', in *Aus der Geisteswelt des Mittelalters* (Beiträge zur Geschichte der Philosophie des Mittelalters, Suppl. III: 1), Münster in Westfalen 1935.

[115] We may note that the term *auctoritas* when used by a writer in the Middle Ages does not denote a person possessed of authority but refers to 'the text itself which was called to witness', see Chenu, *Saint Thomas*, p. 131.

[116] 1a, 1, 8, ad 2: *Auctoritatibus autem canonicae Scripturae utitur proprie, ex necessitate argumentando. Auctoritatibus autem aliorum doctorum ecclesiae, quasi arguendo ex propriis, sed probabiliter'* and cf. the continuation of this passage quoted on p. 48 above. Bonaventure also strongly emphasises the sufficiency of proof from scripture, cf. IV *Sent.* 11, 1, 3, ad 4: *Ecclesia per Scripturam suam potuit probare auctoritatem; qua probata oportet obedire, non aliud testimonium quaerere* (Quaracchi ed. vol. IV, p. 853). G. de Broglie in his 'Note . . . on the Primacy of the Argument from Scripture in Theology', in L. Bouyer, *The Spirit and Forms of Protestantism*, Maryland 1961, p. 230–234, illustrates clearly how formulations such as these must seem offensive and exaggerated to a modern Roman Catholic

Thomas here introduces between proofs from scripture and proofs from tradition in holding that the latter can be used only *probabiliter* is thus an indirect expression of what we have earlier noted in our study, viz. that Thomas adheres to a clear 'scriptural principle'. The idea of tradition as 'a constitutive source of faith standing on an equal line with scripture'[117] is quite lacking in Thomas.[118] This explains why oral traditions are to be regarded primarily as *traditiones servandae*. When he does speak of oral tradition as a source of revelation—and the only specific instance is when he discusses the institution of the sacrament of confirmation—it is in the form of an exception to the general rule of the sufficiency of scripture and is justified by the need to sanction an existing practice of the church.

This adherence to the scriptural principle, however, is not peculiar to Thomas, and in affirming it he is simply expressing an idea commonly found in theologians of the Middle Ages. It is not true, as has at times been alleged, that these theologians merely referred to it occasionally;[119] rather, as has been shown by F. Kropatschek[120] and more recently by P. de Vooght in his exhaustive study of theology in the fourteenth and fifteenth centuries, the question at issue is a principle which is repeatedly brought forward by all the major scholastic theologians when they discuss the transmission of revealed

theologian. Speaking of the passage from Thomas quoted above, de Broglie says: 'According to the literal meaning of the text, it could appear that the argument, from Scripture is the only "necessary", absolutely rigorous, argument in theology' (p. 231). But in Thomas himself the question is one of a statement of principle, the categorical signification of which cannot be made to disappear magically just by saying, 'it could appear'.

[117] The quotation comes from A. Lang, *Die Loci theologici des Melchior Cano und die Methode des dogmatischen Beweises. Ein Beitrag zur theologischen Methodologie und ihrer Geschichte* (Münchener Studien zur historischen Theologie 6), Munich 1925, p. 112, and refers to Melchior Cano, but it may equally well be said to express the intention of the whole of the post-Tridentine theology of tradition inaugurated primarily by him and by Bellarmine.

[118] A typical though indirect expression of this is to be seen in the fact that the abundant citations from Thomas which Diekamp usually includes in his *Dogmatik* are conspicuously absent in section 13, entitled 'Das Wesen der Überlieferung und ihr Verhältnis zur Hl. Schrift', though no explanation for this is offered.

[119] Beumer, *Schriftprinzip*, p. 35. A similar interpretation is not uncommon amongst Protestant writers, see e.g. K. D. Schmidt, *Studien zur Geschichte des Konzils von Trient*, Tübingen 1925, p. 174: 'Es findet sich zwar daneben einzelne Stimmen, die in der hl. Schrift die alleinige Quelle der Kirchenlehre sehen'. Schmidt continues: 'Aber diese Anschauung bedeutet keineswegs eine formale Heresie'—naturally not, since it was a quite conventional idea! Cf. in this connection de Vooght, *Sources*, p. 149.

[120] Kropatschek, *Schriftprinzip*, vol. I, see especially p. 438ff.

knowledge. What we have found in our discussion of Thomas simply confirms that in this regard he subscribed to the general conclusions which are found throughout this period. As P. de Vooght expresses it: 'In the view of scholastic theologians since St. Anselm only one source of Christian doctrine is clearly found—scripture'; '. . . Tradition, considered as an original and independent source of Christian doctrine, is unknown in the theology of the period'.[121] But this also demonstrates that at this point there is a crucial distinction of considerable importance for the history of theology between post-Tridentine Roman Catholic theology, in which the dominant line of thought up to the Second Vatican Council has been that revelation consists of two separate, equivalent and complementary sources, and the medieval theological tradition, of which Thomas is one of the foremost representatives.[122]

[121] de Vooght, *Sources*, p. 28 and 148f. Cf. also p. 32: 'Si on leur demande si toute la vérité chrétienne est révélée dans la Bible? ils répondent en choeur: oui. Seulement, ils se résignent à reconnaître que la règle ne vaut pas toujours. Pour les scolastiques, au XIIe et au XIIIe siècles, ce que le Concile de Trente a appelé les *sine scripto traditiones* se limitaient à quelques "exceptions" '; see also R. Seeberg's article 'Scholastik' in *Realencyklopädie für protestantische Theologie und Kirche* 17, Leipzig 1906, p. 729.

[122] In the light of this fact the insistence of the Reformers on *sola Scriptura* is to be seen not as a sudden breach with previous theological tradition or as a radical innovation within the church, but rather as an attempt to apply in a new way what before had been universally understood as a self-evident and commonly accepted rule. Cf. de Vooght, *Sources*, p. 233, where, in speaking of Hus, he states that 'sa doctrine de la Bible comme source de la théologie chrétienne n'est que la théologie commune de l'époque'. He says the same about Wyclif on p. 259f. It was precisely in maintaining the unique and decisive significance of scripture as the starting-point for theology that the Reformers demonstrated their loyalty to the church and its tradition. In contrast, however, the real novelty is the idea originating at Trent and clearly developed in post-Tridentine theology that the church's tradition is a peculiar source of revelation and on a par with scripture. In this instance it is quite clear that it is in the Reformers and not this later Roman Catholic theology that we can trace the continuity with the main lines of the earlier theological tradition. It is also clear, as Kropatschek, *Schriftprinzip*, vol. I, p. 459, correctly observes, that 'das Wesen der Reformation muss daher wohl in etwas anderem bestehen als in der Aufstellung der Schriftprinzips'. We cannot conclude from all this, as A. Harnack does in his *History of Dogma*, republication of the ET of the 3rd German ed. New York 1961, vol. VI, p. 156, that ' "the formal principle of the reformation" had a representative in the great schoolman', i.e. Thomas. What used to be called in an older term the 'formal principle of the Reformation' does not correspond to the scriptural principle which we find in the theologians of the Middle Ages, for if the former is disjoined from its organic connection with the concept of justification *sola fide* and dealt with in isolation, what results is not the scriptural principle advocated by Luther. The Reformation does not imply any narrowing down of the tradition of the church to include scripture alone: the question with which the Reformers wrestled was what the true tradition was, or, if we prefer, what is the

In summary we could say that for Thomas scripture is not the same as revelation, but it is the necessary means by which revelation is transmitted. Its purpose is to allow the teaching of the prophets and the apostles to be received and heard in each new generation. In his description of how the knowledge given in revelation is transmitted he therefore assigns to scripture a central place as the source from which in every age the revealed truth that is necessary for salvation is to be sought. Around this centre he draws together from the traditional teaching of the church statements which in his view truly interpret what has been revealed and contribute to the church's understanding of it.

In the writings of Thomas we find that the concept of *traditio* has a certain lack of preciseness. This is explained by the fact that tradition cannot be discussed in isolation from the exegesis of scripture. We do not therefore find in Thomas any explanation of tradition, which he regards as something as natural and necessary as the church itself —just as there is a church on earth, so it is necessary that within this church teaching about the goal and means of salvation should be given in each new generation. Formally, even the biblical writings themselves represent one element in this tradition, but materially this *traditio*, which is transmitted within the church, is the continuing exposition throughout the ages of the truth given in scripture. In Thomas tradition is not *complementary* but *interpretative*.[123] Thus the scriptural principle does not mean that scripture is in any way opposed to the interpretation of the church, the tradition of the fathers, and the pronouncements of the *magisterium*. These three elements constitute a unity—and even as early as this we can see the development in theology which gradually led to the dogma of

true interpretation of scripture. The conflict between Luther and scholasticism is not one between a theology which acknowledges scripture alone and another theology which denies this principle—and in both cases the starting-point is essentially the same—but rather the much profounder theological question of the *interpretation* of the prophetic and apostolic message. Some further discussion of this whole problem is to be found in P. E. Persson, 'Quelques réflexions sur l' Écriture et la tradition chez Thomas d'Aquin', in *Positions luthériennes* 5 (1957).

---

[123] Cf. E. Ortigues, '*Écritures et traditions* apostoliques au concile de Trente', in *Recherches de science religieuse* (=*RSR*) 36 (1939), p. 296: 'Par rapport à la Bible, la tradition est-elle complétive ou interprétative? Le moyen âge nous suggère l'idée de l'interprétation', and Chenu, *Saint Thomas*, p. 128: 'The teaching of (theology) had settled, spontaneously and without a break, upon the text of this word of God, upon the collating of the texts of a tradition which interpreted it by congealing around it'.

F

infallibility[124]—but this unity means that the teaching of the church, *doctrina ecclesiae*, is to be understood essentially as *the interpretation of scripture.*

[124] Beumer, *Schriftprinzip*, p. 49 is therefore quite correct in seeing that the characteristic feature of the scriptural principle of scholasticism is that 'die Schrift *nicht allein für sich* genommen wird, sondern *in lebendiger Verbindung mit der kirchlichen Lehrverkündigung*'. There is actually here a clear line from Thomas to the definition of the magisterial office as a *regula proxima fidei* which we can find in Roman Catholic theology before the Second Vatican Council. At this point we can perhaps see most sharply the crucial difference between Thomas and the Reformation. While for the former *sola Scriptura* includes the interpretation of the magisterial office and coincides with it, Luther destroys this unity. This follows from the fact that the interpretation of the content of scripture is in the Reformation itself quite different from what we find in scholasticism, and this necessarily produced a breach at this point. In spite of Thomas's theory of the infallibility of the pope in matters of doctrine, however, the distance which separates him from more recent Roman Catholic theology is at once to be seen in the fact that pre-conciliar Roman Catholic theology would have found the definition, *sola Scriptura canonica est regula fidei*, quite unacceptable.

3

SACRA DOCTRINA AND SACRA SCRIPTURA

As we have seen in the preceding section, the doctrinal tradition of the church is not in Thomas's view an independent source of revelation, parallel to scripture, but is rather the means of transmitting the substance of revelation originally given to prophets and apostles and contained—at least as regards those things which are essential for salvation—in the canonical scriptures. As a theologian, Thomas himself stands within this tradition, and therefore it is important for us to see how he interprets the relationship between what is given in scripture and the task of theology. In this study we shall again take up for discussion questions which were first raised in the introductory section dealing with Thomas's concept of revelation, and which particularly fall within the scope of the present work, viz., the relationship between *ratio* and *revelatio* in the theology of Thomas.

Knowledge of the content of revelation is transmitted within the church through teaching, *doctrina*, but we have also seen how revelation itself, according to Thomas, may be said to have been given *per modum cuiusdam doctrinae* (after the fashion of a certain teaching).[1] Thus Thomas can include within the concept of *doctrina* the original *revelatio* and the continuing transmission of doctrine within the church. This is also the term which he characteristically chooses to describe theology. His noticeably infrequent use of the term *theologia*[2] in comparison with his predecessors and contemporaries is undoubtedly to be explained by the fact that *theologia*, unlike *doctrina*, is incapable of conveying the sense of teaching and the outward activity which clearly for Thomas constitutes the theological task.[3] Theology is not undertaken for its own sake, but as 'instruction of men in the knowledge of salvation,'[4] it is an element

[1] See p. 41 and 44 above.
[2] See in this connection Congar's Letter of Introduction in van Ackeren, *Sacra doctrina*, p. 14, footnote 2.
[3] Cf. van Ackeren, *Sacra doctrina*, p. 121.
[4] van Ackeren, *Sacra doctrina*, p. 118.

in the transmission of revealed truth which is essential for the salvation of men. When the term *theologia* does occur in Thomas, it is used as a comprehensive expression for all 'speech about God' in the sense either of *theologia, quam philosophi consequuntur, quae alio nomine metaphysica dicitur* (the theology known to the philosophers, which is alternatively called metaphysics), or of *theologia, quae in scriptura traditur* (the theology which is found in scripture),[5] but of these only the latter is equivalent to *sacra doctrina*. It is to be distinguished from the purely metaphysical knowledge of God, which is simply a product of man's innate desire to attain perfect knowledge and which can be sought for no other reason than the satisfaction every pursuit of knowledge gives to the individual seeker. *Sacra doctrina*, on the other hand, has its source in a revelation given by God (and therefore it is SACRA *doctrina*) and it is the nature of this revelation that it must be transmitted to other men through teaching (hence it is termed *sacra* DOCTRINA).

Within the church the task of instructing men about salvation and the means of attaining it has been entrusted to the successors of the apostles. To them has been commissioned the task of handing on what has been revealed to the apostles. What is required of them, as Thomas puts it, is to *magis explicite credere* (to believe more explicitly), i.e., to have an understanding of revelation which corresponds to their ministry, and which is greater than the majority of believers are required to have.[6] This deeper understanding of the things of God gives them an intermediate position between God and other men. Their knowledge may be regarded as a participation in God's own knowledge—so far as this is possible on the human level— whether they received it by direct revelation from God (like the apostles) or by study of the holy scriptures.[7] It is within this context

---

[5] *In De Trin* 5, 4; cf. also 5, 1 and 1a, 1, 1, ad 2: *theologia quae ad sacram doctrinam pertinet.* In the light of these passages the interpretation of 1a, 1, 1 which is given by van der Ploeg, *Thomist* 10 (1947), p. 411—'theology is only a part of *sacra doctrina*'—is impossible. We should rather say that *sacra doctrina* is a part of *theologia*, viz, that which teaches what is necesssry for man's salvation.

[6] 2a2ae, 2, 6: *sicut superiores angeli, qui inferiores illuminant, habent pleniorem notitiam de rebus divinis quam inferiores, ut dicit Dionysius, 12 cap. Cael. Hier.; ita etiam superiores homines, ad quos pertinet alios erudire, tenentur habere pleniorem notitiam de credendis et magis explicite credere'; III Sent.* 25, 2, 1, 3: *unusquisque, cui incumbit officium instruendi alios de fide, qui majores dicuntur tenentur tantum scire de ista explicatione quantum pertinet ad officium suum.*

[7] III *Sent.* 25, 2, 1, 4: *illi quibus incumbit officium docendi fidem, sunt medii inter Deum et homines; unde respectu Dei sunt homines, et respectu hominum sunt dii, inquantum divinae cognitionis participes sunt per scientiam Scripturarum vel per revelationem.*

of instruction in revealed, supernatural truth, given by the church throughout the ages, that we are to examine what Thomas says about *sacra doctrina*. As a teacher of theology, he himself stands in this long line of *doctores* when, in the prologue to the *Summa theologiae*, he declares that he wants *cum confidentia divini auxilii*, EA QUAE AD SACRAM DOCTRINAM PERTINENT, *breviter ac dilucide prosequi, secundum quod materia patietur* (trusting in God's help, to pursue the things held by Christian theology, and to be precise and clear, so far as the matter allows).[8]

There is thus an integral relationship between revelation and the task of theology, and to the extent that revelation is given, theology has a task to fulfil. Theological instruction is a *doctrina secundum revelationem divinam*. Thomas begins his *Summa* by showing that man's salvation not only rests on the fact of revelation, but is also dependent on the transmission of the content of this revelation to those who have no knowledge of revealed truth: *Necessarium igitur fuit, praeter philosophicas doctrinas, quae per rationem investigantur, sacram doctrinam per revelationem haberi* (these then are the grounds of holding a holy teaching which has come to us through revelation beyond the discoveries of the rational sciences).[9] This gives Thomas's own work as a theologian and theological instruction in general a systematic place within the broad conception of salvation which is typical of Thomas's own approach and attitude. Salvation means the attainment of the supernatural goal to which God calls man, but which he can neither attain nor merit as a created being. Within this general framework of movement to God *sacra doctrina* constitutes the means by which men are given knowledge of their destiny, and makes it possible for them to attain it.[10] The function of *sacra doctrina* is to transmit what has been revealed.[11]

As we have just noted, the substance of the revelation found in

---

[8] 1a, prol. [9] 1a, 1, 1.

[10] This is particularly stressed by Congar in his Letter of Introduction in van Ackeren, *Sacra doctrina*. Cf. e.g. p. 15f: 'Bref, c'est à l'intérieur d'une forme décisive du grand mouvement par lequel il voit toutes choses, et singulièrement l'homme, revenir à la fin céleste du salut, que S. Thomas situe et comprend la *Doctrina sacra*, l'activité de communication à l'ésprit de ce qui concerne la fin et les moyens de notre destinée surnaturelle'.

[11] Cf. van Ackeren, *Sacra doctrina*, p. 82, where he argues that the statement, 'revelation is the means by which sacred doctrine is carried on', becomes more meaningful if it is reversed to state: 'sacred doctrine is the means by which revelation is carried on'; cf. p. 120, 'revelation . . . signifies the same reality as sacred doctrine but according to its proper mode'.

scripture may be expressed in a brief and simple summary, viz. the articles of faith, which represent in Thomas's view the apostolic confession of faith.[12] In theology, these articles of faith occupy a place which corresponds in the philosophical disciplines to the *principia per se nota* (self-evident principles).[13] They are the fundamental propositions of theology and are not subject to debate nor capable of demonstration, but constitute rather the starting-point and presupposition of theological discussion: *haec doctrina non argumentatur ad sua principia probanda, quae sunt articuli fidei; sed ex eis procedit ad aliquid aliud ostendendum* (this teaching does not argue to establish its premises, which are the articles of faith, but advances from them to make something known).[14] The function of theology is to discuss in detail the substance of these first principles, for the same rule that applies to all scientific study is also applicable here: *in principiis scientiae virtualiter tota scientia continetur* (the entire science is virtually contained in its premises).[15] The first *explicatio*

---

[12] The content and scope of these articles is described in detail in the minor work *In articulos fidei et sacramenta Ecclesiae expositio*. Here and also in other passages Thomas lists the articles as twelve or fourteen, though he always prefers to speak of them as fourteen on the basis of their contents. See III *Sent.* 25, 1, 2; *In decretalem I. expositio; Compend. Theol.* 246; 2a2ae, 1, 6, and 1, 8. When R. Bernard, *La foi*, vol. I, 1941 p. 396, says with regard to the Apostles' Creed that 'Saint Thomas ne pense d'ailleurs pas que ce précieux Symbole épuise la série des grands articles de la foi', and adds on p. 397, 'Au rang des grands articles de foi il faut recevoir aussi certains énoncés majeurs qui, sans avoir été formellement consignés dans l'Écriture, l'ont été ou le seront dans l'Église en vertu de l'infaillibilité dont elle est revêtue en pareil cas', his assertions have no basis in any actual texts of Thomas, but are rather an expression of the author's own wishful thinking about what he thinks they ought to say. We can simply express regret that he does not follow here the excellent principle which he enunciates on p. 227: 'Nous somme d'avis que saint Thomas n'est jamais mieux expliqué que par lui-même'. In rebuttal of Bernard we must emphasise what is said by J. F. Bonnefoy in an essay, 'La théologie comme science et l'explication de la foi selon saint Thomas d'Aquin', in ETL 1937–38 (1938), p. 616: 'Le plus clair, c'est que tous les articles sont contenus dans le Symbole des Apôtres. Sur ce point, le Docteur Angélique n'admet pas de contestation'.

[13] 2a2ae, 1, 7; 2a2ae, 1, 5, ad 2: *Ex his autem principiis ita probatur aliquid apud fideles sicut etiam ex principiis naturaliter notis probatur aliquid apud omnes;* cf. also 1a, 1, 7, and 1, 8. On the first principles of philosophy, see Skydsgaard, *Metafysik*, p. 84f. It is not, however, the principle of identity but rather the principle of contradiction which for Thomas is absolutely primary, cf. 2a2ae, 1, 7: *In quibus principiis ordo quidam invenitur, ut quaedam in aliis implicite contineantur: sicut omnia principia reducuntur ad hoc sicut ad primum, 'Impossibile est simul affirmare et negare', ut patet per Philosophum, in IV Metaphys.;* see also 1a2ae, 65, 2, 1a2ae, 94, 2 and Manser, *Thomismus*, p. 291ff.

[14] 1a, 1, 8; cf. III *Sent.* 25, 1, 1, 1: *Fides autem non inquirit sed supponit ea quae fidei sunt ex testimonio Dei ea dicentis.*

[15] 1a2ae, 3, 6; cf. 1a, 1, 7: *tota scientia virtute contineatur in principiis.*

credendorum, which is given with revelation, must be followed by an *explicatio fidei*, by which the supernatural truth which is essential for salvation is communicated *ad inferiores homines per maiores* (to those of lower degree through those who are over them).[16] The scientific character of theology is thus demonstrated in the fact that it starts from certain given first principles from which in turn certain conclusions can be drawn, and these conclusions constitute a unity since they can be referred to the principles which are the basis and presupposition of scientific knowledge. The criterion by which any science is determined to be a science is that *ex aliquibus notis alia necessario concludantur* (from some things that are known others are necessarily concluded).[17] Unlike the first principles of metaphysics, articles of faith are not self-evident, *per se nota*, i.e. they are not immediately evident to all who have knowledge of them, but this is not because the truth which they contain is in some way more obscure or of a lower order than that dealt with in philosophy. The reverse indeed is true. Revealed truth is *maxime cognoscibilis* (eminently knowable) in itself, and it is only the imperfection of human nature and especially the human intellect *in via* that prevents it from being so.[18] Where this imperfection has been surmounted, for example, by the saints who behold God as he is himself—or, to take what is incomparably the highest form of knowledge of this truth, God's own knowledge of himself—there we see the truth which has been revealed to us as it really is, *per se nota*. The disclosure of this truth by revelation, summarised in the *articuli fidei*, gives the intellect an indescribable perfection and elevation, even though it cannot be seen, but only believed. In this disclosure we gain by faith a

---

[16] 2a2ae, 2, 6.

[17] *In De Trin.* 2, 2. On the question of Thomas's conception of theology, which we cannot deal with fully here, see M.-D. Chenu, 'La théologie comme science au XIIIe siècle in *Archives d'histoire doctrinale et littéraire du moyen âge* (=*AHDLMA*) 2, Paris, 1927, M. R. Gagnebet, 'La nature de la théologie spéculative', in *RT* 46 (1938) (gives an interesting comparison between Thomas on the one hand and Erasmus and Luther on the other); Bonnefoy, *ETL* 14 (1937) and 15 (1938); and Y. M.-J. Congar's article, 'Théologie', in *DTC* 15:1; and also the good historical summary in M. Grabmann, *Die theologische Erkenntnis- und Einleitungslehre des heiligen Thomas von Aquin auf Grund seiner Schrift 'In Boethium de Trinitate'. In Zusammenhang der Scholastik des 13. und beginnenden 14. Jahrhunderts dargestellt* (Thomistische Studien 4), Freiburg in der Schweiz 1948.

[18] 1a, 1, 5, ad 1: *nihil prohibet id quod est certius secundum naturam, esse quoad nos minus certum, propter debilitatem intellectus nostri; In De Trin.* 3, 1: *Ex defectu vero nostro sunt non apparentia res divinae et necessariae, quae sunt secundum naturam maxime notae.*

participation in the knowledge of God and of the saints, *scientia Dei et beatorum*, as far as it is possible for us in our earthly life. Faith enables us to participate in the knowledge of the saints in heaven, inaccessible though it may be to human reason.[19] Faith in the soul is *quasi quaedam sigillatio primae veritatis* (as it were a sealing by the original truth),[20] and the *sacra doctrina* which is based upon this faith may therefore be described as *quaedam impressio divinae scientiae* (an imprint of God's own knowledge).[21]

Since theology thus 'borrows' its principles from a higher knowledge, in terms of a scientific system it represents a parallel to the *scientiae subalternatae* (subordinate sciences) which *procedunt ex principiis notis lumine superioris scientiae* (work from premises recognised in the light of a higher science). The basic initial assumptions of these other sciences are principles which have been derived from higher sciences, and which have been shown to be self-evident in them. Thus music proceeds from principles derived from arithmetic; similarly the physician begins by accepting on trust what the physicist teaches about the four elements.[22] But while these sciences, because of their imperfection, are subordinate to others which stand above them in the hierarchy of science (the highest of all being metaphysics, the *prima philosophia*), theology stands above all other sciences, sub-

---

[19] *In De Trin.* 2, 2: *divinorum notitia . . . ipsa sunt ex se ipsis maxime cognoscibilia, et quamvis secundum modum suum non cognoscantur a nobis, tamen a deo cognoscuntur et a beatis secundum modum suum . . . fit nobis in statu viae quaedam illius cognitionis participatio et assimilatio ad cognitionem divinam, in quantum per fidem nobis infusam inhaeremus ipsi primae veritati propter se ipsam; ib. ad 5: Et hoc modo se habent articuli fidei, qui sunt principia huius scientiae, ad cognitionem divinam, quia ea quae sunt per se nota in scientia, quam deus habet de se ipso, supponuntur in scientia nostra et creduntur ei nobis haec indicanti per suos nuntios, sicut medicus credit physico quattuor esse elementa;* 1a, 1, 2: *Et hoc modo sacra doctrina est scientia: quia procedit ex principiis notis lumine superioris scientiae, quae scilicet est scientia Dei et beatorum.*

[20] *In De Trin.* 3, 1, 4.　　　　　　　　　　[21] 1a, 1, 3, ad 2.

[22] 1a, 1, 2: *duplex est scientiarum genus. Quaedam enim sunt, quae procedunt ex principiis notis lumine naturali intellectus, sicut arithmetica, geometria, et huiusmodi. Quaedam vero sunt, quae procedunt ex principiis notis lumine superioris scientiae: sicut perspectiva procedit ex principiis notificatis per geometriam, et musica ex principiis per arithemeticam notis. . . Unde sicut musica credit principia tradita sibi ab arithmetico, ita doctrina sacra credit principia revelata sibi a Deo; In De Trin.* 2, 2, 5, 5, 1, ad 5 and ad 6; *De Ver.* 14, 9, ad 3; I *Sent.* prol., 1, 3, 3, 2. This idea of a superior or an inferior order in the sciences is derived from Aristotle's *Posterior Analytics I*, see Grabmann, *Erkenntnis- und Einleitungslehre*, p. 142, footnote 1, and it is employed by Thomas, as Chenu, *AHDLMA* 2, p. 62, points out: 'pour rendre raison . . . du caractère apparemment anormal d'une science suspendue à un donné non évident.'

ordinated only to a knowledge which transcends all human powers. Since it takes its starting-point in principles which in their content are immeasurably more sublime than those of metaphysics, in consequence it affords a much deeper and more complete knowledge of God than that attained by philosophy.[23] The fact that its knowledge of the truth contained in the articles of faith is not self-evident is due, therefore, not to its lower status in comparison with other sciences, but simply to the frailty and imperfection of the human intellect.

There is the further truth to be noted in this connection that theological knowledge of God must of necessity be different from that knowledge which is at its perfection in God himself. While God has knowledge both of himself and of all created life *simplici intuitu*, we can attain a deeper understanding of the meaning of revealed truth only *secundum modum nostrum*, viz. *discurrendo de principiis ad conclusiones* (by passing discursively from principles to conclusions).[24] We can proceed from the *articuli fidei* in order to gain knowledge of the things known by God in a perfect way, but we can do so only in a form and manner corresponding to our human limitations. Thus in theology the knowledge of God and of the saints which we receive through infused faith constitutes the basis and presupposition with which the intellect must deal in the only way it can, that is, by use of rational thought, syllogism, and inference: *ipsa, quae fide tenemus, sunt nobis quasi principia in hac scientia et alia sunt quasi conclusiones* (those things which we believe on faith are 'principles' in this science, and other things 'conclusions').[25]

[23] *In De Trin.* 2, 2: *Ex quo patet quod haec scientia est altior illa scientia divina, quam philosophi tradiderunt, cum ex altioribus procedat principiis,* cf. also 1a, 1, 5 and 6.

[24] *In De Trin.* 2, 2: *Et sicut deus ex hoc, quod cognoscit se, cognoscit alia modo suo, id est simplici intuitu, non discurrendo, ita nos ex his, quae per fidem capimus primae veritati adhaerendo, venimus in cognitionem aliorum secundum modum nostrum discurrendo de principiis ad conclusiones.*

[25] *In De Trin.* 2, 2; cf. the conclusion in Manser, *Thomismus*, p. 133: 'Die Prinzipien der Theologie sind die Offenbarungswahrheiten, das, was nur durch göttliches Licht erkennbar ist, mit anderen Worten: die *Glaubensartikel*. Von ihnen geht sie aus, zieht aus dem Geoffenbarten Schlüsse, verbindet sie logisch, und so entsteht die sacra Theologia als wissenschaftliches System'; Grabmann, *Erkenntnis- und Einleitungslehre*, p. 129: 'Die Theologie hat ganz einfach die Form der Wissenschaft und verdient den Namen der Wissenschaft, wenn sie gewisse Wahrheiten der christlichen Lehre, die weniger bekannt oder weniger intelligibel sind, auf andere Wahrheiten gleichfalls der christlichen Lehre, die mehr bekannt oder mehr intelligibel sind, wie Konklusionen auf Prinzipien, entsprechend der Eigenart des menschlichen Erkennens, zurückführt.'

Though it is not possible for us *in statu viae* to comprehend in a proper and demonstrable sense the truths which form the presupposition of theology, and which can only be received in faith, yet it is possible to have sure knowledge of those things *quae concluduntur ex articulis fidei* (which are concluded from the articles of faith).[26]

The object of faith is revealed truth as summarised in the articles of faith,[27] and the task of theology is to disclose the meaning of this truth more fully. But theology itself is not given by revelation, nor can it be the object of faith.[28] It is a human attempt, employing all the resources of natural reason, to reconstruct on the human plane and to reflect *per modum cognitionis* (through a cognitive process) on the knowledge which God possesses of himself and of all created things.[29] As the activity of this reason, theology is a science. This avowedly rationalistic classification of theology as a *scientia* in a hierarchically ordered scientific system distinguishes Thomas in a marked degree, as M.-D. Chenu has shown, from earlier and from contemporary theologians. He is the first to treat theology as a true 'science' in the Aristotelian sense of the term.[30] There is another important difference between Thomas and his predecessors. If the purpose of theology in an earlier period was to arouse and foster in the heart dispositions which better prepared men for their journey to the heavenly goal,[31] for Thomas it is to allow us here and now to anticipate and imitate, so far as such a thing is possible, that perfect

---

[26] See *De Ver.* 14, 9, ad 3; cf. 2a2ae, 1, 5, ad 2 and IV *Sent.* 13, 2, 1, ad 6. Cf. also G. Söhngen, *Die Einheit in der Theologie*, Munich 1952, p. 60.

[27] See 2a2ae, 1, 1–10.

[28] The weakness which is to be found throughout Bonnefoy's otherwise very helpful essays in *ETL* 14 (1937) and 15 (1938) is explained by his failure to notice this fact in his definition of *sacra doctrina*, which means that he regards even the conclusions drawn from the first principles as the object of faith, and thus misses the meaning of what Thomas is saying. For a criticism of Bonnefoy at this point, see Congar in *BT* 1938, p. 500ff. and van Ackeren, *Sacra doctrina*, p. 42ff.

[29] 1a, 1, 6, ad 3; Gardeil, *Le donné*, p. 218; Skydsgaard, *Metafysik*, p. 165: 'Theology is God's knowledge of himself, transplanted into an earthly environment'; and also the same author's essay in *FJN*, p. 286; cf. Congar in *DTC* 15:1, col. 381: 'Il s'agit, pour le théologien, de retrouver et de reconstruire, dans une science humaine, les lignes, les enchaînements, l'ordre de la science de Dieu'.

[30] Chenu, *AHDLMA* 2, p. 33, 57ff., 67: 'En réalité, en poussant à fond l'application du concept de science à la doctrine sacrée, saint Thomas a renouvelé toute la conception et l'économie du travail théologique.'

[31] See especially Gagnebet, *RT* 46 (1938), p. 17–39, 221, 226f.; on the characteristics of the earlier theology cf. also Chenu, *AHDLMA* 2, p. 53: 'la théologie ne s'organise pas selon la méthode rationelle de la science; discipline pieuse et sagesse affective, elle prend le ton de précepte, de l'exhortation, de la prière.'

knowledge of God and heavenly things through which we shall some day attain to our perfection in eternity.[32]

Thus for Thomas theology works by *discurrendo de principiis ad conclusiones*. Its starting-point is the truth given in the revealed articles of faith, and *ex eis procedit (sacra doctrina) ad aliquid aliud ostendendum* (theology proceeds from these things to demonstrate something else). In a critical study of Thomas, G. Söhngen describes his methodological principle as 'a thinking through, on the basis of the given of faith, to new theological truths or insights.'[33] Does this mean that the *explicatio fidei* which is undertaken by theology also opens up *new* truths, which either do not appear in or go beyond the revelation given to us, and which are contained in summary form in holy scripture and the earliest confessions of faith?

As we have seen earlier, the supernatural truth which is transmitted in the church through *sacra doctrina* and which provides the basis of faith, has been directly revealed only to prophets and apostles, i.e. the writers of the canonical scriptures. The two groups are to be distinguished, however, in this regard, that the apostles received a *manifestior revelatio*.[34] Since the truth contained in scripture is summarised in the articles of faith, the primary question to be asked is *utrum articuli fidei secundum successionem temporum creverint* (whether the articles of faith have increased in course of time). This, in fact, is precisely the question which Thomas explicitly discusses: *quantum ad substantiam articulorum fidei, non est factum eorum augmentum per temporum successionem: quia quaecumque posteriores crediderunt continebantur in fide praecedentium Patrum, licet implicite. Sed quantum ad explicationem, crevit numerus articulorum: quia quaedam explicite cognita sunt a posterioribus quae a prioribus non cognoscebantur explicite* (as regards the substance of the articles of faith, they have not received any increase as time went on: since whatever those who lived later have believed, was contained, albeit implicitly, in the faith of the Fathers who preceded them. But

---

[32] One of the ways of stating that theology is in this way an imitation of God's own knowledge is to say that it is at one time a *scientia speculativa* and a *scientia practica, sicut et Deus eadem scientia se cognoscit, et ea quae facit*. It is *magis speculativa quam practica*, however, since in the first place it deals with divine things and has to do with human affairs only *secundum quod per eos ordinatur homo ad perfectam Dei cognitionem, in qua aeterna beatitudo consistit*, 1a, 1, 4.

[33] Söhngen, *Einheit*, p. 25. Söhngen is critical of this 'Konklusions-methode', which involves the risk of 'ein Hinausdenken über die Heilige Überlieferung hinweg', which in his view is clearly to be seen in 'einer sogenannten marianischen Theologie unserer Tage' (ib.).   [34] See p. 32f. above.

there was an increase in the number of articles believed explicitly, since to those who lived in later times some were known explicitly which were not known explicitly by those who lived before them).[35] The 'substance' of the articles, the divine truth, which is the formal object of faith, must always remain the same, for the oneness of the church throughout the ages is contingent upon this unity of belief.[36] On the other hand, the number of the articles of faith manifestly increases. However, this increase proves on closer inspection to be confined to the time *before* Christ. In his discussion of the point, Thomas refers to Ephesians 3:5, where Paul speaks about the 'mysteries of Christ' which were not disclosed in an earlier time, but have now been revealed. In the period of the old covenant, the faith which the fathers had did not differ from that of the apostles, except that they did not see as clearly the full implications of this faith, just as one cannot see as clearly at a distance what can be seen from closer by.[37] That is to say, there is an understanding which gradually grows deeper, the closer one comes to Christ: *illi qui fuerunt propinquiores Christo vel ante, sicut Ioannes Baptista, vel post, sicut Apostoli, plenius mysteria fidei cognoverunt* (those who were nearest to Christ, whether before, like John the Baptist, or after, like the apostles, had a fuller knowledge of the mystery of faith).[38] Thus, what in an earlier period was a general belief in the *mysterium redemptionis* is seen at a later time to mean more exactly the *incarnatio et passio Christi*. The more exact meaning given by these new articles is not to be thought of as an addition to, but as a clarification of what was already implicit in the less definite belief which the fathers had in a salvation given through divine intervention. But this development, by which *fides implicita explicatur in articulos fidei determinatis* (implicit faith is made explicit in the prescribed articles of faith), comes to its conclusion with Christ and the apostles: HAEC EXPLICATIO COMPLETA EST PER CHRISTUM; UNDE EJUS DOCTRINAE QUANTUM AD ESSENTIALIA FIDEI NEC DIMINUERE NEC ADDERE LICET (this explicitation is completed by Christ; with regard to the essential matters of the faith, we may therefore neither subtract from nor add to his teaching).[39] Thomas

---

[35] 2a2ae, 1, 7.   [36] Cf. p. 60 above, footnote 95.   [37] 2a2ae, 1, 7, ad 1.

[38] 2a2ae, 1, 7, ad 4; 2a2ae, 2, 7: *ea quae ad mysteria Christi pertinent tanto distinctius cognoverunt quanto Christo propinquiores fuerunt.*

[39] III *Sent.* 25, 2, 2, 1, ad 5, where the passage quoted continues: *Sed ante Christi adventum non erat completa; unde etiam quantum ad majores crescebat secundum diversa tempora.* This precludes any idea of new *articuli fidei* which are not already to be found in the earliest creed of the church, cf. p. 74 above, footnote 12.

holds that the words of Gregory the Great, *per successiones temporum crevit divinae cognitionis augmentum* (knowledge of God went on increasing as time went on), apply explicitly only to the time *before* Christ.[40]

This whole line of thought must be understood in the light of the fact that for Thomas revelation of divine truth is a gift of grace. Since this, according to the apostle, is given by the Holy Spirit,[41] it is natural that the understanding of this truth came to its climax and perfection in the outpouring of the Spirit on the apostles.[42] The grace given by the Spirit will at no time therefore be given or possessed in a more complete way than when it was given to the apostles. Through the teaching of Christ and the agency of the Spirit, they received the whole truth that is necessary for the attainment of salvation.[43] A fuller and more perfect revelation will be bestowed only *in patria ubi ipsa articulorum veritas plene videbitur* (in heaven, where the truth of the articles will be fully seen).[44]

This unique position of the apostles and of the apostolic age is a natural corollary of the hierarchical movement from higher to lower, which, as we have seen above, applies in Thomas's view both to revelation itself and to the transmission of revealed truth.[45] Within this hierarchical order, the apostles stand at the highest point attainable by man. It follows from this that they also have an understanding of revealed truth which cannot be surpassed. It may be worth noting in this connection that we do not find in Thomas what we frequently find in more recent Roman Catholic theology, the conception that the revelation given to the apostles was a seed which came to its full development only later in the tradition of the church, and then

[40] See 2a2ae, 174, 6, ad 1; *De Ver.* 14, 11; *In ad Heb.*. 1, 1 (10).

[41] Cf. 1a2ae, 111, 4, sed contra.

[42] *De Ver.* 14, 11, ad 6: *veritatis cognitio ad suum complementum pervenerat, quod praecipue factum est in adventu Spiritu sancti;* cf. 1a2ae, 51, 4: *Sicut Apostolis dedit scientiam Scripturarum et omnium linguarum, quam homines per studium vel consuetudinem acquirere possunt, licet non ita perfecte.*

[43] 1a2ae, 106, 4: *Sic etiam status novae legis diversificatur, secundum diversa loca et tempora et personas, inquantum gratia Spiritus Sancti perfectius vel minus perfecte ab aliquibus habetur. Non est tamen expectandum quod sit aliquis status futurus in quo perfectius gratia Spiritus Sancti habeatur quam hactenus habita fuerit, maxime ab Apostolis, qui primitias Spiritus acceperunt;* 1a2ae, 106, 4, ad 2: *Docuit autem Spiritus Sanctus Apostolos omnem veritatem de his quae pertinent ad necessitatem salutis: scilicet de credendis et agendis.* On this special position of the apostles cf. A. Lemonnyer, 'Les apôtres comme docteurs de la foi d'après saint Thomas', in *Mélanges thomistes* (=*MT*) (Bibliothèque thomiste 3), Paris 1934, p. 153 and 167.

[44] III *Sent.* 25, 2, 1, 3.

[45] See p. 42f. above. Cf. 2a2ae, 2, 6.

recognisably changed into something that far transcended what was originally given.[46] Thomas does indeed use this metaphor, but *only* to illustrate the relationship between the Old and New Testaments: *sicut tota arbor continetur in semine . . . per hunc modum nova lex continetur in veteri: dictum est enim quod nova lex comparatur ad veterem sicut perfectum ad imperfectum* (thus, a seed contains the whole tree. It is in this way that the new law is contained in the old: for it has been stated that the new law is compared to the old as perfect to imperfect).[47] The idea that doctrine may develop to a point at which the original revelation given through Christ and the apostles comes to be regarded as imperfect in comparison is simply not to be found in Thomas. His view is rather that the period of Christ and the apostles bears the same relationship to the time of the church as youth bears to the whole of life. Every other period, whether before or after, *vel ante vel post*, is related to this moment of time as the imperfect is related to the perfect.[48] A more complete revelation will be given only when the *visio Dei* is granted, and only in this vision of God which the saints in heaven possess will it be possible to attain the truth which transcends that given to the apostles, and which they summarised in the articles of faith. The *explicatio fidei* which theology provides when it derives conclusions from its first principles does not therefore imply a completion or fulfilment of what has already been given in new truths.[49] The problem is rather that of clarifying *id quod in articulo continetur* (what is contained in the article), and of this task of clarification Thomas says, *quantum*

[46] See e.g. the survey together with the literature cited in K. E. Skydsgaard, 'Schrift und Tradition. Bemerkungen zum Traditionsproblem in der neueren Theologie', in *Kerygma und Dogma*, vol. I, 1955, p. 161ff. The difference between Thomas and more recent Roman Catholic theology is clearly demonstrated in the fact that Gardeil, *Le donné*, p. 151ff., in his chapter 'Le développement du dogme', makes no explicit reference in his discussion to the development from the Old Testament to the New, while Thomas as explicitly confines his discussion to precisely this area.

[47] 1a2ae, 107, 3.

[48] 2a2ae, 1, 7, ad 4: *Quia et circa statum hominis hoc videmus, quod perfectio est in iuventute, et tanto habet homo perfectiorem statum vel ante vel post, quanto est iuventuti propinquior.* If we are to draw any conclusion from this comparison, it must first be that after the period of the apostles there is a decrease rather than an increase in their understanding of revelation! On the difficulties which interpreters of Thomas find in face of these and similar passages, see Bonnefoy *ETL* 15 (1938), p. 504ff.

[49] Cf. van Ackeren, *Sacra doctrina*, p. 120: 'Sacred doctrine as a participation of prophetic revelation will never bring to man any truth that was not communicated to the prophets and apostles.'

ad hoc quotidie potest fides explicari et per studium sanctorum magis explicata fuit (in this regard faith can be made more explicit each day and has been made more explicit by the study of holy men).[50] The function of theology is thus to interpret and explain the meaning of the supernatural knowledge of God which was given once and for all.

As we have seen above, this knowledge of God is found—at least as much of it as is necessary for salvation—in the holy scriptures, and these were passed on by those who had received the revelation *ad instructionem omnium futurorum* (for the instruction of all those who were to come). It is hardly surprising, therefore, to find that in Thomas scripture and theology are integrally related to one another. The primary task of the theologian is to provide knowledge of the content of scripture, for scripture is the source of the truth which it is his function to transmit.[51] For Thomas *sacra doctrina* is directly related to *sacra scriptura*. Scripture is not only the source of knowledge, it is also, as we have seen,[52] the norm of theological instruction. It contains supernatural and saving truth, but for this very reason Thomas also speaks of it as a *regula veritatis* which may be altered neither by subtraction, addition nor false interpretation.[53]

There are several explicit references to this conception of scripture as the norm of theology in Thomas's writings. These are to be found not only in his biblical commentaries, which deal specifically with the exegesis of scripture, but also in his systematic study of *sacra doctrina* in the *Summa theologiae*. Thus, he can lay down the following rule in the *Summa: de Deo dicere non debemus quod in sacra scriptura non invenitur vel per verba, vel per sensum* (we ought not to say about God anything which is not found in holy scripture either explicitly or implicitly).[54] It is not possible to limit oneself in every context to the use of the language and ideas of the Bible, but it is crucially important that the non-scriptural terms which are employed really express the 'sense' of the scriptures. Thomas discusses this problem of translation in a different context, in which he deals with the objection that the concept of 'person' is not found either in the Old

[50] III *Sent.* 25, 2, 2, 1, ad 5.
[51] *Contra impugnantes Dei cultum et religionum*, 2: *Eis autem competit docere qui notitiam habent Scripturarum.*
[52] See p. 51f. above.
[53] *In De div. nom.* 2, 1; see p. 52 above, footnote 57.
[54] 1a, 36, 2, ad 1. An example considered by Thomas is the formula: *Spiritus Sanctus procedit a Filio.* This is not found in scripture, at least in these words, yet it is contained in scripture *quantum ad sensum*, and therefore in Thomas's view must be regarded as a true expression of the biblical teaching on this point.

Testament or in the New, and so should not be used in any theological discussion of the meaning of these scriptures. With a rare flash of humour, Thomas observes that if we were to follow the rule of using only scriptural concepts in theological discussion, and not to vary from that rule, we would be forced to express ourselves in either Hebrew or Greek, and would not be able to speak about God in any other language! The necessity of refuting the heretics has forced men to seek new concepts by which to express in new circumstances and in a different age the meaning of the ancient faith in God. This is not a responsibility to be evaded, but something that is inherent in the theological task. Our obligation is simply to see that the new concepts and formulations are not *a scripturarum sensu discordans*.[55]

Two examples of this general rule can be found in the third part of the *Summa*, where Thomas deals with the regulative function of scripture in determining the content of theology. The context of the passage is a discussion of Christology and the sacraments, and by way of introduction, Thomas raises a problem which proved a point of controversy between the Thomists and the Scotists in the later medieval tradition and indeed in all later Roman Catholic theology. The question is, would the incarnation have occurred if there had never been a fall? Thomas had in fact already dealt with this question in his *Commentary on the Sentences*, where he describes the possible alternatives. In this earlier work he states that in his opinion, both opinions can probably be upheld: it is possible to believe both that the incarnation took place on account of sin and also that it would have taken place in the form of a *humanae naturae exaltatio*, even if man had never fallen.[56] But in the *Summa*, where he expresses his mature and definitive view, he states unequivocally that only the former view can be entertained. The reason for this is simply that in scripture we are given no other explanation of the incarnation than the fact of man's fall. Since it is only through holy scripture that we can know God's will concerning those things which go beyond the demands of nature, it is inadvisable for us to go beyond the words of scripture. Thomas's conclusion is that the incarnation took place on account of sin, even though the idea of an unconditional incarnation is more natural from a purely rational point of view.[57]

---

[55] 1a,29, 3, ad 1.   [56] III *Sent.* 1, 1, 3.

[57] See 3a, 1, 3. The same line of thought is developed in *In 1 ad Tim.* 1, 4 (40). On the conflict between Thomists and Scotists at this point see A. Michel's article, 'Incarnation', in *DTC* 7:2, col. 1495ff.; E. Hugon, *Le mystère de l'Incarnation*, 9th

The second example, directly related to the other, is found in the passage where Thomas rejects the doctrine of the immaculate conception as later advocated by Duns Scotus in particular, and since 1854 exalted to a dogma essential for salvation within the Roman Catholic Church.[58] In his discussion, Thomas asserts first that *nihil in scriptura canonica traditur* (nothing is said in the canonical scriptures) concerning the doctrine. This, however, does not preclude any rational argument—*rationaliter argumentari possumus*—leading to the conclusion that it appears highly probable that Mary was sanctified in her mother's womb, as scripture clearly says Jeremiah (Jer. 1:5) and John the Baptist were (Luke 1:15), and thus before her birth she was cleansed from the taint of original sin.[59] But Thomas lays down limits for any argument based on reason, and decisively rejects the idea that Mary's sanctification could have occurred at the moment of conception. The argument that Mary was freed from sin at a particular moment when she was in her mother's womb is based on biblical evidence, and Thomas refuses to go further on the grounds that to do so would lead to conflict with the clear and unmistakable biblical testimony concerning Christ as *universalis omnium salvator* (the universal Saviour of all). Since scripture expressly speaks of Christ as the Saviour of *all* men, and since he has brought salvation

ed. Paris 1946, p. 76ff.; Diekamp and Jüssen, *Dogmatik*, vol. II, p. 187ff. The article by Michel is of particular interest in this connection, especially col. 1506. He takes his point of departure in a quotation from Bonaventure: *videtur autem primus modus* (i.e. the later so-called Scotist view) *magis consonare iudicio rationis; secundum tamen, ut apparet, plus consonat pietate fidei,* III *Sent.* 1, 2, 2, conclusio (not IV *Sent.* as Michel wrongly states, col. 1502). On the basis of this argument in Bonaventure Michel draws his own conclusion: 'au point de vue de la raison, l'opinion scotiste semble plus satisfaisante'. Cf. also M. Schmaus, *Katholische Dogmatik*, vol. II, 3rd ed. Munich 1949, who on p. 501 takes the Scotist standpoint, reasoning that the incarnation was too great a thing to have taken place simply on account of sin. To say such a thing would mean 'ein der göttlichen Weisheit widersprechendes Missverhältnis zwischen Mittel und Zweck'.

---

[58] On the wording of the dogma see H. Denzinger, *Enchiridion symbolorum definitionum et declarationum de rebus fidei et morum.* 31st ed. by C. Rahner. Barcelona, Freiburg im Breisgau and Rome, 1960, no. 1641.

[59] 3a, 27, 1: *Rationabiliter enim creditur quod illa quae genuit Unigenitum a Patre, plenum gratiae et veritatis, prae omnibus aliis maiora gratiae privilegia accepit: unde legitur, Luc. 1, quod Angelus ei dixit: Ave, gratia plena. Invenimus autem quibusdam aliis hoc privilegialiter esse concessum ut in utero sanctificarentur: sicut Ieremias, cui dictum est, Ierem. 1, Antequam exires de vulva, sanctificavi te; et sicut Ioannes Baptista, de quo dictum est, Luc. 1, Spiritu Sancto replebitur adhuc ex utero matris suae. Unde rationaliter creditur quod Beata Virgo sanctificata fuerit antequam ex utero nasceretur.*

G

from sin, Mary must also in some way be reckoned among sinners, and therefore among those who need to be saved.[60] This principle of confining theological argument to scripture as the source and norm of truth is not, however, an occasional or incidental feature of Thomas's writings. It is expressed as a formal and methodological principle, particularly throughout the important discussion of sacred doctrine which comes at the beginning of the *Summa theologiae*. In Article 1 Thomas states that theology is a *doctrina quaedam secundum revelationem divinam* (schooling in what God has revealed),[61] while in Article 2 he offers a further explanation of the connection between *doctrina* and *revelatio* in the following words: *revelatio divina . . . super quam fundatur sacra scriptura seu doctrina* (divine revelation . . . which is the basis of sacred scripture or doctrine).[62] Scripture and theology are here declared to be synonymous terms. But this statement is by no means an isolated one. In Article 3, for example, where he asks whether theology is a unitary science, *sacra scriptura* and *sacra doctrina* are used as interchangeable terms.[63] In Article 7 he apparently identifies the two elements, as we see clearly in *Objectio* 2 and in the answer which is given to this objection.[64] The same thing is true in Article 8, where the question is asked whether SACRA DOCTRINA *est argumentativa*, and the answer

---

[60] 3a, 27, 2: *Et sic, quocumque modo ante animationem Beata Virgo sanctificata fuisset, nunquam incurrisset maculam originalis culpae: et ita non indiguisset redemptione et salute quae est per Christum, de quo dicitur Matth. 1: Ipse salvum faciet populum suum a peccatis eorum. Hoc autem est inconveniens, quod Christus non sit Salvator omnium hominum, ut dicitur I Tim. 4. Unde relinquitur quod sanctificatio Beatae Virginis fuerit post eius animationem,* cf. also ib. ad 2: *si nunquam anima Beatae Virginis fuisset contagio originalis peccati inquinata, hoc derogaret dignitati Christi, secundum quam est universalis omnium Salvator.* 1a2ae, 81, 3: *secundum fidem catholicam firmiter est tenendum quod omnes homines, praeter solum Christum, ex Adam derivati, peccatum originale ex eo contrahunt: alioquin non omnes indigerent redemptione quae est per Christum; quod est erroneum,* 3a, 14, 3, ad 1 and *Quodl.* 6, 7.

[61] 1a, 1, 1.   [62] 1a, 1, 2, ad 2.

[63] 1a, 1, 3: *Quia igitur* SACRA SCRIPTURA *considerat aliqua secundum quod sunt divinitus revelata, secundum quod dictum est, omnia quaecumque sunt divinitus revelabilia communicant in una ratione formali obiecti huius scientiae. Et ideo comprehenduntur sub* SACRA DOCTRINA *sicut sub scientia una;* cf. also 1a, 1, 4, obi. 2, where Thomas states that SACRA DOCTRINA *dividitur per legem veterem et novam,* which would be an absurd statement if he did not understand *sacra doctrina* to be identical in content with *sacra Scriptura.*

[64] 1a, 1, 7, obi. 2: *Sed in* SACRA SCRIPTURA *determinatur de multis aliis quam de Deo, puta de creaturis; et de moribus hominum. Ergo Deus non est subiectum* HUIUS SCIENTIAE; cf. ib. ad 2: *omnia alia determinantur in* SACRA DOCTRINA, *comprehenduntur sub Deo.*

is given that SACRA SCRIPTURA . . . *disputat cum negante sua principia: argumentando quidem.* . . . (sacred scripture . . . disputes the denial of its principles; it argues. . . .)[65] Thomas then draws his discussion of the question to an end by commenting on the metaphorical language of scripture, without in any way indicating the transition of thought between the two articles, and by asking whether scripture has *plures sensus* (several senses).[66] It is not by any means only here in the introduction to the *Summa* that Thomas affirms this integral connection between theology and scripture. Similar statements can be found, for example, in his commentary on the *de Trinitate* of Boethius, where he speaks of *theologia, quae in sacra scriptura traditur* (theology which is found in holy scripture), and of *theologia sacrae scripturae* (theology of holy scripture).[67] We may also note in this connection that in several parts of the *Summa*, his argument is frequently based on biblical passages, e.g. the seven days of creation,[68] the Old Testament law,[69] or the relatively full account of the life of Jesus given by the four Evangelists.[70] This fact, as M.-D. Chenu has pointed out, clearly distinguishes the *Summa* from the prevailing medieval formulation of doctrine in the form of a commentary on the *Sentences*, in which 'the biblical datum . . . was left outside the *quaestiones*'.[71] This, however, does not mean that Thomas would make a complete identification between scripture and theology. As we have already seen, there is a fundamental distinction between the two—in essence, the canonical scriptures contain the object of faith,[72] and therefore constitute the starting-point for theology, while *sacra doctrina* can never be, as such, the object of faith, but represents the attempt of reason, illuminated by faith, to draw from scripture and reconstruct in a rational and human way the truth which is given in it. The unity of the two is to be sought elsewhere and is given in *id quod docetur* (what is taught).[73] When Thomas insists that *sacra doctrina*

[65] 1a, 1, 8.
[66] 1a, 1, 9 and 10. Cf. article 9, which deals with the question, *utrum* SACRA SCRIPTURA *debeat uti metaphoris;* Thomas in ad 1 immediately goes on to speak of how SACRA DOCTRINA *utitur metaphoris propter necessitatem et utilitatem.*
[67] *In De Trin.* 5, 4: cf. also the use of the terms *sacra doctrina* and *sacra Scriptura* in *CG* IV, 6.   [68] 1a, 67–74.
[69] 1a2ae, 98–105; the articles which deal with the Jewish ceremonial law are discussed in fuller detail than almost any others in the whole of the *Summa*.
[70] 3a, 27–59.
[71] Chenu, *Saint Thomas*, p. 259; cf. also Bonnefoy *ETL* 14 (1937), p. 445f.
[72] See p. 50 above.
[73] We therefore agree with Bonnefoy, *ETL* 14 (1937), p. 445, that 'Identiques, la doctrine sacrée et l'Écriture le seront . . . par leur objet et leur contenu', but we must

is UNA *scientia,* he characteristically does so in a passage in which *sacra doctrina* and *sacra scriptura* appear as interchangeable terms.[74] The unity of the two is grounded on the fact that the subject-matter both of theology and of scripture is subsumed under one and the same *objectum formale,* revealed truth.[75]

We may, therefore, summarise our conclusions as follows: in Thomas's view, there is a direct connection between theology and the scriptures, and this connection is both formal and related to the *contents* of both.

Scripture is an instruction in the revealed truth which is necessary for man's salvation, and it was written *ad instructionem omnium futurorum.* This instruction, mediated by prophets and apostles, is transmitted within the church through the *doctrina* which is taught by the *doctores* of the church. By their teaching they accept and fulfil their part in the commission entrusted to the apostles. Hence in a formal sense there is a direct connection between revelation as the communication of knowledge and the continuing instruction of the church given by Thomas himself, for example.

But as we have already seen, in Thomas's view, there is also a correspondence of content between scripture and theological teaching, or *sacra doctrina.* The function of this teaching is to transmit

reject his conclusion on the same page that there must also be an identity with respect to 'leur origine' and 'leur certitude'. This would mean that theology too was the object of faith and its conclusions as unerringly certain as scripture itself—an absurd idea when we consider what Thomas actually says. Cf. the criticism made on p. 78, footnote 28, and Gilson, *Thomisme,* p. 21, footnote 1: 'Ce que saint Thomas requiert pour la justification de l'homme, c'est la foi dans tous les articles de la foi, mais non point la foi en la science théologique de ces articles'.

---

[74] 1a, 1, 3; the text is quoted on p. 86, footnote 63.

[75] As Bonnefoy, *ETL* 14 (1937), p. 429, correctly points out, what we find in Thomas is a conception of theology which, because it is directly conjoined to scripture, is markedly different from later Roman Catholic theology. Moreover, we do not find in Thomas anything that corresponds to the modern division of theology into different disciplines, e.g., the division between biblical and systematic theology or the distinction frequently made amongst Roman Catholic thinkers between 'positive' and 'speculative' theology. Writers on Thomas have frequently pointed this out and have usually regarded it as a sign of the weakness of modern theology, see e.g. White, *AT* 11 (1950), p. 126, van der Ploeg, *Thomist* 10 (1947), p. 413; van Ackeren, *Sacra doctrina,* p. 116. Chenu, *Saint Thomas,* p. 68, relates the lost unity in theology to the 'controversy against Protestantism, and later against rationalism'. Gilson, *Thomisme,* p. 21, footnote 1, points out how the relation between scripture and theology became a problem simply because theologians abandoned Thomas's starting-point and began to regard theology as 'un en soi et coupé de sa source scripturaire'.

intact the truth once revealed to prophets and apostles, and nothing but this truth. The external form and systematic structure of this teaching may vary according to time and place, but its content must remain the same, viz. the truth which transcends the natural powers of reason, and which can therefore be made accessible only through revelation and instruction based on revelation.[76] For all its earthly imperfections, it is an experience and anticipation of the perfect knowledge of God and the things of God possessed by the saints in heaven, and is therefore, in terms of its own understanding of itself, a *science*.[77] The guarantee of the correctness of teaching is that it can be referred to its origin in scripture and the articles of faith derived from the teaching of the apostles.

Theology is not to be regarded here as an addition to scripture, nor a study which may be pursued independently of scripture: in Thomas's view it is rather the extension of scriptural teaching through the ages, the *traditio* of imparting doctrine which must always be found within the church. Since it is the content of scripture which is being transmitted, *sacra doctrina* and *sacra scriptura* may be used interchangeably as synonyms. This means for Thomas that the subject of theology is preeminently *biblical theology*, and *sacra doctrina* may be regarded, to use an apt expression of Etienne Gilson, as 'holy scripture received in a human intellect'.[78] The theologian, using all the resources at his command as a creature endowed by reason, makes it his task to penetrate and express the meaning and significance of the supernatural knowledge of God given in scripture. The function of *sacra doctrina* is to clarify, vindicate and transmit the truth given in scripture, but it does so through the *ratio* of the theologian, reason, that is, illuminated by faith. And this, in turn, in Thomas's writings, is determined by the recovery of concepts drawn from Greek philosophy and stimulated by the rediscovery of Aristotle, a revival in which Thomas himself took a prominent part. The two lines which are to be found in thirteenth century scholastic thought—

---

[76] Cf. 1a, 1, 1, ad 1: *ea quae sunt altiora hominis cognitione, non sint ab homine per rationem inquirenda, sunt tamen, a Deo revelata. . . Et in huiusmodi sacra doctrina consistit'.*

[77] On the relation between the varying forms of theological instruction and the term *scientia*, see Congar, 'Théologie', in *DTC*, 15:1, col. 379.

[78] Gilson, *Thomisme*, p. 22; cf. also p. 21: 'La théologie porte donc, d'abord et avant tout, sur l'ensemble des écrits inspirés de Dieu que nous nommons *Sacra Scriptura*, l'Écriture Sainte. Disons plus, elle porte *uniquement* (our italics) sur eux, puisqu'elle est la science même que nous en avons'; see also Chenu, *Saint Thomas*, p. 128: 'Theology was the science of a book, of the book of books, the Bible'.

theological instruction centred on the Bible on the one hand, and an enthusiastic advocacy of Greek philosophy on the other—intersect in Thomas's *sacra doctrina* and give it its unique importance in the history of doctrine. All of his theological concepts are ultimately to be understood in the light of his attempt to combine into a synthesis the truth given in scripture with contemporary metaphysics. In this attempt, his 'scriptural principle' in no way prevents him from finding in Aristotle an invaluable aid and indeed an essential basis for the work of theology.[79]

In the present chapter we have seen something of the overriding problem of the relationship between *ratio* and *revelatio* in Thomas's synthesis. We have examined this in discussing the meaning of such concepts as 'revelation' and 'faith', and also in Thomas's definition of theology as a science in the sense in which the term is used in the scientific system of Aristotle. In the following chapter, we propose to concentrate on this relationship as it is expressed at crucial points in his discussion of *sacra doctrina*. After having completed our examination of these points, we will be able to go on to discuss the relationship between *ratio* and *revelatio* in the third and final chapter, and first, see how these are understood by Thomas himself, and second, assess their significance in both the structure and the substance of his theology.

[79] Cf. Gilson, *Thomisme*, 2nd ed. Paris 1922, p. 20: 'Les grands vérités du christianisme . . . trouvent dans la physique d'Aristote leur soutien naturel et leur plus ferme fondement'. We have seen above how the theologians of the Reformation and high scholasticism could be said to be unanimous in regarding theology as a setting forth of the content of scripture. The distance between them is as clearly indicated by their completely different attitude to Aristotle—thus in his criticism of scholasticism Luther, for example, in the first place attacks the use of Aristotelian metaphysics in theology, see e.g. *WA* I: 226 (*Disputatio contra scholasticam theologiam*, 1517), theses 42: *Error est, Aristotelis sententiam de foelicitate non repugnare doctrinae catholicae. Contra Morales;* 43: *Error est dicere: sine Aristotele non fit theologus. Contra dictum commune;* 44: *Immo theologus non fit nisi fiat sine Aristotele;* 50: *Breviter, Totus Aristoteles ad theologiam est tenebrae ad lucem. Contra schol.* See also B. Hägglund, *Theologie und Philosophie bei Luther und in der occamistischen Tradition* (*Lunds universitets årsskrift.* N.F. Avd. 1. Bd 51. Nr 4), Lund 1955, p. 8ff.

II

RATIO AND *REVELATIO* IN *SACRA DOCTRINA*

1

THE SOVEREIGN GOD
CAUSALITY AND THE METAPHYSICS OF EXISTENCE

Principalis intentio huius sacrae doctrinae est Dei cognitionem tradere, et non solum secundum quod in se est, sed etiam secundum quod est principium rerum et finis earum, et specialiter rationalis creaturae (the fundamental aim of holy teaching is to make God known, not only as he is in himself, but also as a beginning and end of all things and of reasoning creatures especially).[1] Having first defined the meaning of *sacra doctrina* in the introductory part of the *Summa theologiae*, Thomas now prefaces the discussion of doctrine which follows with this opening statement. The supreme question of theology is the question of the knowledge of God, and the task of theological instruction is to furnish the answer which is found in revelation. The issue is one of far more than mere theoretical interest. It is a matter of absolute importance for the salvation of men, for their salvation and eternal blessedness depend on their attaining to the knowledge of God, who is their final goal, and on knowing how to achieve this end. Since, therefore, theology deals with a matter of life and death, both man and nature must be brought within its scope in order to indicate their relationship to God, the *principium et finis* of all created things.

Thus the central point of reference for all theological statements is the concept of God, since everything created is *aliqualiter ordinata ad Deum* (somehow related to God),[2] and it is this rigidly theocentric orientation which gives Thomas's discussion in the *Summa* its completeness and finality. God, the beginning and end of all created life, is the organising principle of all theological thought, and theology for Thomas is preeminently, in the primary sense of the term, a *sermo de Deo* (speech about God), whatever else it may deal with

---

[1] 1a, 2, introd.
[2] 1a, 1, 7, ad 2, cf. obi. 2; 1a, 1, 3, ad 1: *sacra doctrina non determinat de Deo et de creaturis ex aequo: sed de Deo principaliter, et de creaturis secundum quod referuntur ad Deum, ut ad principium vel finem.*

from time to time.[3] But God is central to *sacra doctrina*, not only as
the principal object of knowledge but also as the source of saving
knowledge. The knowledge of which the theologian speaks is not
simply knowledge *about* God, it is also a knowledge which comes
from God and is thus to be distinguished from the natural knowledge
of God described in metaphysics.[4] In this, knowledge issues from a
study of the natural creation, while *sacra doctrina* is primarily derived
from revelation. This two-fold theocentric approach to theology is
nowhere expressed more vividly than in Thomas's definition of God
as the *subjectum huius scientiae*.[5] In natural theology God and the
things of God are simply *principia subjecti*, but in the *theologia, quae
in sacra scriptura traditur*, God is the *subjectum scientiae*.[6] He is not
merely the primary subject of theology, but also as the self-revealing
God the basis of cognition in theology.[7]

At a first glance at the *Summa theologiae* it might appear as if the
statement that theology deals principally (*principaliter*) with God
had little if any practical application. The discussion of God and
his nature occupies a comparatively insignificant part of the total
work, which deals mainly with rational creation and its *motus in
Deum*.[8] But when Thomas describes man and creation in extensive
detail, he never ceases to speak about God at any point. He sees
everything, even when he discusses man and creation, *sub ratione
Dei*, for the object of his inquiry is natural creation in its *ordo ad
Deum*. Man is not an autonomous being whose nature can be finally
determined apart from this *ordo*. He exists only in this relationship
to God, because he has his *principium* in God, and because the
destiny to which he moves is God, his *finis*. Behind those frequently
recurring terms there lies a concept which determines the structure
of Thomas's theology at every crucial point, viz. the concept of

---

[3] 1a, 1, 7, sed contra.

[4] Cf. *In De Trin*. 2, 2, ad 1: *non solum de altissimis, sed ex altissimis est.*

[5] 1a, 1, 7: *Omnia autem pertractantur in sacra doctrina sub ratione Dei vel quia sunt
ipse Deus; vel quia habent ordinem ad Deum, ut ad principium et finem. Unde sequitur
quod Deus vere sit subiectum huius scientiae.*

[6] *In De Trin*. 5, 4, and cf. also 2, 2, 5, 1.

[7] The term *subiectum* in this text is often coordinated with 'Gegenstand der
Wissenschaft'. It is a modern tendency to overlook the fact that Thomas is writing
theology and to treat his thought as a form of philosophy.

[8] In the proper sense only 1a, 2–43 deals with God, while 1a, 44–119 speaks of
creation with special reference to angels and men; the most important parts of the
whole work in terms of their contents, 1a2ae and 2a2ae, deal with man and his
activity under the general heading of *motus in Deum*.

cause.[9] All that exists in the created world is to be seen in relationship to God, but when we analyse this relationship more closely, it is always the *ordo* which is found to exist between a cause and its effect.

When Thomas speaks about God in *sacra doctrina*, he does so with explicit reference to him as the highest cause: *sacra autem doctrina propriissime determinat de Deo secundum quod est altissima causa* (holy teaching goes to God most personally as deepest origin and highest end).[10] This means that theology is the highest form of acquired wisdom, *sapientia*, for by definition to be wise means to know the highest cause and to relate every other fact to this cause accordingly.[11] The causal relationship between God and the world is a recurring theme in the writings of Thomas and is expressed in a variety of ways. In his well-known five proofs of the existence of God his basic presupposition in every case is the causal principle. The very imperfection of what exists in the world of our experience points to the perfect existence of God. All change and movement are to be explained by reference to a first cause, which is the ultimate cause in any conceivable series of causes and is therefore unmoved, *immobilis*, for *omnis motus supponit aliquid immobile* (every movement presupposes something immovable).[12] Every effect necessarily implies a preexisting cause which is self-evident.[13] As H. Lyttkens has convincingly demonstrated in his comprehensive study of analogy, even Thomas's concept of the analogy fundamental to his understanding of the nature of man's knowledge of God is based ultimately in all its various forms on causality. The possibility of using human language

---

[9] On the question of the dominance of the idea of causality in Thomas and particularly its significance with regard to the concept of God see G. Aulén, *Den kristna gudsbilden genom seklerna och i nutiden. En konturteckning*, Stockholm 1927, p. 127ff. The parallel which Aulén draws on p. 310f. between Thomas and Schleiermacher is of much theological interest. In both, the causal concept exhaustively defines the way in which the relationship between God and the world is defined, and in both salvation is an elevation, cf. Schleiermacher's term 'Lebenserhöhung' as a synonym for 'Erlösung'. See also Skydsgaard, *Metafysik*, p. 149.

[10] 1a, 1, 6.

[11] *In 1 ad Cor.* 3, 2 (148): *simpliciter sapiens est qui summam causam cognoscit, scilicet Deum, et alio ssecundum Deum ordinat.*

[12] 1a, 84, 1, ad 3; cf. 1a, 2, 3.

[13] 1a, 2, 2: *cum effectus dependeant a causa, posito effectu necesse est causam praeexistere. Unde Deum esse, secundum quod non est per se notum quoad nos, demonstrabile est per effectus nobis notos.* Cf. Gilson, *Thomisme*, p. 113: 'Un ... trait caractéristique est l'emploi qu'elles (i.e. proofs of God) font toutes du principe de causalité. A bien les prendre, en effet, il n'est pas une d'entre elles qui ne démontre Dieu comme la seule cause concevable de l'expérience sensible dont elle est partie'.

about God rests ultimately on the analogical likeness which exists in this special causal relationship between the transcendent, divine cause and its effects in the created world.[14] When, for example, Thomas comes to discuss the relationship between God and the world, the fact that his interpretation of the meaning of the act of creation is immediately preceded by a discussion of God as *prima causa entium* (first cause of beings)[15] is a typical example of the dominance of the concept of causality. Before he even begins to discuss creation, he defines the relationship between God and the world in causal categories.

In defining the causal relationship Thomas takes his starting-point in the categories derived from Greek philosophy. But not all of these, e.g. the four Aristotelian categories, *causa finalis, causa formalis, causa efficiens,* and *causa materialis,*[16] and the *causa exemplaris,*[17] which comes from the Platonic tradition, can be used to define the relationship between God and the world. God may be described as *causa efficiens,*[18] *causa exemplaris,*[19] and *causa finalis,*[20] but never as *causa materialis.* In Aristotelian terminology this term signifies 'that from which' something comes into being; it is a potentiality, that which has the possibility of becoming, but is not yet in being. Since God is pure actuality, this possibility does not exist for him. Nor can God be described as the *causa formalis* of the world, for this would

---

[14] H. Lyttkens, *The Analogy between God and the World. An Investigation of its Background and Interpretation of its Use by Thomas of Aquino,* Uppsala 1952, see e.g. p. 244, 301, 330ff. Lyttkens shows that in the last resort even the so-called *analogia proportionalitatis* presupposes and is an application of 'the causal analogy', see p. 464f. Cf. also Gilson, *Thomisme,* who speaks on p. 154 of Thomas's concept of analogy as 'l'analogie de la cause et de son effet', and A.-D. Sertillanges, *Dieu,* vol. III, 3rd ed. 1935, p. 340.

[15] 1a, 44, introd.

[16] 2a2ae, 27, 3: *Est autem quadruplex genus causae: scilicet finalis, formalis, efficiens et materialis.*

[17] On the question of the historic provenance of these types of cause, see especially G. Schulemann, *Das Kausalprincip in der Philosophie des Hl. Thomas von Aquino* (Beiträge zur Geschichte der Philosophie des Mittelalters 13:5), Münster in Westfalen 1951, p. 8ff. Since it is not possible to discuss fully here the meaning of causality in all of its aspects, we refer to the detailed discussions in J. Gredt, *Die aristotelisch-thomistische Philosophie,* vol. II Freiburg im Breisgau 1935, p. 129ff., J. Legrand, *L'univers et l'homme dans la philosophie de saint Thomas* vol. I (Museum lessianum, Section philosophique (=*ML–SP*) 27), Brussels and Paris, 1946, p. 101ff., or Manser, *Thomismus,* p. 314ff.

[18] 1a, 44, 1; cf. 1a, 44, introd.: *causa efficiens omnium rerum.*

[19] 1a, 44, 3; cf. 1a, 44, introd.: *causa exemplaris rerum.*

[20] 1a, 44, 4; cf. 1a, 44, introd.: *causa finalis rerum,* and 1a, 44, 4, ad 4: *Deus sit causa efficiens, exemplaris et finalis omnium rerum.*

mean that he was comprised in it as an immanent form. But God can never be immanent in his work in this sense, and therefore he may be called the *causa formalis* of the created world only in an improper sense, only *sicut extrinseca a re*, i.e. in the sense of a *causa exemplaris*.[21] The three remaining categories that may be applied to God are all *causae extrinsecae*.[22] God is wholly *extra ordinem totius creaturae* (beyond the whole world of creatures).[23] It is not conceivable to think of him as part of a greater whole, *pars alicuius compositi*, as Thomas demonstrates by comparing God to all known forms of *compositio*, with negative results.[24] Every compound includes by definition a component which is potentially related to some other component, and is therefore incomplete in itself.[25] This means that it is impossible to conceive of God's relationship to the world as an *anima mundi* (world-soul), or as *principium formale omnium rerum* (the formal principle of all things).[26] The world is not a whole of which God is part. God, because he is its cause, transcends the world, not in the sense that he is *apart from* creation but *other than* creation—in his being he is other than the world and therefore distinct from the world of created beings.[27] He is not one of the things within the world, not even the most perfect, but is the cause of the things and beings of this world.

This differentiation of divine causality into different categories does not, however, imply any division in God's own being. The various categories represent different aspects of a single causal relationship, and the differentiation is explained by the fact that the starting-point of theology is the effects of divine causality in the

---

[21] Cf. *In Meta. V,* 2: *Et haec est causa formalis, quae comparatur dupliciter ad rem: Uno modo sicut forma intrinseca et haec dicitur species. Alio modo sicut extrinseca a re, ad cuius tamen similitudinem res fieri dicitur et secundum hoc exemplar rei dicitur forma.*

[22] I *Sent.* 18, 1, 5: *Cum autem causae sint quatuor, ipse (sc. Deus) non est causa materialis nostra; sed se habet ad nos in ratione efficientis et finis et formae exemplaris, non autem in ratione formae inhaerentis.* Manser, *Thomismus,* p. 321: 'Thomas betont den monistischen Tendenzen der Neuplatoniker gegenüber, dass Gott nie seinsinnerliche Formalursache der Dinge genannt werden dürfe, sondern nur causa extrinseca, d.h. Wirk-, Final- und Exemplarursache'.

[23] 1a, 28, 1, ad 3; cf. 1a, 13, 7.   [24] 1a, 3, 1–6.

[25] See e.g. 1a, 3, 7: *in omni composito oportet esse potentiam et actum, quod in Deo non est: quia vel una partium est actus respectu alterius; vel saltem omnes partes sunt sicut in potentia respectu totius.*   [26] 1a, 3, 8.

[27] On the inadequacy and misleading aspect of the terminology of space in attempting to express the significance of the divine transcendence, see J. de Finance, *Être et agir dans la philosophie de saint Thomas,* Paris 1943, p. 149, and Legrand, *L'univers,* vol. I, p. 76.

created world. The primary fact about created things is that they exist, but they are not self-existent—their existence is received from and given by God, the *causa efficiens*. They exist only because God continually gives them their *esse*.[28] This basic, primary effect of the divine causality determines the causal relationship between God and the world. But in every causal relationship, Thomas argues, there is a similarity between an effect and its cause, for *omne agens agit sibi simile* (what a thing does reflects what its active self is).[29] The very fact that a created being exists implies in consequence that there is a similarity between it and its divine, transcendent cause, which is therefore also its *causa exemplaris*. That which is imperfectly realised in the creature has its perfect expression in the divine being which is perfection itself. But the created world is not a collection of static essences, it is filled with movement, life, and change. Just as God is the ultimate cause of the existence and nature of all that is created, so every movement and change, every realisation of the latent possibilities of the creature, is an effect of the divine cause as *causa finalis*. To say that God is *causa efficiens, exemplaris et finalis*, means that everything in the created world, the many forms of existence, movement, and life, depend on the one, active, efficient and indivisible cause—God. But this does not mean that there is only one form of causality. Created things are like God not only because they exist, but also because they themselves are also causes.[30] He is *prima causa*, but created things in their turn are *causae secundae*, each with the activity appropriate to its place in the hierarchy of existence. Hence Thomas can ascribe a particular effect wholly to God and at the same time to some created thing, without in any way finding this a contradiction. There are not two different kinds of activity, which limit or exclude one another. The causality of created things is subordinate to divine causality which it implies, just as a tool implies an agent who puts it to use.[31]

---

[28] *CG*, II, 21: *Esse autem est causatum primum:* 1a, 8, 1: *Cum autem Deus sit ipsum esse per suam essentiam, oportet quod esse creatum sit proprius effectus eius; sicut ignire est proprius effectus ignis. Hunc autem effectum causat Deus in rebus, non solum quando primo esse incipiunt, sed quandiu in esse conservantur.*

[29] See e.g. 1a, 4, 3; 1a, 6, 1; 1a, 19, 2; 1a, 41, 5, etc.

[30] *CG* III, 70: *Non enim hoc est ex insufficientia divinae virtutis, sed ex immensitate bonitatis ipsius, per quam suam similitudinem rebus communicare voluit non solum quantum ad hoc quod essent, sed etiam quantum ad hoc quod aliorum causae essent: his enim duobus modis creaturae communiter omnes divinam similitudinem consequuntur.*

[31] *CG* III, 70: *Virtus enim inferioris agentis dependet a virtute superioris agentis,*

Thomas consequently defines the relationship between God and the world in terms of the relationship which exists between a transcendent cause and its various effects. It necessarily follows that the laws which apply to causality in general are also applicable when we come to describe and define the structure of this particular causal relationship. According to Thomas, a certain order prevails amongst causes. Every action or change implies a transition from potentiality to actuality. Since an actuality, once it has come into being, is always good, whatever its class or category, and therefore also to some extent perfect, for *secundum hoc dicitur aliquid esse perfectum, secundum quod est actu* (things are called perfect when they have achieved actuality),[32] the final cause of every action or change is therefore a good, a *bonum*, which is an object of desire, *appetibile*. The Aristotelian maxim, *bonum est quod omnia appetunt* (good is what all things desire), is in Thomas's view a definitive summary of the meaning of all natural law. This principle corresponds in the area of practice to the rule of contradiction in the realm of theory—it is the first principle which constitutes the basis and presupposition of all other statements and rules of action.[33] This means that the meaning of the good is that it is the object of desire, *appetibile*. But an object of desire must have some form of perfection—a thing can

---

inquantum superius agens dat virtutem ipsam inferiori agenti per quam agit; vel conservat eam; aut etiam applicat eam ad agendum . . . non sic idem effectus causae naturali et divinae virtuti attribuitur quasi partim a Deo, et partim a naturali agente fiat, sed totus ab utroque secundum alium modum: sicut idem effectus totus attribuitur instrumento, et principali agenti etiam totus; 1a, 105, 5: *si sint multa agentia ordinata, semper secundum agens agit in virtute primi: nam primum agens movet secundum ad agendum. Et secundum hoc, omnia agunt in virtute ipsius Dei; et ita ipse est causa actionum omnium agentium.* On this whole problem which we cannot here discuss more fully, see e.g. Gilson, *Thomisme,* p. 245ff.

---

[32] 1a, 4, 1; cf. ib, ad 2: *Oportet enim ante id quod est in potentia, esse aliquid actu: cum ens in potentia non reducatur in actum, nisi per aliquod ens in actu;* 1a, 5, 1: *Intantum est autem perfectum unumquodque, inquantum est actu.*

[33] 1a, 5, 1: *Ratio enim boni in hoc consistit, quod aliquid sit appetibile: unde Philosophus, in I Ethic., dicit quod bonum est quod omnia appetunt;* 1a2ae, 94, 2: *primum principium indemonstrabile est quod non est simul affirmare et negare, quod fundatur supra rationem entis et non entis: et super hoc principio omnia alia fundantur, ut dicitur in IV Metaphys. Sicut autem ens est primum quod cadit in apprehensione simpliciter, ita bonum est primum quod cadit in apprehensione practicae rationis, quae ordinatur ad opus: omne enim agens agit propter finem, qui habet rationem boni. Et ideo primum principium in ratione practica est quod fundatur supra rationem boni, quae est, 'Bonum est quod omnia appetunt'. Hoc est ergo principium praeceptum legis, quod bonum est faciendum et prosequendum, et malum vitandum. Et super hoc fundatur omnia alia praecepta legis naturae.*

be good only as it has perfection.[34] Hence as Thomas uses the terms, goodness and ontological perfection are synonymous concepts.[35] The good is that for the sake of which something happens, in other words, it is *causa finalis*. Every efficient cause, *causa efficiens*, is ultimately dependent on this, for *agens non agit nisi propter finem* (no agent acts except for some end). By definition, therefore, the final cause is antecedent to all causes. It is *causa causarum*, and the presupposition of all others. Apart from it none of the other causes would exist or function, for it is the condition of all other activity.[36] This is true even when we define God as the ultimate cause of all existence and activity: *inter nomina significantia causalitatem divinam, prius ponitur bonum quam ens* (among the epithets signifying divine causality 'good' will precede 'existent').[37] God, as *summum bonum*, is also primarily the final cause, he is the goal and object of all activity. By the very fact that a thing exists, its existence is expressed in the attempt to realise as fully as it can the possibilities inherent within it, i.e. it seeks to perfect itself and attain the goal which is given with its form. *Finis igitur uniuscuiusque rei est eius perfectio* (therefore, the end of each thing is its perfection).[38] Since every crea-

[34] 1a, 4, introd.: *unumquodque, secundum quod perfectum est, sic dicitur bonum;* 1a, 5, 1: *Manifestum est autem quod unumquodque est appetibile secundum quod est perfectum;* cf. 1a, 5, 5; *CG* I, 39: *Ratio autem boni in perfectione consistit. Ergo ratio mali in imperfectione;* cf. also *CG* III, 20.

[35] We may note in this connection that in none of the passages in which Thomas analyses the meaning of 'goodness' (see e.g. 1a, 5 under the heading of *De bono in communi*, 1a, 6, *De bonitate Dei*, or *CG* I, 37–41) does it have the meaning of 'loving kindness', 'mercy', etc. 'Goodness' in Thomas is always synonymous with perfection in the ontological sense, *perfectio*. That God is good is synonymous with saying that his nature is free from any kind of imperfection.

[36] *De principiis naturae: Finis autem non est causa illius quod est efficiens, sed est causa ut efficiens sit efficiens. . . Unde finis est causa causalitatis efficientis, quia facit efficiens esse efficiens; et similiter facit materiam esse materiam et formam esse formam, cum materia non suscipiat formam nisi propter finem et forma non perficiat materiam nisi propter finem. Unde dicitur quod finis est causa causarum, quia est causa causalitatis in omnibus causis.* Cf. J. de Finance 'La finalité de l'être et le sens de l'univers,' in *Mélanges Joseph Maréchal* (=*MJM*) vol. II (*ML–SP* 32), Brussels and Paris 1950, p. 142.

[37] 1a, 5, 2, ad 1: *Bonum autem, cum habeat rationem appetibilis, importat habitudinem causae finalis: cuius causalitas prima est, quia agens non agit nisi propter finem, et ab agente materia movetur ad formam: unde dicitur quod finis est causa causarum. Et sic, in causando, bonum est prius quam ens, sicut finis quam forma: et hac ratione, inter nomina significantia causalitatem divinam, prius ponitur bonum quam ens';* cf. also 1a2ae, 1, 2 and *De Ver.* 28, 7.

[38] *CG* III, 16; 1a, 5, 5: *Ad formam autem consequitur inclinatio ad finem, aut ad actionem, aut ad aliquid huiusmodi: quia unumquodque, inquantum est actu, agit, et tendit in id quod sibi convenit secundum suam formam;* 1a, 6, 1: *Unumquodque autem*

ted *perfectio* with the perfection appropriate to its form[39] is in its creaturely way an image of the divine perfection which is its ultimate cause,[40] there is a direct relationship between the creaturely attempt to attain to its perfection and the gradual realisation of its likeness to God. Thus the *finis* of all created things is God himself, for *omnia, appetendo proprias perfectiones, appetunt ipsum Deum, inquantum perfectiones omnium rerum sunt quaedam similitudines divini esse* (in desiring its own perfection everything is desiring God himself, for the perfections of all things, as we saw, somehow resemble divine existence).[41] We should note, however, that in Thomas's view, the transcendent goal is superior to immanent perfection. The creature comes to its own perfection when it seeks in its creaturely way to emulate divine perfection, *et non e converso* (and not conversely).[42] The attempt to realise its true nature presupposes the action of God, and the immanent goal of the creature, its own goodness and perfection, presupposes the goodness and perfection of God.[43] It is a

appetit suam perfectionem. Perfectio autem et forma effectus est quaedam similitudo agentis: cum omne agens agat sibi simile. Unde ipsum agens est appetibile, et habet rationem boni: hoc enim est quod de ipso appetitur, ut eius similitudo participetur.

---

[39] 1a, 48, 3: *Manifestum est autem quod forma per quam aliquid est actu, perfectio quaedam est, et bonum quoddam.*

[40] *De Ver.* 21, 3: *omne agens invenitur sibi simile agere; unde si prima bonitas sit effectiva omnium bonorum, oportet quod similitudinem suam imprimat in rebus effectis; et sic unumquodque dicetur bonum sicut forma inhaerente per similitudinem summi boni sibi inditam, et ulterius per bonitatem primam, sicut per exemplar et effectivum omnis bonitatis creatae;* 1a, 6, 4: *Sic ergo unumquodque dicitur bonum bonitate divina, sicut primo principio exemplari, effectivo et finali totius bonitatis.*

[41] 1a, 6, 1, ad 2; 1a, 44, 4: *Et unaquaeque creatura intendit consequi suam perfectionem, quae est similitudo perfectionis et bonitatis divinae. Sic ergo divina bonitas est finis rerum omnium;* 1a, 105, 5: *Deus in quolibet operante operatur. Primo quidem, secundum rationem finis. Cum enim omnis operatio sit propter aliquod bonum verum vel apparens; nihil autem est vel apparet bonum, nisi secundum quod participat aliquam similitudinem summi boni, quod est Deus; sequitur quod ipse Deus sit cuiuslibet operationis causa ut finis; CG* III, 18: *Deus igitur sic est finis rerum sicut aliquid ab unaquaque re suo modo obtinendum.*

[42] *CG* III, 24: *Secundum vero quod tendit ad hoc quod sit bonum, tendit in divinam similitudinem: Deo enim assimilatur aliquid inquantum bonum est. . . Propter hoc igitur tendit in proprium bonum, quia tendit in divinam similitudinem, et non e converso. Unde patet quod omnia appetunt divinam similitudinem quasi ultimum finem.* There is a difference in this respect between Thomas himself and Aristotle, who is concerned only with immanent perfection. Cf. de Finance, *Être et agir,* p. 163f.

[43] 1a2ae, 109, 6: *Sic igitur, cum Deus sit primum movens simpliciter, ex eius motione est quod omnia in ipsum convertantur secundum communem intentionem boni, per quam unumquodque intendit assimilari Deo secundum suum modum; De Ver.* 20, 4: *Cuilibet enim creaturae procedenti a Deo inditum est ut in bonum tendat per suam*

H

single activity, and from one side it may be regarded as an attempt, natural to the creature, to become like its ultimate cause, and at the same time as the activity in which this cause seeks to produce a resemblance between itself and its effect.[44] Just as the totality of being consists of many different secondary causes, all dependent on God as *primum agens*, so coherence is given to the whole by the fact that there is a corresponding *ordo* among the goals, according to which every secondary final cause is directly dependent on God as the primary final cause.[45] To the extent that divine causality extends to all created beings, everything in existence is marked by this finality.[46] This is what gives Thomas's whole cosmology a characteristic liveliness,

---

operationem. In cuiuslibet autem boni consecutione creatura Deo assimilatur. Cf. T. Steinbüchel, *Der Zweckgedanke in der Philosophie des Thomas von Aquino* (*BGPM* 11:1), Münster in Westfalen 1912, p. 126: '*wegen des transzendenten Zieles besteht die immanente Ordnung.*'

---

[44] *CG* III, 21: *Eiusdem rationis est quod effectus tendat in similitudinem agentis, et quod agens assimilet sibi effectum: tendit enim effectus in finem in quem dirigitur ab agente.*

[45] *De Pot.* 7, 2, ad 10: *secundum ordinem agentium est ordo finium, ita quod primo agenti respondet finis ultimus, et proportionaliter per ordinem alii fines aliis agentibus; CG* III, 17: *Ad ordinem agentium sequitur ordo in finibus: nam sicut supremum agens movet omnia secunda agentia, ita ad finem supremi agentis oportet quod ordinentur omnes fines secundorum agentium: quidquid enim agit supremum agens, agit propter finem suum. Agit autem supremum actiones omnium inferiorum agentium, movendo omnes ad suas actiones, et per consequens ad suos fines. Unde sequitur quod omnes fines secundorum agentium ordinentur a primo agente in finem suum proprium.* Cf. Legrand, *L'univers*, p. 276: 'Si donc on cherche quel est le principe suprême qui fait la cohésion de l'univers . . . il faudra dire que c'est, plus que leur communauté d'origine dans l'unique source, qu'est la Cause première, leur tendence à la fois la plus intime et la plus transcendante, celle qui les tient suspendus, dans une aspiration tout ensemble universelle et une, à leur Fin dernière unique, qui est Dieu'.

[46] 1a, 22, 2: *Cum enim omne agens agat propter finem, tantum se extendit ordinatio effectuum in finem, quantum se extendit causalitas primi agentis. . . Causalitas autem Dei, qui est primum agens, se extendit usque ad omnia entia. . . Unde necesse est omnia quae habent quocumque modo esse, ordinata esse a Deo in finem.* It has been frequently observed that this finality is prominent in Thomas's thought, cf. R. Johannesson, *Person och gemenskap enligt romersk-katolsk och luthersk grundåskådning*, Stockholm 1947, p. 113: 'The viewpoint of Thomas is markedly teleological', Skydsgaard, *FJN*, p. 275: 'There is hardly any other idea which plays so decisive a role in the philosophy and theology of Thomas as the *concept of finality*', but it is seldom noted that this is based on the fundamental idea of the structure of divine causality. Cf. E. Gilson *The Spirit of Mediaeval Philosophy* (Gifford Lectures 1931–1932), New York 1936, p. 104: 'Born of a final cause, the universe is necessarily saturated with finality,' and also Steinbüchel's monograph, *Zweckgedanke*, already cited.

movement and activity, for everything created is involved in this creaturely attempt to attain to its likeness to God.

The causal relationship between God and the world is not, however, wholly explained by reference solely to the various aspects of this relationship involved in the causal categories listed above and their interconnections. The essential nature of this causality becomes clearer when we understand that in Thomas's view there is no essential, necessary connection between cause and effect. The latter is not immediately given with the former, i.e. there is no essential connection between God and created things in the sense that created things are necessarily implied in the fact of God's own existence. If they were, if creation originated by necessity from God, this would mean that creation was something which God 'needed', something without which he would not be absolutely perfect. The highest perfection, the *summum bonum*, would then not be God alone, but God together with the world of his creation. But if this were the relationship between the Creator and his creation, a relationship of necessity, God would no longer be transcendent in the sense in which Thomas understands his transcendence. To think of God as part of a greater whole is utterly inconceivable,[47] and Thomas decisively rejects any idea of a necessary connection between God and creation.

To illustrate: Thomas will speak of an *ordo creaturae ad Deum*, but never of a corresponding *ordo Dei ad creaturam*. As he puts it; God has no essential relation to creation, *ad alia non ordinatur*.[48] This means that the created world is wholly dependent on God; it has an appointed place in an *ordo ad Deum* who is the beginning and the end of all creation, but God himself is in no way dependent on creation. God alone is the *summum bonum*, and this means that the divine perfection or goodness is as little increased when other beings are created as it is diminished when they cease to be.[49] We can trace this particular emphasis in Thomas's thinking in the passages where he discusses God's will for creation. Every act of a will is directed towards a goal which is its *obiectum proprium*. Like every other act, it is directed towards a value which someone wants to

[47] Cf. p. 96f. above.

[48] 1a, 6, 3: *Ipse etiam ad nihil aliud ordinatur sicut ad finem: sed ipse est ultimus finis omnium rerum;* 1a, 21, 1, ad 3: *ipse ad alia non ordinatur, sed potius alia in ipsum.*

[49] 1a, 104, 3, ad 2: *bonitas Dei est causa rerum, non quasi ex necessitate naturae, quia divina bonitas non dependet ex rebus creatis; sed per liberam voluntatem. Unde sicut potuit sine praeiudicio bonitatis suae, res non producere in esse; ita absque detrimento suae bonitatis, potest res in esse non conservare;* cf. 1a, 19, 3.

achieve or preserve, *omne agens agit propter finem* (every agent acts for some end).[50] The proper object of the will is a good which conforms to the nature of the willing agent,[51] and is the *finis et bonum* (the end and the good) of the volitional act.[52] The will of every *natura rationalis* is directed by a natural necessity towards its highest good. As all men seek their true happiness or *beatitudo* by a natural necessity,[53] so God, who alone is the *summum bonum*, must will himself and his existence.[54] It is therefore God's nature that he *naturaliter vult et amat se* (naturally wills and loves himself).[55] If a creature endowed with will thus necessarily wills its own highest good, this necessity does not apply without qualification to other objects which may be willed. It must act on the assumption that without them it cannot attain its object. But this assumption does not apply in the case of God. He does not need anything in order to be perfect. When we speak of God, the attainment of divine perfection is wholly independent of any attempt by the creature to attain perfection. Since God has no perfection beyond himself and so properly has no object to attain but is his own end, he can necessarily will only himself but not the created world.[56] In relation to the creature, God's will is thus to be conceived as a *liberum arbitrium* (free decision).[57]

[50] See e.g. 1a, 5, 2, ad 1; 22, 2; 1a, 44, 4; 1a2ae, 1, 1; 1a2ae, 1, 2.

[51] 1a, 62, 2: *Naturalis autem inclinatio voluntatis est ad id quod est conveniens secundum naturam.*

[52] 1a, 20, 1: *bonum autem principalius et per se est obiectum voluntatis;* 1a2ae, 1, 1: *Obiectum autem voluntatis est finis et bonum.* The concepts *bonum* and *finis* are used by Thomas as synonyms, cf. 1a, 19, 1, ad 1: *finis enim habet rationem boni,* and 1a, 103, 2: *bonum habet rationem finis.*

[53] 1a2ae, 5, 8 ad 2: *Beatitudo ergo potest considerari sub ratione finalis boni et perfecti, quae est communis ratio beatitudinis: et sic naturaliter et ex necessitate voluntas in illud tendit.*

[54] 1a, 19, 3: *Voluntas enim divina necessariam habitudinem habet ad bonitatem suam, quae est proprium eius obiectum. Unde bonitatem suam esse Deus ex necessitate vult; sicut et voluntas nostra ex necessitate vult beatitudinem;* cf. CG I, 80.

[55] 1a, 41, 2, ad 3: *voluntas, inquantum est natura quaedam, aliquid naturaliter vult; sicut voluntas hominis naturaliter tendit ad beatitudinem. Et similiter Deus naturaliter vult et amat seipsum.*

[56] 1a, 19, 3: *Ea autem quae sunt ad finem, non ex necessitate volumus volentes finem, nisi sint talia, sine quibus finis esse non potest: sicut volumus cibum, volentes conservationem vitae; et navem, volentes transfretare. Non sic autem ex necessitate volumus ea sine quibus finis esse potest, sicut equum ad ambulandum: quia sine hoc possumus ire; et eadem ratio est in aliis. Unde, cum bonitas Dei sit perfecta, et esse possit sine aliis, cum nihil ei perfectionis ex aliis accrescat; sequitur quod alia a se eum velle, non sit necessarium absolute.* Cf. also *De Ver.* 23, 4 and CG I, 81.

[57] *De Pot.* 3, 15: *absque omni dubio tenendum est quod Deus ex libero arbitrio suae voluntatis creaturas in esse produxit nulla naturali necessitate;* 1a, 19, 10; *Cum igitur Deus ex necessitate suam bonitatem velit, alia vero non ex necessitate, ut supra*

Created things do not originate in God by natural necessity, but are wholly dependent on the will of God alone, and therefore we may call his will *causa rerum* (the cause of things).[58]

If then God is self-sufficient, why has he created a world extraneous to himself? Thomas's answer to this question can be best understood by referring to what he says about the nature of *divine love*. To say that God wills, that he has a divine will, is to say also that he loves, that he has a divine love, for love—for which *amor* is the most comprehensive designation[59]—is by definition a function of the will. What is said about God's will applies also *eo ipso* to his love, for love is the *primus actus voluntatis* (first act of the will).[60] Following Aristotle, Thomas also defines the meaning of love as the willing of some good for someone, *velle alicui bonum*.[61] The proper object of love is the same as that of the will, viz, the good, and consequently love can have no other object than goodness and perfection.[62] In this sense all love is primarily self-love.[63] For the will of all created beings capable of willing is to will their own being and perfection. This is also true of God, who therefore, in Thomas's phrase, *naturaliter vult et amat seipsum* (naturally wills and loves himself).[64] In regard to love of others, however, there is a marked distinction between God's love and that of the creature. God's love differs from that of the creature in two respects—first, it is unmotivated, and second, it is creative.

ostensum est; respectu illorum quae non ex necessitate vult, liberum arbitrium habet; see also *De Ver.* 24, 3 and *CG* I, 88.

---

[58] 1a, 19, 4: *necesse est dicere voluntatem Dei esse causam rerum, et Deum agere per voluntatem, non per necessitatem naturae.*

[59] Cf. 1a2ae, 26, 3: *quatuor nomina inveniuntur ad idem quodammodo pertinentia: scilicet in amor, dilectio, caritas et amicitia. Differunt tamen hoc, quod amicitia, secundum Philosophum in VIII Ethic., est quasi habitus; amor autem et dilectio significantur per modum actus vel passionis; caritas autem utroque modo accipi potest. Differenter tamen significatur actus per ista tria. Nam amor communius est inter ea: omnis enim dilectio vel caritas est amor, sed non e converso.*

[60] 1a, 20, 1: *amor naturaliter est primus actus voluntatis et appetitus. . . Unde in quocumque est voluntas vel appetitus, oportet esse amorem: remoto enim primo, removentur alia. Ostensum est autem in Deo esse voluntatem. Unde necesse est in eo ponere amorem.*

[61] See e.g. 1a, 20, 1, ad 3: *Hoc enim est proprie amare aliquem, velle ei bonum;* 1a2ae, 26, 4: *sicut Philosophus dicit in II Rhetoric., amare est velle alicui bonum.*

[62] 1a2ae, 27, 1: *Amoris autem proprium obiectum est bonum.*

[63] See e.g. 1a2ae, 26, 4: *amor quo amatur aliquid ut ei sit bonum, est amor simpliciter: amor autem quo amatur aliquid ut sit bonum alterius, est amor secundum quid.*

[64] 1a, 41, 2, ad 3; 1a, 20, 1, ad 3: *illud bonum quod vult sibi, non est aliud quam ipse, qui est per suam essentiam bonus; I Sent. 45, 1, 2: Unde id quod est volitum primo ab eo est bonitas sua tantum.*

Let us discuss first the question of motivation. In loving others, Thomas maintains, we also gain advantage for ourselves since by loving them we become better and more perfect. But this is never true of God. Since he is already perfect, loving will not make him more perfect than he is nor bring him some enlargement which he lacks. Only the one who is the object of his love gains any benefit.[65] It is inconceivable to suppose that God acts for the sake of gaining some advantage from his act. This does apply to the creature whose perfection is in some way incomplete, but not to God.[66] God's love is absolutely unmotivated, for if it were motivated by something in his creation, this would mean that the final cause of his actions was something other than God himself. But then God would no longer be the primary cause of all other possible causes, and thus no longer God as Thomas conceives him to be, for God is *prima causa*. Thus, in contrast to man's *amor*, God's love for the world is not a grasping but selfless, giving love which gives without thought of its own advantage.[67] Thomas's understanding of the radical distinction between God's love and man's is clearly seen in his use of the term 'liberality' or *liberalitas*, a term not found elsewhere in his writings and taken by Thomas from Avicenna, to describe God's dealings with the world. This liberality is a divine prerogative, *liberalitas est quasi proprium ipsius*.[68]

The significance of this distinction becomes even more clear if we consider the second respect in which God's love differs from human love. It is a mark of human love that it is evoked by goodness,

[65] I *Sent.* 45, 1, 2: *Alia vero vult in ordine ad bonitatem suam: non autem hoc modo ut per ea aliquid bonitatis acquirat, sicut nos facimus circa alios bene operando, sed ita quod eis de bonitate sua aliquid largiatur: et ideo liberalitas est quasi proprium ipsius, secundum Avicennam, tract. XI Metaph.: quia ex operatione sua non intendit aliquod sibi commodum provenire; sed vult bonitatem suam in alios diffundere;* cf. I *Sent.* 18, 1, 3: *illa datio in qua intenditur utilitas dantis nunquam competit Deo.*
[66] II *Sent.* 1, 2, 1, ad 2: *illud quod agit propter desiderium finis, habet finem extra se, quo perficitur. Hoc autem non convenit Deo qui agit propter amorem finis, quia ipsemet est sibi finis a se habitus et amatus;* 1a, 44, 4, ad 1: *agere propter indigentiam non est nisi agentis imperfecti, quod natum est agere et pati. Sed hoc Deo non competit. Et ideo ipse solus est maxime liberalis: quia non agit propter suam utilitatem, sed solum propter suam bonitatem.*
[67] Cf. E. L. Mascall, *He Who Is. A Study in Traditional Theism*, London, New York and Toronto, 1943, p. 108f.: 'So far from diminishing the love shown by God in creation, the doctrine that creation is unnecessary to God enhances it. It is precisely because creation can give nothing whatever to God which in any way enhances his beatitude, that creation is an act of entire giving on the part of God'.
[68] I *Sent.* 45, 1, 2; *De Ver.* 23, 4: *solius actio Dei est pure liberalis, quia nihil sibi accrescit ex his quae vult vel operatur circa creaturam.* See also I *Sent.* 18, 1, 2–3 and 1a, 44, 4. Cf. A.-D. Sertillanges, *La création*, 2nd ed. 1948, p. 182: 'Dieu seul est libéral, puisque lui seul, en agissant, ne reçoit rien'.

i.e. perfection, in what already exists. To say that human love has a will for the good, *velle ei bonum*, means that men desire to preserve and if possible increase the goodness of the object of their love.[69] But God's love is quite different. Unlike human love, it is not evoked by any existing worth, but brings the good into being, *voluntas eius est effectrix boni, et non causata a bono, sicut nostra* (his will, unlike ours, brings the good into being and is not caused by it).[70] As distinct from man's love, the love of God is *infundens et creans bonitatem in rebus* (pours out and creates the goodness in things).[71] God's love is not caused by any human worth. The goodness and worth of man— *omnia existentia, inquantum sunt, bona sunt* (in so far as it is real each is good)[72]—are due simply to the fact that he is loved by God. This creative and unmerited generosity is to be seen not only in the natural relationship between God and man which is given in creation, but also and particularly in the relationship to God which is given by grace and which principally the same structure as the natural one.[73] In relation to God man is first and always the recipient, according to Thomas,[74] but this does not mean that God is in any way constrained to give what he gives to man. Precisely because he is absolutely perfect even without his creation, he is utterly free to give or not to give, and therefore his relationship to the creation is never one of indebtedness. This is simply a different way of saying, as we said above, that there is no necessary connection between God and creation.[75]

---

[69] 1a, 20, 2: *voluntas nostra non est causa bonitatis rerum, sed ab ea movetur sicut ab obiecto, amor noster, quo bonum alicui volumus, non est causa bonitatis ipsius: sed e converso bonitas eius, vel vera vel aestimata, provocat amorem quo ei volumus et bonum conservari quod habet, et addi quod non habet: et ad hoc operamur.*

[70] *De Ver.* 27, 1; *In Joan.* 5, 3 (3): *Cum enim bonum solum sit amabile; aliquod bonum potest se dupliciter ad amorem habere: scilicet vel ut causa amoris, vel ut ab amore causatum. In nobis autem bonum causat amorem. . . Sed in Deo aliter est: quia ipse amor Dei est causa bonitatis in rebus dilectis: quia enim Deus diligit nos, ideo boni sumus: nam amare nihil est aliud quam velle bonum alicui.* See also II *Sent.* 26, 1, 1; *In ad Rom.* 1, 4 (67); 1a, 23, 4; 1a2ae, 110, 1.

[71] 1a, 20, 2.

[72] 1a, 20, 2, where the text quoted continues: *ipsum enim esse cuiuslibet rei quoddam bonum est, et similiter quaelibet perfectio ipsius.*

[73] See also *De Ver.* 27, 1; *CG* III, 150; 1a2ae, 110, 1.

[74] Cf. Sertillanges, *La création*, p. 240f.: "Au sens propre des mots, Dieu n'acquiert jamais rien, puisque non seulement il a toute perfection, mais il EST cette perfection même. Par l'action de la créature, c'est donc toujours et exclusivement la créature qui est gratifiée.

[75] 1a, 21, 1, ad 3: *Et licet Deus hoc modo debitum alicui det, non tamen ipse est debitor: quia ipse ad alia non ordinatur, sed potius alia in ipsum;* cf. also 1a2ae, 111, 1, ad 2.

The nature of the causal relationship which Thomas says exists between God and the world is determined in the first instance by the fact that he conceives God to be absolutely transcendent and independent of creation. The act of creation, like all God's dealings with his creation, is an act of sovereign freedom since it does not come about by any natural necessity but only by his free will. This means that we cannot posit any *causa* of this act but simply offer such *a posteriori* arguments, *rationes*, as seem appropriate.[76] Statements about goodness, such as that it seeks to give itself to others, also apply by definition to God.[77] Even though the act of God in creation is not a natural necessity, it is not on that account contrary to nature but in a sense in accordance with God's own nature.[78] We are to note, however, that for Thomas these *rationes* never represent the final explanation, for if they did, it would no longer be possible for him to maintain that the will of God is unmotivated, and this Thomas is clearly anxious to affirm. Thus the causal relationship is not ultimate, for God exists and he is absolutely perfect, apart altogether from those things of which he is cause. For Thomas there is thus no final answer to the ultimate question of *why* God acts, other than to refer to the will of God, because to give any answer would mean that there is a knowable cause in response to which God is presumed to act and which would then be something other than God—and this in turn would mean that God had ceased to be what he is. On the other hand, Thomas does give an answer to the question of *how* God acts, and he does so in terms of the causal relationship. It is from this aspect that Thomas defines the significance of what God has bestowed upon men.

The love of God is thus unmotivated, both from the standpoint of God—for he does not gain any advantage by loving men—and also from the standpoint of men. He is not moved to love by reason of any worth in man, but he himself creates this worth. His love is therefore a free gift, a love which does not seek its own, but gives rather to others. Hence Thomas can say of this gracious activity that God *intendit solum communicare suam perfectionem* (he intends only to communicate his own completeness),[79] or that he *produxit . . . res*

---

[76] See in addition to 1a, 19, 5 *CG* 1, 86 and 87 in particular, and Sertillanges, *Dieu*, vol. III, p. 308f.

[77] This line of argument is found especially in 1a, 19, 2.

[78] 1a, 19, 3, ad 3: *non est naturale Deo velle aliquid aliorum, quae non ex necessitate vult. Neque tamen innaturale, aut contra naturam: sed est voluntarium;* cf. also the conclusion of *CG* I, 82.

[79] 1a, 44, 4.

in esse propter suam bonitatem communicandam creaturis (brought things into existence so that his goodness might be communicated to creatures).[80] This might seem to contradict the assertion made above that for Thomas the basic form of all love is self-love. But there is no such contradiction in Thomas. There is such a contradiction only if we treat 'self-love' and 'altruistic love' as mutually exclusive and define the former exclusively in terms of personal advantage. But in Thomas's view we simply cannot do this in regard to God's love, which is not a copy of human love but a love *sui generis*. God's love for the world is included within the divine love of its own perfection, and the two are by no means antithetical. This becomes clear when we see how Thomas defines the *finis* of God's activity in the world. The object of this activity, that for the sake of which it exists, is not the creature itself, *potentia autem Dei non ordinatur ad effectum sicut ad finem, sed magis ipsa est finis sui effectus* (God's power is not subordinate to its effect as to its end, but is rather itself the end of the effect).[81] God and God alone is the final object, not the communication of good, *communicatio bonitatis non est ultimus finis, sed ipsa divina bonitas* (the communication of goodness is not the ultimate end, but the divine goodness itself).[82] Hence God wills both his own existence and that of the creature, but *se ut finem, alia vero ut ad finem* (himself as the end, and others as to that end).[83] Since he who is *summum bonum* is also *ultimus finis*, there can be no other object of his activity than this. The same is true of created things. For every creature God is the end of its existence from the moment when it first comes into being, for God is *finis rerum omnium* (the final cause of all things).[84]

God wills the creature *propter suam bonitatem*, but *propter* does not here mean 'for the benefit of', for he gains no advantage from the existence of the creature, nor does it mean that his goodness requires a created world. The phrase is in fact equivalent to *in ordine ad bonitatem suam*. If the creature but not the creator were the ultimate object of his divine activity, this would be contrary to God's own

---

[80] 1a, 47, 1.   [81] 1a, 25, 2, ad 2.   [82] *De Pot.* 3, 15, ad 14.
[83] 1a, 19, 2: *Sic igitur vult et se esse, et alia. Sed se ut finem, alia vero ut ad finem, inquantum condecet divinam bonitatem etiam alia ipsam participare;* 1a, 19, 3: *Alia autem a se Deus vult, inquantum ordinantur ad suam bonitatem ut in finem;* CG I, 74: *Ultimus autem finis est ipse Deus: quia ipse est summum bonum;* CG I, 86: *Deus autem vult bonitatem suam tanquam finem, omnia autem alia vult tanquam ea quae sunt ad finem.*
[84] 1a, 44, 4; cf. p. 99ff. above.

being and goodness, and would mean that he denied his nature—
'and this would be a mortal sin in God', as R. Garrigou-Lagrange
observes.[85] Creation exists for God's sake, since it is directed towards
him as its end, but God does not exist for the sake of creation.
Profoundly, this is the meaning of the somewhat obscure expression
used by Thomas to summarise his discussion of the question: *vult
ergo hoc esse propter hoc: sed non propter hoc vult hoc* (he wills this to
be because of that, but he does not will this because he wills that).[86]
Hence the existence of creation can be understood only by reference
to God's free and sovereign will, which is to give himself to other
beings than himself as the end of their own existence, i.e. to allow
them to reproduce the divine perfection on their own separate plane,
and thereby attain their own being and perfection.[87] To say that
God gives himself means that by establishing the causal relationship between himself and things, he gives himself to them as
their end or *finis*.[88] And to say that God 'wills' or 'loves' them
is the same as saying that they exist in the image of God, repro-
ducing this image and producing representations of it on a different
plane.

This love of God for all of his creation is ultimately identical with
the causality which relates them to him.[89] By the very fact of its
existence the creature has a certain perfection or *bonum*, which
simply means that God loves the creature, for *amare est velle bonum*

---

[85] R. Garrigou-Lagrange, *God. His existence and His Nature. A Thomistic Solution
of Certain Agnostic Antinomies* (translated from the fifth French ed.), sixth printing.
St Louis and London 1955, vol. II, p. 106: 'If He were not to ordain us for Himself,
it would be both 'a disorder and a barbarity'. It would be a disorder, for the final
end of the creative act would no longer be God Himself, but the creature. God in
creating us would cease to love the supreme Good above all things. He would be
preferring a finite good to Himself, just as the miser prefers his gold to his honor.
It would be tantamount to a mortal sin in God or the extreme in absurdities'. Cf.
Sertillanges, *Dieu*, vol. III, p. 280: 'Dieu, lui, ne veut rien pour un autre, si ce n'est
en raison de son propre bien, qui est suprême et qu'il ne peut point ne pas reconnaître comme tel', and *De Ver.* 22, 1, ad 11: *Fini ergo ultimo non competit tendere
in finem, sed seipso fine fruitur.*

[86] 1a, 19, 5.   [87] See especially *Compend. Theol.* 103.

[88] Cf. 1a, 20, 3, ad 2: *Bonum autem quod Deus creaturae vult, non est divina essentia,*
and 1a, 19, 1, ad 1: *licet nihil aliud a Deo sit finis Dei, tamen ipsemet est finis respectu
omnium quae ab eo fiunt. Et hoc per suam essentiam, cum per suam essentiam sit
bonus, ut supra ostensum est: finis enim habet rationem boni.* It is clear that in the
theology of Thomas any idea of God's giving of himself has no place and is indeed
impossible. We shall return to this whole problem later, see p. 222 and 286f.

[89] See also A. Nygren, *Filosofi och motivforskning*, Stockholm 1940, p. 56ff. and
Gilson, *Thomisme*, p. 171: 'Dire que la volonté de Dieu est cause de toutes choses,
c'est donc dire que Dieu aime toutes choses'.

alicui (loving is no other than willing good to someone).[90] Therefore, the degree of *esse* in accordance with which the creature takes
its place in the hierarchy of existence is *eo ipso* a direct expression
also of the degree of God's love for that creature. The higher it is
in the hierarchy, i.e. the greater its perfection and consequently its
likeness to God, the stronger is the effect produced by the divine
causality, in other words, the greater is God's love for it.[91] Likeness
to God is at once both a consequence of God's love and a measure
of the degree of his love.[92] The same is also true of man, and therefore Thomas can say that God loves us to the extent that we resemble
him, *Deus intantum diligit nos, inquantum ei assimilamur* (God loves
us to the extent that we become like him).[93] This identification of
divine love and causality is discussed by Thomas particularly in the
context of God's love for sinners. Insofar as men live and therefore
have their being from God, he loves them, but insofar as they are
sinners, *peccatores*, he does not love them, for their sinfulness implies
a privation of being, *ab esse deficiunt*.[94]

---

[90] 1a, 20, 2: *voluntas Die est causa omnium rerum: et sic oportet quod intantum
habeat aliquid esse, aut quodcumque bonum, inquantum est volitum a Deo. Cuilibet
igitur existenti Deus vult aliquid bonum. Unde, cum amare nil aliud sit quam velle bonum
alicui, manifestum est quod Deus omnia quae sunt, amat.*

[91] III *Sent.* 32, 4: *sic Deus dicitur magis diligere unum quam aliud inquantum vult
ei majus bonum; et ex hoc etiam habet majorem effectum in illo, quia voluntas ejus
est causa rerum.*

[92] Cf. 1a, 20, 4: *necesse est dicere . . . quod Deus magis diligat meliora. Dictum est
enim quod Deum diligere magis aliquid, nihil aliud est quam ei maius bonum velle:
voluntas enim Dei est causa bonitatis in rebus. Et sic, ex hoc sunt aliqua meliora, quod
Deus eis maius bonum vult. Unde sequitur quod meliora plus amet.*

[93] *In Joan.* 4, 2 (14).

[94] 1a, 20, 2, ad 4: *Deus autem peccatores, inquantum sunt naturae quaedam, amat:
sic enim et sunt, et ab ipso sunt. Inquantum vero peccatores sunt, non sunt, sed ab esse
deficiunt: et hoc in eis a Deo non est. Unde secundum hoc ab ipso odio habentur.* This
is the point at which we can see a clear distinction between Thomas and the New
Testament conception of love which we find presented by A. Nygren in his *Agape
and Eros*, London 1957. The characteristics of the divine love which are given on
p. 75ff. would all be accepted by Thomas; divine love is both 'unmotivated',
'creative', and 'the initiator of fellowship' (the initiative in establishing fellowship
lies with God), and in one sense is also 'indifferent to value', since God does not
love man on the basis of a value which already exists in man before God loves him.
From another point of view, however, the divine love is not 'indifferent to value',
for it creates of itself a scale of values, as can be seen most clearly in the fact that it is
impossible to conceive of God as loving the sinner as sinner. Thus Thomas is
unable to give expression to the New Testament language about God's love as a
'coming down' or a 'giving of himself'. It is here that we see most clearly the
distinction between the New Testament concept of love and that which we find in
Thomas. It has to be said, however, that Thomas does give clear expression to the

This brief discussion of Thomas's understanding of the love of God also sheds some light on the repeated emphasis on finality which, as we saw above, is a distinctive aspect of his interpretation of the causal relationship between God and the world. Ultimately, the basis of this absolute finality is the belief that God is known to be *causa efficiens* only when he is understood to be *causa finalis*. The ultimate point of reference in causality is the divine perfection. When God is efficient cause *in ordine causando*, i.e. when he causes created things to be, from the first moment of their existence he is the object towards which they move.[95] The particular forms of existence which are to be found in creation are not, therefore, to be regarded, according to Thomas, as an emanation from the divine being, but rather as the first step on the journey back to God which is the goal of creation, for the general rule that *principium . . . executionis est primum eorum quae sunt ad finem* (the principle in execution is the first of the things which are ordained to the end),[96] also applies to the divine causality.

As we have seen, divine perfection in Thomas's view is something quite independent of the existence of created things. Creation is wholly and completely dependent on God, for all that it is and all that it includes comes from him, but God himself is in no way dependent on creation. Thomas is at his clearest in discussing this relationship between creation and God. A relation means an *ordo unius ad alterum*, a connection usually expressed in Thomas by such terms as *ad aliud* or *ad aliquid*.[97] He does, however, make a helpful distinction among these relationships when he seeks to establish a definition of

view—without abandoning the idea that the primary form of love is self-love—that the mark of divine love is an unselfish willingness to give, though Nygren fails to convey this in his discussion of Thomas's doctrine of love, *Agape and Eros*, p. 642ff.

[95] Cf. *CG* III, 65: *In finem autem ultimum quem Deus intendit, scilicet bonitatem divinam, ordinantur res non solum per hoc quod operantur, sed etiam per hoc quod sunt: quia inquantum sunt, divinae bonitatis similitudinem gerunt.*

[96] 1a2ae, 1, 4; cf. A.-M. Carré, *Le Christ de saint Thomas d'Aquin*, Paris 1944, p. 14: 'tout être doit retourner à Dieu pour y trouver sa fin. Le premier don de Dieu à sa créature, l'existence, est aussi le premier pas qu'elle fait vers lui, et tous les déploiements de sa nature, mise en oeuvre des dons de Dieu, ne sont que les étapes successives qui, dans un perpétuel progrès, la ramènent à lui;' cf. de Finance, *MJM*, vol. II, p. 149: 'Créer, c'est identiquement pour Dieu, convertir vers soi'.

[97] 1a, 28, 1: *Ea vero quae dicuntur ad aliquid, significant secundum propriam rationem solum respectum ad aliud;* see too—and also for a discussion of Thomas's doctrine of relation—the numerous passages quoted by A. Krempel in his very thorough study, *La doctrine de la relation chez saint Thomas. Exposé historique et systématique*, Paris 1952, p. 40ff. See also the lucid analysis in H.-F. Dondaine, *La Trinité*, vol. I, 1943, p. 232ff.

the connexion which he conceives to exist between God and the world. At times, for instance, Thomas will speak of a group of relationships which are implicit in the nature of things, i.e. it is a necessary part of their being to be related to some other thing or things, and in this instance we speak of a *relatio realis*. At other times the relationship has no correspondence whatever to reality, but it simply a conceptualisation in the mind of the person who compares two different things, and in such a case we speak of a *relatio secundum rationem tantum* or a *relatio rationis tantum* (merely a logical relation).[98] A particular example of this, and one frequently cited by Thomas, is the comparison which he found in Aristotle between knowledge (*scientia*) and that which may be known (*scibile*). There is no real relationship between what can be known and the actual mental knowledge of it, for when we know something, our knowing does not mean anything to what is knowable (*scibile*), for that which we can know was already in existence before our act of cognition and is in no way dependent upon it. On the other hand, it has to be said that there is a real relationship between knowledge (*scientia*) and that which can be known (*scibile*) since knowledge is completely dependent on having an object which can come to be known. Apart from this there can be no such thing as knowledge.[99]

A corresponding relationship is to be understood to exist between God and the world. The act of creation does not imply that anything new comes into being or any change is made in the divine being— anything new that comes into being does so 'outside' God. When something new comes into existence, the new thing is an effect of the divine causality. But this effect is wholly dependent upon God who gave it its existence, or, to express it in a different way, there is a real relation between the created thing and its transcendent cause. *Relationes consequuntur actiones* (relations result from actions),[100] and this relation is simply another aspect of the divine *actio* in the created world, i.e. the whole meaning of creation is comprehended in

[98] 1a, 28, 1: *Qui quidem respectus aliquando est in ipsa natura rerum; utpote quando aliquae res secundum suam naturam ad invicem ordinatae sunt, et invicem inclinationem habent. Et huiusmodi relationes oportet esse reales. . . Aliquando vero respectus significatus per ea quae dicuntur ad aliquid, est tantum in ipsa apprehensione rationis conferentis unum alteri: et tunc est relatio rationis tantum.*
[99] See e.g. III *Sent.* 1, 1, 1, ad 1; *De Ver.* 1, 5, ad 16; *De Pot.* 7, 10; *CG* II, 12; 1a, 6, 2, ad 1; 1a, 13, 7. See also H. Kusch, 'Der Titel Gottes "Dominus" bei Augustinus und Thomas von Aquino', in *Festschrift Franz Dornseiff* (=*FFD*), Leipzig 1953, p. 197f.
[100] 1a, 34, 3, ad 2.

the term relation.[101] There is no change in God when he brings created things into existence, *creando, producit res sine motu* (in creating he produces a thing without motion in the making), and properly speaking no change occurs in the creature itself when it is brought into being, for this would imply that through the act of creation something in existence before creation received a new mode of existence. It would not then be possible to speak of a *creatio ex nihilo*. If we eliminate every form of change, *motus* or *mutatio*, from the fundamental relationship of *actio* and *passio*, only the simple causal relationship of cause and effect remains.[102] For Thomas creation means that the creature is related to God as its ultimate and primary cause, and this relationship of dependence on the part of the creature inheres in its being.[103]

Once we have defined the meaning of this dependence, we have also described what creation is. Consequently, when Thomas comes to discuss the relationship established in creation, he does not regard the concept of time as of any constitutive significance. Even if the world had always been in existence, it would still have been 'created', for creation simply means *ipsa dependentia esse creati ad principium a quo statuitur* (the very dependency of the created actual being upon the principle from which it is produced).[104] Time does not exist before the act of creation, and so creation does not occur *in* time—rather, time comes into existence with the act of creation. Where there is no change or motion there is no time, for time is the measure of change, *mensura motus*,[105] and therefore something created.[106] We can and must

---

[101] Cf. Sertillanges, *La création*, p. 253: 'l'idée de création correspond à l'idée d'une dépendance totale, mais transcendante et extratemporelle de l'être à l'égard de sa Source. Cette idée se définit par celle de relation'.

[102] 1a, 45, 3: *Quia quod creatur, non fit per motum vel per mutationem. Quod enim fit per motum vel mutationem, fit ex aliquo praeexistenti: quod quidem contingit in productionibus particularibus aliquorum entium; non autem potest hoc contingere in productione totius esse a causa universali omnium entium, quae est Deus. Unde Deus, creando, producit res sine motu. Subtracto autem motu ab actione et passione, nihil remanet nisi relatio, ut dictum est* (cf. 1a, 45, 2, ad 2). *Unde relinquitur quod creatio in creatura non sit nisi relatio quaedam ad Creatorum, ut ad principium sui esse;* cf. *De Pot.* 3, 2 and 3; *CG* II, 17 and 18.

[103] This relation may therefore also be defined as *aliqua res*, see e.g. *De Pot.* 7, 9 or *CG* II, 18: *Cum enim effectus creatus realiter dependeat a creante, oportet huiusmodi relationem esse rem quandam.*

[104] *CG* II, 18, cf. the words which follow: *Et sic est de genere relationis.* See also Sertillanges, *La création*, p. 188: 'le monde eût-il toujours existé, il ne serait pas moins créé, c'est à dire la créature de Dieu, sa créature permanente'.

[105] 1a, 10, 1: *ex hoc quod numeramus prius et posterius in motu, apprehendimus tempus; quod nihil aliud est quam numerus prioris et posterioris in motu;* 1a, 10, 4: *aeternitas est mensura esse permanentis, tempus vero est mensura motus.*

[106] 1a, 46, 3, ad 1: *simul cum tempore caelum et terra creata sunt.*

speak of time, but only because there is a created world whose distinctive mark is change. Even though the world had always been in existence, this would not mean that it was eternal, for *quod mutabilitati subjacet, etiam si semper sit, aeternum esse non potest* (what is subject to change, even though it has always existed, cannot be eternal).[107] Eternity is not the same as unending time, but differs qualitatively from time in the same way as God differs from the world.[108] Eternity transcends creaturely existence, for *aeternitas non est aliud quam ipse Deus* (eternity and God are the same thing).[109] The activity of God does not take place *within* time, rather time is an effect of the divine activity and begins as soon as the creature itself comes in to existence.[110] Temporal categories cannot therefore be applied to God but only to the creature. Hence it is as inconceivable to suppose that God *began* his creative work after a period of inactivity[111] as it is to hold that he existed *before* creation in any temporal sense.[112] The 'new' which comes into being with creation is new only 'outside' God and in the sphere of the creature. The divine activity *active accepta* is simply God himself and is therefore of necessity eternal, and temporal categories apply only to the result of this activity, to the activity *passive accepta*, i.e. to the creature.[113] As a causal relationship, the relation between God and the world is primarily and essentially a timeless one, since time is a purely

---

[107] *De Pot.* 3, 14, ad 1.

[108] Cf. Mascall, *He Who Is*, p. 99: 'Eternity means existence *outside time*'.

[109] 1a, 10, 2, ad 3. This means that eternity is defined as something other than and outside the creaturely sphere—it belongs to God alone. Even though it may be said of the saints in heaven that they participate in 'eternal' life, 'eternal' is used here in an improper sense. The eternity of which they have part is like the divine eternity, but it is a *participatio* on the creaturely sphere.

[110] On this whole problem see especially Sertillanges, *L'idée de création et ses retentissements en philosophie*, Paris 1945, p. 48ff.

[111] Sertillanges, *La création*, p. 245: 'Dieu n'agit pas *après* n'avoir point agi, puisqu'il est immuable'.

[112] Sertillanges, *La création*, p. 255: 'À la vérité, Dieu précédant son oeuvre en durée, cela n'a pas de sens. De quelle durée serait-il question? S'il s'agit d'une durée créée, elle fait partie de l'oeuvre et Dieu en est entièrement dehors . . . S'agit-il de la durée incréée, de l'éternité? Mais l'éternité, si elle précède le temps d'une priorité de nature et de causalité . . . elle ne se place point avec lui sur une même ligne, au même plan de réalité, ni en ordre de succession'.

[113] On these terms cf. *De Pot.* 3, 3; 1a, 45, 4, ad 1, and Gilson, *Thomisme*, p. 176, footnote 2. Cf. Garrigou-Lagrange, *God*, vol. II p. 138: 'The creative act . . . is a formally immanent action not distinct from God's essence. But it is said to be virtually transitive in that it produces an external fact'; see also p. 149ff. de Finance, *Être et agir*, p. 133 says: 'L'action créatrice, en produisant des effets *ad extra*, comme le ferait une opération transitive, reste de caractère strictement immanent'.

accidental element within it and since the relation between God and the world is not affected by the question of time.[114]

Since time is not a constituent element in his understanding of *creatio*, Thomas in effect identifies creation with *conservatio*. Creation is a continuous process which is actualised to the extent that things exist 'outside' the divine being. The mode of their existence remains essentially the same from first to last, for they are utterly dependent for their continued existence on the divine causality.[115] The two concepts simply express the same reality, and the distinction between them is explained by the revealed knowledge that creaturely existence begins at some point. *Creatio* and *conservatio* both refer to the same relationship between God and the creature, according to which the fact of creaturely existence 'outside' God implies the dependence of the creature on the one who gives it its existence.[116] When we use the concept *creatio*, we also imply with its use the *novitas essendi* (newness of being) of which revelation bears witness, though this does not necessarily belong to the concept itself.[117] It is possible by means of rational demonstration to determine the structure of the relationship established in creation, but impossible to prove *quod mundum non semper fuisse* (that the world has not always existed): this, like the revealed knowledge of the triune being of God, must be received by faith.[118] The element of cause in creaturely existence is more apparent,

[114] Sertillanges, *La création*, p. 251: 'La succession, et par suite le commencement, est accidentelle à la causalité'.

[115] 1a, 9, 2: *Sicut autem ex voluntate Dei dependet quod res in esse producit, ita ex voluntate eius dependet quod res in esse conservat: non enim aliter eas in esse conservat, quam semper eis esse dando, unde si suam actionem eis subtraheret, omnia in nihilum redigerentur;* 1a, 104, 1, ad 4: *conservatio rerum a Deo non est per aliquam novam actionem; sed per continuationem actionis qua dat esse, quae quidem actio est sine motu et tempore; De Pot.* 5, 1, ad 2. Thomas can also refer explicitly in this connection to John 5:17, for instance in I *Sent.* 37, 1, 1.

[116] Mascall, *He Who Is*, p. 101: 'There is no real distinction between God's creation of the world and his preservation of it. Both are aspects of one extra-temporal act by which the world in the whole of its history receives its existence'; Sertillanges, *L'idée de création*, p. 67: 'Dans le langage courant, on ne dit pas que l'univers est actuellement créé, mais qu'il a été créé, que notre âme a été créée, etc. En réalité toutefois, c'est bien à tout moment que l'univers ou chaque être est suspendu à Dieu par cette relation de dépendance qui est la création même'.

[117] *De Pot.* 3, 3: *sic creatio nihil est aliud realiter quam relatio quaedam ad Deum cum novitate essendi;* 1a, 45, 3, ad 3: *creatio importat habitudinem creaturae ad creatorem cum quadam novitate seu incoeptione;* cf. *De Pot.* 3, 3, ad 6: *Sed in hoc non est diversitas nisi secundum nomen, prout nomen creationis potest accipi cum novitate, vel sine.*

[118] 1a, 46, 2: *quod mundum non semper fuisse, sola fide tenetur, et demonstrative probari non potest: sicut et supra de mysterio Trinitatis dictum est.* It is not possible

however, if it is seen to have had a beginning than if it has always been in existence, and therefore revelation simply gives, in Thomas's view, a fuller confirmation and corroboration of the causal structure of creation.[119]

Thomas accordingly expresses the relationship between Creator and creature in terms of the relationship between eternity and time, between absolute and relative, and between the perfection of the transcendent cause and its *effectus* which are realised in varying degrees of imperfection.[120] This relationship, however—the relationship established in creation between Creator and creature—is not implied in the divine being itself, but, if we may so speak, is a unilateral relationship which exists *realiter* only in the creature.[121] It is of the nature of the creature to be dependent on God, but there is no necessary connection between God's being and creation—the relationship between God and creation is only a *relatio secundum rationem*. Since he is called Creator, God may indeed be said to have a relationship to creation, but such a statement has no real correspondence in the nature of God. The reality corresponding to this statement is found only on the side of the creature: *sic Deus dicitur relative ad creaturam quia creatura refertur ad ipsum* (so that God is said to be related to a creature because the creature is related to

---

to prove that there is a beginning to the existence of things; it is, however, possible to show that this not contrary to reason. See Thomas's argument in *De Pot.* 3, 17 and also in his *De aeternitate mundi*. Cf. A. Rohner, *Das Schöpfungsproblem bei Moses Maimonides, Albertus Magnus und Thomas von Aquin. Ein Beitrag zur Geschichte des Schöpfungsproblems im Mittelalter* (*BGPM* 11:5), Münster in Westfalen 1913, p. 95; Sertillanges, *L'idée de création*, p. 25ff. and the same author's *La création*, p. 254ff.

---

[119] 1a, 46, 1, ad 6.
[120] Cf. R. Prenter, *Thomismen*, Copenhagen 1952, p. 84f. When Thomas defines *creatio*, he does not really say anything different from what he says in his discussion of the proofs of God—a thing exists, but it does not exist of itself, it is caused by something outside itself which does not receive but *is* its own existence. Cf. E. L. Mascall, *Existence and Analogy. A Sequel to 'He Who Is'*, London, New York and Toronto 1949, p. 71: 'The Five Ways are therefore not so much five different demonstrations of the existence of God as five different methods of manifesting the radical dependence of finite being upon God'. It is characteristic that none of Thomas's proofs of God proceed *ex suppositione novitatis mundi*. No part of his argument is altered by the assumption of a *motus* which has neither beginning nor end in a temporal sense. Cf. Sertillanges, *La création*, p. 246 and 251; Gilson, *Thomisme*, p. 96f.
[121] Sertillanges, *L'idée de création*, p. 46: 'Une relation unilatérale de dépendance, et rien d'autre. C'est cela, la création, dans sa réalité effective'.

I

him).[122] Because the relationship of creation to God is one of real dependence, we may speak of him as 'Creator' and 'Lord', but it is not essential to the divine being to be, for instance, Creator. This is simply an *ex tempore* designation applied to God. To say that he is Creator does not mean that when creation comes into being he becomes other than he was, but only that something new and distinct from him was brought into being. He is no more changed by the fact that created things exist than a pillar is changed when someone near it moves to a different position, so that whereas formerly the original pillar was on the left it is now on the right. He is Creator and Lord not because he comes to be related to something outside himself in a new way but because this external reality comes to be related to him in a new way.[123]

The reason that we cannot say that God 'becomes' something other than he was, is that in Thomas's view becoming implies change, and it is of the nature of change that it involves a change from potentiality to actuality: *movere enim nihil aliud est quam educere aliquid de potentia in actum* (to cause change is to bring into being what was previously only able to be).[124] With the existence of the creature its nature or *essentia* is also given, along with the potentialities which are inherent in this nature. When these potentialities are realised, a change in the creature occurs which may also be represented as an accretion,[125] for when it achieves these possibilities, the creature becomes more perfect than it was before in accordance with the principle: *secundum hoc enim dicitur aliquid esse perfectum, secundum quod est actu* (things are called perfect when they have achieved actuality).[126] It is a characteristic of the creature that it is *aliquo modo*

---

[122] 1a, 13, 7, ad 4; 1a, 13, 7: *Cum igitur Deus sit extra totum ordinem creaturae, et omnes creaturae ordinentur ad ipsum, et non e converso, manifestum est quod creaturae realiter referuntur ad ipsum Deum; sed in Deo non est aliqua realis relatio eius ad creaturas, sed secundum rationem tantum, inquantum creaturae referuntur ad ipsum*; 1a, 28, 1, ad 3: *in Deo non est realis relatio ad creaturas. Sed in creaturis est realis relatio ad Deum: quia creaturae continentur sub ordine divino, et in earum natura est quod dependeant a Deo;* see also the detailed discussion in *De Pot.* 7, 8–11 and also *CG* II, 11–14.

[123] See also *De Pot.* 7, 11; I *Sent.* 14, 1, 1; I *Sent.* 30, 1, 1; 1a, 13, 7: *Et sic nihil prohibet huiusmodi nomina importantia relationem ad creaturam, praedicari de Deo ex tempore: non propter aliquam mutationem ipsius, sed propter creaturae mutationem; sicut columna fit dextera animali, nulla mutatione circa ipsam existente, sed animali translato.* See also ad 1, ad 4 and ad 5, and also 1a, 43, 2, ad 2. Cf. Kusch, *FFD*, p. 195ff.

[124] 1a, 2, 3.

[125] 1a, 9, 1: *omne quod movetur, motu suo aliquid acquirit, et pertingit ad illud ad quod prius non pertingebat.*   [126] 1a, 4, 1.

mutabilis—it can become something different from what it was, and this is true in regard both to its own inherent possibilities and to its relationship to God.[127] At its deepest level the *mutabilitas* of the creature consists in the fact that it has no existence of its own, but is constantly liable to a *reduci in non esse* (reduction to nothingness).[128] But no such postulate can be predicated of God. There is no un-realised potency in God, no unfulfilled need. Since he is *perfectus* and *infinitus*, he can add nothing to himself which he does not already have, nor is there any place in which he is not already present. We cannot posit *motus* or *mutatio* of God either in the metaphysical sense of transition from potentiality to actuality or in the ordinary localised sense of movement or change.[129] In dealing with this question Thomas answers an objection raised by a passage in the New Testa-ment which appears to contradict this definition of God as *immu-tabilis*, viz. James 4:8, 'Draw near to God, and he will draw near to you.'[130] When scripture speaks of God in terms of movement, Thomas argues, it is to be understood only metaphorically—it is in no way to be understood in a literal sense at this point. By way of illustration he refers to the expression, 'The sun "comes in" to a room', when in fact it is its rays that enter, not the sun. We can no more speak of the sun being changed by 'coming in' to a room (though the room is changed, by becoming brighter) than we can say in any proper sense that God 'draws near' to us or 'goes away' from us. The reality which underlies this metaphorical language is rather that of a change which takes place in the sphere of the creature. God is said to 'approach' us or 'go away from' us according to the varying degree in which we participate in the divine perfection.[131] Thomas also discusses other objections to the doctrine of the immutability of God which are found elsewhere in scripture, and his answers are particularly illu-minating when we attempt to determine his conception of the rela-tionship between God and the world. Thus, it is said in scripture that

---

[127] 1a, 9, 2.

[128] 1a, 9, 2: *Sic igitur per potentiam quae est in altero, scilicet in Deo, sunt mutabiles, in-quantum ab ipso ex nihilo potuerunt produci in esse, et de esse possunt reduci in non esse.*

[129] 1a, 9, 1: *Deus autem, cum sit infinitus, comprehendens in se omnem plenitudinem perfectionis totius esse, non potest aliquid acquirere, nec extendere se in aliquid ad quod prius non pertingebat.* On God's attributes of perfection and infinity see also 1a, 4, 1–3 and 1a, 7, 1–4. [130] 1a, 9, 1, obi. 3.

[131] 1a, 9, 1, ad 3: *huiusmodi dicuntur de Deo in Scripturis metaphorice. Sicut enim dicitur sol intrare domum vel exire, inquantum radius eius pertingit ad domum; sic dicitur Deus appropinquare ad nos vel recedere a nobis, inquantum percipimus influentiam bonitatis ipsius, vel ab eo deficimus.*

God 'repents' (Genesis 6:6, Jeremiah 18:8), which appears to indicate that God's will at least is changeable. But since the divine will is one with the divine nature, it must, like God himself, be *omnino immutabilis* (altogether immutable).[132] Thomas's explanation is that here, too, the scripture speaks *metaphorice*. Scripture is simply using a metaphor drawn from human experience. When a man repents, he expresses his repentance by undoing what he has done.[133] A distinction must be made at this point, Thomas holds, between saying that the will of God itself is changed—which is *a priori* impossible—and saying—and this is the only way in which it is possible to speak of 'change'—that the will of God, which is itself unchangeable, wills that there should be a change at some point in the created world. Only there can any change or alteration take place.[134] There is a further objection: God commands obedience to certain laws, only to annul them later. Does this not imply a *voluntas mutabilis* (variable will)?[135] Here again Thomas gives the same answer: this does not mean that God's will is changed, but that he wills a change.[136] There is a further example in his explanation of the meaning of passages in the Bible which speak of God's wrath. For Thomas the divine will is to be described as a *voluntas beneplaciti*, a will to do good. By definition, therefore, it cannot be a wrathful will. The concept of wrath includes a *passio* and therefore an imperfection which cannot be attributed to God. Thomas accordingly concludes that *ira de Deo nunquam proprie dicitur* (anger properly so-called is never attributed to God). However, since scripture does in fact frequently speak of God's wrath, this is also to be understood metaphorically, i.e. in certain of the effects of the divine causality we recognise something akin to human anger. But these effects cannot be ascribed to any wrath on God's part, and we can speak of his wrath only in an improper sense—in fact, we speak of something which exists only in the

---

[132] 1a, 19, 7.
[133] 1a, 19, 7, ad 1. The same subject is discussed also in *In ad Rom.* 11, 4 (925).
[134] 1a, 19, 7: *voluntas Dei est omnino immutabilis. Sed circa hoc considerandum est, quod aliud est mutare voluntatem; et aliud est velle aliquarum rerum mutationem;* see also ib. ad 1 and ad 2. Cf. the commentary in *Vollständige, ungekürzte deutsch-lateinische Ausgabe der Summa Theologica* (*Die deutsche Thomas-Ausgabe*), vol. II, Salzburg 1934, p. 318: 'Weil das Werk, das Gott wirkt, eine Ähnlichkeit hat mit jenen Werken, die bei uns aus der Reue hervorgehen, deshalb sagen wir auch von Gott, Er habe Reue. Im Wirkenden selbst besteht jedoch nichts dergleichen'.
[135] 1a, 19, 7, obi. 3.
[136] 1a, 19, 7, ad 3: *ex ratione illa non potest concludi quod Deus habeat mutabilem voluntatem; sed quod mutationem velit.*

created world where it is an 'effect' of the immutable will of God. There is nothing in God's nature which corresponds to punishment, but since punishment is commonly a sign of wrath, on this basis we speak of God's wrath, though improperly.[137] Thomas argues in this way that many of the statements made about God in the Bible refer rather to something which takes place in the world, since they contradict the metaphysical interpretation of the divine perfection.[138]

God is the final cause of all change and movement of any kind, but he himself is always *omnino immutabilis* (altogether unchangeable),[139] or, to use another expression which we frequently find in Thomas, he remains *primum movens immobile* (the unchanging first cause of change).[140] In relation to immutability, every form of mutability or affectional change is to be regarded as deficient and imperfect. As a general rule, nothing which implies deficiency (*defectus*) can be imputed to God. To impute deficiency to God would, of course, be to detract from his honour and this would be nothing less than blasphemy.[141] It is a mark of all animate and

---

[137] 1a, 19, 11: *in Deo quaedam dicuntur proprie, et quaedam secundum metaphoram, ut ex supradictis patet. Cum autem aliquae passiones humanae in divinam praedicationem metaphorice assumuntur, hoc fit secundum similitudinem effectus: unde illud quod est signum talis passionis in nobis, in Deo nomine illius passionis metaphorice significatur . . . hoc distat inter voluntatem et iram, quia ira de Deo nunquam proprie dicitur, cum in suo principali intellectu includat passionem: voluntas autem proprie de Deo dicitur. Et ideo in Deo distinguitur voluntas proprie, et metaphorice dicta. Voluntas autem proprie dicta, vocatur voluntas beneplaciti: voluntas autem metaphorice dicta, est voluntas signi, eo quod ipsum signum voluntatis voluntas dicitur;* cf. 1a, 3, 2, ad 2: *ira et huiusmodi attribuuntur Deo secundum similitudinem effectus: quia enim proprium est irati punire, ira eius punitio metaphorice vocatur; In ad Rom.* 9, 4 (793): *Non enim dicitur ira in Deo secundum affectus commotionem, sed secundum effectus vindictae;* 1a, 59, 4, ad 1; *CG* I, 96.

[138] Thomas has to continue to make a distinction here between statements which are properly made about God and those which are made only in a figurative or metaphorical sense, cf. e.g. *CG* I, 91: *Ex praedictis autem excluditur error quorundam Iudaeorum attribuentium Deo iram, tristitiam, poenitentiam, et omnes huiusmodi passiones, secundum proprietatem, non distinguentes quid in Scripturis Sacris proprie et metaphorice dicatur.* It can hardly be fortuitous that Thomas finds these statements made by Jews. In Hebrew thought they clearly do not present the difficulties which make them unacceptable to Thomas. For Thomas there is nothing that can conceivably correspond ontologically in God to 'wrath', while the statement that God is 'good' does have a fully acceptable equivalent in the metaphysical concept of *bonitas*. But this concept has a significance which fails to express what are perhaps the decisive aspects of the biblical statements concerning the goodness of God, cf. p. 100 above, footnote 35.

[139] 1a, 9, 1; see also *CG* I, 13 and 14; *Compend. Theol.* 4; 1a, 10, 3.

[140] 1a, 3, 1.

[141] 3a, 16, 4, ad 2: *si ea quae ad defectum pertinent Deo attribuantur secundum divinam naturam, esset blasphemia, quasi pertinens ad diminutionem honoris ipsius.*

inanimate life that it embodies potentiality and actuality, whereas God by definition is free from every form of potentiality. As we saw above,[142] we cannot conceive of God as forming part of a larger whole, not even if this larger whole were wholly perfect. For the same reason we cannot define the divine being as the sum of several components which together constitute God, for he is *omnino simplex* (altogether simple).[143] But if we accept that *esse autem in potentia, omnino removetur a Deo* (potentiality is to be altogether ruled out from God),[144] we conclude that God must be pure actuality, which in fact is what Thomas means by the phrase *actus purus* (sheer actuality), a term commonly found in his writings as a designation of God.[145]

We have already discussed Thomas's understanding of the relationship between *ratio* and *revelatio*, and this may be the appropriate time to consider what part, if any, revelation plays in his total picture of the relationship between God and the world. His fundamental concept of cause is derived in its essentials, as we noted, from Greek philosophy, and his definition of God as *actus purus* and *primum movens immobile* appears at first glance to coincide with the 'Unmoved Mover' of Aristotelian cosmology. It is commonly supposed by those who have some acquaintance with Thomas that he works primarily with a natural theology based wholly on reason and introduces revelation only when particular theological doctrines are involved, e.g. the Trinity, grace, or the incarnation.[146] From this point of view it would appear that two separate strands can be isolated in his thinking, first, a basic substructure of purely philosophical speculation on which he imposes a superstructure consisting of the additional knowledge of God given by revelation. In philosophical speculation both the concept of God and the structure of the relationship between God and the world must be defined in purely rational terms without reference to any revealed knowledge, and therefore the relationship between theology and philosophy is simply one of supplementation, in which two essentially separate entities are added to one another. Quite obviously, however, this

---

[142] See p. 97 above.   [143] 1a, 3, 7.   [144] 1a, 3, 6.
[145] 1a, 3, 2: *Deus est purus actus, non habens aliquid de potentialitate*, and also 1a, 9, 1; 1a, 12, 1; 1a, 14, 1, ad 1, etc.
[146] Cf. e.g. N. Söderblom, *Naturlig religion och religionshistoria. En historik och ett program*, Stockholm 1914, p. 32ff., Aulén, *Gudsbilden*, p. 127ff., R. Bring, *Teologi och religion*, Lund 1937, p. 68 or R. Prenter, *Skabelse og genløsning*, vol. II, Copenhagen 1952, p. 150f.

interpretation is hardly adequate to express the thought of Thomas, for he does not regard the philosophical elements in theology as autonomous but subordinate rather to revelation.[147] He was primarily a theologian, and a philosopher only that he might more effectively fulfil this primary function.[148] One example of this was his criticism of Aristotle. Despite the esteem in which Aristotle was held as *Philosophus*, Thomas (unlike the Latin Averroists) never regarded his philosophy as infallible or identical with human reason itself.[149] As any work of philosophy or historical theology indicates, Thomas rejected those elements in Aristotle which contradicted the traditional doctrines of the immortality of the individual soul or divine providence. To accept this fairly widely held interpretation of Thomas as the basis for understanding his thought would mean that we could determine his natural theology by bringing together the philosophical ideas which were left when the rejected Aristotelian concepts had been extracted. This would mean that revelation was then primarily a limiting factor which had no real effect either on the content or on the structure of this 'natural' theology. However, a brief comparison with some of the main philosophical ideas of the Aristotelian and neo-Platonic tradition, on which Thomas was chiefly dependent in formulating his own view of the relationship between God and the world, will indicate that this particular solution of the problem is altogether too easy.[150]

[147] On the other hand this definition would quite adequately express the position of Descartes, if he also had been a theologian. Descartes attempts to think philosophically without reference to revelation, cf. E. Gilson, *God and Philosophy*, New Haven, 1941, p. 77f.

[148] Cf. p. 12 above.

[149] Cf. E. Gilson, *Reason and Revelation in the Middle Ages*, New York 1938, p. 79f.: 'Whereas Thomas Aquinas would follow Aristotle when he was right, but no further, and because he was right, but on no other ground, the Averroists would consider Averroës, Aristotle and human reason, as three different words for one and the same thing'; see also A. C. Pegis, *Saint Thomas and the Greeks* (The Aquinas Lecture 1939), 2nd ed. Milwaukee 1943, p. 8.

[150] In any such comparison it is important to bear in mind that these entities did not mean for Thomas what they mean for us. This is particularly true of Platonism. Neither Thomas nor his contemporaries had any acquaintance with a great many of the dialogues of Plato, though these have come to occupy a central place in modern philosophical and historical study, which concentrates primarily on the system of ideas. The encounter between Christianity and Platonism brought about by neo-Platonism was primarily an encounter between two religious traditions, and the elements which were held to be of greatest significance for the Christian tradition were what we should regard today as peripheral matters, particularly the myths about the immortality of the soul and the creation of the world which are to be found in the *Phaedo* and *Timaeus*. On the other hand, however, the encounter with

At first glance it would seem that the cosmology which we find in Thomas is in complete accord with Greek thought. He speaks, apparently in Aristotelian terms, about a world in movement, brought into being by a first Unmoved Mover, and in its hierarchical arrangement of different degrees of perfection we discern the cosmology common to neo-Platonism and Greek thought in general. On closer examination, however, we discover that even though we seem to find in Thomas, in Gilson's phrase, 'the very cosmography of Aristotle, and consequently a view of the world in the physical sense which is in agreement with that of Aristotle, the real question is not one of physics but of metaphysics, and in this respect Thomas differs markedly from Aristotle.[151]

The first obvious fact is that despite his use of Aristotelian terms Thomas has a conception of God which is qualitatively different from that of the Greek philosopher. The difference is not simply that whereas in line with his view of nature Thomas speaks of a single First Mover, *primus motor*, Aristotle posits no fewer than fifty-five such unmoved movers on the basis of his astronomical calculations.[152] The difference lies much deeper. As the highest object of desire the First Mover of Aristotelian metaphysics causes all existing change and movement, but to say this is also to express in full the causal relationship between this First Mover and the world. He is, indeed, the cause of all that is created, but as such he is

Aristotelianism, which had been transmitted by Arabic philosophers, was primarily a confrontation between a religion and a philosophy. In addition to offering a natural philosophy, Aristotle provided a philosophical technique—it is significant that the position of theology is included in a scientific system as one *scientia* among other *scientiae* only from the thirteenth century—while in their basic religious ideas, theologians generally remained loyal to the Platonic tradition. We cannot therefore simply say that Aristotelianism replaced or superseded Platonism at that time, since they did not function, as it were, on the same plane. On this whole question, see especially E. Gilson, 'Le Christianisme et la tradition philosophique' in *Revue des sciences philosophiques et théologiques* (= *RSPT*) 30, 1942, p. 252ff. Even Aristotelianism was revised in a strongly neo-Platonic direction. The article, 'God', by M. Chossat in *DTC* 4:1, 1911, col. 1183 gives some illuminating examples of how indistinct the dividing-lines between the two actually were. The compendium of Proclus known as the *Liber de Causis*, which was of such importance in medieval thinking, was understood by Thomas in an Aristotelian sense, though it is clear that he classified Proclus as a Platonic thinker. A further illustration of this blurring of the lines of division is found in Thomas's discussion of Pseudo-Dionysius who, Thomas held, followed Plato in his theology but Aristotle in his physics.

[151] Gilson, *Spirit*, p. 74.
[152] Cf. de Finance *Être et agir*, p. 12f. and Gilson, *Spirit*, p. 44f.

properly speaking only the final cause.[153] The only link between him and the world is the desire he arouses from eternity, and this desire is inherent in things, it was not implanted within them by the First Mover. By reason of his perfection the Aristotelian God actuates the self-originated movement of the creature, but he is not the ultimate cause of the existence of this movement. In the words of Gilson, he is not only in an ontological sense 'distinct from all else' in relation to the world, he is also 'ontologically absent from all else'.[154] The only activity which can be ascribed to him is thinking—he is Thought that conceives itself from all time. The Aristotelian cosmos has nothing in it that corresponds to the divine ordering of the world which we find in Plato's *Timaeus*, and even less the idea of a creation of the world.[155] Aristotle does not conceive the cosmos with its hierarchy of immanent entelechies to be brought forth by the First Mover, but to have been in existence like him from all eternity. The God of Aristotle may indeed be said to be the cause of *what the world is*, since the aspiration to pure form common to all material forms gives it its coinherence, but he is not the cause of the fact *that it is*.[156]

---

[153] H. Meyer, 'Thomas von Aquin als Interpret der aristotelischen Gotteslehre', in *Aus der Geisteswelt des Mittelalters* (*BGPM* Suppl. III:1), Münster in Westfalen 1935, p. 683: 'Gleich den platonischen Ideen ist der aristotelische Gott nur Ursache im Sinne der Zweckursache'. . . 'Für Aristoteles war der Satz, Gott bewege die Welt als Gegenstand des Verlangens, wie das Geliebte den Liebenden, die Formulierung für das Kausalverhältnis überhaupt, in dem Gott zur Welt steht'.

[154] Gilson, *Thomisme*, p. 121.

[155] Meyer, *BGPM*, Suppl. III:1, p. 682: 'Es darf als gesichertes Forschungsresultat gelten, dass Aristoteles weder eine Weltschöpfung noch eine Weltbildung im Sinne Platons gekannt hat. Der aristotelische Gott ist nur Weltbeweger. Der Seinskosmos mit den ihr immanenten zielstrebigen Kräften ist nicht von Gott hervorgebracht'; cf. the same author's *Thomas von Aquin. Sein System und seine geistesgeschichtliche Stellung*, Bonn 1938, p. 297f.; J. Hessen, *Platonismus und Prophetismus. Die antike und biblische Geisteswelt in strukturvergleichender Betrachtung*, Munich 1939, p. 44: '*der Begriff der Schöpfung ist dem Aristoteles wie überhaupt dem antiken Denken völlig fremd*'; the same author's *Thomas von Aquin und wir*, Munich 1955, p. 128f; Gilson, *God and Philosophy*, p. 33f.: 'The pure Act of the self-thinking Thought eternally thinks of itself, but never of us. The supreme god of Aristotle has not made this world of ours; he does not even know it as distinct from himself, nor consequently, can he take care of any one of the beings or things that are in it.' Cf. Thomas's own statement in *In articulis fidei et sacramenta Ecclesiae expositio: Tertius est error Aristotelis, qui posuit mundum a Deo factum non esse, sed ab aeterno fuisse*. On the debated question of Thomas's commentaries on texts of Aristotle, in which it seems at times as though he assumed that Aristotle was acquainted with the idea of a creation, see Pegis, *Saint Thomas and the Greeks*, p. 101ff.

[156] Gilson, *God and Philosophy*, p. 33: 'The world of Aristotle is there, as something that has always been and always will be. It is an eternally necessary and necessarily eternal world. The problem for us is therefore not to know how it has come into being but to understand what happens in it and consequently what it is.'

For Thomas, however, God is the cause both of the movement and of the existence of the creature: in other words, he is not only *causa finalis* but also *causa efficiens*. This implies, however, that Thomas differs from Aristotle not only in his conception of God but also in his understanding of the things of the world. The difference between the two is clearly illustrated by reference to the differentiation between actuality and potentiality. Though both Thomas and Aristotle conceive of the relationship between God and the world in causal terms, on closer analysis we shall see that in Thomas the causal relationship is understood in a completely different sense and has a much broader significance than it has in Aristotle, and also that terms like *actus* and *potentia* are invested with a much profounder meaning than they have in Aristotle. In Aristotle the corresponding concepts are form and matter. The term *actus purus* as an attribute of God is therefore in Aristotle equivalent to immateriality, the state of being without body or substance. Immateriality is an attribute both of the movers of the heavenly spheres and of the First Mover, and the difference between them is a qualitative difference of divine perfection. The new meaning which Thomas gives to potentiality and actuality in his metaphysical interpretation will best be understood by examining what Thomas and Aristotle mean when they say that something 'is' or has 'being'. For Aristotle, the existence of a thing is necessarily inherent in its essence: the question of the meaning of τὸ ὄν is inseparable from that of the οὐσία of the thing, i.e. from 'what it is', or from what was termed in later scholasticism the *essentia, natura* or *quidditas* of a thing.[157] By this latter term is meant the whatness of a thing—it represents the answer to the question, *quid sit*. The crucial difference between the metaphysics of Thomas and Aristotle's metaphysics of essence is that Thomas gives an added dimension to the question by extending the reference to the plane of existence. To Thomas, *esse*—or more precisely, *ipsum esse*—does not mean '*that which is*', but the *very act by which a thing is*, its *existence*. This existence does not belong inherently to the nature of a thing, as in Aristotle, that is, the existence of a thing is not equivalent to its *essentia*, but is distinct *realiter* from its nature, since the thing does not exist in and of itself. We thus find that, over and above the distinction which Aristotle makes between form and matter, Thomas introduces a further distinction between essence

[157] See in this connection E. Gilson, *L'être et l'essence*, Paris 1948, p. 53ff. and the same author's *Thomisme*, p. 64.

and existence, and by doing so radically alters metaphysics. This means that there are two kinds of potentiality in Thomas: there is, first, in the case of things which consist of form and matter, the potentiality of matter in relation to its determining form, and in addition a new kind of potentiality which we may call the potentiality of essence, consisting of form and matter, in relation to its existence.[158] The very act of existence is not something that things have in and of themselves—it comes to them from outside, it is given to them at every moment of their existence, and may be taken away from them at any moment. This is true not only of the lower beings in the hierarchy of existence where form is usually accompanied by matter, but also of immaterial intelligences, the angels, who have an important place in his view of the universe. An angel is a purely immaterial being and as such is pure form, but this does not mean— as Aristotle says of corresponding beings—pure actuality. Moreover, the nature of the angel is potentially related to the act by which it exists, but the existence of the angel too must be given at every moment by God.[159] In addition to all this, however, we also find in

---

[158] See e.g. 1a, 54, 3: *In omni autem creato essentia differt a suo esse, et comparatur ad ipsum sicut potentia ad actum.*

[159] 1a, 50, 2, ad 3: *licet in angelo non sit compositio formae et materiae, est tamen in eo actus et potentia. Quod quidem manifestum potest esse ex consideratione rerum materialium, in quibus invenitur duplex compositio. Prima quidem formae et materiae, ex quibus constituitur natura aliqua. Natura autem sic composita non est suum esse, sed esse est actus eius. Unde ipsa natura comparatur ad suum esse sicut potentia ad actum. Subtracta ergo materia, et posito quod ipsa forma subsistat non in materia, adhuc remanet comparatio formae ad ipsum esse ut potentiae ad actum. Et talis compositio intelligenda est in angelis;* In De Trin. 5, 4, ad 4: *actus et potentia sunt communiora quam materia et forma; et ideo in angelis, etsi non inveniatur compositio formae et materiae, potest tamen inveniri in eis potentia et actus . . . quia non habet esse a se ipso angelus, ideo se habet in potentia ad esse quod accipit a deo, et sic esse a deo acceptum comparatur ad essentiam eius simplicem ut actus ad potentiam. Et hoc est quod dicitur quod sunt compositi ex 'quod est' et 'quo est', ut ipsum esse intelligatur 'quo est', ipsa vero natura angeli intelligatur 'quod est'.* Thomas always reads his own distinction between *essentia* and *esse* into the distinction between *quod est* and *esse* which first appears in Boethius (see e.g. the *De hebdomadibus* of Boethius, *MPL* 64, 1311 B: *Diversum est esse et id quod est*). This distinction always appears in later writers in the form of *quod est* and *quo est*. It is clear, however, that the term as used in Boethius—and in almost the entire theological tradition after him up to Thomas— has quite a different meaning from what it has in the metaphysics of Thomas. In earlier theological tradition *esse* does not mean the act of existence, as it does in Thomas, but the nature of a thing, its *essentia*, while *quod est* denotes the actual, existing thing—in Thomas's terminology, the *suppositum*. See here particularly de Finance, *Être et agir*, p. 84f. and M. D. Roland-Gosselin, *Le 'De ente et essentia' de S. Thomas d' Aquin. Texte établi d'après les manuscrits parisiens.* Introduction, notes et études historiques (*BT* 8), Paris 1948, p. 142ff.

Thomas, when we compare him with Aristotle, not only a new type of potentiality but a completely new type of actuality as well. The *esse* of a thing is related to its *essentia* as actuality is related to potentiality.[160] We are speaking here of a much deeper and profounder kind of actuality than is expressed in the form of the thing, for in spite of its immateriality it is potentially related to the act of existence itself, *actus essendi*. Thomas can therefore say, *esse est actualitas omnium rerum, et etiam ipsarum formarum* (the act of existing is the ultimate actuality of everything, and even of every form).[161] The form is that by which a thing is what it is, *quo est*, but it itself must in turn be actualised by *ipsum esse*, if the thing which is determined by its form is also really to exist. The act of existence is related to form as form is related to matter—it is the *quo est* of form.[162] Hence *esse* expresses also a higher perfection than *forma: esse est actualitas omnium actuum, et propter hoc est perfectio omnium perfectionum* (the act of existing is the actuality of every act, and is therefore the perfection of every perfection).[163] A thing is perfect insofar as it *is*, i.e. its perfection or goodness is simply another expression for the degree of *esse* which makes it an existing thing.[164] Here it is the act of existence but not form that constitutes the highest type of actuality, which means that in Thomas the distinction between act and potency is given a new and profounder meaning than it originally had in Aristotle.[165] This is also true in regard to the

---

[160] 1a, 3, 4: *esse est actualitas omnis formae vel naturae: non enim bonitas vel humanitas significatur in actu, nisi prout significamus eam esse. Oportet igitur quod ipsum esse comparetur ad essentiam quae est aliud ab ipso, sicut actus ad potentiam.*
[161] 1a, 4, 1, ad 3.
[162] Cf. e.g. *CG* II, 54: *ad ipsam etiam formam comparatur ipsum esse ut actus. . . Unde in compositis ex materia et forma nec materia nec forma potest dici ipsum quod est, nec etiam ipsum esse. Forma tamen potest dici quo est, secundum quod est essendi principium; ipsa autem tota substantia est ipsum quod est; et ipsum esse est quo substantia denominatur ens.* Cf. E. Gilson, *L'être et l'essence*, Paris 1948, p. 109: 'Le rapport de l'exister à l'essence se présente donc comme celui d'un acte qui n'est pas une forme, à une potentialité qui n'est pas une matière, c'est-à-dire à une certaine sorte de potentialité.'
[163] *De Pot.* 7, 2, ad 9.
[164] 1a, 5, 1: *Intantum est autem perfectum unumquodque, inquantum est actu: unde manifestum est quod intantum est aliquid bonum, inquantum est ens: esse enim est actualitas omnis rei; CG* I, 28: *Omnis enim nobilitas cuiuscumque rei est sibi secundum suum esse. . . Sic ergo secundum modum quo res habet esse, est suus modus in nobilitate.*
[165] de Finance, *Être et agir*, p. 117: 'En réalité, sous toutes ces formules, héritées de la philosophie grecque, saint Thomas glisse un sens entièrement nouveau. Tandis qu'Aristote voit dans l'existence une propriété nécessaire de la forme

meaning of the term *actus purus* as a definition of God. God is pure actuality, not because he is pure form—even the angels are such— but because his nature is the act of pure existence, *ipsum esse per se subsistens* (self-subsistent being itself).[166] There is no potentiality in God, since the divine essence does not depend for its existence on any other thing or on any other being than himself. His essence is *ipsum esse*, and therefore in God *essentia* and *esse* constitute a unity.[167]

This for Thomas is the crucial dividing line between God and all animate and inanimate life. The dividing line between God and man is not simply the difference of degree which Aristotle makes between pure form in the sense of immateriality and all other forms within the world found in combination with matter. There is also a difference of kind, since there is an insuperable distinction between God, who is *ipsum esse*, and all other things which do not have existence of themselves, but *receive* it as that which is caused by something other than themselves.[168] All that is created is thus dependent by the very fact of its creation on an ultimate cause outside creation. If there ceased to be this dependence even for a moment, the creation would cease to exist, since the *esse* of creation is not its own but from God.[169]

comme telle, la matière introduisant seule la contingence, si bien que toute essence est éternellement réalisée de par sa seule consistance métaphysique, saint Thomas voit dans *l'esse* un acte qui doit à la forme sa détermination, mais lui donne la réalité, s'en distingue et la domine comme la forme elle-même, dans les composés, domine le principe matériel. C'est l'existence, et non la forme, qui représente, dans le thomisme, le type achevé de l'actualité,' Cf. Manser, *Thomismus*, p. 558ff.

---

[166] 1a. 4. 2.

[167] 1a, 3, 4: *Cum igitur in Deo nihil sit potentiale, ut ostensum est supra, sequitur quod non sit aliud in eo essentia quam suum esse; CG I, 22: Si ergo divina essentia est aliud quam suum esse, sequitur quod essentia et esse se habeant sicut potentia et actus. Ostensum est autem in Deo nihil esse de potentia, sed ipsum esse purum actum. Non igitur Dei essentia est aliud quam suum esse.*

[168] *De ente et essentia, 4: Non autem potest esse quod ipsum esse sit causatum ab ipsa forma vel quiditate rei, causatum dico sicut a causa efficiente, quia sic aliqua res esset causa sui ipsius et aliqua res seipsam in esse produceret, quod est impossibile. Ergo oportet quod omnis talis res cuius esse est aliud quam natura sua habeat esse ab alio. Et quia omne quod est per aliud reducitur ad illud quod est per se sicut ad causam primam, oportet quod sit aliqua res que sit causa essendi omnibus rebus ex eo quod ipsa est esse tantum. . . Patet ergo quod intelligencia est forma et esse et quod esse habet a primo ente quod est esse tantum, et hec est causa prima que Deus est* (quotation from the critical edition of the text in Roland-Gosselin, *Le 'De ente et essentia'*, p. 35. Cf. Gilson, *Thomisme*, p. 253: 'Une créature, en effet, c'est essentiellement ce qui tient d'autrui son exister, par opposition à Dieu, qui ne tient son exister que de soi-même, et subsiste indépendamment'.

[169] 1a, 104, 1: *Dependet enim esse cuiuslibet creaturae a Deo, ita quod nec ad momentum subsistere possent, sed in nihilum redigerentur, nisi operatione divinae virtutis conservarentur in esse.*

Thomas uses the metaphor of light in this connection to explain his meaning. According to the Aristotelian metaphysics the sky is permeated by the light which comes from the sun, which means that the sky itself becomes 'light'. But this does not mean that 'lightness' is a constituent element in the nature of sky, though it is an essential element of the sun to be light. This means that the sky at once ceases to be light whenever the sun is concealed from view, *quia non habet radicem in aere, statim cessat humen, cessante actione solis* (since it has no root in the air, the light ceases with the action of the sun).[170] Just as the sky in this way 'participates' in the light of the sun, without in any way participating thereby in the nature of the sun, so likewise created things share in *esse* as something caused by God, without existing in the same way as God himself.[171] God is the only being to whom it belongs by nature to exist, and it is as impossible for the sky to become sun as it is for anything created to become God, i.e. to have its existence inherent in its *essentia*. In contrast to that of God, the *esse* of the creature is an *esse per participationem* (existence by participation), or more accurately, since it is *causatum ab alio* (caused by another), it is an *esse receptum* (received existence).[172] In other words, while *esse* and *essentia* are one and the same in God, the *esse* of the creature is something other than its *essentia*, and it

---

[170] 1a, 104, 1.

[171] 1a, 104, 1: *Sic autem se habet omnis creatura ad Deum, sicut aer ad solem illuminantem. Sicut enim sol est lucens per suam naturam, aer autem fit luminosus participando lumen a sole, non tamen participando naturam solis; ita solus Deus est ens per essentiam suam, quia eius essentia est suum esse; omnis autem creatura est ens participative, non quod sua essentia sit eius esse.* Cf. *In ad Heb.* 1, 2(31). The difference between the existence of God and that of created things is often defined by Thomas as the difference between *esse per essentiam* and *esse per participationem*. It should be noted here that for Thomas *participare* in this context never means to have part in another entity. The term is rather to be understood in quite the opposite sense, or, as Gilson expresses it in his *Thomisme*, p. 182, footnote 3: 'participer, en langage thomiste, ne signifie pas être une chose, mais ne pas l'être; participer à Dieu, c'est ne pas être Dieu'. *Esse per participationem* has thus primarily the sense correctly given to it in R. J. Deferrari and M. I. Barry, *A Lexicon of St Thomas Aquinas*, Baltimore 1948–49, p. 376: 'existence which is received from another', though it must be noted, however, that the 'receiving' self does not exist prior to the act of receiving itself, but is rather constituted by this act. By this divine gift of *esse* man possesses a distant likeness to the Giver who is *ipsum esse*. See also L.-B. Geiger, *La participation dans la philosophie de S. Thomas d'Aquin* (*BT* 23), Paris 1942, especially p. 48f. and 239.

[172] 1a, 7, 2: *forma creata sic subsistens habet esse, et non est suum esse, necesse est quod ipsum eius esse sit receptum; 1a, 44, 1, ad 1: ex hoc quod aliquid per participationem est ens sequitur quod sit causatum ab alio. Unde huiusmodi ens non potest esse, quin sit causatum.*

may therefore be said that there is a real distinction between the two.[173]

In order to understand this 'real distinction'[174] between the *esse* and *essentia* of created things, it is important, as Gilson in particular points out, that we have a correct understanding of the word *esse*.[175] In studying the various passages in which it appears we must always remember that *esse*, like every verb, denotes an activity and not a state. When we say that a thing *is* we indicate not simply the fact that it is but also the *act* that causes it to be. We are not to conceive of essence and existence as two distinct components which by being added to one another constitute an existing thing. To say that things are 'composed' of *essentia* and *esse* is an oversimplified assumption, and to conceive of their relationship in this way means to accept without questioning the assumption that *esse* is an essence or a thing. When we do this, we cannot do justice to Thomas's thought. But 'existence is not a thing, but the act that causes a thing both to be and to be what it is'.[176] When, therefore, we define God as *ipsum esse per se subsistens*, this does not mean that he is to be conceived in terms of static essence, but that he is pure activity, 'the pure act of existence'.[177] Like Aristotle, Thomas regards the world in a dynamic sense as filled with movement and activity, but he gives a

---

[173] 1a, 54, 3: *In omni autem creato essentia differt a suo esse, et comparatur ad ipsum sicut potentia ad actum;* 1a, 61, 1: *Solus enim Deus est suum esse: in omnibus autem aliis differt essentia rei et esse eius. . . Et ex hoc manifestum est quod solus Deus est ens per suam essentiam: omnia vero alia sunt entia per participationem. Omne autem quod est per participationem, causatur ab eo quod est per essentiam: sicut omne ignitum causatur ab igne;* cf. Gilson, *God and Philosophy,* p. 70: 'The definition of no empirically given thing is existence; hence its essence is not existence, but existence must be conceived as distinct from it'.

[174] Only in one passage, *De Ver.* 27, 1, ad 8, does Thomas use the expression *realis compositio* in reference to what is described in all later works on Thomas as 'the real distinction between essence and existence'. It is absolutely clear, however, that the idea itself is one of the most profound and fundamental in Thomas's metaphysics, cf. e.g. N. del Prado, 'La vérité fondamentale de la philosophie chrétienne selon saint Thomas', in *RT* 18 (1910), p. 209ff; L. Rougier, *La scolastique et le thomisme,* Paris 1925, p. 124ff. and 460ff.; see also H. Meyer, *Thomas von Aquin,* p. 112f.; de Finance, *Étre et agir,* p. 94ff.; Roland-Gosselin, *Le 'De ente et essentia',* p. 197ff.; E. Gilson, *Being and Some Philosophers,* Toronto 1949, p. 174ff.; Manser, *Thomismus* p. 537f.; on p. 493, footnote 1, Manser provides a survey of the extensive literature dealing with the problem.

[175] Cf. also de Finance, *Étre et agir,* p. 79: 'Toute la signification, toute la valeur du thomisme dépendent de la façon dont il conçoit l'*esse*'.

[176] Gilson, *God and Philosophy,* p. 70; the same author's *Thomisme,* p. 52; *Spirit,* p. 88f.; and his *Being and Some Philosophers,* p. 172.

[177] Gilson, *Thomisme,* p. 53.

deeper meaning to Aristotle's dynamic, in which form is primary, by interpreting it to signify that God, who is both pure form and *ipsum esse*, causes a thing to be and to be what it is. His view of God as well as of the divine activity is altogether different from that of Aristotle.

Thomas, however, differs at crucial points not only from Aristotle, but also from neo-Platonism, the second major stream of Greek philosophy from which he borrowed elements in the formation of his synthesis. We do not have the opportunity here to examine this relationship more fully, but will confine ourselves to his interpretation of the neo-Platonic axiom, *bonum est diffusivum sui* (the good is generous of itself), a frequently debated proposition in the medieval tradition.[178] As J. Peghaire has shown, this definition had its origin in the neo-Platonic concept of the world as an emanation of the highest principle, the One, or, to use the synonymous term, the Good.[179] It is the nature of the Good to 'emanate' or flow over its limits—this is the explanation of the origin of the world which exists outside the One. Just as the sun cannot be sun unless it shines and thus emits its rays until they become lost in darkness, so all existence flows from the One on a continually decreasing scale. Of necessity this emanation has continued from all eternity, for if the first principle should allow the emanation of the world from itself to cease even for a moment, it would cease to be the highest Good. By eternal necessity the One thus acts as *causa efficiens* of the world, while at the same time it constitutes the end of the whole world process.[180] The concept of emanation is thus the very nerve of neo-Platonic cosmology.

In interpreting this axiom, Thomas does not begin by defining *diffusivum*—which for the neo-Platonists would have been the most

[178] All of the passages in Thomas which deal with this axiom are listed by J. Peghaire in 'L'axiome "Bonum est diffusivum sui" dans le néo-platonisme et le thomisme', in *Revue de l'Université d'Ottawa* (=*RUO*), Section spéciale, vol. I 1932, p. 19*f. In speaking of this concept Thomas often refers (see e.g. 3a, 1, 1) to ch. 4 of the *De divinis nominibus* of Pseudo-Dionysius, in which, however, the customary formula is not found. The text as Thomas found it read: . . . *ea quae est bonum, ut substantiale bonum, ad omnia existentia extendit bonitatem*, see Peghaire, *RUO*, Section spéciale, 1932, p. 7.

[179] Peghaire, *RUO*, Section spéciale, 1932, p. 10ff. J. Guitton, *Le temps et l'éternité chez Plotin et saint Augustin*, Paris 1933, p. 89: 'Ainsi, Plotin repousse violemment, toutes les fois qu'il la rencontre, la notion de *création*, c'est-à-dire qu'il refuse à l'Etre premier toute indépendance par rapport au monde. A cette notion il substitue celle de *procession*: il met dans l'être divin une nécessité d'écoulement, de production et de rayonnement'; cf. also de Finance, *Être et agir*, p. 65ff.

[180] Peghaire, *RUO*, Section spéciale, 1932, p. 12ff.

natural step—but rather by seeking to explain the meaning of *bonum*. As we saw earlier,[181] *bonum* in Thomas's metaphysics corresponds to *finis*, and so he frequently explains the meaning of the axiom in the following way: *bonum dicitur diffusivum sui esse, eo modo quo finis dicitur movere* (good things are said to pour forth their being in the same way that ends are said to move one).[182] The crucial point is that Thomas conceives of *bonum* as final cause, not as *causa efficiens*. Underlying this conception is the basic distinction which he sees to exist between *bonum* and *esse*. In neo-Platonic thought *bonum* is prior to *esse*, for it is the nature of the good to emanate and bring into existence some thing other than itself, and so for neo-Platonism *bonum* is the presupposition of *esse*. If we apply this reasoning to God, and conceive of him primarily as the highest Good (from which his other attributes are then derived), this would mean that he would have a necessary relationship to something which emanated from him. It would be his nature to produce something *ad extra*, for 'a supreme Good without effect would be a pure contradiction.'[183] But then it would be very difficult to introduce the idea of 'creation', except in the sense of pure emanation. Hence in neo-Platonic cosmology the world is an eternal and necessary complement to the One.[184]

While *bonum* is primary in neo-Platonic cosmology, Thomas gives metaphysical priority to *esse*. While it is true that the *transcendentalia* of Thomas coincide, *ens et verum et unum et bonum convertuntur* (being, truth, unity and goodness are convertible),[185] *ens* is primary —a thing can be good or perfect only if it exists.[186] In Thomas's

---

[181] See p. 103f. above.
[182] 1a, 5, 4, ad 2. The argument is presented most fully in *De Ver.* 21, 1, ad 4; cf. also I *Sent.* 34, 2, ad 4 and *CG* I, 37.
[183] Peghaire, *RUO*, Section spéciale, 1932, p. 28.
[184] On the neo-Platonic view of the relation between God and the world cf. Pegis, *Saint Thomas and the Greeks*, p. 74f.: 'The universe is mysteriously implied within the nature of being and shares with God its eternal community. In thus sharing existence with the universe, God must recognise the universe as His constant companion and as the constant limit of His perfections. However good, however perfect, however free we may now consider God, He is neither so good nor so perfect nor so free that He can be without the universe'.
[185] See e.g. *De Ver.* 21, 2–3; 1a, 16, 3; 1a, 17, 4, ad 2; 1a2ae, 55, 4, ad 2.
[186] Cf. Gilson, *Thomisme*, p. 149: 'Il en est de l'un comme du bien; ce n'est pas l'un qui est, c'est l'être qui est un, comme il est bon, vrai et beau. Ces propriétés, qu l'on nomme souvent les *transcendentaux*, n'ont de sens et de réalité qu'en fonction de l'être qui les pose toutes en se posant'; Peghaire, *RUO*, Section spéciale, 1932, p. 26; 'Ces propriétés d'unité et de bonté sont sans doute inséparables de l'être et identiques

K

cosmology, as we have seen, the highest actuality—and therefore perfection—is not *what* a thing is but the fact that it *is*.[187] This is true also of God, who is supreme perfection—he does not exist because he is *summum bonum*, but he is *summum bonum*, because he *IS*.[188] Since for Thomas the perfection or goodness of a thing presupposes its *esse*, the ultimate cause of all that exists, *causa efficiens*, is to be sought in something which itself is *esse*, while as *bonum* it cannot primarily be *causa efficiens* but properly only *causa finalis*. Thomas thus gives the neo-Platonic axiom a different meaning from what it had originally, and forces it to express final rather than efficient causality.[189] God is perfect because he is *ipsum esse*, but this means that he does not require anything other than himself and his own existence for his perfection. Thus we come from a different starting-point back to the problem of the relationship between God and the world which we discussed above[190] when we examined Thomas's view of the will of God and his love for created things, We now see more clearly, however, both the limits within which he discusses the sovereign transcendence of God and also his definitive interpretation of divine causality. Since God as *ipsum esse* is absolutely perfect even without creation, his relationship to creation is one of sovereign freedom, not of necessity. It is by no means essential to

à lui, *ens, unum et bonum convertuntur*, mais elles le supposent, elles lui sont donc postérieures. C'est à cette hauteur métaphysique qu'il faut s'élever pour découvrir la raison véritable de la divergence entre saint Thomas et les disciples de Platon'.

---

[187] See p. 127f. above.

[188] Cf. Garrigou-Lagrange, *God*, vol. II p. 26f.; Gilson, *Spirit*, p. 54.

[189] Cf. Gilson, *Thomisme*, p. 185, footnote 2; 'C'est pourquoi l'axiome néo-platonicien: *bonum est diffusivum sui*, ne doit pas s'entendre chez saint Thomas au sens platonicien d'une causalité efficiente du Bien, mais seulement au sens de la cause finale'. See also de Finance, *Être et agir*, p. 70; L.-B. Geiger, *Le problème de l'amour chez saint Thomas d'Aquin* (Conférence Albert-le-Grand (=*CAG*) 1952), Montreal and Paris 1952, p. 58, footnote 29; M.-J. Nicolas, 'Bonum diffusivum sui', in *RT* 63 (1955), p. 363ff. When A. Hayen, *Saint Thomas d' Aquin et la vie de l'Église* (Essais philosophiques (=*EP*) 6), Louvain and Paris 1952, p. 55, footnote 3, apparently interprets Thomas in quite the opposite sense—'Il est significatif de voir comment saint Thomas interprète de plus en plus par la causalité efficiente et non pas finale l'adage néoplatonicien: *bonum est diffusivum sui*,—he means in fact the same thing. He is merely using 'causalité efficiente' in its *Thomistic* sense, while Gilson refers to its 'sens platonicien'. Cf. Hayen, *Saint Thomas et la vie de l'Église*, p. 88: 'il métamorphose du dedans l'univers antique en consacrant le triomphe de la cause efficiente sur la cause finale,—en faisant de chaque être un existant fait à l'image . . . et ressemblance de l'Acte pur d'exister,—plus exactement encore, en substituant peu à peu à l'émanatisme grec, son propre 'réalisme théologal'' '; cf. also the quotation from Gilson on p. 75.

[190] See p. 103ff. above.

his perfection that he should be the *causa efficiens* of anything—it is not an essential attribute of his being that he should cause anything. But when he does cause something, of necessity he becomes primarily its *final* cause, for the divine activity cannot have any other end than itself. If we consider God in his causal relationship *in ordine causando*, he is primarily *bonum*, but this presupposes that *simpliciter* he is *esse*. Thus, the very structure of the causal relationship, which Thomas holds to exist between the world and God, is dominated by his metaphysics of existence, for *esse absolute praeintelligitur causae* (to be is presupposed to being a cause).[191]

By so referring every metaphysical statement to the plane of existence, Thomas breaks decisively with the neo-Platonic tradition. That is to say, he not only dismisses the concept of a chain of emanations in which each subsequent grade in the hierarchy of being emanates from the nearest above it,[192] but by giving *esse* in the metaphysical sense priority over *bonum*, he completely changes the very concept of emanation. There is no necessary procession of things from God, and no other cause of the existence of creation than God's free and sovereign will,[193] who wills that there shall be finite forms of existence, analogous to himself, which in their own way participate in his love of divine perfection. Against the necessitarianism of neo-Platonism, as represented particularly by Avicenna, Thomas affirms the absolute contingency of the creature.[194] One example of this difference between Thomas and the neo-Platonic thinkers is that the characteristic neo-Platonic idea of 'centrifugal' movement is transformed by Thomas into a 'centripetal' movement by which the whole world is characterised. The existence of every thing is wholly dependent upon God who, by defining the existence in which it participates also defines the finality of the nature which it is appointed to have from the first moment of its existence.[195]

---

[191] Cf. the passages quoted on p. 100 above, footnotes 36 and 37, and also 1a, 13, 11, ad 2: *hoc nomen bonum est principale nomen Dei inquantum est causa, non tamen simpliciter: nam esse absolute praeintelligitur causae.*

[192] This is how Lyttkens, *Analogy*, p. 350f., represents the difference between Thomas and neo-Platonism.

[193] 1a, 46, 1: *Non est ergo necessarium Deum velle quod mundus fuerit semper. Sed eatenus mundus est, quatenus Deus vult illum esse: cum esse mundi ex voluntate Dei dependeat sicut ex sua causa.* See also p. 104f, and the passages referred to in footnotes 56–58.

[194] See especially in this connection Pegis, *Saint Thomas and the Greeks*, p. 50ff.

[195] de Finance, *Être et agir*, p. 121: 'En réalité l'essence, considérée en soi, indépendamment de son rapport à l'*esse*, n'est rien. Le sujet qui reçoit l'*esse* est posé dans l'être en même temps que l'acte reçu'.

All other effects of the divine causality point back to and presuppose the first effect, the *ipsum esse*, for *movere praesupponit esse* (to cause change presupposes existence).[196] Existence itself is an act, but every act as act is at the same time a striving towards an end.[197] Thus, the dominating idea of the whole *Summa theologiae* (*'motus in Deum'*[198]) presupposes ultimately Thomas's particular interpretation of the relation between *esse* and *bonum*, or, and in the end the meaning is the same, between *esse* and *essentia*.[199]

[196] *Supra librum de causis*, 18; *Compend. Theol.* 68: *Primus autem effectus Dei in rebus est ipsum esse, quod omnes alii effectus praesupponunt, et supra quod fundantur.*

[197] Gilson, *Being and Some Philosophers*, p. 186: 'To be (*esse*) is to act (*agere*), and to act is to tend (*tendere*) to an end wherein achieved being may ultimately rest'. This is also, we may say, the basic thesis of de Finance's *Être et agir*, see e.g. p. 2: 'l'objet de ce travail est de montrer comment la métaphysique de l'agir résulte, dans le thomisme, de la métaphysique de l'être, ou, si l'on veut, comment l'affirmation de l'existence appelle l'affirmation de l'activité.

[198] See 1a, 2, prol. Cf. p. 94 above.

[199] As Gilson in particular has pointed out, Thomas's interpretation of the relation between *esse* and *essentia* separates him not only from Greek philosophy but also from his predecessors and contemporaries in Christian theology who were influenced by the Platonic tradition. Although Thomas is not the first to draw a distinction between essence and existence (on the history of this distinction from Boethius, Arabic philosophy, and the first clear formulation in William of Auvergne, up to Thomas's contemporaries, see in particular de Finance, *Être et agir*, p. 81ff., Roland-Gosselin, *Le 'De ente et essentia'*, p. 137ff. and Manser, *Thomismus*, p. 508ff.), what is original is his interpretation, which starts from the act of existence. The central concept of the metaphysics of the Platonic tradition is *essentia*; see the interesting discussion in R. J. Henle, *Saint Thomas and Platonism. A Study of the Plato and Platonici Texts in the Writings of Saint Thomas*, The Hague 1956, p. 369ff. Thus for Augustine God is primarily *summa essentia*, the Unchanging in contrast to the changeability of all that is created (Gilson, *Thomisme*, p. 76, 137, 191). The same starting-point is to be found in Anselm and may be seen, e.g., in the well-known so-called ontological argument for God in the Proslogion. The whole problem is really reduced to the question of whether *essentia*, which by definition means 'that which is', can be understood to mean non-existent, and to this, of course, the answer must be no. Instead of adopting this realistic starting-point in the concept of essence—which according to Thomas proves nothing about a real existence (cf. 1a, 2, 1, ad 2)—Thomas takes quite a different starting-point in actual, existing things in order to deduce from them the existence of a first cause, which must therefore be *ipsum esse*; Gilson, *Thomisme*, p. 85f.). Other representatives of the 'théologie de l'essence' are Richard of St Victor, Alexander of Hales, and Bonaventure (Gilson, *Thomisme*, p. 78ff.). An interesting example of how dependence on the neo-Platonic concept of the metaphysical primacy of the diffusive Good over *esse* is decisive even in what seem to be very subtle questions may be found in Bonaventure's theology of the Trinity, which starts from the definition, *Pater quia generat* (I *Sent.* 27, 1, 2, Quaracchi ed., vol. I, p. 469), while Thomas says, *quia generat, est Pater* (1a, 40, 4). Cf. de Finance, *Être et agir*, p. 77: 'Pour le Docteur Angélique, l'ordre des concepts exige qu'on se représente le Père subsistant en soi, avant de se représenter sa communication de nature. Pour saint Bonaventure, au contraire, c'est l'acte même d'engendrer qui constitue le Père dans sa propre subsistance, et

The ultimate explanation of what is distinctive in Thomas's line of thought is that he interprets the *essentia* of God to be identical with his *esse*, while in the creature there is a real distinction between the two.[200] The same is true in regard to the strong emphasis on divine *transcendence*, God's 'otherness', which we have already noted in his writings. God is *omnino simplex* because, unlike the things of the created world, his *esse* is not derived *ab alio*. As *ipsum per se subsistens*, he is perfect and independent of all others, and the expression of this perfection and independence is that there is no real relation between him and creation.[201] God is therefore absolutely self-existent and remains for ever beyond human grasp, and so can never be regarded as a 'thing' within the *ordo* of existence.[202] The equivalent of this relationship in the sphere of knowledge is that he remains the great Unknown, even when reason is illuminated by faith. We can know only *that* he is; with regard to *what* he is we cannot go beyond an analogous knowledge, which, though true in itself is still entirely inadequate, since we know of *esse* only as limited by an *essentia*. What *ipsum esse* is in itself remains incomprehensible to us.[203] As we saw above, the divine transcendence may also be

c'est cet acte qu'il faut d'abord concevoir. Simples différences de point de vue, mais révélatrices de deux 'saisies' différentes de l'être'. In his vast work, *La scolastique et le thomisme*, Paris 1925, a work, however, which is not always to be relied on in its details, L. Rougier offers the interesting suggestion that the theological success of Thomism is dependent on the fact that its thesis concerning the real distinction between essence and existence proved to be better suited to explaining central points of Christian dogma, e.g. the Trinity and the incarnation, than any other metaphysical principle; see e.g. p. 129ff., 372 and 534ff.

[200] Gardeil, *Le donné*, p. 313: 'Pas une ligne de la *Somme* qui ait été écrite indépendamment de cette vérité fondamentale: En Dieu l'essence et l'existence sont un: dans l'être créé l'essence et l'existence ne s'impliquent pas'.
[201] Cf. p. 112ff. above.
[202] Cf. p. 96f. above. For this reason, too, it is impossible to define God. Thomas expressly rejects the idea that a definition such as *actus purus* could be regarded as a definition, *De Pot.* 7, 3, ad 5: *Deus definiri non potest. Omne enim quod definitur, in intellectu definientis comprehenditur; Deus autem est incomprehensibilis ab intellectu; unde cum dicitur quod Deus est actus purus, haec non est definitio ejus.* See also *CG* I, 25; 1a, 1, 7, ad 1; 1a, 3, 5.
[203] *In ad Rom.* 1, 6 (114): *Sciendum est ergo quod aliquid circa Deum est omnino ignotum homini in hac vita, scilicet quid est Deus; CG* I, 12: *in Deo idem esse essentiam et esse, scilicet id quod respondetur ad quid est, et ad quaestionem an est. Via autem rationis perveniri non potest ut sciatur de Deo quid est;* 1a, 12, 13, ad 1: *licet per revelationem gratiae in hac vita non cognoscamus de Deo quid est, et sic ei quasi ignoto coniungamur; tamen plenius ipsum cognoscimus, inquantum plures et excellentiores effectus eius nobis demonstrantur.* Cf. Skydsgaard, *Metafysik*, p. 104ff.; Gilson, *Thomisme*, p. 158: 'Que savons-nous de Dieu? Ceci, indubitablement,

expressed by defining God as *omnino immutabilis*,[204] but this may also be traced back to the metaphysics of existence—the ultimate reason why God cannot 'become' something is that he *IS*.[205] Both the *causal relationship* between God and the world and Thomas's *attitude to value* are ultimately based on this assumption. Since God is *ipsum esse*, he can be the cause of all that exists,[206] and it is by existing that a thing is also good, a *bonum*.[207]

Thus there is already clearly present in Thomas's so-called natural theology something which cannot be derived from ancient philosophy. The explanation is not that Thomas corrected neo-Platonism with Aristotelian categories of thought, for even though Thomas follows Aristotle in expressing the basic antithesis of the world in terms of the related concepts of actuality and potentiality, yet he goes beyond

que la proposition "Dieu existe" est une proposition vraie, mais ce que c'est pour Dieu que d'exister, nous n'en savons rien, car *est idem esse Dei quod est substantia, et sicut ejus substantia est ignota, ita et esse* (*De Pot.* 7, 2, ad 1)'. In his *Approaches to God*, New York 1954, J. Maritain has drawn attention to Thomas's terminology in connection with the so-called arguments for God. He avoids the term *demonstratio*, and speaks only of *viae*: 'God is not *rendered evident* by us. He does not receive from us and from our arguments an evidence which He would have lacked. . . Our arguments do not give us evidence of the divine existence itself or of the act of existing which is in God and which is God himself. . . They give us only evidence of the fact that the divine existence must be affirmed, or the truth of the attribution of the predicate to the subject in the assertion "God exists" '; cf. 1a, 3, 4, ad 2. It is true even of analogical knowledge of God that its meaning is properly understood only against the background of the distinction between essence and existence, cf. Gilson, *Thomisme*, p. 182f. When Meyer says this of *docta ignorantia*, that 'den Aquinaten mehr als manche Thomisten wahr haben wollen, gefangen hält', *Thomas von Aquin*, p. 53f., his remarks properly apply to any attempt to use analogy in Thomas to reach positive knowledge about the being of God. Cf. Gilson, *Thomisme*, p. 155: 'Faire dire par saint Thomas que nous avons une connaissance au moins imparfaite de ce que Dieu est, c'est donc trahir sa pensée telle qu'il l'a expressément formulée à mainte reprise'.

---

[204] Cf. p. 118ff. above.
[205] Gilson, *Being and Some Philosophers*, p. 180: 'Where existence is alone, as is the case in God, Whose essence is one with His existence, there is no becoming. God is, and, because He is no particular essence, but the pure act of existence, there is nothing which He can become, and all that can be said about Him is, *He is*.
[206] Cf. p. 126ff. above. 1a, 45, 5: *creare non potest esse propria actio nisi solius Dei. Oportet enim universaliores effectus in universaliores et priores causas reducere. Inter omnes autem effectus, universalissimum est ipsum esse. Unde oportet quod sit proprius effectus primae et universalissimae causae, quae est Deus;* 1a, 45, 6: *creare est proprie causare sive producere esse rerum.* Gilson, *Spirit*, p. 73: 'The relation of effect to cause that links up nature with God lies in the order and on the plane of existence itself'.
[207] Cf. p. 133f. above. 1a, 20, 2: *omnia existentia, inquantum sunt, bona sunt: ipsum enim esse cuiuslibet rei quoddam bonum est.*

Aristotle in his interpretation of these terms by giving them a significance which they do not have in Aristotle. What is the source of this new interpretation? A possible answer is provided by considering elements common to all thinkers for whom the relation between existence and essence is a real problem. These, without exception, belong either to a Jewish, Mohammedan, or Christian tradition. Apart from representatives of Christian scholasticism we have in mind such names as Al-Farabi, Avicenna, Al-Gazzali, Averroes, and Moses Maimonides.[208] For men like these, though not for those who belonged to the purely Greek tradition in philosophy, the problem of existence is of crucial significance for metaphysics. The common starting-point for each of them in formulating this hypothesis is the characteristic Old Testament conception of God as the omnipotent Creator, who at the beginning made heaven and earth, but who is also constantly at work in the world of his creation, directly maintaining it by his power. In all this it is clear that we are dealing with a nexus of ideas which we have summed up in the term *revelatio*, for the writings of the Old Testament are included within the holy scriptures which according to Thomas contain the revelation of God.

In the eternal and uncreated world of Greek philosophy the essences of things are what they have been from all eternity, and they cannot be understood in any other way. That which is *is* by natural necessity, and the only form of contingency which is given is dependent upon the intractability of matter or the gradual assimilation of things into immaterial and unchangeable reality. There is simply no question of contingency for immaterial beings. The only causality of which we may speak is that which explains the phenomenon of change and movement.[209] In such a world to ask what causes a thing *to be* is an irrelevant question which would not even have been raised but for the fact that the Bible has a particular conception of creation, and this un-Hellenistic manner of thought alters the very structure of metaphysics. The problem is thus created by revelation, and for

[208] An introductory survey of Arabic and Jewish speculation on this point, of interest from many points of view, is given in Rougier, *La scolastique*, p. 297–371. On Arabic philosophy see also Roland-Gosselin, *Le 'De ente et essentia'*, p. 150–159. A comparative discussion of passages from Arabic philosophers and Thomas is found in A. Forest, *La structure métaphysique du concret selon saint Thomas d'Aquin* (*EPM* 14), Paris 1931, p. 139–165 and Gilson, *L'être et l'essence*, p. 62–77.

[209] Cf. Gilson, *Spirit*, ch. IV, 'Beings and their contingence', p. 66–83. On the problem of contingence in Aristotle see also Roland-Gosselin, Le '*De ente et essentia*', p. 140f.

Thomas—we do not have opportunity to consider here any earlier discussion of the question—the answer is provided by the 'real distinction' between *esse* and *essentia*. We also find in Thomas a radical contingency that is quite foreign to Greek thought. No thing exists of itself, no thing, no being, not even pure forms are self-existent, but are all at every moment dependent on the fact that their existence is given to them by God, who alone *is* his *esse*. That is to say, a real distinction is to be made between the act by which a thing exists—between that upon which it depends for what it is and for what it has—and its *essentia*, since its *esse* is *ab alio*, and at the beck of the Creator may at any moment cease to be.[210] It might even be said that the biblical concept of God's dealings with creation and salvation as a free gift requires this more profound metaphysical interpretation in order to be expressed with clarity within the scope of Thomas's thought. Only a God who as *ipsum esse* is absolutely transcendent and independent of the world can give in pure *liberalitas*, since by his giving he does not gain any benefit for himself, and the absolute dependence of the creature conveys the truth that all things come from God. However far this abstraction may be from the concrete world of the biblical narrative, Thomas's metaphysics of existence is thus an attempt to express the immediate relationship between God and the creature which is communicated by revelation. The point at issue is not whether Thomas adequately translated the biblical concept but simply that we cannot comprehend this general conception, which is fundamental to Thomas's synthesis, without seeing it in its relationship to the problem of reason and revelation.[211] It is in this context that the real distinction between *esse* and *essentia* performs its function.[212] A clear indication of the fact that Thomas

[210] Gilson, *L'être et l'essence*, p. 94: 'l'existence reste dans l'être créé comme une donation perpétuellement révocable au gré du donateur. De quelque manière qu'on se représente la distinction thomiste d'essence et d'existence, c'est là le fait qu'elle a pour objet de formuler. L'existence peut bien être *dans* l'essence . . . mais elle n'est jamais *de* l'essence'.

[211] de Finance, *Être et agir*, p. 352: 'Le créationnisme chrétien a pour corrélatif une valorisation nouvelle de *l'existence*. Et c'est sous cet aspect formel qu'il convient, pensons-nous, de l'envisager, pour déterminer quelle est exactement, dans la pure ligne de l'aristotélisme, l'innovation de saint Thomas. Car cette innovation consiste, à notre avis, en ce que, pour le thomisme, l'actualité suprême, la perfection des perfections, n'est plus située dans la forme, mais dans l'acte d'exister.

[212] Cf. Forest, *La structure*, p. 162: 'D'une façon générale la distinction d'essence et d'existence est en rapport avec la doctrine de la création'. We cannot here discuss the philosophical difficulties which are raised by the real distinction between essence and existence, see e.g. Rougier, *La scolastique*, p. 520ff., 563ff. The question

himself took this position can be seen in the *Summa contra gentiles* where he explicitly states that the basic presupposition of the real distinction, namely the identity of essence and existence in God, is something revealed by God himself: *Dei igitur essentia est suum esse. Hanc autem sublimem veritatem Moyses a Domino est edoctus: qui cum quaereret a Domino, Exod. III, dicens: Si dixerint ad me filii Israel, Quod nomen eius? quid dicam eis? Dominus respondit: ego sum qui sum. Sic dices filiis Israel: Qui est misit me ad vos, ostendens suum proprium nomen esse QUI EST . . . Unde relinquitur quod ipsum divinum esse est sua essentia vel natura* (His essence is, therefore, his being. This sublime truth Moses was taught by the Lord. When Moses asked the Lord: 'If the children of Israel say to me: what is his name? What shall I say to them?' The Lord replied: 'I am who I am . . . Thou shalt say to the children of Israel: HE WHO IS hath sent me to you' (Exod. 3:13, 14) . . . It remains, then, that the divine being is God's essence or nature').[213]

In this passage revelation appears as a factor which carries certain ideas in Greek philosophy (e.g. the distinction between act and potency) far beyond the inherent possibilities of Greek metaphysics. The biblical idea of creation implies a radical reorientation in metaphysics, but this does not mean that metaphysics thereby ceases to be metaphysics.[214] The primary modes of thought come from Greek philosophy, and though new formulations may in fact really be new when compared with earlier thought, they do not abrogate existing categories but rather bring existing lines of thought to completion. We

remains, however, whether, when Meyer, *Thomas von Aquin*, defines the real distinction, e.g. on p. 115, as 'widersinnig', this judgment is dependent on the fact that he regards Thomas's world of thought as 'pure' philosophy, abstracted from the revelation which it seeks to express in its own way. If we adopt such a position, which has no basis on anything Thomas actually says, we deprive ourselves altogether of the possibility of understanding what Thomas really means.

[213] *CG* I, 22; cf. *CG* II, 52; 1a, 13, 11 and 2a2ae, 174, 6.
[214] It is therefore quite misleading when Gilson, *Spirit*, speaks on p. 433, note 9, of 'a metaphysic of Exodus', or on p. 51, footnote 1 of the second French edition, *L'esprit de la philosophie médiévale* (*EPM* 33), 2nd ed., Paris 1948, refers to 'le primat . . . de l'être tel que l'enseigne la Bible'. See the critical views expressed in A.-M. Dubarle, 'La signification du nom de JHWH', in *RSPT* 35 (1951), p. 3–21. Even if biblical statements provide the occasion of and are taken as the starting-point of a new metaphysical orientation, this does not in any way mean that the idea of God which is thereby expressed corresponds to what the Old Testament says about God. Gilson does not in fact at any point deal with the all-important question of the nature of the concept of God in the comparison which he makes on p. 40–63 of *Spirit* between Greek philosophy and the Christian concept of God.

see from this that even Thomas's 'natural theology' raises the problem with which he constantly deals and which he expresses in the phrase, *gratia non tollit naturam, sed perficit* (grace does not scrap nature but brings it to perfection).[215] Theology is given a positive significance in relation to philosophy, since its correction of philosophical speculation implies for philosophy a perfection in the sense that human thought now achieves the result which would never have been attained apart from revelation.[216]

We shall, however, get a full picture both of Thomas's conception of the relation between God and the world and also of the logical connection between *ratio* and *revelatio* only by discussing his *doctrine of the Trinity*,[217] The explanation of this is, first, that Thomas's whole thought is much more strongly determined by the doctrine of the Trinity than earlier commentators have indicated, and, secondly, that Thomas himself repeatedly cites the Trinity as a particular example of a knowledge of God which only revelation could give.[218] We now move, therefore, into the sphere of theology proper, in which, according to Thomas, we deal with a truth which far transcends the natural powers of reason.

When we turn to Thomas's discussion of the doctrine of the Trinity in the first part of the *Summa theologiae*, we find first of all that, following Aristotle, Thomas makes a distinction between two types of acts, the immanent which remain in the acting subject, and the transcendent, which pass into an effect outside the subject itself. Transcendent acts constitute a causal relationship, whereas immanent acts, such as knowing (*intelligere*) and willing (*velle*), do not.[219] As Thomas attempts to show, heresies have arisen in the history of the doctrine of the Trinity simply because the theologians have failed to observe this distinction when interpreting passages in scripture which

---

[215] 1a, 1, 8, ad 2.

[216] It is this basically Thomistic view of the relation between theology and philosophy as a positive relationship so far as philosophy is concerned which lies behind Gilson's vigorous advocacy of a 'Christian philosophy'; see especially *Spirit*, p. 414–426 and his detailed discussion of the problem.

[217] We do not propose to offer any exhaustive list of references at this point; our purpose is simply to draw attention to certain aspects of Thomas's interpretation of the meaning of the Trinity in reference to citations already given. See further the summary and outline given in Dondaine, *La Trinité*, vol. I, 1943, and vol. II, 1950.

[218] See e.g. *Compend. Theol.* 36; *CG* IV, 1; 1a, 12, 13, ad 1; 1a, 32, 1; 2a2ae, 171, 3; 2a2ae, 174, 6.

[219] 1a, 27, 1; cf. 1a, 18, 3, ad 1: *sicut dicitur in IX Metaphys., duplex est actio: una, quae transit in exteriorem materiam, ut calefacere et secare; alia, quae manet in agente, ut intelligere, sentire et velle*, see also 1a, 14, introd. and 1a, 54, 2.

speak of *processiones* within the divine nature (e.g. John 8:42, 15:26) and have begun instead with the causal relationship. For Arius the Son is a created *effectus* of the divine cause—which means that the unity of the divine nature is destroyed—while for Sabellius a new effect extraneous to the divine cause means that it is possible to speak of God the Father also as *Filius*—and this means that any real distinction between the persons disappears. Arius and Sabellius both begin with the transcendent causal relationship, *uterque accepit processionem secundum quod est ad aliquid extra* (both took procession to be going forth to something outside).[220] But this prevents them from saying anything about what happens *within* God, for causality always implies a *diversitas*—an effect is always different from its cause.[221] Thus the relationship of cause and effect, by which the relationship of God to the world is defined, does not apply within the godhead itself. The only analogy therefore left to use is the second type of acts referred to in Aristotle's distinction as immanent acts, *in divinis non est processio nisi secundum actionem quae non tendit in aliquid extrinsecum, sed manet in ipso agente* (in God procession corresponds only to an action which remains within the agent himself, not to one bent on something external).[222]

In seeking to explain what the Bible means when it speaks about the procession of the Son and the Spirit from the Father, Thomas conforms to the established procedure of the western theological tradition since Augustine by employing a psychological analogy. In man, as in every intellectual nature, there is not only an *actio intellectus* (action of the intellect) but also an *actio voluntatis* (action of the will).[223] But according to scripture God also has knowledge and will,[224] as rational thought can also demonstrate. It follows from

---

[220] 1a, 27, 1: *divina Scriptura, in rebus divinis, nominibus ad processionem pertinentibus utitur. Hanc autem processionem diversi diversimode acceperunt. Quidam enim acceperunt hanc processionem secundum quod effectus procedit a causa. Et sic accepit Arius, dicens Filium procedere a Patre sicut primam eius creaturam. . . Alii vero hanc processionem acceperunt secundum quod causa dicitur procedere in effectum, inquantum vel movet ipsum, vel similitudinem suam ipsi imprimit. Et sic accepit Sabellius, dicens ipsum Deum Patrem Filium dici, secundum quod carnem assumpsit a Virgine. . . Si quis autem diligenter consideret, uterque accepit processionem secundum quod est ad aliquid extra: unde neuter posuit processionem in ipso Deo.*
[221] 1a, 27, 1, ad 2: *id quod procedit secundum processionem quae est ad extra, oportet esse diversum ab eo a quo procedit;* 1a, 33, 1, ad 1: *hoc nomen 'causa' videtur importare diversitatem substantiae.*
[222] 1a, 27, 3.   [223] 1a, 27, 3; 1a, 27, 5.
[224] 1a, 14, 1, sed contra (Rom. 11:33); 1a, 19, 1, sed contra (Rom. 12:2); see also the full biblical documentation in *CG* IV, 2, 3, 15 and 17.

the affirmation that God is *actus purus* that he must also possess an *intelligere*, for as Aristotle teaches the capacity to know is related to the degree of actuality: *secundum modum immaterialitatis est modus cognitionis* (the capacity to know is in proportion to the degree of freedom from matter).[225] Where there is an intellect there must also be a will which wills the good that is conceived by the intellect, and so there must also be a *voluntas* within the divine nature: *in quolibet habente intellectum, est voluntas . . . Et sic oportet in Deo esse voluntatem, cum sit in eo intellectus* (anything with a mind has a will . . . Consequently, there must be a will in God because he has a mind).[226] But to say this also means that there is love in God, for *amor naturaliter est primus actus voluntatis* (love of its nature starts all activity of will).[227]

Thomas finds confirmation of this psychological analogy in the fact that revelation speaks of the second person of the godhead as *Verbum Dei*, John 1:1ff. As we can establish in the human act of cognition, a concept of the object of knowledge is formed by the *actio* of the intellect, and this concept, *conceptio* or *verbum cordis* remains in the knowing subject as an image of the known object. This intrinsic image may thus in turn be expressed extrinsically in the spoken word, *verbum vocis*. Thomas holds that we are to interpret the term *Verbum Dei* as analogous to this human *verbum cordis* or *verbum mentis*.[228] To say that God has knowledge of himself means that there is a procession of a 'Word' in the divine nature, and this is the meaning of the trinitarian term, *generatio*.[229] It is the nature of the cognitive act to produce something that resembles the object of knowledge. In this particular case we are dealing with the highest

[225] 1a, 14, 1; 1a, 14, 3: *Tanta est autem virtus Dei in cognoscendo, quanta est actualitas eius in existendo: quia per hoc quod actu est, et ab omni materia et potentia separatus, Deus cognoscitivus est;* see also *CG* I, 44 and IV, 11.

[226] 1a, 19, 1; see also *CG* I, 72 and 73, IV, 19: *in omni natura intellectuali est voluntas; Deus autem intelligens est, ut in Primo ostensum est: oportet quod in ipso sit voluntas.*

[227] 1a, 20, 1; see also *CG* I, 91; IV, 19: *amare autem quoddam velle est.*

[228] 1a, 27, 1: *Quicumque enim intelligit, ex hoc ipso quod intelligit, procedit aliquid intra ipsum, quod est conceptio rei intellectae, ex vi intellectiva proveniens, et ex eius notitia procedens. Quam quidem conceptionem vox significat: et dicitur verbum cordis, significatum verbo vocis.* 1a, 34, 1: *Dicitur autem proprie verbum in Deo, secundum quod verbum significat conceptum intellectus.* The fullest analysis of the concept 'word' is to be found in *CG* IV, 11 and *In Joan.* 1, 1 (1).

[229] 1a, 27, 2: *processio verbi in divinis dicitur generatio, et ipsum verbum procedens dicitur Filius. In Joan.* 1, 1 (1): *Patet etiam quod, cum in qualibet natura illud quod procedit, habens similitudinem naturae eius a quo procedit, vocetur filius; et hoc Verbum procedat in similitudine et identitate naturae ejus a quo procedit; convenienter et proprie dicitur Filius; et productio ejus dicitur generatio.*

possible form of identity, since both the knowing subject, who is the *origo* of the procession, and the 'Word' which proceeds from the knowing subject, both have the same divine nature. Thus even the biblical affirmation that the Son is the image of the Father is to be understood in terms of this psychological analogy, according to which *conceptio intellectus est similitudo rei intellectae* (what the intellect conceives is the likeness of what is understood),[230] for *omne generans generat sibi simile* (every begetter produces its own like).[231] A typical example of this use of a psychological analogy to explain the doctrine of the Trinity is to be seen in the part of the *Summa* where Thomas refers explicitly to the second person of the godhead. The section is admittedly headed *De persona Filii*, but in fact it consists entirely of an analysis of the term *Verbum*.[232]

Since the *intelligere* of Aristotelian psychology provides a starting-point for understanding the procession of the second person of the godhead from the Father, it is quite natural that *velle* should help to explain the procession of the Holy Spirit. For this there is no biblical basis, as there is in the case of the *Verbum*, but this does not seem to have disturbed Thomas.[233] The procession of the third person of the godhead is undoubtedly to be defined as an *actio voluntatis* (action of the will), or, more accurately, a *processio amoris* (procession of love).[234] When he begins to explain the meaning of this love more

---

[230] 1a, 27, 2; see also 1a, 35, 1–2. *CG* IV, 11: *Verbum autem interius conceptum est quaedam ratio et similitudo rei intellectae.*

[231] 1a, 27, 4.   [232] 1a, 34, 1–3.

[233] In 1a, 37, 1, where Thomas answers the question *Utrum Amor sit proprium nomen Spiritus Sancti* in the affirmative, no objection of this kind is raised amongst the *obiectiones* offered. Nor do we find in Thomas the explanation which Augustine offers, that the idea is not found in scripture for pedagogical reasons (*De Trinitate*, 15: 17, 27 [*MPL* 42, 1080]: *Ut autem nos exerceret sermo divinus . . . majore studio fecit inquiri*). Having listed at length biblical passages which refer to the Spirit in *CG* IV, 18, Thomas then goes on immediately in ch. 19 to deal with *voluntas* and *Amor*, when he considers *qualiter huiusmodi veritas utcumque accipi debeat, ut ab impugnationibus infidelium defendatur*. Cf. Dondaine, *La Trinité*, vol. II, p. 331.

[234] 1a, 27, 3: *praeter processionem verbi, ponitur alia processio in divinis, quae est processio amoris;* 1a, 45, 7: *Processiones autem divinarum Personarum attenduntur secundum actus intellectus et voluntatis, sicut supra dictum est: nam Filius procedit ut Verbum intellectus, Spiritus Sanctus ut Amor voluntatis.* This psychological analogy makes it not simply possible but absolutely necessary to maintain the *filioque* of the Western tradition, for a *processio amoris* of necessity presupposes a *processio verbi*. There can be no object of love unless as the ground of the act of love there exists in the intellect a concept of the thing that is loved: *de ratione amoris est quod non procedat nisi a conceptione intellectus*, 1a, 27, 3, ad 3; cf. 1a, 36, 2: *Filius procedit per modum intellectus, ut verbum; Spiritus Sanctus autem per modum voluntatis, ut amor. Necesse est autem quod amor a verbo procedat: non enim aliquid*

fully, however, Thomas, as we would expect, moves away from the main tradition of psychological trinitarian teaching, which had begun with Augustine and was most notably represented in scholasticism by Richard of St. Victor.[235] The Spirit is defined in this tradition as the mutual love of Father and Son.[236] For Thomas, who takes Aristotelian psychology as his point of departure, the emphasis lies not so much on the act of love itself as on the object of this love, and therefore he comes to stress the idea—which also goes back to Augustine—of the Spirit as God's self-love.[237] He regards love as the primary function of the will, an *actio* directed towards the perfection which constitutes its *finis—necesse est quod Deus primo et principaliter suam bonitatem et seipsum amet* (necessarily it is first and principally his goodness and himself that God loves).[238] Thomas does indeed discuss the concept of mutual love, but when he tries to define the nature of the procession of the third person, his primary starting-point is the idea of God's love for his own goodness and perfection.[239] As *ipsum esse* God is from all eternity, but as such he is also from all eternity Father, the *origo*[240] from whom the Son and the Spirit proceed. The Son thus proceeds from the Father as the act through which God has perfect knowledge of his being from all eternity, and the third person of the godhead is the eternal act of love with which God loves himself from all eternity.[241] It is characteristic of Thomas

amamus, nisi secundum quod conceptione mentis apprehendimus. Unde et secundum hoc manifestum est quod Spiritus Sanctus procedit a Filio.

---

[235] See Dondaine, *La Trinité*, vol. II, p. 393ff. The difference between Thomas and Richard has been discussed with some passion by M. T.-L. Penido 'Gloses sur la procession d'amour dans la Trinité' in *ETL* 14 (1937), p. 33–68: see also the same author's article, 'A propos de la procession d'amour en Dieu', in *ETL* 15 (1938), p. 338–344.
[236] Cf. Nygren, *Agape and Eros*, p. 653.
[237] Penido, *ETL* 14 (1937) p. 48ff.; Nygren, *Agape and Eros*, p. 653f.
[238] *CG* IV, 19.
[239] Dondaine, *La Trinité*, vol. II, p. 397f.: 'saint Thomas relègue au second plan l'amour mutuel: il n'a pas été invoqué pour introduire la seconde procession, en la question 27; dans notre question 37, il est rappelé comme une donnée traditionnelle dont la théorie doit rendre compte'; p. 400f.: 'le Saint-Esprit est l'Amour que Dieu porte à sa Bonté . . . il convient de prendre pour image créée du Saint-Esprit non point de prime abord l'amitié qui unit deux personnes, mais plutôt l'amour qu'un être spirituel a pour soi-même'. In the analysis of Thomas's doctrine of the Trinity in Diekamp, *Dogmatik*, vol. I, p. 335ff., we find no trace of this important line of thought which we find in Thomas, but the idea rather of 'die gegenseitige Liebe des Vaters und des Sohnes'.   [240] Cf. 1a, 33, 1, ad 1.
[241] 1a, 27, 5, ad 2: *processiones . . . verbi et amoris, secundum quod Deus suam essentiam, veritatem et bonitatem intelligit et amat;* 1a, 37, 2, ad 3: *ita diligit (Pater)*

in this context that he defines the meaning of divine beatitude *before* he turns to the doctrine of the Trinity. God's beatitude is not a blessed communion of the persons of the Trinity—it is his knowledge and love of his own perfection.[242]

The idea of these two 'processions', *secundum actionem intellectus* and *secundum actionem voluntatis,* also provides a basis for the doctrine of relationship from which Thomas goes on to discuss the concept of personality in the Trinity.[243] Since both the *procedens* and *id a quo procedit* in this case belong to the same nature, the only way by which we can conceive a distinction to exist between them is to assume the mutual relationships which inhere in the *actiones* of the intellect and will within the divine being.[244] As we noted earlier,[245] Thomas makes a distinction in his doctrine of relations between real relations which belong to the nature of a thing and *relationes rationis tantum* (logical relations only), which have no real counterpart in the nature which is said to be related to something else. Since God and the world are not complementary parts of the same total *ordo,* there can be no real relation to creation in the divine being. The relations which exist, however, between the persons of the godhead must be considered real, for both 'processions' by which they are what they are take place within the same nature.[246] But to the extent that we are dealing with a real relation, we may also speak of it as *quaedam*

se et omnem creaturam Spiritu Sancto, inquantum Spiritus Sanctus procedit ut amor bonitatis primae, secundum quam Pater amat se et omnem creaturam; 1a, 93, 8: *Verbum autem Dei nascitur de Deo secundum notitiam sui ipsius, et Amor procedit a Deo secundum quod seipsum amat. CG IV, 20: Spiritus Sanctus procedit per modum amoris quo Deus amat seipsum;* see also *CG* IV, 23 and *De Pot.* 10, 2, ad 6.

---

[242] 1a, 26, 1: *Nihil enim aliud sub nomine beatitudinis intelligitur, nisi bonum perfectum intellectualis naturae; cuius est suam sufficientiam cognoscere in bono quod habet.* . . . *Utrumque autem istorum excellentissime Deo convenit, scilicet perfectum esse, et intelligentem. Unde beatitudo maxime convenit Deo.* This *quaestio* on the divine blessedness comes immediately before the extended discussion of the doctrine of the Trinity in q. 27–43.

[243] On the question of relationships in Thomas's doctrine of the Trinity, see Dondaine, *La Trinité,* vol. I, p. 232ff. and especially Krempel, *La doctrine de la relation,* p. 537ff.

[244] 1a, 34, 3, ad 2: *relationes consequantur actiones;* 1a, 28, 4: *relationes reales in Deo non possunt accipi, nisi secundum actiones secundum quas est processio in Deo, non extra, sed intra;* 1a, 29, 4: *Distinctio autem in divinis non fit nisi per relationes originis.*   [245] See p. 113 above.

[246] 1a, 28, 1: *Cum autem aliquid procedit a principio eiusdem naturae, necesse est quod ambo, scilicet procedens et id a quo procedit, in eodem ordine conveniant: et sic oportet quod habeant reales respectus ad invicem. Cum igitur processiones in divinis sint in identitate naturae, ut ostensum est, necesse est quod relationes quae secundum processiones divinas accipiuntur sint relationes reales.* We should note

res, i.e. we may conceive it to have independent subsistence.[247] Hence the relation may be what constitutes the distinction between the persons of the godhead and therefore these persons themselves. The relationships which are found within the godhead—*paternitas, filiatio*, and *processio*—fulfil all the requirements which must be met to enable us to speak of persons in accordance with the ancient definition derived from Boethius and held by scholastic theologians: *persona est rationalis naturae individua substantia* (person is an individual substance of a rational nature).[248] All of them are to be found in a *natura rationalis*, and they are also *incommunicabiles*, in that none of them can be applied to any of the others and therefore they connote something individual and peculiar to each; such a relationship, furthermore, has an immediate subsistence, since essence and existence constitute a unity in God.[249] Thus, for example, *paternitas* constitutes the first person in distinction from the others, while *filiatio*, as a relationship existing within the godhead is another expression for *Filius Dei*.[250]

that it is only *actiones* which can give rise to real relations. Static relations between the persons, e.g. their *aequalitas*, have no real counterpart in the divine essence: 1a, 28, 4, ad 4: *aequalitas et similitudo in Deo non sunt relationes reales, sed rationis tantum.*

---

[247] 1a, 28, 3: *Relativa autem oppositio in sui ratione includit distinctionem. Unde oportet quod in Deo sit realis distinctio, non quidem secundum rem absolutam, quae est essentia, in qua est summa unitas et simplicitas; sed secundum rem relativam;* 1a, 40, 1: *relatio . . . est quaedam res in divinis.*

[248] 1a, 29, 1, introd. On Thomas's concept of person see Dondaine, *La Trinité*, vol. I, p. 237ff.

[249] 1a, 29, 3, ad 4: *Deus potest dici 'rationalis naturae', secundum quod ratio non importat discursum, sed communiter intellectualem naturam. 'Individuum' autem Deo competere non potest quantum ad hoc quod individuationis principium est materia: sed solum secundum quod importat incommunicabilitatem. 'Substantia' vero convenit Deo, secundum quod significat existere per se.*

[250] 1a, 29, 4: *Persona igitur, in quacumque natura, significat id quod est distinctum in natura illa. . . Distinctio autem in divinis non fit nisi per relationes originis. . . Relatio autem in divinis non est sicut accidens inhaerens subiecto, sed est ipsa divina essentia: unde est subsistens, sicut essentia divina subsistit. Sicut ergo deitas est Deus, ita paternitas divina est Deus Pater, qui est persona divina. Persona igitur divina significat relationem ut subsistentem;* 1a, 30, 1: *hoc nomen 'persona' significat in divinis relationem, ut rem subsistentem in natura divina;* 1a, 30, 2, ad 1: *Sed hae tres relationes, paternitas, filiatio et processio, dicuntur 'proprietates personales', quasi personas constituentes: nam paternitas est persona Patris, filiatio persona Filii, processio persona Spiritus Sancti procedentis.* See also P. Vanier, 'La relation trinitaire dans la Somme théologique de saint Thomas d'Aquin', in *Sciences ecclésiastiques* (=*SE*) 1 (1948), p. 153ff. and the same author's *Théologie trinitaire chez saint Thomas d'Aquin. Évolution du concept d'action notionelle* (Université de Montréal. Publications de l'institut d'études médiévales 13), Montreal and Paris 1953, p. 67ff.

In Thomas's view the doctrine of the Trinity cannot be separated from the relationship between God and the world—thus in the *Summa theologiae* the trinitarian section of 1a, 27–43 comes right before his discussion of the procession of created things from the first cause in 1a, 44–47. Since the ultimate cause of creation is the triune God and *omnis effectus aliqualiter repraesentat suam causam* (any effect some-how copies its cause), it is possible to find in everything that is created a *repraesentatio Trinitatis*.[251] The common essence of the three persons of the godhead is *ipsum esse*, the act of existence, and when a thing is brought into existence, a likeness to the divine cause is given with its very *esse*.[252] But the resemblance does not end here, for with its existence the nature of the thing is given a structural likeness to its first cause. As an existing thing, *id quod est*, its *subsistence*, which is the presupposition of its own development, constitutes a likeness to the first person of the godhead, who is the *causa et principium* of all things. Within the divine being the Father is the *principium* or *origo* of the 'processions' of the other persons. Again, the *form* of the thing, *id quo est*, that which makes up its nature and distinctiveness, consti-tutes a likeness to the *Verbum* of the divine being, *secundum quod forma artificiati est ex conceptione artificis* (as the form of a work of handicraft derives from the conception of the craftsman). Lastly, the *ordo* of a thing, the movement towards a particular end innate in its nature, is to be attributed to the divine *Amor*, the love of God, be-cause *ordo effectus ad aliquid alterum est ex voluntate creantis*. Thus from our revealed knowledge of God we can find in all created things a distant resemblance to the trinitarian nature of the Creator.[253] In addition to these *vestigia Trinitatis*, however, there is a more pro-found and more perfect resemblance to the triune God in rational beings in creation, and this allows us to speak of them as having an *imago Trinitatis*. This image of the divine nature consists in their being endowed with reason and will and in having, like God though only in an analogous sense, *verbum conceptum et amor procedens* (the word conceived and the love proceeding).[254]

---

[251] 1a, 45, 7.

[252] 1a, 45, 6: *creare est proprie causare sive producere esse rerum. Cum autem omne agens agat sibi simile, principium actionis considerari potest ex actionis effectu: ignis enim est qui generat ignem. Et ideo creare convenit Deo secundum suum esse: quod est eius essentia, quae est communis tribus Personis.*

[253] See I *Sent.* 3, 2, 1–3; *CG* IV, 26; 1a, 45, 7; 1a, 93, 6.

[254] 1a, 45, 7: *Processiones autem divinarum Personarum attenduntur secundum actus intellectus et voluntatis ... nam Filius procedit ut Verbum intellectus, Spiritus Sanctus*

L

Thus there is a structural resemblance—a resemblance grounded on the concept of cause—between what is and is done in the created world and what takes place in God himself. All that is brought into being *ad extra* bears varying degrees of resemblance to what takes place *ad intra* in the divine being. As we shall have occasion to see in what follows, this is a central theme in the theology of Thomas. This causal relationship, however, has not been given by necessity. We have seen earlier that God by necessity can will only himself, which means that the existence of creation is radically contingent in regard to God.[255] It is precisely our revealed knowledge of the Trinity, Thomas argues, that keeps us from falling into the error of emanationist views. Because there is in God a *Verbum* by which he has knowledge of his own perfection from all eternity, and also an *Amor* with which he loves and wills himself from all eternity, clearly nothing else is necessary to express his perfect being.[256] The divine Word and the divine Love eternally proceed in God *ad intra*—it is here in God that the natural necessity rules which Avicenna held should also apply to the effects *ad extra* of the divine causality. According to Thomas, the natural necessity which is expressed in the idea of emanation applies *within* the Trinity, and only there. But this limitation to the immanent acts of God is consequent on the fact that in and with these acts the circle has already been closed, and therefore unlike ourselves God has no need of anything outside himself in order to attain perfection.[257] In Thomas's view the sovereign freedom of the Creator's act presupposes God's perfect life within the Trinity.[258]

ut Amor voluntatis. In creaturis igitur rationalibus, in quibus est intellectus et voluntas, invenitur repraesentatio Trinitatis per modum imaginis, inquantum invenitur in eis verbum conceptum et amor procedens; see also *De Ver.* 10, 7; *De Pot.* 10, 1, ad 5; *CG* IV, 26; 1a, 93, 6 and 8.

[255] See p. 140 above.

[256] 1a, 32, 1, ad 3: *cognitio divinarum Personarum fuit necessaria nobis . . . ad recte sentiendum de creatione rerum. Per hoc enim quod dicimus Deum omnia fecisse Verbo suo, excluditur error ponentium Deum produxisse res ex necessitate naturae. Per hoc autem quod ponimus in eo processionem amoris, ostenditur quod Deus non propter aliquam indigentiam creaturas produxit, neque propter aliquam aliam causam extrinsecam; sed propter amorem suae bonitatis.*

[257] Cf. *De Pot.* 9, 9: *Est ergo tam in nobis quam in Deo circulatio quaedam in operibus intellectus et voluntatis: nam voluntas redit in id a quo fuit principium intelligendi: sed in nobis concluditur circulus ad id quod est extra, dum bonum exterius movet intellectum nostrum, et intellectus movet voluntatem, et voluntas tendit per appetitum et amorem in exterius bonum; sed in Deo iste circulus clauditur in seipso.*

[258] This is the viewpoint which is maintained in particular by Garrigou-Lagrange, *God*, vol. II, p. 169ff. He does not appear to have noted, however, that Thomas nowhere takes the axiom *bonum est diffusivum sui* as the basis and starting-point of

Furthermore, the Trinity is not only essential for a true under-standing of creation, but indispensable also *et principalius* for an understanding of the redemption which is wrought through the in-carnation of the Son and the gift of the Spirit.[259]

How, then, does the relationship between *ratio* and *revelatio* appear at this central point in his theology? A knowledge of the Trinity is given only by revelation.[260] Philosophy can do no more than teach us that God is one and the cause of all existence, but unaided reason has no conception at all of God as three in one. But once this truth has been revealed and faith illuminated by reason, a whole new field of activity is opened up for reason, since it has the function now of interpreting the inner meaning of the truth that has been disclosed. This truth cannot be proved, but it can be shown to be deserving of credence, since all it does is to provide further clarification and confirmation of what philosophy already teaches us concerning the causal relationship between God and the world. To use Thomas's own terminology, revelation does not give us a *probatio* but a *manifestatio*, by means of which a hypothesis unprovable in itself can be shown to be deserving of belief through its correspondence with already known facts.[261] Reason can thus defend truth against unbelievers and demonstrate that *non esse impossibile quod praedicat fides* (what faith upholds is not impossible).[262]

his interpretation of the Trinity, in part because for Thomas *esse* and not *bonum* has metaphysical priority. Cf. Peghaire, *RUO*, Section spéciale, 1932, p. 25, de Finance, *Être et agir*, p. 74ff, and p. 136 above, footnote 199.

[259] 1a, 32, 1, ad 3: *cognitio divinarum Personarum fuit necessaria nobis . . . et principalius, ad recte sentiendum de salute generis humani, quae perficitur per Filium incarnatum, et per donum Spiritus Sancti.*

[260] 1a, 32, 1: *impossibile est per rationem naturalem ad cognitionem Trinitatis divinarum Personarum pervenire.*

[261] 1a, 32, 1, ad 2: *ad aliquam rem dupliciter inducitur ratio. Uno modo, ad probandum sufficienter aliquam radicem: sicut in scientia naturali inducitur ratio sufficiens ad probandum quod motus caeli semper sit uniformis velocitas. Alio modo inducitur ratio, non quae sufficienter probet radicem, sed quae radici iam positae ostendat congruere consequentes effectus: sicut in astrologia ponitur ratio excentricorum et epicyclorum ex hoc quod, hac positione facta, possunt salvari apparentia sensibilia circa motus caelestes. . . Primo ergo modo potest induci ratio ad probandum Deum esse unum, et similia. Sed secundo modo se habet ratio quae inducitur ad manifesta-tionem Trinitatis: quia scilicet, Trinitate posita, congruunt huiusmodi rationes; non tamen ita quod per has rationes sufficienter probetur Trinitas Personarum.*

[262] 1a, 32, 1. Thus the doctrine of relation makes it possible for Thomas to interpret the Trinity without ending up in contradictory statements—the one God *is* three with respect to mutually distinct relations within the godhead and therefore three persons. Cf. Krempel, *La doctrine de la relation*, p. 93: 'En Dieu seul la relation . . . nous permet d'écarter toute contradiction du mystère de la Trinité'.

We must realise, however, in this connection that the psychological analogy is not primary in the sense that it gives Thomas a starting-point from which he can come through rational demonstration to the Trinity. It is simply an *a posteriori* construction, subsequent to revelation. Furthermore, it is merely an analogy, and cannot therefore give us any clear knowledge of God's being.[263] Even though there is a resemblance between the creature and God—and this is implicit in the causal relationship itself, for *omne agens agit sibi simile*—and even though this resemblance increases the higher we go in the hierarchy of existence, we cannot reverse the statement and say that God is also like the creature: *licet aliquo modo concedatur quod creatura sit similis Deo, nullo tamen modo concedendum est quod Deus sit similis creaturae* (although we may admit is a way that creatures resemble God, we may in no way admit that God resembles creatures).[264] That is to say, divine transcendence does not ultimately mean only that God is more perfect than man in every way. If it were simply a question of a difference of degree increased by the distance between them, we could freely speak of a resemblance between God and the creature, though it would be a distant and gradually decreasing resemblance. But for Thomas the distinction between God and the varying degrees of perfection in the hierarchically ordered world is neither the difference of degree which can be found among different individuals of the same species, nor that which exists among different species: the distinction goes much deeper, for God is *omnino existens extra genus* (in no way at all does God belong to a genus).[265] There is an unbridgeable gulf between God and creation, between *ipsum esse per se subsistens* and *esse receptum*, and this is brought out also in what Thomas says concerning the nature of the statements that we make about God when we take creation as our starting-point. When we say that man is like God in that he is a creature possessing reason and will, we still have not explained what we mean by terms like 'reason', 'will' or

---

[263] Statements about a *repraesentatio Trinitatis* are expressly stated in *De Ver.* 10, 7 to be *secundum analogiam*.

[264] 1a, 4, 3, ad 4; cf. *CG* I, 29: *Non igitur Deus creaturae assimilatur, sed magis e converso.* Thomas's concept of God cannot therefore by any means be said to be an *imago hominis* writ large. On the question of an alleged anthropomorphism in Thomas's doctrine of the Trinity, see especially M. T.-L. Penido, *Le rôle de l'analogie en théologie dogmatique* (*BT* 15), Paris 1931, p. 258ff.

[265] *De Pot.* 7, 3, ad 3; cf. *De Pot.* 7, 3; *CG* I, 25; *Compend. Theol.* 12; 1a, 3, 5; 1a, 88, 2, ad 4.

'word' when these are applied to God.[266] What we mean by the term *intellectus* does not apply univocally to man and God,[267] and because of the limitations of our reason it is impossible for us to know what it means when what it describes is identical with *ipsum esse*.[268] But this is not to say that concepts which we borrow from the created world are merely symbols—they do really correspond to truth, they do not apply to God *pure aequivoce* but *analogice*, and so they are true, though inadequate, statements.[269] This means that despite their imperfection they can be used to explain the meaning of revealed truth. They do not contradict revelation, since both natural and supernatural knowledge come from the same God.[270]

Revelation is therefore primary in Thomas's doctrine of the Trinity, in the sense that only by revelation can we know that God in his being is three persons. Furthermore, this revelation specifically gives us a knowledge otherwise inaccessible to us of the deepest meaning of the natural world, since the light of revelation enables us to see that the created world reflects the divine Trinity. The revelation of the Trinity also discloses why the relationship between the creature

[266] On the crucial distinction between the human and the divine *verbum internum*, see the analyses in *In Joan.* 1, 1 (1–4) and *CG* IV, 11.

[267] 1a, 32, 1, ad 2: *Similitudo autem intellectus nostri non sufficienter probat aliquid de Deo, propter hoc quod intellectus non univoce invenitur in Deo et in nobis.*

[268] Cf. *In De div. nom.* prol.: *hoc ipsum quod Deus est, cum excedat omne illud quod a nobis apprehenditur, nobis remanet ignotum.* See also p. 137 above, footnote 203.

[269] It is striking that when Thomas speaks about the meaning of our analogical statements about God, he totally rejects the idea that they might apply *univoce*, indeed, he suggests the opposite by such terms as *non pure aequivoce* or *non omnino aequivoce*, cf. 1a, 13, 5: *Et hoc modo aliqua dicuntur de Deo et creaturis analogice, et non aequivoce pure, neque univoce.* In addition to this text see also *De Pot.* 7, 7 and *CG* I, 33. Analogy implies an affirmation, at the same time, of likeness and unlikeness, but it is clear that the accent here falls on unlikeness. Cf. Gilson, *Thomisme*, p. 152f.: 'Il ne semble pas avoir jamais dit que les noms que nous donnons à Dieu ne soient pas équivoques, mais seulement qu'ils ne sont pas purement équivoques. . . Cette manière de parler 'pas tout à fait équivoquement' de Dieu, c'est précisément ce que saint Thomas nomme l'analogie'. Thus in Thomas the analogy between God and the world is also ultimately an expression of God's inaccessible transcendence, but this important emphasis is often overlooked, especially in Protestant theology where it is usually held that analogy in Thomas is an expression of the continuity between God and the world and therefore a means of attaining positive knowledge about God. It is on the basis of such an interpretation that Karl Barth makes his well-known statement: 'I regard the *analogia entis* as the invention of Antichrist', *Church Dogmatics*, vol. I, *The Doctrine of the Word of God*, part I, p. X. The function of the doctrine of analogy, as Mascall has correctly noted in *Existence and Analogy*, p. 124, 'is not to furnish us with knowledge of God, but to explain how we come to have it'. On Thomas's concept of analogy and its antecedents, see particularly Lyttkens, *Analogy*, together with the literature cited on p. 486ff.

[270] See also in this connection p. 232f. below.

and the transcendent cause is wholly one of contingency. Here again we see that revelation also exercises a direct influence on that part of the Thomistic synthesis which is sometimes called, though the term is clearly inadequate, 'natural' theology. But at the same time the meaning of what has been revealed—and this applies not only to the knowledge principally within reach of human *ratio* but also to the knowledge of the Trinity—is further clarified from our knowledge of man's nature and the causal context of existence which we attain in a purely rational way by the exercise of reason. The 'new' that is given is coordinated with existing knowledge and interpreted in terms of this knowledge—and in this sense therefore it could be said that *ratio* is primary, even in regard to the doctrine of the Trinity.

This necessarily brief account of Thomas's view of the relation between God and the world may perhaps have shown that the relationship between *ratio* and *revelatio* within his thinking is more complicated than might be assumed at first glance. The two entities are quite clearly not related to each other in a simple complementary fashion, and we find rather a continual interaction between them throughout his whole theological work. On the one hand, we find that for Thomas revelation is of crucial significance even for the basic outlines of his metaphysics, which means that he defines the relationship between God and the world in a markedly different way from Greek philosophy. On the other hand, he defines the meaning of the knowledge given by revelation ultimately in terms of a rational knowledge that is independent of revelation. In this whole process two different worlds of thought confront us, since Thomas borrows terms from Greek thought in order to translate the biblical idea of the living God who is at work in his creation without ceasing to be its sovereign Lord.

One particular expression of this is that in Thomas's cosmology the basis of all creation is the free and unconditional will of the Creator. He sustains his creation in power by giving life and existence to all animate and inanimate beings in a continuing creative act. The nature of the relationship between God and the world is such that the world exists only by continually receiving from God. If this unilateral dependence were to cease even for a moment, the world would cease to be, for the relationship is one in which 'everything comes from God'. It has been held by some that Thomas's doctrine of creation would somehow obscure the central religious significance of the Christian doctrine of creation, viz. the idea of the sovereignty of God in relation to the creature[271] but the only possible answer to this is that nothing is affirmed by Thomas with greater frequency or conviction than the idea of God's absolute sovereignty and the equally radical contingency of creation. Nothing that Thomas says anywhere would permit us to state that in Thomas the line between God and the world is obliterated in the sense that as first cause God becomes 'a part of the world and man a piece of divine being',[272] for nothing is more strongly emphasised by Thomas himself than the insuperable line of separation between the absolutely transcendent God and the world. He is, indeed, the cause of our world, but he cannot be enclosed within its categories, since we can by no means conceive of him as forming 'part' of some other thing: *Deus non potest esse pars alicuius compositi* (God cannot be a component of anything).[273] Man is indeed stamped with the image of God, but he can never become a divine being, because of the absolute distinction between man and God, the distinction between *ipsum per se subsistens* and *esse receptum*. This uncompromising affirmation of God's sovereignty and transcendence undeniably expresses an essential aspect of the biblical concept of God. Another question which we cannot yet discuss more fully is whether this definition of divine transcendence is not such that it becomes impossible to express other parts of the biblical message which are equally indispensable. We have already sensed something of the nature of this problem in the difficulties which certain passages in the Bible present to Thomas, for instance, those which speak about the 'wrath' of God'[274]

Thomas was concerned to express the biblical concept of God, even if it meant having to use such apparently irresoluble terms as *immutabilis* or *actus purus* in order to describe his nature. The terms do not imply that God is to be conceived of as reposing in total inactivity; on the contrary, as *actus purus* he is wholly activity.[275]

---

[271] G. Aulén, 'Kristendom och idealism', in *Svensk teologisk kvartalskrift* (=*STK*) 8 (1932), p. 14.

[272] Aulén, *STK* 8 (1932), p. 14f.

[273] 1a, 3, 8; cf. p. 97 above.

[274] See p. 120 above.

[275] 1a, 25, 1: *Manifestum est enim quod unumquodque, secundum quod est actu et perfectum, secundum hoc est principium activum alicuius. . . Deus est purus actus, et simpliciter et universaliter perfectus . . . Unde sibi maxime competit esse principium activum;* cf. the definition of God in 1a, 9, 1 as *immutabilis*, because he is *primum ens* and thus *actus purus*. Cf. Garrigou-Lagrange, *God*, vol. II, p. 171: 'When we say that God is immutable, we do not mean that He is therefore inert. We affirm, on the contrary, that as He is plenitude of being or pure act, He is essentially activity itself and has no need of transition to act that He may act'.

It is significant that Thomas includes his discussion of the *vita Dei* in the section in which he deals with the *operationes Dei*.[276] The life of God is the supreme activity. And when we say that God is *ipsum esse*, this does not mean that he is a remote supreme Being, but rather the pure act of existence. Thomas's metaphysics of existence, which, as we saw in the previous section, distinguishes him from Greek philosophy, is in the last resort nothing more than an attempt to translate into the language of metaphysics the statements made in Hebrew thought about the living and active God.[277]

The world, as Thomas sees it, is not static but filled with movement, life, and force. And all that happens in the world is a direct expression of divine causality; nothing is done apart from God. Both the *esse* and the *operatio* of the things are given to them by God. Hence when Aulén says in his *Den kristna gudsbilden* that 'the typical medieval way of looking at things' sees God as 'enthroned in an infinite remoteness', this is an inadequate statement, at least as far as Thomas is concerned. It is equally untrue to say that the idea of God's presence and his direct action 'do not appear in any living form'.[278] Aulén's assertions are refuted by such an eminent scholar as Gilson, who has a profound acquaintance with Thomas's view of the world which he describes as 'a sacred world, impregnated in its innermost fibres with the presence of a God whose sovereign existence saves it for ever from nothingness.'[279] It is also refuted by a great many of Thomas's own statements in which he says that God *est in omnibus rebus . . . et intime* (exists and exists intimately in everything).[280] In Thomas's view God may indeed be inexorably transcendent in relation to the world, but this does not mean that he

---

[276] Cf. 1a, 14, introd. and 1a, 18, 1–4. 'Life' for Thomas is identical with personal activity, and the more perfect such activity is, i.e. the less dependent a nature is on an activity external to itself, the more perfect is its life. God, therefore, being independent of all determination, possesses *vitam perfectissimam et sempiternam*, 1a, 18, 3. See also M. Grabmann, *Die Idee des Lebens in der Theologie des hl. Thomas von Aquin*, Paderborn 1922.

[277] Cf. Mascall, *Existence and Analogy*, p. 52f.: 'St Thomas's uncompromisingly existential interpretation of the "sublime truth", as he calls it, that the most proper name of God is "He who is" . . . brings back into Christian thought a sense of the divine energy and activity which comes ultimately from the Hebraism of the Bible and which it cannot afford to ignore. I do not think that Luther was the first person to realise this'; see also p. 63.

[278] Aulén, *Gudsbilden*, p. 173; cf. R. Prenter, *Spiritus Creator*, Philadelphia 1953, p. 21: 'The scholastic system holds that God is the distant one'.

[279] Gilson, *Thomisme*, p. 147.

[280] 1a, 8, 1.

reigns far away from his creation. By the very fact of their existence things are brought into direct and intimate association with God who *immediate in omnibus agit* (acts in everything without intermediary).[281] This concept of God's presence as immediately active in all that exists and in all that is done in the created world is one of the central ideas of Thomas's theology.

In this preliminary section we have dealt with the dominant aspects of Thomas's view of the relationship between God and the world. We now pass on to focus more closely in what follows on the nexus of ideas implied in his interpretation of God's presence. We do so for two reasons.

1. This narrowing of the field of view obviously does not imply any arbitrary restriction of the discussion to a single specific question, interesting though it may be in itself. On the contrary, it clearly implies a concentration on the kind of questions which must be central in any theological discussion. That is to say, the phrase, 'presence of God', has reference not only to *God's general presence* in creation but also to *the doctrine of grace* and *the incarnation*, as Thomas makes quite clear in a passage in his commentary on Colossians: *Tribus enim modis est Deus in rebus. Unus est communis per potentiam, praesentiam, et essentiam; alius per gratiam in sanctis; tertius modus est singularis in Christo per unionem* (There are three modes of God's presence in things: one, the general, by power, presence, and essence; the second, in the righteous by grace; the third, uniquely, in Christ, by being one with him).[282] This also gives us a procedure to follow in the remainder of the chapter. Having looked at what Thomas has to say about God's presence in creation, we shall go on to discuss his particular presence in grace, in order to try to explain, lastly, the meaning of his presence in Christ.

2. In order to reach a more conclusive definition of the relationship between *ratio* and *revelatio* which is found in Thomas's world of thought, it is necessary for us to move from the more general statements which we have made up to this point to a fuller examination of a limited area in which we can get to the heart of the problem. When we do this we shall find that, even when we approach the problem from this side, Thomas's view of the presence of God in the world provides a convenient starting-point, for we are dealing here with what is clearly a *revelatio* feature in his theology. There is a crucial

[281] 1a, 8, 1, ad 3.
[282] *In ad Col.* 2, 2 (97); see also I *Sent.* 37, 1, 2.

distinction here between Thomas and the general idea which we find in Greek philosophy of the supreme principle as 'ontologically absent' from the world, whether we have in mind Aristotle's 'Unmoved Mover' who is unaware of the world and its affairs, or the 'One' of neo-Platonism who is elevated above the rest of the world and its imperfections. It is our hope, therefore, that, when we have concluded our discussion, of the concept of presence, which is so central to Thomas's thought, and the accentuation of this idea in the doctrine of the incarnation, we shall then be able to sum up our discussion by pointing up and elucidating the primary question which has been before us throughout, viz. the relationship between reason and revelation in the theology of Thomas Aquinas.

2

GOD'S GENERAL PRESENCE IN CREATION

With reference to a phrase widely current among scholastic writers since Peter Lombard[1] Thomas can say that God is in his created world *per potentiam* in the sense that in the last resort everything is dependent on him and is subject to his dominion, *per praesentiam* in the sense that nothing lies beyond divine Providence, and *per essentiam* because he creates and sustains all existence and is thus its *causa essendi* (cause of existence).[2] But when he comes to define the meaning of this divine presence more fully, he concentrates on the last of these three.

Once again we see that in Thomas's thought the relationship between God and the world is determined by the category of cause: *Deus est supra omnia per excellentiam suae naturae: et tamen* EST IN OMNIBUS REBUS, UT CAUSANS OMNIUM ESSE (the perfection of his nature places God above everything, and yet as causing their existence he also exists in everything).[3] For Thomas God is absolutely transcendent, because his nature is *ipsum esse*. This means that he is other than and incomparably more perfect than any other thing or being in creation, for it is a mark of the creature that its *esse* is not coincident with its nature.[4] God, therefore, is as radically independent of things as they are radically dependent on him for their existence. He is also therefore *infinitus*[5] and *immutabilis*, while it is a mark of the

---

[1] I *Sent.* 37; cf. Diekamp, *Dogmatik*, vol. I, p. 160f.
[2] 1a, 8, 3: cf. I *Sent.* 37, 1, 2; *In Joan.* 1 5 (2); *In ad Col.* 2, 2 (96); 1a, 43, 3; 3a, 6, 1, ad 1.
[3] 1a, 8, 1, ad 1.   [4] See p. 129ff. above.
[5] 1a, 7, 1: *Cum igitur esse divinum non sit esse receptum in aliquo, sed ipse sit suum esse subsistens, ut supra ostensum est; manifestum est quod ipse Deus sit infinitus.* It may be noted in this connection that the aversion to infinity which is characteristic of Greek philosophy in general—which holds that this attribute may not be applied even to the divine—seems to be bound up with the fact that in Greek philosophy, in contrast to Thomas, *bonum* and not *esse* has metaphysical primacy. As long as *bonum* does have metaphysical primacy, infinity implies an imperfection, while, if *esse* is primary, it becomes a necessary quality of the divine, for *ipsum esse* in itself precludes any form of limitation. Cf. de Finance, *Être et agir*, p. 45ff. (where a number of passages from Greek philosophy are discussed) and Gilson, *Spirit*, p. 54f.

creature that it is always in some sense finite and *mutabilis*.[6] But Thomas does not conceive this transcendence in such a way that it precludes an immediate divine immanence in creation—on the contrary, such immanence is necessarily presupposed.[7] If God were simply one cause among others within the world of time and change, there would be no possibility of showing how he is immediately at work in the present time. Had he been simply the first cause within the sphere of time, then however perfect he was and however much the 'first' cause, he would have had to be confined to the beginning of time as the initiator of time, separated from subsequent developments. Thomas's God, however, is not a deistically conceived first cause, far removed from the world, but a God who is present and active in the world. And it is just this which is presupposed by his absolute transcendence as *ipsum esse per se subsistens*. In the thought of Thomas God really is *in* his creation, but in no way does he coincide with it. It is not possible to express his thought about God in deistic terms, nor is there any question of any form of pantheism. God *IS*, even without the world, and his perfection would not in the least way be diminished, even if there were no world. The creature is thus radically contingent as regards its being, and in this sense is distinct from God. In the metaphysical sense there is an infinite distance between God and the creature, and it is impossible for anything that is created to be identical with God, When we say that God is *esse omnium* or define his presence as a presence *per essentiam*, this does not mean that the creature participates in God's *esse* but that its *esse* is caused by God: *Deus est esse omnium non essentiale, sed causale* (God is not the essential being of all things, but the cause of their existence).[8] Thus God's 'presence' is simply for Thomas a different way of expressing the causal relationship which links the world to its transcendent ultimate cause.

God is in his creation as a cause is in its effect. He is in the world through the act by which he creates and sustains it as a world which exists in an existence given by and therefore distinct from him. Seen from the standpoint of the divine being this act is eternal and in-

---

[6] 1a, 7, 2; 1a, 9, 2: *solus Deus est omnino immutabilis: omnis autem creatura aliquo modo est mutabilis . . . universaliter omnes creaturae communiter sunt mutabiles secundum potentiam Creantis, in cuius potestate est esse et non esse earum.*

[7] Cf. 1a, 7, introd. On the meaning of God's transcendence and immanence, see especially de Finance, *Être et agir*, p. 148ff.

[8] I *Sent.* 8, 1, 2; 1a, 3, 8, ad 1: *deitas dicitur esse omnium effective et explariter: non autem per essentiam.*

finite and coincides with God's *essentia*, but it can also be seen from the standpoint of its *effectus*, the actual, existing things. Here, as in every other causal relationship, *causa est in effectu per modum effectus* (a cause is in its affect according to the mode of the effect).[9] The form of the divine action in the thing which is its result and object is thus determined by the level in the hierarchical order of the universe which is given with the form of the thing itself. The things and beings in creation which receive their *esse* as a gift of God through his continuing act of creation do not possess this gift as it exists in the giver but in the manner which corresponds to the limited power of their nature to use it. As things exist in God *per modum Dei* (according to God's mode) in the sense that their imperfect nature has a perfect image and counterpart in the *ideae* which exist in the divine intellect,[10] so also God is in the things *per modum rerum* (according to the mode of things), and not in the same way that he is in himself.[11] In the sphere of the creature his *actio* is identical with its results, viz. existing things. In God himself it is eternal and indivisible, but in things it differs according to their varying degrees of perfection and their consequent variation of life and activity. Creation is not identical with God, but its existence is an expression of the fact that God is at work, for the power, *virtus*, which at every moment keeps a thing from reverting to *non esse*, does not arise from the thing itself, and is therefore no part of its *essentia*. Nor is it an accident, *accidens*, imposed upon an existing substance, *substantia*, but rather it comes from God, and is his own direct action in the thing. He is in the thing *sicut agens adest ei in quod agit* (as an agent is present to that in which its action is taking place).[12] God is present wherever this

---

[9] *De Pot.* 3, 15: *Omne autem quod est in aliquo, est in eo per modum ejus in quo est; In De causis, 12: hoc modo causa est in effectu, et e converso, secundum quod causa agit in effectum, et effectus recipit actionem causae. Causa autem agit in effectum per modum ipsius causae; effectus autem recipit actionem causae per modum suum: unde oportet quod causa sit in effectu per modum effectus, et effectus sit in causa per modum causae.* See also Legrand, *L'univers*, p. 160ff.

[10] See 1a, 15, 1–3. The difficulties which this implies, particularly with regard to *materia prima* as a created thing which should therefore have its prefiguration in God, have been pointed out and analysed by R. L. Patterson, *The Conception of God in the Philosophy of Aquinas*, London 1933, p. 125ff. and Lyttkens, *Analogy*, p. 177ff.

[11] I *Sent.* 37, 2, 3, ad 3: *Deus enim est in rebus temporaliter per modum rerum, sed res ab aeterno in Deo per modum Dei; quia omne quod in altero est, est in eo per modum eius in quo est, et non per modum sui.*

[12] I *Sent.* 37, 1, 1, ad 1: *quamvis essentia divina non sit intrinseca rei quasi pars veniens in constitutionem ejus; tamen est intra rem quasi operans et agens esse*

power is at work, not *absolute* as he is in himself, but *per operation-em*.[13] Thus for Thomas God is not only like the Aristotelian First Mover, *causa movens*, but divine causality goes far deeper than this, for in speaking of the operation of God we must observe that he *agit creando* (acts by creating).[14] According to Thomas—and Aristotle —the degree of activity is equivalent to the degree of actuality in the efficient cause: *unumquodque, inquantum est actu, agit* (activity is consequent upon actuality).[15] The higher the degree of actuality a cause has, so much the more far-reaching is its effect and the deeper its immanence in its *effectus*.[16] The immanence of a cause in its effect is thus in direct proportion to its transcendence—the greater its transcendence, the greater also its immanence, just as the warming effect of fire penetrates further in relation to the degree of warmth.[17] Since there is no cause in the whole realm of being which is com-mensurable in terms of actuality with God, who, as *ipsum esse*, is therefore also absolutely transcendent, there is no causality either that extends further or is immanent to such an extent in things. God is *prima causa omnium* (first cause of all things), and therefore it follows that *sua virtus est immediatissima omnibus* (his power is immediately present in all things).[18] Since he and he alone is the cause of the *esse* of a thing, and nothing in a thing is *magis intimum* than the act by which it exists, it follows that *Deus est unicuique intimus, sicut esse proprium rei est intimum ipsi rei* (God is intimately present to each thing as the existence that is proper to it is intimately present

uniuscujusque rei; 1a, 8, 1: *Deus est in omnibus rebus, non quidem sicut pars essentiae, vel sicut accidens, sed sicut agens adest ei in quod agit;* 1a, 112, 1: *Dei enim proprium est ubique esse: quia cum sit universale agens, eius virtus attingit omnia entia; unde est in omnibus rebus.*

---

[13] I *Sent.* 37, 1, 2: *Essentia autem ejus cum sit absoluta ab omni creatura, non est in creatura nisi in quantum applicatur sibi per operationem;* cf. I *Sent.* 37, 3, 1, ad 5. See also the passages cited in connection with the discussion on p. 114f. above on the divine activity.

[14] *In Joan.* 1, 5 (1).

[15] 1a, 5, 5; 1a, 25, 1, ad 1; 1a, 50, 5: *unumquodque operatur secundum quod est actu, operatio rei indicat modum esse ipsius,* etc.

[16] *De Pot.* 3, 7: *Quanto enim aliqua causa est altior, tanto est communior et efficacior, et quanto est efficacior, tanto profundius ingreditur in effectum, et de remotiori potentia ipsum reducit in actum.*

[17] 1a2ae, 66, 1: *Semper enim est potior causa suo effectu: et in effectibus, tanto aliquid est potius, quanto est causae propinquius;* CG III, 74: *Quanto autem aliqua causa est superior, tanto est maioris virtutis: unde eius causalitas ad plura se extendit;* CG III, 77: *Quanto virtus alicuius agentis est fortior, tanto in magis remota suam operationem extendit: sicut ignis, quanto est maior, magis remota calefacit.*

[18] I *Sent.* 37, 1, 1, ad 4.

to the thing itself).[19] Everything that is created is utterly dependent on this effect of the divine causality, without which it can neither come into being nor continue to exist, for nothing *exists* which is not wholly dependent by its very existence on the fact that *he* who *IS* effects and bestows its *esse* at every moment.[20] This 'effect' of divine causality is *intimior* than any other effect and therefore also presupposes every other effect.[21] The presence of God is thus for Thomas primarily a different manner of expressing the truth that God is *causa essendi* in regard to the world. But as such he is also *causa movens*, since he gives to the thing not only its *esse* but also the *forma* and *operatio* through which it receives the tendency that is given with its form: *inquantum est actu, agit, et tendit in id quod sibi convenit secundum suam formam* (activity is consequent upon actuality, and things gravitate towards what is natural to them).[22] Insofar as a thing has *esse*, it is also directly *agens*, just as God himself is perfect activity with regard to his being since he is *ipsum esse*. Moreover, God is also *causa exemplaris*, and God's general presence in the created

---

[19] I *Sent.* 37, 1, 1: *illud quod est causa esse, non potest cessare ab operatione qua esse datur, quin ipsa res etiam esse cessat. . . Ex quibus omnibus aperte colligitur quod Deus est unicuique intimus, sicut esse proprium rei est intimum ipsi rei, quae nec incipere nec durare posset, nisi per operationem Dei; In Joan.* 1, 5 (2): *Cum ergo esse sit intimum cuilibet rei, Deus, qui operando dat esse, operatur in rebus ut intimus agens;* 1a, 8, 1: *Esse autem est illud quod est magis intimum cuilibet, et quod profundius omnibus inest: cum sit formale respectu omnium quae in re sunt . . . Unde oportet quod Deus sit in omnibus rebus, et intime.* The statement which is frequently to be found in works on Thomas that God is 'plus en nous que nous; plus présente à notre âme que notre âme n'est présente à elle-même' (the expression is from A. Gardeil, *La structure de l'âme et l'expérience mystique*, vol. II, 2nd ed. Paris 1927, p. 81; cf. also A. Villard, *L'Incarnation d'après saint Thomas d'Aquin*, Paris 1908, p. 177; R. Morency. *L'union de grâce selon saint Thomas* (Studia collegii maximi immaculatae conceptionis 8), Montreal 1950, p. 118; and the references given by Skydsgaard, *Metafysik*, on p. 116 and 121]—this kind of statement does not correspond to anything that can be found anywhere in Thomas, and is to be understood primarily as a rhetorical accentuation of Thomas's own more cautious statement.

[20] 1a, 8, 4: *oporteret in omnibus esse Deum: quia nihil potest esse nisi per ipsum.*

[21] *De Pot.* 3, 7: *Ipsum enim esse est communissimus effectus primus et intimior omnibus aliis effectibus. Compend. Theol.* 68: *Primus autem effectus Dei in rebus est ipsum esse, quod omnes alii effectus praesupponunt, et supra quod fundantur.*

[22] 1a, 5, 5; 1a, 8, 2: *Deus . . . est in omnibus rebus, ut dans eis esse et virtutem et operationem;* 1a, 105, 5, ad 3: *Deus non solum dat formas rebus, sed etiam conservat eas in esse, et applicat eas ad agendum, et est finis omnium actionum.* According to Thomas Paul in his Areopagus speech (Acts 17:28) gives expression precisely to this divine omnicausality: 1a, 18, 4, ad 1: *hoc modo intelligendum est verbum Apostoli dicentis, 'in ipso vivimus, movemur et sumus': quia et nostrum vivere, et nostrum esse, et nostrum moveri causantur a Deo.* Cf. *In ad Heb.* 1, 2 (31): *ad subtractionem virtutis divinae cessat et esse, et fieri, et subsistere omnis creaturae,* and *In ad Rom.* 9, 3 (772).

world may therefore also be described as a presence *secundum similitudinem . . . divinae bonitatis* (after the likeness of the divine goodness).[23] Since, furthermore, the divine ubiquity is held to imply a relation between God and creation that is based on his *operatio* in creation, a relation that has in fact no corresponding reality in God himself,[24] it becomes all the more clear that in spite of all he says about God's general presence, Thomas is not really saying anything new beyond what he says in general terms, as we saw earlier, in his interpretation of the causal relationship between God and the world. He says nothing at this point that adds to what he says when he attempts to explain the meaning of God's creation and maintaining of the world in terms of his general metaphysics of existence.[25]

Based as it is on the biblical idea of creation, it is this metaphysics of existence which makes it possible for Thomas to express in the strongest terms both the absolute transcendence of God and his active and direct immanence in creation. If the former expresses the otherness, the absolute aseity and independence of the divine being, the latter implies the equally radical dependence of things—through and through they are dependent upon God. In the last resort here (as when he interprets the meaning of *creatio* and *conservatio*)[26] Thomas reduces God's presence or immanence in creation to a relation of dependence which receives its most obvious expression in the doctrine of the unilateral real relation between creation and God. To say that God is in the creature is simply to say that without him nothing at all *is*: *oporteret in omnibus esse Deum: quia nihil potest esse nisi per ipsum* (it must need be that God exists in them, since nothing can exist except through him).[27] His presence is expressed in the fact that things and beings *are*, but they do not get their *esse* from themselves. Their being presupposes rather the existence of some one who IS and who can therefore be the cause of all existence.

[23] I *Sent.* 37, 1, 2.
[24] I *Sent.* 14, 2, 1, 2, ad 1: *cum dicitur Deus esse ubique, importatur quaedam relatio Dei ad creaturam, quae quidem realiter non est in ipso, sed in creatura;* I *Sent.* 37, 2, 3: *cum dicitur, Deus est ubique, importatur quaedam relatio Dei ad creaturam, fundata super aliquam operationem, per quam Deus in rebus dicitur esse.*
[25] Cf. de Finance, *Être et agir*, p. 149: 'La théorie de l'immanence divine est, chez saint Thomas, entièrement dépendante de la métaphysique de l'*esse* et de la création'.
[26] See p. 116ff. above.
[27] 1a, 8, 4. Cf. *CG* IV, 21: *ubicumque est aliquis effectus Dei, ibi sit ipse Deus effector.*

3

GOD'S PRESENCE IN THE RIGHTEOUS
MISSIO INVISIBILIS

The statements concerning a divine presence which we have so far discussed apply to all created things. By the very fact that a thing exists, God is also in what he creates as the cause is in its effect. Since the subject of this discussion is the second and particular form of his presence according to which God is *in justis* or *in sanctis*, our field of view is now limited to that part of the created world which consists of men. That is to say, in the hierarchical order of existence it is only in human nature that we find the presupposition of this special divine presence.

What is it, then, that distinguishes man from all other creatures that are inferior to him? Since man is *aliquid compositum ex anima et corpore* (composed of soul and flesh).[1] he possesses all that is distinctive of both the inorganic world and plants and animals. Thus Thomas can speak of man, following Aristotle, as a *minor mundus* (little world).[2] There is, however, something in man which transcends even the most highly developed animals, since his soul, which possesses the characteristics of both the *anima vegetabilis* of plants and the *anima sensibilis* of animals, is, in addition, also an *anima rationalis*.[3] This is man's *forma substantialis*: it determines both his *esse* and his *operatio*, and, united to the body as the matter whose potencies it realises, it makes man a particular, existing unity.[4] Since he is at once both spiritual and corporal, man is thus a being midway between the creatures endowed with reason who are pure form

---

[1] 1a, 75, 4.

[2] 1a, 91, 1: *Et propter hoc homo dicitur minor mundus, quia omnes creaturae mundi quodammodo inveniuntur in eo.*

[3] This is not to be understood to imply that there are two or three separate souls in man; rather, *anima rationalis* includes within itself all the properties of the others. See *De spiritualibus creaturis*, 3: *Sic etiam anima intellectiva virtute continet sensitivam, quia habet hoc, et adhuc amplius; non tamen ita quod sint duae animae; De anima*, 11: *in homine sit tantum una anima secundum substantiam, quae est rationalis, sensibilis et vegetabilis;* see also 1a, 76, 4.

[4] *De spiritualibus creaturis*, 2; *De anima*, 1; 1a, 76, 1; 1a, 76, 4.

—the angels—amd all other creatures not endowed with reason—
animate and inanimate beings who always, like him, also possess a
material element.[5]

Man shares with the angels the property of being a *creatura
rationalis*, but since he possesses a body and because of his consequent potentiality in regard to the object of his knowledge, compared to them he is *infimus in ordine intellectuum* (lowest in the order
of intelligence). From the beginning his soul is a *tabula rasa* in which
intellectual powers are realised only through external impulses.[6] As
pure form, therefore, the angel is *imago Dei* in a more perfect way
than man,[7] but even man, because he is a reasonable being, is *imago
Dei*. He is to be distinguished from all creatures inferior to him by the
fact that he possesses a soul endowed with reason, *intellectus sive
mens*, and it is this and nothing else that makes him the *imago Dei*.
As we have already seen, there is a resemblance to the divine cause in
everything that is created. Common to all existing things is the
primary likeness to God which is given in the very fact of existence,
but there is also a higher degree of resemblance in things which do
not merely exist, but are also characterised by their own form of
activity, i.e. life. The highest expression of likeness to God is ultimately found in those beings which do not merely exist and live, but
are also possessed of intellect and will.[8] All other likeness to God can
be styled a *similitudo per modum vestigii* (in the manner of a trace),
but only the latter is a *similitudo per modum imaginis* (in the manner
of an image). Consequently, only the highest part of man's soul is
properly speaking the *imago Dei*, while the lower functions of the
soul and the body possess simply the *vestigia Dei*.[9] The more closely

[5] *De anima*, 1: *Si igitur anima humana, inquantum unitur corpori ut forma, habet esse
elevatum supra corpus non dependens ab eo; manifestum est quod ipsa est in confinio
corporalium et separatarum substantiarum constituta;* cf. also 1a, 77, 2.

[6] 1a, 79, 2: *Intellectus igitur angelicus semper est in actu suorum intelligibilium,
propter propinquitatem ad primum intellectum, qui est actus purus, ut supra dictum est.
Intellectus autem humanus, qui est infimus in ordine intellectuum, et maxime remotus
a perfectione divini intellectus, est in potentia respectu intelligibilium, et in principio
est sicut tabula rasa in qua nihil est scriptum, ut Philosophus dicit in III de Anima.*
On Thomas's theory of knowledge see p. 21f. above together with the references
cited in footnote 12.

[7] 1a, 93, 3: *Et sic imago Dei est magis in angelis quam sit in hominibus: quia intellectualis natura perfectior est in eis.*

[8] 1a, 93, 2: *Assimilantur autem aliqua Deo, primo quidem, et maxime communiter,
inquantum sunt; secundo vero, inquantum vivunt; tertio vero, inquantum sapiunt vel
intelligunt.*

[9] 1a, 93, 6: *cum in omnibus creaturis sit aliqualis Dei similitudo, in sola creatura
rationali invenitur similitudo Dei per modum imaginis . . . in aliis autem creaturis per*

the creature resembles the Creator, the greater the perfection of the creature.[10] The relatively perfect likeness to God which is expressed by the term *imago* can be seen only on the plane of the *anima rationalis* within the hierarchy of creation, for only this soul, by virtue of the fact that it possesses reason and will, has the capacity to imitate God's own knowledge and love for himself. We are dealing here with an analogical likeness to God's own trinitarian being, which simply means that in God there is also a *verbum conceptum et amor procedens* (word conceived and love proceeding).[11] This image of God is permanent and indestructible in man, since it is the image that makes man what he is. The soul is also *incorruptibilis*.[12] Thus Thomas holds, following Augustine, that the *imago Dei* is present, though only potentially, even in those who lack understanding, just as it is also to be found even in sinners, though in this case it is obscured and is clearly disclosed only in the righteous.[13] Since the image of God in the proper sense is present in a man only in his *anima rationalis*, Thomas insists that a theologian who proposes to discuss the meaning of man in any work of *sacra doctrina* need be concerned only with this particular soul.[14] To say what we mean by the *mens* of man is also to define his relation to God. In the prologue to the second main part of the *Summa theologiae*, Thomas argues that the best perspective from which to formulate a theological anthropology is the *imago Dei*.[15]

Theologically, the ultimate explanation of the centrality of this doctrine of the *imago Dei* is that the very gifts of intellect which

modum vestigii. Id autem in quo creatura rationalis excedit alias creaturas, est intellectus sive mens. Unde relinquitur quod nec in ipsa rationali creatura invenitur Dei imago, nisi secundum mentem. In aliis vero partibus, si quas habet rationalis creatura, invenitur similitudo vestigii.

---

[10] *In Joan.* 17, 3 (1): *uniuscujusque perfectio nihil est aliud quam participatio divinae similitudinis. In tantum enim sumus boni inquantum Deo assimilamur.*

[11] 1a, 45, 7; 1a, 93, 4: *Imitatur autem intellectualis natura maxime Deum quantum ad hoc, quod Deus seipsum intelligit et amat;* 1a, 93, 8: *Attenditur igitur divina imago in homine secundum verbum conceptum de Dei notitia, et amorem exinde derivatum;* see also p. 143ff. above.

[12] 1a, 75, 6.

[13] 1a, 93, 8, ad 3: *imaginem Dei semper diximus permanere in mente: sive haec imago Dei ita sit obsoleta, quasi obumbrata, ut pene nulla sit, ut in his qui non habent usum rationis; sive sit obscura atque deformis, ut in peccatoribus; sive sit clara et pulchra, ut in iustis, sicut Augustinus dicit, XIV de Trin.;* cf. 1a, 93, 7, ad 4.

[14] 1a, 75, prol.: *Naturam autem hominis considerare pertinet ad theologum ex parte animae.*

[15] 1a2ae, prol.: *postquam praedictum est de exemplari, scilicet de Deo . . . restat ut consideremus de eius imagine, idest de homine.*

allow us to speak of man as the *imago Dei* also make him *capax Dei*.
Since the task of *sacra doctrina* is to define the goal of salvation and
the way by which man may obtain it, the primary possibility given
with human nature must be the axle around which everything else
in sacred doctrine revolves.[16] Since Thomas defines the meaning of
salvation as a *perfectio rationalis seu intellectualis naturae* (perfection
of a nature endowed with reason or intellect),[17] the precondition for
obtaining this goal is that man is a *creatura rationalis*.[18] But to be a
creatura rationalis also means that man is *capax Dei* (capable of
God), or—and this is the same thing—*capax beatitudinis* (capable of
blessedness), for the goal of salvation for man is a permanent and
abiding affinity to God's own blessedness in knowing and loving God
as perfectly as he can, and thus in imitating his blessedness, which
means knowing and loving himself.[19] Because of the direct relationship between likeness to God and man's supernatural goal, the
imago Dei comes to have crucial significance for Thomas: *similitudo
imaginis attenditur in natura humana secundum quod est capax Dei,
scilicet ipsum attingendo propria operatione cognitionis et amoris* (the
resemblance of the image is looked for in human nature insofar as
it is capable of God, viz. by attaining to him through its own operation of knowledge and love).[20] We may therefore define the attainment of this goal as a gradual increase of man's likeness to God until
he reaches absolute perfection.

It is a distinctive feature of Thomas's anthropology that he does
not define this likeness to God in static categories, and all that he has
to say about it is subsumed under the title which he gives to the introduction of the *Summa theologiae*, '*motus rationalis creaturae in
Deum*' (the journey to God of reasoning creatures).[21] Thus the term

[16] Skydsgaard, *Metafysik*, p. 222: 'This makes plain what part the image of God
plays in Thomas's understanding of the Christian faith. The doctrine of the *imago
Dei* is the axis of his understanding of Christianity . . . it is the formally determinative central point of his understanding of the faith. It is therefore theologically
absolutely indispensable.

[17] 1a, 62, 1; cf. 1a, 12, 1: *ultima hominis beatitudo in altissima eius operatione
consistat, quae est operatio intellectus;* 1a2ae, 3, 4: *essentia beatitudinis in actu
intellectus consistit.*

[18] *De Ver.* 22, 2, ad 5: *sola creatura rationalis est capax Dei, quia ipsa sola potest
ipsum cognoscere et amare explicite.*

[19] 1a, 26, 2: *Attribuenda ergo est Deo beatitudo secundum intellectum, sicut et aliis
beatis, qui per assimilationem ad beatitudinem ipsius, beati dicuntur;* cf. *De Pot.* 9, 9:
conformitas, quae in solis sanctis invenitur, qui idem intelligunt et amant quod Deus.

[20] 3a, 4, 1, ad 2; cf. 2a2ae, 25, 3, ad 2; 3a, 6, 2; 3a, 9, 2; 3a, 23, 1.

[21] 1a, 2, prol.

imago Dei has also primarily a dynamic sense of movement towards man's goal: *imago Dei attenditur in anima secundum quod fertur, vel nata est ferri in Deum* (the image of God is looked for in the soul insofar as it brings itself to bear on God, or is of a nature to do so).[22] Not even the first man in creation was in a state of blessedness—even for Adam this was a goal to strive for.[23] For Thomas, this orientation towards a goal, which is the distinguishing mark of all that is created, comes to expression in the statement of the creation narrative that man was created *ad imaginem Dei*. This means that man was not and is not now created perfect, but was and is created to realise more fully the imperfect likeness to God which belongs to his very nature as man. The phrase, *ad imaginem*, indicates a *motus tendentis in perfectionem* (movement of tendency to perfection).[24] It indicates further that as a created being man never is nor can ever become an *imago Dei perfecta*, for only the second person of the godhead can be said to be such. He alone is *Deo connaturalis*, and therefore we do not refer to him as *ad imaginem* but only as *Imago*.[25] The phrase *ad imaginem* thus points at the one time to man's finiteness as a creature and to the final goal which is set before him by the very fact of his creation and is rendered necessary by his very finiteness. In his nature he is *perfectibilis*, and any increase of his likeness to God always implies a concurrent perfection of human nature itself as such.

When he speaks of this *motus in Deum*, Thomas describes it as a development in three stages. At the lowest stage there is the *imago* which is common to all men and consists in the natural capacity to know and love God inherent in the rational soul. On the natural plane there already exists a *Dei cognitio et dilectio* (knowledge and love of God),[26] for 'the whole of human nature is a movement towards a goal, that is, to God, who is naturally known and naturally

---

[22] 1a, 93, 8.
[23] *De Ver.* 18, 1, ad 5: *homo factus erat ad videndum Deum non in principio, sed in ultimo suae perfectionis; et ideo quod in principio suae conditionis Deum per essentiam non vidit, non fuit ex hoc quod obstaculo impediretur; sed solum proprio defectu, quia nondum ei inerat perfectio illa quae requiritur ad videndum Deum per essentiam.*
[24] 1a, 35, 2, ad 3: *Et ideo ad designandam in homine imperfectionem imaginis, homo non solum dicitur imago, sed ad imaginem, per quod motus quidam tendentis in perfectionem designatur;* 1a, 93, 1: *Et hoc significat Scriptura, cum dicit hominem factum ad imaginem Dei: praepositio enim ad accessum quendam significat, qui competit rei distanti.*
[25] 1a, 35, 2; 1a, 93, 1, ad 2; *In 1 ad Cor.* 11, 2 (604).
[26] 1a, 93, 8, ad 3; cf. 1a, 93, 4.

loved as Creator'.[27] Man is created to attain knowledge of God and to love him. This natural capacity is the presupposition of the greater perfection, which means that the image of God is raised to an *imago per conformitatem gratiae* (image by conformity to grace). The 'conformity' to God's own triune being here referred to is of a much higher kind than natural conformity, and it is found only among the righteous. But even this likeness to God is imperfect in comparison with the ultimate perfection of man, the *imago gloriae*, concerning which Thomas says that *homo Deum actu cognoscit et amat perfecte* (man actually knows and perfectly loves God), and which is found only among the blessed in heaven who have attained the supernatural goal of salvation.[28]

This brings us to the second form of God's presence in the world which Thomas defines as a presence *per gratiam in sanctis*.[29] Before we turn to examine the statements in which Thomas speaks explicitly of grace as a form of the divine presence, it may be necessary to describe certain of the essential features in Thomas's general understanding of the meaning of grace, and we shall take as our starting-point the doctrine of the *imago Dei* already outlined.[30]

We may therefore begin with the observation that in Thomas's view grace is a heightening of the likeness to God given by nature. It is human nature and not something else that comes by grace to its final perfection in the beatific vision of God. Grace does not mean that a new and more perfect likeness to God is added to human 'nature' from without in order to supplement the natural *imago*, but it is precisely this nature which is perfected through grace. Thomas in fact says as much by using the term *imago* in each of the three stages.

[27] Skysdgaard, *Metafysik*, p. 206.　　[28] 1a, 93, 4.　　[29] See p. 156f. above.
[30] For a fuller study of the doctrine of grace in Thomas reference should be made in particular to R. Garrigou-Lagrange's classical work, *De gratia. Commentarius in Summam theologicam S. Thomas* IaeIIae q. 109–114, Turin 1947. In spite of the second part of the title, however, this author's tendency to introduce questions in a modern form means that he does not always reproduce Thomas's own point of view. The same tendency is also found to some extent in R. Mulard, *La grâce*, 2nd ed. 1948, which is also a commentary on 1a2ae, 109–114. A study limited to the *Summa contra Gentiles* is offered in H. Lais, *Die Gnadenlehre des heiligen Thomas in der Summa contra Gentiles und der Kommentar des Franziskus Sylvestris von Ferrara* (Münchener theologische Studien, Syst. Abt., Band 3), Munich 1951. A work which aims at providing a picture of the doctrine of grace which is actually to be found in Thomas's writings and which is therefore strikingly and helpfully different from many others by reason of its precise historical method is H. Bouillard, *Conversion et grâce chez S. Thomas d'Aquin. Étude historique* (Théologie 1), Paris 1944. Skydsgaard's *Metafysik* is also of importance here, even though its point of departure is neo-Thomism rather than Thomas himself. See p. 109ff. in particular.

We do not find in Thomas the usual distinction which Protestant theologians make in their interpretation of Roman Catholic anthropology between *imago* and *similitudo* as designations respectively of nature and supernature. For Thomas *similitudo* is a comprehensive term which includes all degrees of likeness to God existing in creation, from *similitudo vestigii* (likeness of a trace) to *similitudo gloriae* (likeness of glory).[31] The term *imago* does not refer exclusively in Thomas to the image of God given by nature, but expresses the special form of *similitudo* which is to be found in that part of creation which is endowed with reason, angels and men.

Thomas often speaks of grace as a *donum*,[32] by which he means that it is given to man—it is a *qualitas*[33] that comes to man from without, though it is inherent in the soul—but this new quality of the soul does not mean that a new level of potentiality is added to the natural potentialities already present in man.[34] Grace is not the same thing as new potentialities or a new nature added to the old. It is, rather, in Thomas's words, a *forma accidentalis*, infused into the essence of the soul and dwelling habitually within the soul, by which the natural potencies of creation are made perfect.[35] Thus the *virtutes* which flow from grace, such as faith and love, are not added from without to the natural powers of gaining knowledge and of willing which are possessed by the *anima rationalis*; rather, it is these very *potentiae animae* (potentialities of the soul)[36] that are brought to perfection through grace. It is the intellect that believes and the will that

[31] See e.g. 1a, 33, 3; 1a, 93, 1, 2 and particularly 9.

[32] 1a2ae, 110, 2: *aliquod habituale donum*; also 1a2ae, 111, 2; 1a2ae, 112, 1, etc.

[33] 1a2ae, 110, 2.

[34] R. Johannesson, *Person och gemenskap*, expresses it thus, p. 135ff., though without providing any textual evidence to support his argument. On this basis he is able to speak on p. 136 of the tendency in Thomas to divide the nature of man into two strata independent of one another, but this is just a caricature of the relation between nature and supernature which we find in Thomas.

[35] 1a2ae, 110, 2, ad 2: *gratia . . . est forma accidentalis ipsius animae.*

[36] On reason and will as *potentiae animae*, see 1a, 77, 5 and 8. Cf. 1a2ae, 110, 4: *gratia . . . habeat subiectum prius potentiis animae: ita scilicet quod sit in essentia animae. Sicut enim per potentiam intellectivam homo participat cognitionem divinam per virtutem fidei; et secundum potentiam voluntatis amorem divinum, per virtutem caritatis; ita etiam per naturam animae participat, secundum quandam similitudinem, naturam divinam;* ib. ad 1: *sicut ab essentia animae effluunt eius potentiae, quae sunt operum principia; ita etiam ab ipsa gratia effluunt virtutes in potentias animae, per quas potentiae moventur ad actus.* 3a, 62, 2: *gratia, secundum se considerata, perficit essentiam animae, inquantum participat quandam similitudinem divini esse. Et sicut ab essentia animae fluunt eius potentiae, ita a gratia fluunt quaedam perfectiones ad potentias animae, quae dicuntur virtutes et dona, quibus potentiae perficiuntur in ordine ad suos actus.*

loves.[37] Grace, therefore, does not mean the addition of a new 'storey' to the edifice of nature, but rather the perfection of nature itself from within its own inmost activity. Man is not changed into a new being by the grace which God gives and effects, but in the most literal sense of the word he becomes a *better* man than he was before.[38] This is what Thomas means by describing grace as an elevation, *gratia . . . est quaedam perfectio elevans animam ad quoddam esse supernaturale* (grace is a perfection raising the soul to a certain supernatural existence).[39] Just as an object gets warmer the closer it comes to the fire or lighter the closer it is brought to the source of light, so man's nature is perfected according as he is raised to God's own eternal perfection.[40] But this raising presupposes in the first instance that man is a rational being and therefore *factus ad imaginem Dei* (made in the image of God) and *capax Dei* (capable of God).[41] Grace presupposes and perfects nature, and in this sense there is a continuous line from human nature as such to its final perfection *in patria*.

This continuity, however, should not be interpreted to mean that *gratia* and *gloria* merely imply a development of man's natural endowments. A direct continuity such as this is to be found only between the two last stages of the soul's *motus in Deum*, in that the life of grace inaugurates and anticipates the vision of God that is granted to the redeemed in heaven, *gratia nihil est aliud quam quaedam inchoatio gloriae in nobis* (grace is simply the beginning of glory in us).[42] This direct connection is to be seen in the fact that by

---

[37] 2a2ae, 4, 2: *Credere autem est immediate actus intellectus: quia obiectum huius actus est verum, quod proprie pertinet ad intellectum;* 2a2ae, 23, 2: *necesse est quod ad actum caritatis existat in nobis aliqua habitualis forma superaddita potentiae naturali, inclinans ipsam ad caritatis actum;* 2a2ae, 24, 1: *caritatis subiectum . . . est . . . appetitus intellectivus, idest voluntas.*

[38] 1a, 43, 3, ad 1: *per donum gratiae gratum facientis perficitur creatura rationalis;* cf. E. Mersch, *Morale et Corps Mystique*, vol. II (Museum lessianum, Section théologique (=*ML–ST*) 37), 3rd ed. Brussels and Paris 1949, p. 32: 'La grâce . . . son effet premier est de nous faire plus hommes que l'homme ne peut l'être par lui seul'.

[39] *De Ver.* 27, 3; cf. *De Ver.* 27, 2; 1a, 12, 4, ad 3; 3a, 7, 1.

[40] *Compend. Theol.* 214: *Inquantum autem creatura aliqua magis ad Deum accedit, intantum de bonitate ejus magis participat, et abundantioribus donis ex ejus influentia repletur; sicut et ignis calorem magis participat qui ei magis appropinquat;* cf, 3a, 7, 13.

[41] 2a2ae, 175, 1, ad 2: *ad modum et dignitatem hominis pertinet quod ad divina elevetur, ex hoc ipso quod homo factus est ad imaginem Dei;* cf. also 3a, 9, 2, ad 3.

[42] 2a2ae, 24, 3, ad 2; *De Ver.* 27, 2, ad 7: *Gratia . . . est sicut dispositio quae est respectu gloriae, quae est gratia consummata.*

the help of grace a man can merit salvation by his works, but there is no such direct route from nature to grace. A man cannot merit grace by any effort or exertion, however perfect, for grace, unlike salvation, is not accorded to works, *ex operibus*.[43] A man can no more deserve to be created than he can deserve grace once he has been created. Nor is grace necessary in order to fulfil his natural endowments, for nothing more is needed to realise a man's natural potencies than he already possesses within his own nature. Thus grace is not a necessary endowment of man in the sense that his gifts of intellect are. If grace were something to which he could lay claim by virtue of his merits or of a potency inherent in his nature which required grace for its fulfilment, then grace would no longer be *grace*, for the *gratuitas* of grace excludes by definition every form of *debitum*, whether it is a *debitum meriti* (debt arising from merit) or a *debitum naturae* (debt arising from nature).[44]

Thomas explicitly deals with this aspect of grace as *indebitum naturae* in speaking of the *duplex finis* which God has set before man. Like all created things, man's nature has its appointed end, *proprium est naturae rationalis ut tendat in finem* (it is proper to rational nature to tend to an end).[45] As a created nature, man, like all other natures in the hierarchy of existence, has been given a *finis naturae creatae proportionatus*, which he can attain by developing and perfecting the talents that are naturally his as a man. In other words there is a direct relationship between this goal and his natural endowments. Thomas speaks of this *finis* as the *contemplatio divinorum* (contemplation of heavenly things) or *felicitas* of which the philosophers spoke in their writings as man's final end and perfection. Thus even on the natural plane man is appointed to attain to a knowledge of God and a love for him appropriate to his circumstances, and to this there corresponds a *beatitudo proportionata humanae naturae* (blessedness proportionate to human nature). He would have lacked nothing

---

[43] 1a, 62, 3, ad 3: *gloria . . . est finis operationis ipsius naturae per gratiam adiutae. Gratia autem non se habet ut finis operationis, quia non est ex operibus; sed ut principium bene operandi;* 1a, 95, 1, ad 6: *gloriam meremur per actum gratiae, non autem gratiam per actum naturae.*

[44] 1a2ae, 111, 1, ad 2: *gratia, secundum quod gratis datur, excludit rationem debiti. Potest autem intelligi duplex debitum. Unum quidem ex merito proveniens. . . Aliud est debitum ex conditione naturae: puta si dicamus debitum esse homini quod habeat rationem et alia quae ad humanam pertinent naturam. . . Dona igitur naturalia carent primo debito, non autem carent secundo debito. Sed dona supernaturalia utroque debito carent: et ideo specialius sibi nomen gratiae vindicant.*

[45] 1a2ae, 1, 2.

of what could make him perfect as a man, if God had done no more than this. But now in addition *sola liberalitate divina* God has set before man simultaneously with the act of creation a new and higher goal, the attainment of which infinitely exceeds all man's natural gifts. This is the *visio Dei* of the life eternal, in relation to which every other natural *felicitas* is merely a *beatitudo imperfecta* (imperfect blessedness).[46] There is no relation between this new goal and man's nature as such, and if he is to be able to achieve it, he must be changed, for *nihil . . . potest ordinari in aliquem finem, nisi praeexistat in ipso quaedam proportio ad finem* (nothing can be directed to any end unless there pre-exists in it a certain proportion to the end).[47] It is precisely the *donum gratiae* that establishes such a relation between man and his supernatural goal, and it is ultimately from this insufficient conformity between human nature and man's divinely appointed end that the need for grace arises.[48] Grace, therefore, is not necessary primarily for the sake of sin, for it is an essential requirement as much before as after the fall: *homo post peccatum ad plura indiget gratia quam ante peccatum*, SED NON MAGIS (man does not need grace more after sin than before it, but he needs it for more things.)[49] Before the fall *in statu integritatis* nature was free from imperfection and man had the ability *per sua naturalia* to achieve

---

[46] *De Ver.* 27, 2: *Homo autem secundum naturam suam proportionatus est ad quemdam finem, cuius habet naturalem appetitum; et secundum naturales vires operari potest ad consecutionem illius finis: qui finis est aliqua contemplatio divinorum, qualis est homini possibilis secundum facultatem naturae, in qua philosophi ultimam hominis felicitatem posuerunt. Sed est aliquis finis ad quem homo a Deo praeparatur, naturae humanae proportionem excedens, scilicet vita aeterna, quae consistit in visione Dei per essentiam, quae excedit proportionem cuiuslibet naturae creatae;* 1a, 23, 1: *Finis autem ad quem res creatae ordinantur a Deo, est duplex. Unus, qui excedit proportionem naturae creatae et facultatem: et hic finis est vita aeterna, quae in divina visione consistit, quae est supra naturam cuiuslibet creaturae . . . Alius autem finis est naturae creatae proportionatus, quem scilicet res creata potest attingere secundum virtutem suae naturae;* 1a2ae, 62, 1: *Est autem duplex hominis beatitudo sive felicitas. . . Una quidem proportionata humanae naturae. . . Alia autem est beatitudo naturam hominis excedens;* the same applies also in the case of angels, see 1a, 62, 2. See also II *Sent.* 1, 2, 2; *De Ver.* 14, 2; *De Caritate* 2; 1a2ae, 5, 5; 1a2ae, 68, 2.

[47] *De Ver.* 14, 2; 1a2ae, 7, 2; 1a2ae, 96, 1.

[48] *CG* III, 147: *Ea enim quae sunt ad finem, necesse est fini esse proportionata. Si igitur homo ordinatur in finem qui eius facultatem naturalem excedat, necesse est ei aliquod auxilium divinitus adhiberi supernaturale, per quod tendat in finem.*

[49] 1a, 95, 4, ad 1. The passage quoted continues: *Quia homo, etiam ante peccatum, indigebat gratia ad vitam aeternam consequendam, quae est principalis necessitas gratiae.* See also the discussion on p. 35ff. above of the meaning of grace in our earlier analysis of Thomas's concept of revelation.

the goal of perfection which was appointed for him as a natural being. But even then grace was absolutely essential for the attainment of a higher blessedness. The gift of grace was lost through the fall, but more than this occurred—nature was *deordinata* (disordered) and could no longer attain even its natural end.[50] This means that in addition to its proper function of lifting up, grace has also now a work of renewing and restoring to do. But grace is what it is because it is *gratia elevans*, and in relation to this its function as *gratia sanans* (healing grace) is simply an accidental consequence resulting from man's condition after the fall.[51] Thomas thus defines the necessity of grace primarily from the standpoint of how man's metaphysically appointed nature is to be defined, and not from the standpoint of sin and its consequences.[52] What is said in the biblical revelation of

[50] It should be noted that for Thomas the fall is not primarily to be understood as the loss of grace or a supernatural endowment, but the loss rather of *iustitia originalis* and the consequent *deordinatio naturae*, by which is meant that concupiscence and the lower potencies of the soul gained ascendancy over reason contrary to nature. Since Thomas regards *iustitia originalis* as a *dispositio quaedam ad illud auxilium quo mens humana ordinatur ad videndum Deum*, De Malo 5, 1, the loss of the *donum supernaturale* is not the primary but a secondary consequence of the fact that the primal disposition of man is no longer a reality. On this line of thought in Thomas which distinguishes him from much that is currently said in modern Roman Catholic theology, see R. Bernard, *Le péché*, vol. II, 1931, p. 340ff. It is characteristic of Thomas that he defines the nature even of *sin* from the standpoint of the metaphysical determination of human nature: 1a2ae, 109, 2, ad 2: *peccare nihil aliud est quam deficere a bono quod convenit alicui secundum suam naturam*, see also 1a, 63, 9; 1a2ae, 94, 3; 1a2ae, 109, 8, and other passages. Correspondingly, original sin, *peccatum originale*, is defined by Thomas as *quaedam habitualis deordinatio naturae*, 3a, 86, 2, ad 1, see also 1a2ae, 82, 1 and 3. Thomas thus draws the conclusion that nothing that takes place in accordance with human nature can be sin: *Quod autem secundum naturam fit, non est peccatum, In Joan.* 8, 6 (4). On the relation between Thomas and Aristotelian ethics on this point, cf. A. M. Festugière, 'La notion du péché présentée par St Thomas, I, II, 71 et sa relation avec la morale aristotélicienne', in *The New Scholasticism. A Quarterly Review of Philosophy* (=*NS*) 5 (1931), p. 332ff.

[51] 1a2ae, 109, 2: *Sic igitur virtute gratuita superaddita virtuti naturae indiget homo in statu naturae integrae quantum ad unum, scilicet ad operandum et volendum bonum supernaturale. Sed in statu naturae corruptae, quantum ad duo: scilicet ut sanetur; et ulterius ut bonum supernaturalis virtutis operetur;* see also 1a2ae, 109, 3. Hence too Mulard, *La grâce*, p. 314, defines the healing work of grace as 'accidentel à la grâce'. Cf. also Diekamp and Jüssen, *Dogmatik*, vol. II, p. 438: 'In Beziehung auf unser *übernatürliches Endziel* ist die Gnade nicht nur notwendig, weil die menschliche Natur gefallen und verwundet ist, sondern auch deswegen, weil dieses Ziel die Ordnung unserer Natur wesentlich übersteigt. Der zweite Grund ist der durchschlagendste'.

[52] Skydsgaard in particular has drawn attention to this point; see his *Metafysik*, p. 109ff. and especially p. 133. Corresponding to this basic idea of the relationship between nature and grace is the idea of the possibility of a *status naturae purae* which we find in Thomistic literature dealing with the doctrine of grace, i.e. of a

sin and the fall is merely a supplementary disclosure which essentially changes nothing in the existing scheme of things.

Grace restores the relation (*proportio*) which must exist between man and his supernatural goal if he is to be able to achieve it, but which he lost in the fall. Through grace his impaired nature is healed, and at the same time raised to a plane from which it becomes possible for him to resume the *motus in Deum* which was interrupted by the fall. In relation to man's natural endowments, however, the perfect *visio Dei* of the redeemed in heaven is something utterly *supra naturam*; it is beyond the reach of man's own powers, and he would not even be aware of this end had it not been disclosed to him from outside through the revelation of supernatural knowledge. When Thomas speaks of a *potentia ad scientiam beatorum* (potentiality to attain the knowledge of the blessed)[53] in man, he is referring simply to the attitude of obedience to the Creator on the part of all created things, or, to use another phrase, their *potentia obedientiae*.[54] In

state in which man is created without at the same time being endowed with grace, see e.g. Diekamp and Jüssen, *Dogmatik*, vol. II, p. 141; Skydsgaard, *Metafysik*, p. 124; Garrigou-Lagrange, *De gratia*, p. 18f., cf. p. 326f. Though this point is simply not discussed by Thomas—for which reason H. de Lubac, *Surnaturel. Éudes historiques* (Théologie 8), Paris 1946, p. 101ff., suggests that it should be rejected as basically alien to Thomas—yet there is some evidence that contemporary Thomistic interpretation at this point does express an idea which is to be found in Thomas himself; see e.g. II *Sent.* 31, 1, 2, ad 3: *Poterat Deus a principio quando hominem condidit, etiam alium hominem ex limo terrae formare, quem in conditione naturae suae relinqueret, ut scilicet mortalis et passibilis esset, et pugnam concupiscentiae ad rationem sentiens; in quo nihil humanae naturae derogaretur, quia hoc ex principiis naturae consequitur,* cf. also *De Malo* 4, 1, ad 14. We see this more clearly particularly if we note that Thomas always speaks of death as something that belongs to man's nature. He defines man as *animal rationale mortale* (1a, 29, 4, ad 2), hence it follows that *mors in hominibus semper est naturalis* (*In Joan.* 10, 4 (5)). See also in particular III *Sent.* 16, 1, 1, ad 2 and ad 5; *In ad Rom.* 5, 3 (416); *CG* IV, 52. While Thomas defines *sin* as 'unnatural' (cf. footnote 50 just above), he regards death as something essentially unrelated to sin, and a consequence rather of the fact that man is *ex contrariis compositum*. This in fact is how he explains the possibility that Christ could die, though he was free from sin; he assumed *naturam humanam absque peccato in illa puritate in qua erat in statu innocentiae,* 3a, 14, 3; cf. III *Sent.* 16, 1, 2; III *Sent.* 18, 4, 2; 3a, 14, 2. Thus the characteristic view of early Christian theology that sin and death constitute a unity in which both are unnatural is abandoned by Thomas. Underlying his view is the distinction between nature and the supernatural which is not found in the earlier tradition. Yet Anselm connects mortality with *natura corrupta* and not *natura pura*, see *Cur Deus homo* 2, 11 (*MPL* 158, 410ff.).

---

[53] Thus e.g. 3a, 9, 2.
[54] 3a, 11, 1: *Est autem considerandum quod in anima humana, sicut in qualibet creatura, consideratur duplex potentia passiva: una quidem per comparationem ad*

relation to God creation is 'open' to a fuller perfection that lies beyond the *bonitas* which is given with its nature. Thus grace is at the one time *supra naturam* (beyond nature) and *secundum naturam* (in accordance with nature); it is something wholly *indebitum naturae* (due to nature), and yet at the same time it is *nature* that is perfected.[55] This presupposes in the first instance that man is *capax Dei*, but to say this is not to imply a *habere* (possession) in man but a *posse habere* (capacity to possess).[56] Salvation is not the completion of creation as such, but is primarily something that far transcends creation. It does, indeed, mean the perfection of creation, but on a plane which is far above and essentially distinct from the natural plane. Only when grace is defined in this way can its character of *grace* be assured, for grace is primarily *aliquid supernaturale*.

What does Thomas mean when he speaks of God's special presence in the world through grace? As we have already seen, God is already present in the world as the One on whom all things are dependent, since he gives to all existing things their *esse et virtutem et operationem* (existence, power and activity).[57] Thomas holds that in addition to this general presence there is a second form of divine presence, but we can speak of this only in connection with a *creatura rationalis*. Only in such a case can we assume this form of presence, for it means that God is in man *sicut cognitum in cognoscente et amatum in amante* (as the object known is in the knower, and the beloved in the lover), and only a creature endowed with reason and will can gain knowledge of God and love him. But this knowledge of God and love for him are not found in all men, only in those to whom God has given *gratia gratum faciens* (sanctifying grace).[58] Of those who are in a state of grace it may be said not only that God is 'in

agens naturale; alia vero per comparationem ad agens primum, qui potest quamlibet creaturam reducere in actum aliquem altiorem, in quem non reducitur per agens naturale; et haec consuevit vocari potentia obedientiae in creatura. For a fuller examination of this important concept in Thomas's doctrine of grace see Skydsgaard, *Metafysik*, p. 208f. and 220ff.

[55] 3a, 9, 2, ad 3.   [56] Skydsgaard, *Metafysik*, p. 228.   [57] 1a, 8, 2.
[58] 1a, 43, 3: *Est enim unus communis modus quo Deus est in omnibus rebus per essentiam, potentiam et praesentiam, sicut causa in effectibus participantibus bonitatem ipsius. Super istum modum autem communem, est unus specialis, qui convenit creaturae rationalis, in qua Deus dicitur esse sicut cognitum in cognoscente et amatum in amante. . . Sic igitur nullus alius effectus potest esse ratio quod divina Persona sit novo modo in rationali creatura, nisi gratia gratum faciens;* 1a, 8, 3, see especially ad 4: *nulla alia perfectio superaddita substantiae, facit Deum esse in aliquo sicut obiectum cognitum et amatum, nisi gratia: et ideo sola gratia facit singularem modum essendi Deum in rebus.*

them', *esse in*, but that he 'resides' in them—that there is an *in-dwelling*, an *inhabitatio*, of God in their souls.[59] This is simply one among several expressions which Thomas uses to describe this special form of presence. Thus, for instance, he speaks of it as a *sending* of the persons of the godhead to the righteous man. Underlying this phrase, of course, there is the language of the Bible itself. The New Testament speaks both of God's sending of his Son and of the sending of the Holy Spirit upon the disciples. In the first instance the reference is to the incarnation, and, as we shall see further on, for Thomas the term *missio* includes also Christ's becoming man. He speaks of this 'mission' as a *missio visibilis*,[60] but using language which goes back to Augustine and which is found frequently among scholastic writers, he also speaks of the presence of God in grace as a *missio invisibilis*.[61]

We propose now to limit our inquiry into what Thomas means by the presence of God in grace to an analysis of this concept, and we have three reasons in particular for doing so. In the first place, Thomas investigates the meaning of this form of presence only in the context of a general discussion of the sending of the persons of the Trinity.[62] In the second place, the term *missio* is derived from the biblical writings and not from the language of philosophy, and we may therefore expect that a study of the term will shed further light on the central question of the present study, namely, the relation between *ratio* and *revelatio* in the theology of Thomas. Lastly, the term also includes the incarnation, and thus we have a given starting-point for our discussion of Thomas's interpretation of God's presence in Christ.

It is perfectly clear, then, that in the *Summa theologiae*, where Thomas could arrange the traditional material of theology in accordance with his own dogmatic principles—there was no corresponding freedom of treatment in his *Commentary on the Sentences*—*missio* occupies a key position. In *Quaestio* 43 of Part I, where he deals with the sending of the persons of the godhead, Thomas elaborates his doctrine of the Trinity, but the passage provides at the same time a transition to the completely new section which begins with *Quaestio* 44, *De processione creaturarum a Deo*. Coming as it does between a

---

[59] *In Joan.* 2, 3 (2); *In 1 ad Cor.* 3, 3 (173); *In 2 ad Cor.* 6, 3 (240); 1a, 43, 5 and 6.
[60] See e.g. 1a, 43, 2.
[61] Dondaine, *La Trinité*, vol. II, refers in this connection to Augustine, *De Trinitate*, books 2 and 4, especially book 2, 18–21.
[62] The passages which most fully deal with this are I *Sent.* 14, 15 and 16 and 1a, 43, 1–8.

discussion of the nature of God and a section in which he deals with created things, the position of *Quaestio* 43 indicates that the term *missio* is of particular importance in showing how Thomas conceives the relationship between God and the world.

We have already seen[63] how Thomas regards the doctrine of the Trinity not only as a theological locus in the traditional understanding but also as a vital and determinative element in the whole of his theological thinking. This is true also with regard to the doctrine of grace, as we clearly see from the fact that Thomas defines God's presence in grace as a *missio invisibilis*, for it means that any discussion of what happens to a man in the state of grace must begin with the activity of the divine Trinity itself. The term 'sending' presupposes that someone is sent by another who sends him: *per hoc quod aliquis mittitur, ostenditur processio quaedam missi a mittente* (that anyone be sent implies a certain kind of procession of the one sent from the sender).[64] Since, however, we are here discussing a 'sending out' of persons of the godhead, to be more precise, the Son and the Spirit, we must eliminate anything that may imply imperfection from the term *missio* if we are to use it of God.[65] There is thus no suggestion in the word of any *motus localis*, in which the one who is sent out leaves the one who sends him and goes to somewhere else. God is already in every place, and we cannot say of any of the persons of the godhead that he *incipit esse ubi prius non fuerat, ita nec desinit esse ubi fuerat* (begins to exist where he did not previously exist, or ceases to exist where he was).[66] The only possible conclusion is that the act of proceeding here understood must coincide with the eternal *processio* by which one of the persons of the godhead eternally proceeds from the Father as the *origo* or *principium* of his procession.[67] If we consider the person who is sent, his *missio* is simply the eternal, immanent act by which this person of the godhead is a real, subsisting relation within the divine being.[68] *Missio* thus implies nothing new in regard to the person who is sent, but its eternal *processio* is one part of the totality to which Thomas refers when he speaks of *missio*, or, as he sometimes expresses it, *processio temporalis*. But since the scriptures speak in connection with the Spirit of a real sending *into the world*, the concept must refer to

[63] See p. 149 above.   [64] 1a, 43, 1.
[65] 1a, 43, 1, ad 3; cf. 1a, 27, 1. The term *missio* presents such vast difficulties when used of the persons of the godhead that Thomas simply says that it is used of them *aequivoce*, see 1a, 112, 2, ad 3.
[66] 1a, 43, 1, ad 2.   [67] Cf. 1a, 33, 1 and ad 3.   [68] See p. 148 above.

something that takes place in the created world in addition to this eternal activity within the Trinity. For Thomas, as we saw earlier, the relation between God and the world is in the last resort a causal one which also applies in this case, since MISSIO INCLUDIT PROCESSIONEM AETERNAM, ET ALIQUID ADDIT, SCILICET TEMPORALEM EFFECTUM (mission includes the eternal procession, with the addition of a temporal effect).[69] In this new effect of the divine causality, the person of the godhead is said *esse novo modo in aliquo* (to exist in a new way in something). God cannot begin to be where he was not previously, but his presence must be understood to mean that he is present in a new way, *quodam modo novo*, wherever by virtue of his omnipresence he is already present.[70] This 'new' presence cannot in any way mean that God himself changes, since he is unchangeable, but the change that is implied when we say that God is present in the world of his creation in a new way must rather be one that takes place entirely within creation.[71] Since God's general presence is conceived in causal categories as the presence of the transcendent cause in its effect, and a presence *quodam novo modo* presupposes this primary presence,

---

[69] 1a, 43, 2, ad 3; *De Pot.* 10, 4, ad 14: *missio divinae personae intelligatur secundum aliquem effectum in creatura . . . in missione non intelligatur auctoritas mittentis ad personam quae mittitur, sed causalitas ad effectum, secundum quem dicitur mitti persona; In De Trin.* 3, 4, ad 11: *filius et spiritus sanctus dicuntur missi a patre, non quod essent ubi prius non fuerant, sed ut essent aliquo modo quo prius non fuerant, quod est secundum aliquem effectum in creatura;* 1a, 43, 8: *Quia cum dicitur aliqua Persona mitti, designatur et ipsa Persona ab alio existens, et effectus visibilis aut invisibilis, secundum quem missio divinae Personae attenditur.* The crucial importance of this causal concept for Thomas's interpretation of the term *missio* is emphasised in particular by L. Chambat, *Présence et union. Les missions des personnes de la Sainte Trinité selon saint Thomas d'Aquin,* Abbaye S. Wandrille 1943, see e.g. p. 113: 'L'idée mère, qui exprime le *propter quid,* la raison d'être des missions et qui engendre tout le traité jusque dans ses moindres détails, c'est la causalité des personnes divines vis-à-vis des créatures . . . d'un bout à l'autre, comme on le voit, tout est sous le signe de la causalité et s'explique par elle'; see also especially p. 176 and 193.

[70] 1a, 43, 6: *missio de sui ratione importat quod ille qui mittitur vel incipiat esse ubi prius non fuit, sicut accidit in rebus creatis; vel incipiat esse ubi prius fuit, sed quodam modo novo, secundum quod missio attribuitur divinis Personis.* Cf. *In Joan.* 14, 6: *Non est autem intelligendum quod per motum localem ad nos veniat, sed quia quodam modo in eis esse debeat, quo prius non fuerat.*

[71] I *Sent.* 15, 1, 1: *Quia autem omnis imperfectio amovenda est ab his quae in divinam praedicationem veniunt, ideo missio in divinis intelligitur non secundum exitum localis distantiae, nec secundum aliquam novitatem advenientem ipsi misso, ut sit ubi prius non fuerat; sed secundum exitum originis ab aliquo ut a principio, et secundum novitatem advenientem ei ad quem fit missio, ut novo modo persona missa in eo esse dicatur;* cf. I *Sent.* 17, 1, 1: *oportet quod illa creatura, in qua speciali mode Deus esse dicitur, habeat in se aliquem effectum Dei, quem alia non habeat.*

this 'new' presence must logically be understood to be a change wrought in the creature, *mutatio creaturae*, by the divine causality.[72] The divine presence thus becomes equal to *quoddam temporale* (something temporal), which as such can be a reality only within the creaturely sphere (as distinct from the Creator).[73] Even when scripture speaks of a sending of one of the persons of the godhead into the world, God remains transcendent. Once again we find the expression of what this transcendence means in the conception of the relationships between God and the creature. The new thing that begins does not establish any new relationship in the divine being beyond the relationships which are expressed in the eternal *processiones* of the divine will and intellect. The 'new' that is brought about exists, so to speak, 'outside' God, in the soul of man. By being endowed and perfected by an *effectus* or *donum* of God, man is brought into a new relationship to God.[74] On man's side this relation is a real one, but it has no counterpart in the being of God. Thomas explicitly says that we have a parallel to this whenever we state *ex tempore* something about God which does not correspond to what he actually is, but we say it, if improperly, because by saying it we imply something on the part of the creature, as for instance when we say that God is *Dominus*.[75] Since something new happens to us, bringing us into a relationship to God other than that which existed

---

[72] 1a, 43, 2, ad 2: *dicendum quod divinam Personam esse novo modo in aliquo . . . non est propter mutationem divinae Personae, sed propter mutationem creaturae;* I *Sent.* 15, 3, 1: *Missio enim, ut dictum est, importat duo: scilicet missum esse ab alio . . . et iterum effectum secundum quem novo modo in aliqua creatura Spiritus sanctus dicitur. Unde sensus est: Spiritus sanctus mittitur: id est, est ab aliquo, et fit novo modo in aliquo, nulla tamen mutatione facta circa ipsum;* III *Sent.* 13, 3, 1, ad 9.

[73] 1a, 43, 2: *Personam autem divinam haberi ab aliqua creatura, vel esse novo modo existendi in ea, est quoddam temporale;* cf. Villard, *L'Incarnation,* p. 203f.

[74] I *Sent.* 14, 1, 1: *et sic dicetur processio temporalis ex eo quod ex novitate effectus consurgit nova relatio creaturae ad Deum.*

[75] Cf. p. 118 above. I *Sent.* 14, 1, 1 ad 2: *inquantum per amorem, qui est Spiritus sanctus, aliquod donum creaturae confertur, nulla mutatio vel variatio fit in ipso amore, sed in eo cui per amorem aliquid datur; si tamen mutatio, et non potius perfectio dici debet. Et ideo ille temporalis respectus non ponitur circa Spiritum sanctum realiter, sed solum secundum rationem; realiter autem in creatura quae mutatur; sicut fit cum dicitur Deus Dominus ex tempore;* I *Sent.* 14, 2, 1, 2, ad 1: *cum dicitur Deus esse ubique, importatur quaedam relatio Dei ad creaturam, quae quidem realiter non est in ipso, sed in creatura. Contingit autem ex parte creaturae istas relationes multipliciter etiam diversificari secundum diversos effectus quibus Deo assimilatur; et inde est quod significatur ut aliter se habens ad creaturam quam prius. Et propter hoc Spiritus sanctus, qui ubique est, secundum relationem aliquam creaturae ad ipsum potest dici de novo esse in aliquo, secundum novam relationem ipsius creaturae ad ipsum.* See also Morency, *L'union de grâce,* p. 66f.

N

before, we may say that God is related to us in a new way, though this is an improper way of speaking and does not really correspond to anything in God himself.[76] In the last resort, therefore, Thomas reduces the term *missio* to a combination of two types of real relations. In speaking, for example, of the sending of the Holy Spirit, he has reference on the one hand to the relation constituted by the eternal procession of the third person of the Trinity from the Father and Son within the godhead, and on the other hand to the relation to the transcendent, divine cause which follows from a change that God brings about in the creature.[77] The causal relationship which links God and the world also unites the activity of the Trinity within the godhead to that which occurs within the creature, for the former is by definition the *ratio et causa* (reason and cause) of the latter.[78] Thus here, too, in discussing salvation we come back ultimately to a causality that has the same structure as that all-inclusive structure of which Thomas speaks in his discussion of the general relation between God and the world that is given in creation. The basic difference between creation and salvation is a distinction in regard to the 'effect' of which the same divine causality is the cause.[79]

The new *effectus* which distinguishes salvation from creation is grace.[80] Grace is the expression of the new presence in man. God's

---

[76] I *Sent.* 14, 2, 1, 2: *secundum hoc enim ipse (scil. Spiritus sanctus) dicitur referri ad nos, secundum quod nos referimur in ipsum.* I *Sent.* 14, 2, 1, 2, ad 3: *non dicitur ipsemet in nos procedere, quia circa ipsum aliquid fiat; sed quia ex eo quod nos ad ipsummet aliter nos habeamus, ipse potest significari sub alio respectu se habere ad nos.*

[77] I *Sent.* 14, 3: *in processione temporali . . . duo sint; scilicet respectus aeternus, quo Spiritus sanctus exit a Patre et Filio, et respectus temporalis, qui consurgit ex eo quod creatura per donum susceptum novo modo se habet ad ipsum.* Cf. Dondaine, *La Trinité,* vol. II, p. 425f. and 431.

[78] I *Sent.* 14, 1, 2: *Processio autem est duplex, vel gemina, ratione duorum respectuum in duo objecta, scilicet in aeternum et temporale: quorum unus, scilicet aeternus, realiter est in ipso procedente; alius autem secundum rationem tantum in Spiritu sancto, sed secundum rem in eo in quem procedit. Horum tamen respectuum primus includitur in secundo, sicut ratio et causa ejus; unde secundus se habet ex additione ad primum;* see also ib. ad 6.

[79] Skydsgaard is therefore wrong, at least in the case of Thomas, when in his *Metafysik,* p. 122, he restricts the causal relationship to the relationship of creation to God and defines salvation thus: 'Creation is raised up from the simple causal relation to God to a participation in God's own inner life, not *per causalitatem* but *per unionem*'. Cf. F. Bourassa, 'Les missions divines et le surnaturel chez saint Thomas d'Aquin', in *SE* 1 (1948), p. 51f.: 'Or, cette transcendance de la présence et de l'operation divine, S. Thomas la retrouve dans toute l'étendue de l'oeuvre surnaturelle; et partout le même problème est résolu par la production d'un effet créé intrinsèque à la créature: grâce sanctifiante, charité, lumière de gloire'.

[80] Cf. 1a2ae, 111, 3, ad 1: *gratia significat effectum temporalem.*

presence in man, that is to say, differs from his general presence: *nullus alius effectus potest esse ratio quod divina Persona sit novo modo in rationali creatura, nisi gratia gratum faciens* (no other effect can be put down as the reason why the divine person is in the rational creature in a new way, except sanctifying grace).[81] When Thomas speaks of the presence in grace as the indwelling of God, he means that the whole Trinity is in man through the *effectus gratiae*. We can speak of *missio* only with regard to the indwelling of the Son and the Spirit, since only these persons of the godhead come *ab alio* and by their *processio* can participate in the idea of sending. Unlike the Son and the Spirit, only the Father is *origo*, which simply means that we cannot say of the Father that he 'is sent'.[82] The difference between *inhabitatio* and *missio* is thus above all a distinction which originates in the relations between the persons of the Trinity, and grace itself, like every other act of God *ad extra*, is an effect of the whole Trinity.[83] But since this effect appears in a being endowed with reason and will, a *creatura rationalis*, this means that it comes to be expressed in a particular way.

As cause, God is at once *causa efficiens*, *causa exemplaris*, and *causa finalis*. With regard to grace, as CAUSA EFFICIENS he is also present in the soul by reason of the fact that something is given in the soul that is an effect of the divine causality, *ubicumque est aliquis effectus Dei, ibi sit ipse Deus effector* (wherever there is an effect of God, there God himself is at work).[84] But he is also present in the soul as CAUSA EXEMPLARIS, and the expression of this presence is our conformity to God himself through grace.[85] Endowed as he is with reason and will, man is already the *imago Dei*, and since grace implies a perfection of nature, it means that these endowments are perfected in order that they may function better and more in accordance with the divine original. When Thomas speaks of the invisible sending of the persons of the godhead, it is to this that he refers. The sending of the Son thus means a perfection of man's intellect through

---

[81] 1a, 43, 3, where the passage quoted continues: *Unde secundum solam gratiam gratum facientem, mittitur et procedit temporaliter Persona divina*; cf. 1a, 8, 3, ad 4: *sola gratia facit singularem modum essendi Deum in rebus.*

[82] 1a, 43, 5: *per gratiam gratum facientem tota Trinitas inhabitat mentem;* 1a, 43, 4, ad 2: *licet effectus gratiae sit etiam a Patre, qui inhabitat per gratiam, sicut et Filius et Spiritus Sanctus; quia tamen non est ab alio, non dicitur mitti.*

[83] Cf. Dondaine, *La Trinité*, vol. II, p. 369f.; Morency, *L'union de grâce*, p. 67.

[84] *CG* IV, 21. The *effectus* referred to is in fact supernatural *caritas.*

[85] 1a, 43, 5, ad 2: *anima per gratiam conformatur Deo*. On this *assimilatio* see especially the exhaustive analysis in Morency, *L'union de grâce*, p. 120ff.

being conformed to the divine Word by the *donum sapientiae* (gift of wisdom),[86] while the sending of the Spirit means an *assimilatio* of the will to the divine Love by the *donum amoris*. In this way man himself is lifted up to a higher plane on which he attains a degree of God-likeness far above his natural endowment, where these gifts of grace bring about a special affinity between his created reason and will and the corresponding realities in the divine being itself.[87] Through grace, these eternal real relations within the Trinity have a created counter-part in the new real relations which are established in the creaturely sphere with the increase of the affinity between the faculties of the human soul and the divine Word and Love. The persons of the god-head are thus present in man in a way most nearly comparable to the presence of a thing in its own image or copy. Since the relation-ships within the Trinity are thus reflected in man's soul, *dicuntur personae divinae in nobis esse, secundum quod novo modo eis assimi-lamur* (the persons of the godhead are said to be in us as we are made like them in a new way).[88] In fact, the image of God which we have by nature is itself an *imago Trinitatis* in that the soul's faculties

[86] The *sapientia* referred to, as distinguished from the *sapientia acquisita* of theology, is a perfection of the intellect through grace, see 2a2ae, 8, 6; 2a2ae, 45, 1, ad 2.

[87] *CG* IV, 21: *ea quae a Deo in nobis sunt, reducuntur in Deum sicut in causam efficientem et exemplarem. In causam quidem efficientem, inquantum virtute operativa divina aliquid in nobis efficitur. In causa quidem exemplarem, secundum quod id quod in nobis a Deo est, aliquo modo Deum imitatur. Cum ergo eadem virtus sit Patris et Filii et Spiritus Sancti, sicut et eadem essentia; oportet quod omne id quod Deus in nobis efficit, sit, sicut a causa efficiente, simul a Patre et Filio et Spiritu Sancto. Verbum tamen sapientiae, quo Deum cognoscimus, nobis a Deo immissum, est proprie repraesentativum Filii. Et similiter amor quo Deum diligimus, est proprium repraesen-tativum Spiritus Sancti;* cf. I *Sent.* 15, 4, 2; 1a, 43, 5, ad 1. Cf. Bourassa, *SE* 1 (1948), p. 72: 'la présence surnaturelle, ou la vie surnaturelle, est la vie intime de Dieu—mais dans une créature'.

[88] I *Sent.* 15, 4, 1: *in reductione rationalis creaturae in Deum intelligitur processio divinae personae, quae et missio dicitur, inquantum propria relatio ipsius personae divinae repraesentatur in anima per similitudinem aliquam receptam, quae est exemplata et originata ab ipsa proprietate relationis aeternae; sicut proprius modus quo Spiritus sanctus refertur ad Patrem, est amor, et proprius modus referendi Filium in Patrem est, quia est verbum ipsius manifestans ipsum. Unde sicut Spiritus sanctus invisibiliter procedit in mentem per donum amoris, ita Filius per donum sapientiae; in quo est manifestatio ipsius Patris, qui est ultimum ad quod recurrimus. Et quia secundum receptionem horum duorum efficitur in nobis similitudo ad propria personarum; ideo secundum novum modum essendi, prout res est in sua similitudine, dicuntur personae divinae in nobis esse, secundum quod novo modo eis assimilamur; et secundum hoc utraque processio dicitur missio;* see also *De Ver.* 27, 2, ad 3. Cf. Bourassa, *SE* 1 (1948), p. 45: 'Et ainsi, en autant qu'une chose est contenue en son image, on peut dire que les personnes divines sont en nous, dans la mesure où nous leur sommes assimilés d'une nouvelle manière'.

of reason and will proceed from its *essentia* just as in God Word and Love proceed from the Father, and the convergence must be even greater in the higher likeness to God that is constituted by grace.[89] It is in the essence of the soul that habitual grace resides, and this *radix gratiae* (root of grace) is the source of those acts by which the faculties of the soul are brought to a fuller perfection in an *illuminatio intellectus* (illumination of the intellect) and an *inflammatio affectus* (kindling of the affection). Since grace is a reflection in man of God's own intra-Trinitarian life, *sapientia* cannot exist without *caritas*. The very presence of grace in a man means that both acts must be brought about if the whole man is to be perfected, just as in God there can be no procession of the Son without a procession of the Spirit *per modum voluntatis*.[90] It is at this profound level that we see why for Thomas faith, in order to be saving faith, must be *caritate formata* (directed by love). A *fides informis* (dead faith) cannot save if it lacks a love that is conjoined to faith, a God-given love for the truth it possesses, for a man who has only an unformed faith lacks the *gratia gratum faciens* which brings the *whole* man to perfection or salvation. Since faith can be conceived to exist without a concomitant supernatural perfection of the will, Thomas defines the perfection of the intellect by grace as *sapientia* and not as *fides*.[91] But this brings us to the ultimate meaning of God's presence through grace as CAUSA FINALIS, which is the principal aspect of this causal relationship. For it is the inclination given through grace to attain to our supernatural destination and not simply the increase of our likeness to God that makes what is done to us in the *missio invisibilis*

---

[89] *De Ver.* 27, 6, ad 5: *imago creationis consistit et in essentia et in potentiis, secundum quod per essentiam animae repraesentatur unitas essentiae divinae, et per distinctionem potentiarum distinctio personarum; et similiter imago recreationis consistit in gratia et virtutibus.*

[90] I *Sent.* 15, 4, 2: *una missio nunquam est sine alia;* 1a, 43, 5, ad :3 *Si autem quantum ad effectum gratiae, sic communicant duae missiones in radice gratiae, sed distinguuntur in effectibus gratiae, qui sunt illuminatio intellectus, et inflammatio affectus. Et sic manifestum est quod una non potest esse sine alia: quia neutra est sine gratia gratum faciente, nec una Persona separatur ab alia.*

[91] *In 1 ad Cor.* 3, 3 (173): *cognitio sine dilectione non sufficit ad inhabitationem Dei;* 1a, 43, 5, ad 2: *Non igitur secundum quamlibet perfectionem intellectus mittitur Filius: sed secundum talem instructionem intellectus, qua prorumpat in affectum amoris;* cf. I *Sent.* 14, 2, 2, ad 3. *Sapientia* presupposes faith, see 1a2ae, 68, 4, ad 3; 1a2ae, 113, 4, ad 2; 2a2ae, 45, 1, ad 2, but is a deepening and perfecting of its *cognitio simplex articulorum*, just as acquired *sapientia* presupposes and perfects the simple knowledge of first principles, see III *Sent.* 35, 2, 1, 1, ad 1, and Morency, 'L'union du juste à Dieu par voie de connaissance et d'amour', in *SE* 2 (1949), p. 49ff. and the same author's *L'union de grâce*, p. 197ff.

grace, and so distinguishes it from every natural form of the *imago Trinitatis*.[92] Grace and grace alone can impel us towards the higher goal that God has set before us apart from any merit or need of ours, *gratia gratum faciens est forma quaedam in homine, per quam ordinatur ad ultimum finem* (sanctifying grace is a certain form in man whereby he is ordered to his ultimate end).[93] Even when he speaks of grace as a sending of the persons of the godhead or their dwelling in the human soul, Thomas includes it within the finality by which in his view the whole of existence, both on the natural and the supernatural plane, is marked. *Missio pertinet ad reditum creaturae in finem* (mission relates to the return of the creature to its end),[94] and therefore grace means the completion of the *motus in Deum*, and for Thomas this is the intent of the work of salvation. It is a fundamental rule for all things created that *ultimum per quod res unaquaeque ordinatur ad finem, est eius operatio* (it is through its activity that a real being is ultimately ordered to its end),[95] and therefore we are not to understand grace in the first instance as a static possession but as an activity or *operatio*. But the meaning of final causality is also determined by the fact that what is being described is something that takes place in a *creatura rationalis*. Since this creature is to be distinguished from others by reason of the fact that it has cognitive and volitional functions, Thomas defines the presence of the divine cause as a presence *sicut cognitum in cognoscente et amatum in amante* (as the object known in the knower, and the beloved in the lover).[96] God is the *finis* or *objectum operationis* of the soul in the sense that he is

---

[92] In his monograph on the concept of *missio* in Thomas, *Présence et union*, Chambat has failed to notice what Thomas himself regarded as the crucial final aspect of the divine causality, a serious lack in what is otherwise a study of basic importance. At this point Chambat's work requires to be supplemented, as Bourassa indicates in *SE* 1 (1948), p. 45ff. It is not true that 'l'assimilation de la grace' is to be distinguished from natural *assimilatio*, in that the former is 'voulue', as P. Galtier states in *L'habitation en nous des trois personnes. Le fait—la mode*, Paris 1928, p. 238. The author does not quote a single passage from Thomas to sustain his argument, which is understandable, since for Thomas creation as much as salvation is dependent on the will of God.

[93] *CG* III, 151; cf. also 1a2ae, 111, 5: *Gratia autem gratum faciens ordinat hominem immediate ad coniunctionem ultimi finis*, and many passages of a similar nature which are quoted by Morency, *L'union de grâce*, p. 148ff.

[94] I *Sent*. 15, 5, 1, 1, ad 3; cf. also the reference given on p. 184 above in footnote 88 from I *Sent*. 15, 4, 1. Morency, *L'union de grâce*, p. 72: 'S. Thomas insiste de façon toute spéciale sur les rapports qui existent entre les missions divines et l'ordre de la finalité'.

[95] *CG* III, 22.

[96] 1a, 43, 3.

the object of its knowledge and of its desire.[97] As we have already seen, grace in Thomas's view is primarily a lifting up of human nature, but this *elevatio* occurs *per operationem*.[98] Following Augustine in his use of the terms *uti* and *frui*, Thomas maintains that man by grace not only possesses the gifts of God but by making use of them can also enjoy God and know him and love him. When he speaks of grace as a possessing of God, *habere Deum*[99] or describes the invisible sending as a giving by God of himself, it is this final character of grace to which he refers. God not only gives a perfection inherent in man, he also gives himself as an 'object' together with the gift of perfection.[100] Grace is *id per quod fruibili conjungimur* (that by which we are united to the source of our joy).[101] Thus we cannot properly describe Thomas's view of the meaning of grace simply by defining it as an immanent quality or *donum creatum*. Since God is not only *causa efficiens et exemplaris*, but also and above all *causa finalis*, this immanent quality must always be related to the transcendent cause or *donum increatum*.[102]. Through the *donum creatum* we possess God as the object of knowledge or of desire. This perfection, of course, is an immanent one, but it is produced only by the transcendent *objectum* or *finis*.

---

[97] II *Sent*. 1, 2, 2: *ipsamet divina bonitas potest acquiri a creatura rationali ut perfectio quae est objectum operationis, inquantum rationalis creatura possibilis est ad videndum et amandum Deum. Et ideo singulari modo Deus est finis in quem tendit creatura rationalis*. On *operatio* as a particular instance of final causality see Morency, *L'union de grâce*, p. 148: 'c'est parce qu'il est l'objet de l'opération surnaturelle du juste, que Dieu est la fin du juste', see also ib. p. 240f. and Bourassa *SE* 1 (1948), p. 48f.

[98] 3a, 2, 10: *Elevatur autem humana natura in Deum . . . per operationem: qua scilicet sancti cognoscunt et amant Deum.*

[99] Cf. I *Sent*. 18, 1, 5, ad 6: *dicitur autem Deus justorum specialiter, secundum rationem finis quem contingunt; et ideo dicitur etiam ab eis haberi.* On the meaning of *habere Deum* see also I *Sent*. 14, 2, 1; I *Sent*. 14, 2, 2, ad 2; 1a, 38, 1.

[100] I *Sent*. 14, 2, 1, 2, 1: *ipsemet Spiritus sanctus procedit temporali processione, vel datur, et non solum dona ejus. . . Cum igitur in acceptione donorum ipsius non solum relatio nostra terminetur ad dona, ut ipsa tantum habeamus, sed etiam ad Spiritum sanctum, quia aliter ipsum habemus quam prius; non tantum dicentur dona ipsius procedere in nos, sed etiam ipsemet; secundum hoc enim ipse dicitur referri ad nos, secundum quod nos referimur in ipsum;* see also ib. ad 2; 1a, 43, 3, ad 1: *per donum gratiae gratum facientis perficitur creatura rationalis, ad hoc quod libere non solum ipso dono creato utatur, sed ut ipsa divina Persona fruatur. Et ideo missio invisibilis fit secundum donum gratiae gratum facientis, et tamen ipsa Persona divina datur.* Thomas uses this idea of the divine self-giving as a giving of the object of desire in his interpretation of John 3:16, see *In Joan*. 3, 3, (1): *In hoc autem quod dicit 'Habeat vitam aeternam', indicatur divini amoris immensitas: nam dando vitam aeternam, dat seipsum. Nam vita aeterna nihil aliud est quam frui Deo. Dare autem seipsum, magni amoris est indicium.*

[101] I *Sent*. 14, 2, 2, ad 2.   [102] Bourassa, *SE* 1 (1948), p. 49ff.

Thomas thus employs the same causal scheme to express the presence of God in grace as he does—we noted this earlier—to express his general presence. In dealing with the general presence he applied the rule *causa est in effectu per modum effectus* (a cause is in its effect according to the mode of the effect).[103] He does so here too, but having regard to the nature of man he states the general definition more precisely as *cognitum autem est in cognoscente secundum modum cognoscentis* (the thing known is in the knower according to the mode of the knower),[104] or, *est autem amatum in amante secundum quod amatur* (the thing loved is in the lover so far as it is loved).[105] God is present in the righteous, as Thomas puts it, *per ipsorum sanctorum operationem . . . nam diligens et cognoscens dicitur in se habere cognita et dilecta* (through the activity of the righteous themselves . . . for one who loves and knows is said to possess what is known and loved).[106] This presence does not mean that God is in any way changed. His absolute transcendence remains. But since something new takes places in what Thomas describes as God's *esse quodam novo modo* in the world, this 'new' must exist entirely on the side of the creature and therefore Thomas focuses his attention on the change that occurs in the creature. Nor does grace imply anything new for God in the sense that in relation to his general *actio* in creation, grace is to be considered as some sort of new and supernatural act. We may define God as *finis naturalis* and *finis supernaturalis*, but this in no way implies any division in God's being, and the distinction between these two definitions is simply a way of stating that something new has taken place on the human plane. As Bouillard has convincingly shown, there is nothing in Thomas comparable to the idea widely found in more recent Roman Catholic theology of a *gratia actualis* that is distinct from God's

---

[103] See p. 160f. above.

[104] 1a, 12, 4; 2a2ae, 1, 2; cf. 1a, 8, 3: *Deus dicitur esse in re . . . sicut obiectum operationis est in operante: quod proprium est in operationibus animae, secundum quod cognitum est in cognoscente, et desideratum in desiderante. Hoc igitur . . . modo, Deus specialiter est in rationali creatura, quae cognoscit et diligit illum actu vel habitu. Et quia hoc habet rationalis creatura per gratiam . . . dicitur esse hoc modo in sanctis per gratiam.*

[105] *CG* IV, 19. Cf. Bourassa, *SE* 1 (1948), p. 85: 'La présence de l'aimé dans l'aimant s'explique donc dans le théorème général de la causalité, suivant lequel la cause est présente en son effet dans la mesure où elle le cause. . . Et ainsi le bien aimé est présent dans l'aimant dans la mesure où il est aimé, i.e. dans la mesure où il cause l'amour, tout comme le vrai est dans l'intellect dans la mesure où il est cause de l'intelliger'.

[106] *In 2 ad Cor.* 6, 3 (240).

general activity in the world: 'The divine motion . . . in itself is neither natural nor supernatural, but *general* or *universal.*'[107] The 'new' that distinguishes supernature from nature is not something new in God but is the habitual perfection that is given with *gratia gratum faciens* and transcends all natural expectations, claims and merits.[108] This is *grace* and *aliquid supernaturale* simply because it does not have its origin in man, being quite beyond his capacity, but in God; but the *operatio* which grace sets in motion and renders possible is in fact the *operatio* of a man's own natural abilities perfected by grace. There could be no *actio* common to God and man in which each had a part to play. This would contradict God's transcendence. All that is done on man's side is created; it is man's own *motus in Deum*. But even man's *operatio*, creaturely function though it is, comes to him from God, for it is received from God and dependent upon him at every moment. Thus even God's presence in grace—the sending of the persons of the godhead to men —may apparently be related to the elements characteristic of the causal relationship between God and the world as an 'effect' produced in the creature and as its real relation to its final, transcendent cause, or (as Bouillard expresses it), 'The divine motion, then, is simply the movement of the creature, in so far as it depends on God as its source'.[109]

In the section that follows we shall see how Thomas interprets God's presence in Christ, and then go on to show briefly in the final chapter how this throws light on the problem of the relationship

[107] Bouillard, *Conversion*, p. 202: 'il est impossible de prouver que saint Thomas a distingué deux sortes de motion, l'une naturelle, l'autre surnaturelle. Jamais il ne rapporte le qualificatif de *supernaturale* à la motion divine'. Bouillard's work is a stimulating example of the advantage of approaching the texts from a strictly historical standpoint without assuming, as Roman Catholic theologians have tended, perhaps unconsciously, to assume that what is to be found in contemporary theology must in some way or another be found in all earlier theologians of the church. In this regard Thomas displays a freshness and originality by his use of Aristotelian elements clearly distinct from patristic theology, but also in clear contrast to Roman Catholic theology after the Reformation.

[108] Cf. Bouillard, *Conversion*, p. 201: 'Une opération, un acte est naturel ou surnaturel. Mais ce n'est pas la motion divine qui le différencie; c'est la forme dont il procède. Il est naturel ou surnaturel, selon qu'il procède d'une forme naturelle ou d'une perfection infuse. La motion divine ne fait qu'actuer la forme'.

[109] Bouillard, *Conversion*, p. 198, where the passage cited continues: 'Elle est, si l'on préfère, la relation à Dieu du mouvement créé'. Cf. Bourassa, *SE* 1 (1948), p. 73: 'il s'agit d'une présence de Dieu nouvelle, non pas éternelle, d'une présence de Dieu hors de lui-même, non pas en lui, d'une présence acquise à la créature, par voie de causalité divine, et donc contenue dans des relations de cause à effet'.

between *ratio* and *revelatio* in the doctrine of grace. Even at this point, however, the immediate impression received from a reading of certain passages in Thomas may suggest some preliminary observations. The discussion of God's presence in the righteous has concentrated on two concepts which are both manifestly biblical in origin and for Thomas are simply different aspects of the same reality, viz. *gratia* and *missio*. It has become increasingly clear that Thomas's general principle that grace at every point presupposes nature determines the content which is given to these concepts. It is not simply that the necessity for grace is determined primarily from a philosophical concept of nature; it must also be asked whether this starting-point may not also ultimately determine how Thomas answers the question of what grace essentially is. *Vita gratiae . . . praesupponit vitam naturae rationalis* (the life of grace presupposes the life of the rational nature),[110] not only in the sense that salvation is something that has reference to man and presupposes his existence, but in such a way also that 'the structure of the state of grace is determined beforehand in the spiritual structure of the *mens* its subject'.[111] The answer to the question of the meaning of grace is structurally pre-determined by a philosophical analysis of the nature of man as a *natura rationalis*, and is such because it completes the general outlines of this analysis. The influence of *ratio* in determining both the meaning and content of *missio* is strong. Scripture does not speak of an invisible sending of the Son (though it does, of course, speak of Christ's indwelling), but the need to speak of a *missio invisibilis Filii* is dictated by the necessity of supplying in the case of the intellect a parallel to the perfection of the will through the sending of the Spirit, to which scripture explicitly testifies.[112] This necessity in turn is determined by the assumption that the Spirit is a divine counterpart to the act of will in the human soul.

The fact that for Thomas the concept of *missio* also includes the incarnation apparently indicates that we may expect to find ourselves dealing with a similar kind of problem when we turn from our discussion of God's general presence in creation and his special presence in grace to consider the third form of his presence, viz. his presence in Christ.

[110] 3a, 71, 1, ad 1.
[111] Dondaine, *La Trinité*, vol. II, p. 446. See also Gardeil, *La structure*, vols. I and II, in which this whole idea is central.
[112] There is no discussion of this whole idea in the introductory section of Chambat, *Présence et union*, which deals with the question of biblical theology, see p. 15ff.

4

GOD'S PRESENCE IN CHRIST
MISSIO VISIBILIS

If Thomas seems to go beyond revelation when he speaks of a *missio Filii invisibilis*, he is quite clearly on a biblical basis when he speaks of incarnation in terms of *missio*.[1] The New Testament, in particular the Johannine writings but also Paul, often speaks of the 'sending' of the Son into the world: *Filium suum unigenitum misit Deus in mundum* (I John 4:9, Vulgate).[2] Our task is to see how Thomas interprets a statement like this.

Here too, as we shall find, his starting-point is God's life within the Trinity. The Son is born from all eternity in that he eternally proceeds from the Father, and since moreover by being sent into the world he is also born in time, the fact that we may speak of his birth in time presupposes his birth in eternity.[3] As we saw when discussing the invisible sending of the persons of the godhead into the world, the activity of God within the Trinity is comprehended within the incarnation. As we noted earlier, also, Thomas defines the meaning of the sending of one or other of the persons of the godhead in the words, *missio includit processionem aeternam, et aliquid addit, scilicet temporalem effectum* (mission includes the eternal procession, with the addition of a temporal effect),[4] and this definition applies here too without further qualification. The new thing that takes place in what we speak of as the *missio visibilis* does not take place on God's side but on man's, and is expressed as an *effectus visibilis*.[5] To be more precise, this does not mean that the Son is sent in an invisible manner *ut sit in homine* (to dwell in man), as he is in the case of grace, but in a visible manner, *ut etiam sit homo* (to become man as well).[6]

---

[1] *In Joan.* 6, 7 (7): *Missio enim Filii Dei est ejus incarnatio.*
[2] See e.g. John 3:17; 5:23f., 37; 10:36; 17:18, etc.; Rom. 8:3; Gal. 4:4.
[3] 1a, 43, 2, ad 1 : *ex hoc ipso Filius habet quod possit mitti, quod est ab aeterno genitus.*
[4] 1a, 43, 2, ad 3; Diekamp, *Dogmatik*, vol. I, p. 350: 'Von den göttlichen Hervorgängen sind die Sendungen also dadurch verschieden, dass sie *eine zeitliche Wirkung hinzufügen*'.
[5] 1a, 43, 8.   [6] 1a, 43, 2.

This implies not only a divine indwelling in the soul of man but an activity also which includes the body as well. Thus, in speaking about the incarnation in terms of Paul's words in I Corinthians 2:9, *in quo inhabitat omnis plenitudo divinitatis corporaliter*, Thomas can speak of *ipsum corpus Christi* as *templum Dei*.[7] By the incarnation Christ is in the world as man, and a man has both soul and body. The visible sending of the Son into the world does not imply any change on God's part, but a visible *effectus*, produced in the world by the triune God, which thus forms an addition to the eternal activity within the godhead.[8]

Thomas, however, can also interpret the distinction between the invisible and visible sending of the Son to mean that the latter implies union with God *non solum secundum operationem, sed etiam secundum esse* (not only in accordance with his activity but also in accordance with his being).[9] It is quite evident that for Thomas God's presence in Christ includes the form which we have just discussed according to which God *est in mentibus sanctis per operationem, quae per amorem et cognitionem attingunt Deum* (is by his activity in righteous minds, which attain God through love and knowledge),[10] but there is another kind of presence also, that SECUNDUM ESSE. Thomas employs the same terminology when in a different context he speaks of grace as an *elevatio* of human nature *in Deum . . . per operationem*, but he also speaks of another kind of *elevatio* which applies only to Christ, and in this case he is referring to an elevation of human nature *per esse personale* (by personal actuality).[11] We are here at the very heart of Thomas's interpretation of the classical doctrine of the incarnation which originates in the early church and speaks of 'one person in two natures', for the *esse personale* to which Thomas makes reference here is simply the act by which the second person of the godhead exists. But at the same time we also come once more to the centre of

---

[7] *In Joan.* 2, 3 (2); *In ad Col.* 2, 2 (97): *alii sancti inhabitantur solum secundum animam . . . sed in Christo divinitas inhabitat corporaliter;* cf. 3a, 2, 10, ad 2.

[8] Cf. Dondaine, *La Trinité*, vol. II, p. 429f.: 'si l'on regarde l'Incarnation de ce point de vue des trois Personnes, ce qui se passe là n'est point d'abord un événement: c'est toujours l'éternelle et immuable Naissance du Verbe, c'est la Procession éternelle. Mais à ce prodigieux échange de vie au sein de Dieu, vient s'adjoindre . . . par l'opération des Trois un effet fini, bénéficiaire dans le temps de la divine Naissance: la sainte Humanité est unie au Fils'.

[9] I *Sent.* 37, 1, 2.   [10] *In ad Col.* 2, 2 (96).

[11] 3a, 2, 10: *Elevatur autem humana natura in Deum dupliciter. Uno modo, per operationem: qua scilicet sancti cognoscunt et amant Deum. Alio modo, per esse personale: qui quidem modus est singularis Christo.*

Thomas's metaphysics of existence, the main outlines of which we traced in the introductory section of the present chapter. For Thomas, the fundamental distinction between God and the creature is that in God *esse* and *essentia* constitute an inseparable unity, while in the case of the creature *esse* is really distinct from *essentia* because it is constantly received *ab alio*, and so we may also say that it is a mark of the creature that it consists of *esse* and *essentia*.[12]

Our task, therefore, will be to see how Thomas understands the traditional dogmatic concepts of 'nature' and 'person'.[13] Turning first to the concept of nature, we find that *natura* for Thomas is synonymous with *essentia*.[14] But since the *essentia* of a creature is to be distinguished *realiter* from *esse*, *essentia* cannot mean 'that which exists', *quod est*, but 'that in accordance with which something exists' and which is indicated is its definition, viz. *quo est*, or, to use Thomas's own definition of the relation between nature and existence: *Esse autem pertinet . . . ad naturam . . . sicut ad id* QUO *aliquid habet esse* (the act of existence pertains to nature as to that by which something has existence).[15] We may therefore speak of the nature of man by using the term *humanitas*, which expresses what all men have in common and defines the conditions, limits and means in accordance with which every actual human being exists as a being consisting of form and matter.[16] *Natura* thus expresses the manner in which a thing exists and the means by which it is distinguished from other things of a different species. To designate the individuality which is peculiar to particular things and which distinguishes them from other things of the same species Thomas uses the term *suppositum* or its Greek equivalent *hypostasis*. In speaking of rational creatures he also

[12] See p. 129f. above.
[13] On this terminology see especially the discussion in Villard, *L'Incarnation*; p. 250ff.; E. Hugon, *Le mystère de l'incarnation*, 9th ed. Paris 1946, p. 144ff., Ch.-V. Héris, *Le Verbe incarné*, vol. I, 2nd ed. 1927, p. 279ff. and vol. III, 2nd ed. 1954, p. 290ff.
[14] 1a, 29, 1, ad 4: *communiter essentia uniuscuisque rei, quam significat eius definitio, vocatur natura;* 3a, 2, 2: *Natura enim significat essentiam speciei, quam significat definitio.*
[15] 3a, 17, 2.
[16] 1a, 3, 3: *in rebus compositis ex materia et forma, necesse est quod differant natura vel essentia et suppositum. Quia essentia vel natura comprehendit in se illa tantum quae cadunt in definitione speciei: sicut humanitas comprehendit in se ea quae cadunt in definitione hominis: his enim homo est homo, et hoc significat humanitas, hoc scilicet quo homo est homo;* 3a, 17, 2: *natura enim significatur per modum formae, quae dicitur ens ex eo quod ea aliquid est, sicut albedine est aliquid album, et humanitate est aliquis homo;* ib. ad 4: *hoc totum compositum ex anima et corpore, prout significatur nomine humanitatis, non significatur ut quod est, sed ut quo aliquid est.*

uses the term *persona* as a synonym of *hypostasis,* meaning by this a particular individual within this species.[17] *Persona* or *suppositum* and *natura* differ from one another in their relationship to *esse.* As Thomas expresses it, *esse consequitur naturam, non sicut habentem esse, sed sicut qua aliquid est: personam autem, sive hypostasim, consequitur sicut habentum esse* (existence follows on nature, not as on that which possesses existence, but as on that by which something exists. On the contrary, it follows on the person or subsisting subject as on that which possesses existence).[18] The act of existence thus properly belongs to the person, not to nature: *ipsum esse est personae subsistentis* (actual existence belongs to the subsisting person)[19]—it is the person that exists, but it does so in accordance with the conditions that are given with its nature. One can also say that the person 'subsists', for the verb *subsistere* implies that a thing exists as a substance distinct from other substances, i.e. with an existence of its own as distinguished from that which exists *in alio* and is therefore accidental to it.[20] In a creature consisting of form and matter, therefore, *suppositum* differs from *essentia,* while among beings, such as angels, whose essence consists of pure form, person and essence coincide, since the form itself as such constitutes the actual subsistence.[21] But since on their case there is a real distinction between *esse* and *essentia,* there is also a difference between *suppositum* and *esse*: 'The idea of subsistence is by no means identical to the idea of existence'.[22] *Suppositum* designates that which exists, not

---

[17] Cf. our earlier discussion on p. 148 above of the concept of person in Thomas. See also 1a, 29, 2; 3a, 2, 2; 3a, 2, 3; 3a, 17, 2. Héris, *Le Verbe incarné,* vol. I, p. 280: 'Pour exprimer cette sorte d'autonomie et d'indépendance par laquelle la substance se trouve constituée en un tout distinct et se tenant par soi, subsistant séparément des autres substances, nous disons qu'elle est un suppôt ou une hypostase, et s'il s'agit d'une substance intelligente, nous lui donnons le nom de personne', cf. 3a, 2, 3: *persona supra hypostasim non addit nisi determinatam naturam, scilicet rationalem; De unione Verbi incarnati,* 1: *persona nihil aliud sit quam suppositum rationalis naturae.*

[18] 3a, 17, 2, ad 1.

[19] 3a, 17, 2, ad 4.

[20] I *Sent.* 23, 1, 1: *subsistere autem dicit determinatum modum essendi, prout scilicet aliquid est ens per se, non in alio, sicut accidens;* see also ib. ad 2 and 1a, 29, 2.

[21] 1a, 3, 3: *in rebus compositis ex materia et forma, necesse est quod differant natura vel essentia et suppositum . . . unde id quod est homo, habet in se aliquid quod non habet humanitas. . . In his igitur quae non sunt composita ex materia et forma, in quibus individuatio non est per materiam individualem, idest per hanc materiam, sed ipsae formae per se individuantur, oportet quod ipsae formae sint supposita subsistentia. Unde in eis non differt suppositum et natura;* cf. 3a, 2, 2.

[22] Héris, *Le Verbe incarné,* vol. I, p. 282.

existence itself as such. Only in the case of God himself do *natura*, *persona* and *esse* constitute a single, indivisible unity.[23]

We may now pass over to the particular case of the incarnation, by which it is meant that one of the persons of the godhead possesses at one time both a divine and a human nature. The Son exists from all eternity identical with the divine nature itself, *in Deo, ibi non est aliud secundum rem suppositum et natura* (in God, in whom the subsisting subject and nature are not really distinct).[24] But since the nature of God is *ipsum esse*, the nature of the Son is simply 'the pure act of existence'. Nothing can be added to this eternal divine existence, and the human nature which Christ assumes in the incarnation does not mean a new *esse personale*.[25] As it is the person that has existence and not his nature, Christ's human nature cannot have any existence of its own apart from his *esse* as one of the persons of the godhead. If indeed it had, his nature would itself have been a person (*qoud est*), but this would be to deny what is affirmed in the doctrine of the incarnation. In this instance the sole function of human nature is to determine the conditions by which the person exists. From the moment of his incarnation the Son exists not simply *secundum divinam naturam* but also as man, i.e. *secundum humanam naturam*, but since there is only one person who exists in two distinct modes, there can only be one *esse*.[26] The uniqueness of Christ is thus that the *esse* of the preexistent, divine Word becomes the act through which from a particular moment of time a human nature also exists in union with this Word. Like every other man Christ has body and soul, and this individual human nature would normally constitute a human person, as it does in other men. But this human person is lacking in Christ, its place being taken by the eternal and divine Word.[27] This means that to understand Thomas we must free

[23] See Hugon, *Incarnation*, p. 174ff., Héris, *Le Verbe incarné*, vol. I, p. 279ff. and Vol. III, p. 290. It is clear that at this point these writers have a more adequate interpretation than we find in Michel's article, 'Hypostase', in *DTC* 7: 1, col. 423, in which *suppositum* is held to coincide with the actual act of existence.   [24] 3a, 2, 2.

[25] 3a, 17, 2: *cum humana natura coniungatur Filio Dei hypostatice vel personaliter ... consequens est quod secundum humanam naturam non adveniat sibi novum esse personale.*

[26] See III *Sent.* 6, 2, 2; *Quodl.* 9, 3; *Compend. Theol.* 212; 3a, 17, 2. On the problem raised by the apparent difference in formulation in the *De unione Verbi incarnati*, 4, ad 1: *esse humanae naturae non est esse divinae*, see Héris, *Le Verbe incarné*, vol. III, p. 329ff.

[27] 3a, 2, 5, ad 1: *Et propter hoc ex unione animae et corporis in Christo non constituitur nova hypostasis seu persona: sed advenit ipsum coniunctum personae seu hypostasi praeexistenti;* 3a, 17, 2, ad 2: *illud esse aeternum Filii Dei quod est divina*

ourselves of all modern psychologising concepts of person in which 'person' is understood virtually as synonymous with, 'personality' or some such term. For Thomas *persona* is simply a 'pure principle of existence'—to use the apposite term of Congar[28]—and therefore the fact that it is not a human person who bears that humanity represents no infringement of Christ's human nature. That which makes a man man does not belong to the person as such but to his nature. It would be inconceivable for Thomas to suggest that the true humanity of Christ is somehow incomplete because we understand his human nature to be 'impersonal', for it is the concept of nature and that alone that gives him his doctrinal understanding of Christ as *perfectus homo*. We may speak of God's presence in Christ as a *missio visibilis* precisely because a fully human nature possessing body and soul was united with God in the hypostatic union. Through the mediation of the soul even the body of Christ coexists with the eternal *esse* of the second person of the godhead.[29]

This does not mean, however, that this human nature itself is eternal or divine. However intimate the connection between the human soul and the body, the soul no more makes the body *incorruptibilis* than human nature participates through the incarnation in the divine attributes such as eternity or immutability. It remains a human *essentia*: it is created, even though it subsists with an uncreated and divine *esse*. Its natural potencies and possibilities may indeed be perfectly realised through its affinity with one of the persons of the godhead, but this perfection never transcends the limits defined by its own very nature itself.[30] Both natures have been united in Christ in such a way that *proprietas utriusque naturae inconfusa permansit* (the properties of both natures remained unconfused).[31] In Part III of the *Summa theologiae* Thomas discusses in some detail what later

---

natura, fit esse hominis, inquantum humana natura assumitur a Filio Dei in unitate personae.

---

[28] Y. M.-J. Congar, *Christ, Our Lady and the Church*, London, New York and Toronto 1957, p. 47, but see the French original, *Le Christ, Marie et L'Église*, Paris 1952, p. 59: 'La personne, au sens métaphysique qui est aussi le sens de la théologie, est donc un pur principe d'existence, et c'est de la nature que relèvent à titre immédiat le contenu, les qualifications, les facultés et la structure des actes selon lesquels l'être existe'. See also E. L. Mascall, *Christ, the Christian and the Church. A Study of the Incarnation and its Consequences*, London, New York and Toronto 1946, p. 36.　[29] Cf. 3a, 6, 1.　[30] Cf. Héris, *Le Verbe incarné*, p. 293ff. [31] 3a, 10, 1; 3a, 13, 1: *in mysterio incarnationis ita facta est unio in persona quod tamen remansit distinctio naturarum, utraque scilicet natura retinente id quod sibi est proprium.*

theological writings referred to as the communication of properties, *communicatio idiomatum*,[32] and his intention at this point is mainly to draw a clear distinction between statements about Christ which have exclusive reference to his divine nature and those which apply only to his human nature. For Thomas the rule is that when we speak of a divine or human property, we should always do so *cum determinatione*, i.e. with a clear indication of the nature referred to.[33] This applies particularly in the case of the properties which belong to the human nature.[34] Thus we may indeed say that Christ has suffered, but not that his divine nature has suffered, for he endured his suffering *secundum humanam naturam*.[35] As we might expect, the doctrine of perichoresis between the two natures of Christ, which was a prominent feature in the theology of the early church, does not appear in Thomas.[36] Ultimately, however, it is the distinction

[32] We may refer, for instance, to 3a, 16, 1–12 and particularly to articles 4 and 5. The actual term *communicatio idiomatum* seems to be used only once in Thomas in the *De unione Verbi incarnati*, 5, ad 9: *in Christo est communicatio idiomatum; non quod sit aliqua proprietatum naturalium confusio; sed quia proprietates utriusque naturae dicuntur de eodem supposito.*

[33] Cf. *Compend. Theol.* 211: *Si ergo referatur ad suppositum, indifferenter sunt praedicanda de Christo humana et divina. Est tamen discernendum secundum quid utrumque dicatur, quia divina dicuntur de Christo secundum divinam naturam, humana vero secundum humanam;* 3a, 16, 4: *Quamvis igitur non distinguantur ea quae praedicantur de Christo, distinguuntur tamen quantum ad id secundum quod utrumque praedicatur. Nam ea quae sunt divinae naturae, praedicantur de Christo secundum divinam naturam: ea autem quae sunt humanae naturae, praedicantur de eo secundum humanam naturam.*

[34] 3a, 16, 5, ad 3: *ea quae sunt humanae naturae, nullo modo possunt dici de divina;* 3a, 16, 8: *non est absolute dicendum quod Christus sit creatura, vel minor Patre: sed cum determinatione, scilicet, secundum humanam naturam;* 3a, 20, 2: *Sed ea quae conveniunt sibi secundum humanam naturam, sunt ei potius attribuenda cum determinatione.* Cf. 3a, 16, 11: *magis est ista neganda: Christus, secundum quod homo, est Deus, quam sit affirmanda.*

[35] 3a, 16, 5, ad 1. The whole problem is reduced ultimately to a question of the proper use of logic—according to Thomas we must use here concrete terms to refer to the divine person who exists in accordance with two distinct natures, and not abstract terms which are applicable only to the natures. Cf. 3a, 16, 1, ad 2: *In mysterio autem incarnationis naturae quidem, quia distinctae sunt, de invicem non praedicantur secundum quod significantur in abstracto, non enim natura divina est humana: sed quia conveniunt in supposito, praedicantur de invicem in concreto.* See also Hugon, *Incarnation*, p. 192ff. and Diekamp and Jüssen, *Dogmatik*, vol. II, p. 256ff. It is significant that M. B. Schwalm, *Le Christ d'après saint Thomas d'Aquin* (Leçons, notes et commentaires, recueillis et mis en ordre par le R. P. Menne), 8th ed. Paris 1910, p. 185, attacks the term *communicatio idiomatum* as 'aussi barbare comme inutile' and asks why it cannot be replaced by the more adequate 'l'échange logique des propriétés'.

[36] A useful point of comparison is provided in 3a, 2, 1, ad 3: *sicut Damascenus dicit, natura divina dicitur incarnata, quia est unita carni personaliter: non quod sit in*

O

between *esse* and *essentia* that makes it possible to keep both natures of Christ absolutely intact. Since *esse est personae subsistentis* and since it is therefore really distinct from human nature, this latter remains at every point a human and created nature, despite its union with one of the persons of the godhead and in spite of the fact that it was assumed to subsist with the eternal and uncreated *esse* of the Son. The same relationship that holds in creation holds also in Christology, where there is a real distinction between existence and essence, a distinction that denotes the insurmountable line of division between the Creator and the creature, divine and human.[37]

When Thomas says that God sent his Son into the world, he does not mean by this that after the incarnation the Son was present where he had not been before, for as God he was already in the world in an invisible mode, *sicut causa efficiens et conservans*.[38] The incarnation no more implies a movement away from the One who sends than does the invisible sending.[39] Nor does it imply a putting off of the divine majesty, and thus it cannot be understood on the analogy of a king who sends his subject or a master his servant.[40] When scripture

---

naturam carnis conversa. Similiter etiam caro dicitur deificata, ut ipse dicit, non per conversionem, sed per unionem ad Verbum, salvis suis proprietatibus. The passage in John Damascene to which Thomas refers (*De fide orthodoxa* III, 17) states that the *deificatio* of human nature is caused by the perichoresis, but we simply do not find this in Thomas. The significant addition *salvis suis proprietatibus* has no counterpart in the passage quoted from the Damascene. See also I. Backes, *Die Christologie des hl. Thomas von Aquin und die griechischen Kirchenväter* (Forschungen zur christlichen Literatur- und Dogmengeschichte 17:3/4), Paderborn 1931, p. 154 and 248f. Cf. Diekamp and Jüssen, *Dogmatik*, vol. II, p. 258, who state that 'Die beiden Naturen in Christus durchdringen sich gegenseitig und sind in einander' is a *sententia communis*, but they do not quote a single passage from Thomas in evidence.

---

[37] On the importance of the real distinction in Thomas's theology of the incarnation, see, in addition to the works of Villard, Hugon and Héris already referred to on p. 193, footnote 13, Garrigou-Lagrange, *God*, p. 555; Rougier, *La scolastique*, p. 543ff.; de Finance, *Être et agir*, p. 108; Roland-Gosselin, *Le 'De ente et essentia'*, p. 193ff. In connection with this absolute distinction between divine and human which is based on the metaphysics of existence we are to note, as Penido points out in *Le rôle de l'analogie*, p. 383ff., that Thomas rejects monophysitism as intellectually absurd and untenable from a purely metaphysical point of view, while he rejects Nestorianism almost exclusively by arguments from scripture.

[38] *In Joan.* 1, 5 (1).

[39] *In Joan.* 16, 7 (4): *Sicut autem exitus a Patre ab aeterno non est localiter, ita nec adventus ejus in mundum est localis: quia cum Filius sit in Patre, et e converso; sicut Pater omnia implet, ita et Filius; nec est quo localiter moveatur.* Cf. p. 179 above.

[40] *In ad Gal.* 4, 2 (202): *Similiter non misit eum quasi ministrum, quia sua missio fuit assumptio carnis, non depositio maiestatis;* cf. 1a, 43, 1, ad 1; 3a, 1, 2, ad 3.

speaks of the 'descent' of Christ, this reference to the divine Word must be understood only in a metaphorical sense, for it does not mean that he left heaven, but that he *incipit* NOVO MODO *esse* (begins to be in a new way) on earth.[41] He is in the world as the cause is in its effect, and it seems that even God's presence in Christ is likewise to be expressed in causal categories, for Thomas defines this *novus modus* more precisely as a presence *per* NOVUM EFFECTUM *in terris* (by a new effect on earth).[42] Here again we find the same terminology as we found in discussing the invisible sending of the persons of the godhead, except that in this case we are speaking of a visible *effectus*. God is also *causa efficiens* in the incarnation, since the whole Trinity causes a human nature to be united with the second person of the godhead.[43] What is the meaning of this union that has been wrought between human and divine through the sending of the Son?

Obviously the union cannot imply anything new for the person who is sent. The very fact that we define God as *actus purus* excludes any possibility of change. It belongs to the perfection of his divine nature that it cannot be changed and become something other than it is. Any such change would imply the destruction of that which is specifically divine, and God is absolutely *incorruptibilis*. Nor can any other thing become God, for since he is *ingenerabilis*, he cannot be created by any other.[44] It is equally impossible to conceive of the union of the two natures as a compound or *mixtio*, for since the divine nature eternally transcends the human in every respect, this would simply imply the destruction of human nature and only the divine nature would remain.[45] The divine Word is not united with human nature as the soul is united with the body as its form,

---

[41] *In ad Phil.* 2, 2 (57): *descendit de caelo, non quod desineret esse in caelo, sed quia incepit esse novo modo in terris; In Joan.* 3, 2 (4): *Sic descendit de caelo, quod tamen est in caelo; descendit enim de caelo, non quidem desinens esse sursum, sed assumens naturam quae est deorsum;* see also *In Joan.* 1, 6 (1); *In ad Eph.* 4, 3 (208–209); *CG* IV, 23; *CG* IV, 30; 1a, 112, 1; 3a, 5, 2, ad 1.

[42] III *Sent.* 22, 3, 1, ad 2: *Dicitur etiam metaphorice . . . descendisse secundum divinam naturam . . . inquantum per novum effectum fuit in terris, secundum quem ibi ante non fuerat.*

[43] 3a, 3, 4: *Tres enim personae fecerunt ut humana natura uniretur uni personae Filii.* Cf. in regard to creation 1a, 45, 6 and to grace 3a, 3, 4, ad 3. Dondaine, *La Trinité,* vol. II, p. 370, thus regards the incarnation as 'ce que Dieu produit dans le monde'.

[44] 3a, 2, 1: *natura divina est omnino immutabilis. . . Unde nec ipsa potest converti in aliud, cum sit incorruptibilis: nec aliud in ipsam, cum ipsa sit ingenerabilis.* See also *Compend. Theol.* 206.

[45] 3a, 2, 1: *Et secundum hoc, cum natura divina in infinitum excedat humanam, non potest esse mixtio, sed remanebit sola natura divina.*

forma, for as we have already seen, we cannot conceive of God as part of a whole in which the other element consists of something created.[46] Thus in the incarnation as well as in his relation to creation or his bestowal of grace God remains *immutabilis* and, with respect to historical events, absolutely transcendent.[47]

Since something new does, however, happen when God sends his Son into the world, it must be something that occurs wholly within the sphere of the creature. The 'new' thing is in fact the human nature of Christ—it is this that is unique.[48] Even in the case of the *missio visibilis* we are not to understand God's sending of his Son as *secundum aliquam novitatem advenientem ipsi misso* (something new occurring to the one who is sent), but *secundum novitatem advenientem ei ad quem fit missio* (something new occurring to those to whom he was sent).[49] In his study of the incarnation which he bases on Thomas, Hugon attempts to explain what the incarnation means by using the metaphor of a pilgrim who comes to Rome and sees the dome of St Peter's for the first time. Something new takes place when he sees it, but it takes place wholly within the observer who gains through his new experience a knowledge that he previously lacked. The thing that he sees, however, is not changed in any way.[50] How, then, does Thomas deal with John 1:14, ὁ λόγος σὰρξ ἐγένετο, or, as he read in his Latin Bible, *Verbum caro factum est*, and with other similar passages? He has a detailed discussion of these questions in the *Summa theologiae* in the context of his study of the related phrase found in the Nicene Creed, *Deus factus est homo*—God was made man—and in the exposition of Romans 1:3 in his Commentary on the Epistle to the Romans. Thomas takes his starting-point in the

[46] 3a, 2, 1: *divina natura non potest esse forma alicuius, praesertim corporei;* 3a, 5, 1, ad 2: *per hoc quod Filius Dei verum corpus assumpsit, in nullo est eius dignitas diminuta. . . Non enim Filius Dei sic assumpsit verum corpus ut forma corporis fieret, quod repugnat divinae simplicitati et puritati.* Cf. p. 96f. above.

[47] Villard, *Incarnation*, p. 161: 'Si Dieu n'éprouve aucun changement en lui-même quand il crée les mondes, il ne change pas davantage alors qu'il sanctifie la créature raisonnable et même quand il appelle celle-ci au partage de son être personnel'.

[48] The passage from Villard cited in the above note continues: 'Cependant quelque chose de réel, et qui n'existait pas auparavant, est produit chaque fois que s'exerce la divine puissance; mais quelque chose qui ne peut entrer en Dieu, ni faire partie de sa substance'; Dondaine, *La Trinité*, vol. II, p. 429: 'Toute la nouveauté est dans l'effet créé'. J. A. Dorner, *History of the Development of the Doctrine of the Person of Christ*, Edinburgh 1865, Division Second, vol. I, p. 308, has also drawn attention to this point: 'The incarnation was not a new mode of being or "habitus" of God Himself, but simply a new thing relatively to men, or a new operation of God'. It may be noted that 'operation' is an inadequate translation of the German 'Wirkung'.

[49] *I Sent.* 15, 1, 1.   [50] Hugon, *Incarnation*, p. 58.

rule, *unumquodque dicitur esse factum illud quod de novo incipit praedicari de ipso* (whenever a new predicate is attributed to a subject we speak of the subject's being made whatever it is that the predicate signifies).[51] By this he means, roughly, that when in speaking of something or someone we say that he or it 'became' something, this must simply mean that from a given moment we can apply to a particular subject a quality or predicate which we could not properly apply before. This 'becoming' does not necessarily imply any change or *mutatio* in the subject, as is clear from relational statements that express how the subject is related to what is external to it. It is just such a relationship, says Thomas, that we are dealing with here, and he illustrates his meaning as follows: We can say of a man who is sitting in a certain place that at a particular moment he is no longer 'on the left' but instead is 'on the right'—as Thomas puts it, *fit dexter*—though no change has occurred in the man himself. The explanation, of course, is simply that someone beside him moved. The change was that the other person, not the one sitting, created a new relationship which is indicated by saying that the seated man is now 'on the right'.[52] It is by this analogy, says Thomas, that we are to understand the meaning of the incarnation.

We find here essentially the same scheme as we found earlier in dealing with creation and the doctrine of grace. When God acts, something new comes into being 'outside' the divine being—either something begins to exist or something that already exists is changed and by being changed is related in a new way to the transcendent cause that effects the change. This effect also establishes a new relation between the creature and God.[53] Since a part of the created world is in a new relationship to God, we may say—though only in an improper sense—that God's relationship to the creature is new. This is what is meant when we speak of God as 'Creator' and 'Lord', and,

---

[51] 3a, 16, 6; there is a different formulation of the rule in ib. ad 2: *fieri importat quod aliquid praedicetur de novo de altero.*

[52] 3a, 16, 6, ad 2: *Ea vero quae relative dicuntur, possunt de novo praedicari de aliquo absque eius mutatione: sicut homo de novo fit dexter absque sua mutatione, per motum illius qui fit ei sinister; In ad Rom.* 1, 2 (37): *Unde cum dicitur 'factus est' non intelligitur secundum conversionem sed secundum unionem, absque divina mutatione. Potest enim aliquid de novo dici relative de aliquo absque eius immutatione, puta: aliquis, non immobiliter sedens, fit dexter, per mutationem eius qui transfertur; In Joan.* 1, 7 (1): *Hoc autem quod dicitur, 'Verbum caro factum est', non aliquam mutationem in Verbo, sed solum in natura assumpta de novo in unitatem personae divinae dicit.* See also III *Sent.* 7, 2, 1.

[53] I *Sent.* 14, 1, 1: *ex novitate effectus consurgit nova relatio creaturae ad Deum, ratione cujus oportet Deum sub nova habitudine ad creaturam significari.*

as Thomas explicitly states, this is how we are to understand the miracle of the incarnation, the fact that the Son became man.[54] In the incarnation we speak of God being united with the creature *ex hoc quod creatura unita est ei* (since the creature is united to him).[55] For Thomas it is precisely this union between divine and human that constitutes God's presence in Christ: *praesentia autem Dei in Christo intelligitur secundum unionem humanae naturae ad divinam personam* (the presence of God in Christ is by the union of human nature with the divine person),[56] and therefore it is necessary for us to define the meaning that he attached to the term *unio*. We find that the reality of this hypostatic union subsists wholly in something that belongs to the creaturely sphere, in that *unio* refers to the real, unilateral relation to God of Christ's humanity. There is nothing in the divine being that corresponds to this or any other relation between God and creation. It is simply a relation *secundum rationem* in the divine being, whereas it does really exist in human nature, and therefore we may speak of it as *quoddam creatum* (something created).[57] Thus in the last resort even the biblical word, *Verbum caro*

---

[54] The passage from *In ad Rom.* 1, 2 (37) quoted in footnote 52 just above continues: *Et sic Deus dicitur ex tempore Dominus vel creator per mutationem creaturae; et eadem ratione dicitur de novo factus, secundum illud Psalmi: 'Domine refugium factus es nobis', Quia igitur unio relatio quaedam est, per mutationem creaturae Deus dicitur de novo factus homo, scilicet unitum in persona humanae naturae.* Cf. Héris, *Le Verbe incarné*, p. 293.

[55] 3a, 2, 7, ad 1. Cf. how in III *Sent.* 1, 1, 1, ad 1 Thomas applies the relation between *scientia* and *scibile* referred to on p. 113 above to the incarnation: *contingit in relativis aliquid relative dici, non quia ipsum referatur, sed quia alterum refertur ad ipsum, ut dicitur in V. Meta.; sicut scibile relative dicitur ad scientiam. . . Nulla enim mutatione facta circa scibile, incipit esse a me scitum per mei mutationem. . . Et ideo Deus dicitur uniri non per mutationem sui, sed ejus cui unitur.*

[56] 3a, 7, 13.

[57] 3a, 2, 7: *unio de qua loquimur est relatio quaedam quae consideratur inter divinam et humanam, secundum quod conveniunt in una persona Filii Dei. Sicut autem in Prima Parte dictum est* (cf. 1a, 13, 7), *omnis relatio quae consideratur inter Deum et creaturam, realiter quidem est in creatura, per cuius mutationem talis relatio innascitur: non autem est realiter in Deo, sed secundum rationem tantum, quia non nascitur secundum mutationem Dei. Sic igitur dicendum est quod haec unio de qua loquimur, non est in Deo realiter, sed secundum rationem tantum: in humana autem natura, quae creatura quaedam est, est realiter. Et ideo oportet dicere quod sit quoddam creatum.* See also III *Sent.* 2, 2, 2, 3, 3: III *Sent.* 5, 1, 1, 1; *In Joan* 1, 7 (1); *In ad Gal.* 4, 2 (204); Héris, *Le Verbe incarné*, p. 294: 'L'union hypostatique doit être considérée, elle aussi, comme une production de la puissance divine, réalisée dans le temps. Elle rentre donc à ce titre dans le domaine des choses créées; H.-M. Manteau-Bonamy, *Maternité divine et Incarnation. Étude historique et doctrinale de saint Thomas à nos jours* (BT 27), Paris 1949, p. 59: 'suivant qu'on la regarde en Dieu ou dans l'humanité, l'Incarnation a une valeur différente: *logique*, du côté de Dieu

factum est, is to be understood metaphorically, and if we attempt to understand it from God's perspective, it does not essentially mean anything different from for instance the statement that 'God is our refuge'.[58] For Thomas the real meaning of John 1 :14 is that a change has been wrought by God in a particular part of creation which implies a new relation to the transcendent first cause. By reason of this change which occurred 'outside' God, we may state, though improperly, that God 'became' man. Krempel faithfully represents Thomas's thought at this point when he concludes his study of the concept of relation in the theology of the incarnation with these words: 'Expressions like incarnation, union, assumption, becoming man or being made flesh do not admit the shadow of a *processus* in God'.[59] Thomas also emphasises in this connection the absolute sovereignty and 'otherness' of God in relation to the created world.

We are not to conclude from what we have said so far that for Thomas the incarnation is merely a metaphor, or that he does not treat the *reality* of the incarnation seriously. The very fact that a human nature exists in the hypostatic union with its dependence upon God also means for Thomas that God is *really* incarnate, for this particular human nature is preeminently real. Since this 'real' incarnation occurs wholly within the creaturely sphere,[60] Thomas therefore concentrates on this.

In the incarnation God is not only the *causa efficiens* of the union of human nature with God, but also *causa exemplaris* and *causa finalis*. We shall see more clearly what this means, Thomas holds, if we study what takes place in Christ's human nature, a human nature that is united with God. The new relation which it has to the transcendent divine cause, is based, like every other *ex tempore* relation, on a *mutatio*.[61] The incarnation is an event by which a particular

immuable, elle est *réelle* dans la nature humaine qui est unie au Verbe'. See also Krempel, *La doctrine de la relation*, p. 563ff.

---

[58] Cf. *De Pot.* 7, 8, ad 5: *per hoc quod in creatura aliqua mutatio fit, aliqua relatio de Deo incipit dici. Unde ipse non potest dici factus nisi metaphorice; quia se habet ad similitudinem facti, inquantum de Deo aliquid novum dicitur. Et sic dicimus: 'Domine refugium factus es nobis', Psalm. 89, 1.* Cf. *In ad Rom.* 1, 2 (37).
[59] Krempel, *La doctrine de la relation*, p. 581.
[60] Cf. Penido, *Le rôle de l'analogie*, p. 448: 'Dieu est dit Créateur, et le Verbe est dit Incarné; et ce n'est point là 'flatus vocis', puisque à ces relations de raison, correspondent vraiment, dans le créé, des relations réelles'.
[61] 3a, 2, 8: *Omnis autem relatio quae incipit esse ex tempore, ex aliqua mutatione causatur.*

human nature was changed—more specifically changed in the sense of being perfected. The change was that of *melioratio* or *perfectio*.[62] This perfection is such that in the incarnation humanity is brought to its highest expression: *natura humana in ipsa incarnatione est perducta ad summam perfectionem* (by the incarnation human nature is raised to its highest perfection).[63] The closer a creature comes to God, the more perfect it becomes, just as light and heat grow more intense the closer we get to their source. Thomas employs this metaphor also to illustrate how Christ's human nature is perfected in the incarnation. It helps to explain the character of the causal relationship itself, for as Thomas puts it, just as the sky grows brighter the closer we come to the sun, so the influence of the divine cause becomes stronger in proportion as it is brought to bear on something. Human nature can not only be perfected as nature, but being *capax Dei*, it can also attain through grace the perfection which lies far beyond its own capacities. Since no human soul can come closer to the divine first cause than the Christ's, whose soul, coexisting as it does with his eternal *esse*, is the soul of one of the persons of the godhead, its union with God results in its being endowed with the fullest measure of grace.[64] Hence Thomas speaks both of a *gratia unionis*, which is unique to Christ, and of a *gratia habitualis*, which is not essentially different from the grace which other men experience. The former is simply *ipsum esse personale* which Christ's human nature possesses apart from any previous merits. This grace is given to the *whole* of his human nature, since his body and his soul are

---

[62] *In ad Phil.* 2, 2, (61): *natura humana . . . sic advenit divinae personae, quod non mutavit ipsam; sed mutata est in melius;* 3a, 2, 6, ad 1: *humana natura assumpta a Verbo Dei est meliorata, ipsum autem Verbum Dei non est mutatum;* 3a, 3, 1, ad 1: *non Deus, sed homo perficitur.*

[63] 3a, 1, 6.

[46] *Compend. Theol.* 214: *Inquantum autem creatura aliqua magis ad Deum accedit, intantum de bonitate ejus magis participat, et abundantioribus donis ex ejus influentia repletur; sicut et ignis calorem magis participat qui ei magis appropinquat. Nullus autem modus esse aut excogitari potest, quo aliqua creatura propinquius Deo adhaereat, quam quod ei in unitate personae conjungatur;* 3a, 7, 1: *Quanto enim aliquod receptivum propinquius est causae influenti, tanto magis participat de influentia ipsius;* 3a, 7, 9: *quanto aliquod receptivum propinquius est causae influenti, abundantius recipit. Et ideo anima Christi, quae propinquius coniungitur Deo inter omnes creaturas rationales, recipit maximam influentiam gratiae eius;* 3a, 7, 13: *Gratia enim causatur in homine ex praesentia divinitatis, sicut lumen in aere ex praesentia solis. . . Praesentia autem Dei in Christo intelligitur secundum unionem humanae naturae ad divinam gersonam. Unde gratia habitualis Christi intelligitur ut consequens hanc unionem, sicut splendor solem.* See also Schwalm, *Le Christ*, p. 55ff. and Hugon, *Incarnation*, p. 218ff.

raised to exist with divine *esse.*[65] *Gratia habitualis,* on the other hand, is for Thomas a consequence of this elevation, and like every other created grace is present only in the soul as a perfection of its essence.[66] Thomas frequently refers in this connection to the passage in John's Gospel which speaks of the glory of the only-begotten Son as 'full of grace and truth',[67] and he interprets this phrase 'full of grace' (*plenum gratiae*) to mean that grace was given here in such perfection that there could not conceivably be any increase of it in Christ.[68] Since grace as the perfection of the soul *eo ipso* also implies a perfection of its cognitive and volitive potentialities, these potentialities must also have reached exceptional perfection in the soul of Christ.[69]

As God, Christ possessed in respect of his divine nature the perfect knowledge which belongs to God's own being. But since his human soul could not by reason of its createdness admit within itself anything eternal or uncreated, it would not have had any knowledge at all if Christ had only had this *scientia increata* (uncreated knowledge).[70] His soul must therefore have had a *scientia creata,* like that of any other man.[71] And his intellect, as *intellectus possibilis,*

[65] The divine *esse* of Christ inheres not only in his soul but also in his body. Thomas expresses this by saying, for example, that even in his death—which Thomas interprets as a separation between body and soul—Christ's body remains united with the divine Word, see 3a, 50, 2.

[66] 3a, 6, 6: *in Christo ponitur gratia unionis, et gratia habitualis. . . Gratia enim unionis est ipsum esse personale quod gratis datur humanae naturae in persona Verbi. . . Gratia autem habitualis, pertinens ad specialem sanctitatem illius hominis, est effectus quidam consequens unionem;* 3a, 2, 10, ad 2: *gratia habitualis est solum in anima: sed gratia, idest gratuitum Dei donum quod est uniri divinae personae, pertinet ad totam naturam humanam, quae componitur ex anima et corpore.* On *gratia unionis* as something given without *merita,* see 3a, 2, 11. See also Héris, *Le Verbe incarné,* vol I, p 254f. and A. Vugts, *La grâce d'union d'après S. Thomas d'Aquin,* Tilburg 1946, especially p. 95f.

[67] *Compend. Theol.* 213 and 214; 3a, 6, 6; 3a, 7, 9; 3a, 7, 10; 3a, 8, 1; 3a, 10, 4.

[68] The reference by Luke in his Gospel to Jesus' increase in wisdom and favour (Luke 2:52) applies, Thomas holds, only to those outward works by which the grace of Christ was made manifest. These became even more perfect, but this cannot be said of his habitual grace itself as such, for this was absolutely perfect *a primo instanti suae conceptionis.* See 3a, 7, 12 and especially ib. ad 3.

[69] 3a, 7, 2: *cum gratia Christi fuerit perfectissima, consequens est quod ex ipsa processerint virtutes ad perficiendum singulas potentias animae, quantum ad omnes animae actus.*

[70] 3a, 9, 1, ad 1: *Christus cognovit omnia per scientiam divinam operatione increata, quae est ipsa Dei essentia: Dei enim intelligere est sua substantia, ut probatur in XII Metaphys. Unde hic actus non potuit esse animae humanae Christi: cum sit alterius naturae. Si igitur non fuisset in anima Christi alia scientia praeter divinam, nihil cognovisset.*

[71] On the question of the *scientia Christi,* see also the detailed analysis in Schwalm, *Le Christ,* p. 243ff. and Hugon, *Incarnation,* p. 168ff.

must have had a corresponding *scientia acquisita vel experimentalis* (acquired or empirical knowledge) derived from the things of creation, though not in the sense that any man or angel instructed him, for this would have contradicted his perfection and honour.[72] This form of knowledge came to its highest perfection in Christ, and he was thus the greatest genius who ever lived on the earth,[73] and therefore the intellectual powers of the soul reached their highest natural perfection in his soul. But the human intellect by virtue of the *potentia obedientiae* (potentiality of obedience) is also capable of receiving by the direct intervention of God a *scientia indita vel infusa* (imparted or communicated knowledge). By this is meant the kind of knowledge which normally belongs to the metaphysical status of the angels, but which may also from time to time be given to a man through the *donum sapientiae* (gift of wisdom) or the *donum prophetiae* (gift of prophecy). It must be assumed that this potentiality was also fully realised in the human nature of Christ. But since there is no question of any imperfection in his human nature, we cannot, here speak of a *passio transiens* (impermanent experience)[74] as we do in the case of other recipients of revelation, but rather of his habitual knowledge of all that can be given to men through revelation.[75] Christ thus possesses in his human nature not only *gratia unionis* and *gratia habitualis* but in the fullest measure also all *gratiae gratis datae*. He is thus the first and principal Teacher of the faith, *fidei primus et principalis Doctor*, since the highest earthly expression of the revealed knowledge of God is to be found in him.[76] As we saw above, moreover, every man as a rational being has been created

[72] 3a, 9, 4; 3a, 12, 1–4.

[73] 3a, 12, 1: *per scientiam acquisitam scivit omnia illa quae possunt sciri per actionem intellectus agentis;* cf. Héris, *Le Verbe incarné*, vol. II, p. 327: 'Ainsi le Christ, qui possédait le plus puissant génie qui ait jamais existé, pouvait-il, au contact des expériences que la vie lui offrait, dégager les lois universelles du monde, et développer sa science humaine bien au-delà de ce que peuvent les autres hommes'.

[74] See p. 27 above, de Ver. 12, 13, ad 3.

[75] 3a, 9, 3: *oportet in Christo scientiam ponere inditam, inquantum per Verbum Dei animae Christi, sibi personaliter unitae, impressae sunt species intelligibiles ad omnia ad quae est intellectus possibilis in potentia: sicut etiam per Verbum Dei impressae sunt species intelligibiles menti angelicae in principio creationis rerum;* 3a, 11, 1: *per hanc scientiam cognovit Christus omnia illa quae per revelationem divinam hominibus innotescunt: sive pertineant ad donum sapientiae, sive ad donum prophetiae, sive ad quodcumque donum Spiritus Sancti. Omnia enim ista abundantius et plenius ceteris cognovit anima Christi;* see also the whole of 3a, 11, 1–6 and *Compend. Theol.* 216. Cf. too Héris, *Le Verbe incarné*, vol. II, p. 346ff.

[76] 3a, 7, 7: *manifestum est quod in Christo fuerunt excellentissime omnes gratiae gratis datae, sicut in primo et principali Doctore fidei:* cf. also 3a, 7, 8 and p. 25 and 32 above.

ad imaginem Dei and is therefore *capax beatitudinis*. This capacity of a *potentia ad scientiam beatorum* (potentiality for the knowledge of the blessed) must also be perfectly realised in the soul of Christ, or else its *perfectio* would be incomplete, and so once again we are dealing with the question of a *visio seu scientia beata* (beatific vision or knowledge). As God, Christ possesses in respect of his divine nature the *beatitudo increata* (uncreated blessedness) by which God enjoys his own perfection from all eternity, but his human nature cannot experience this blessedness. It possesses instead a *beatitudo creata* by which it is conformed to and imitates the divine blessedness on its own plane. In and with this beatific vision Christ's human nature has attained the supreme supernatural goal which God has set before men, but which at the same time is the highest conceivable perfection of what is human.[77] To use the earlier metaphor of sunlight once again, a created intellect is endowed with greater knowledge the closer it comes to God, who is Truth itself. Since nothing that is human is brought closer to God than the soul of Christ, his soul receives more of the light that comes from the *prima veritas* than any other, and therefore it is more blessed than other *beati*, for in Thomas's view the degree of blessedness is equal to the degree of intellectual perfection.[78] Christ thus lived at one time the intellectual life both of ordinary men (*scientia acquisita*) and of angels (*scientia infusa*) and the blessed (*scientia beata*). There is a perfect harmony, however, between all these different kinds of knowledge, each of which participates, though on its own distinct plane, in the same divine light, the difference between them consisting in a distinction in the degree of perfection.[79]

[77] 3a, 9, 2, ad 2: *Sed praeter beatitudinem increatam, oportuit in natura humana Christi esse quandam beatitudinem creatam, per quam anima eius in ultimo fine humanae naturae constitueretur;* see also this article in its entirety and also 3a, 10, 1–4.

[78] 3a, 10, 4: *divinae essentiae visio convenit omnibus beatis secundum participationem luminis derivati ad eos a fonte Verbi Dei. . . Huic autem Verbo Dei propinquius coniungitur anima Christi, quae est unita Verbo in persona, quam quaevis alia creatura. Et ideo plenius recipit influentiam luminis in quo Deus videtur ab ipso Verbo, quam quaecumque alia creatura. Et ideo prae ceteris creaturis perfectius videt ipsam primam veritatem, quae est Dei essentia; Compend. Theol.* 216: *Conveniens etiam fuit ut prae ceteris creaturis illa anima divina visione beatificaretur quae Deo propinquius conjungebatur: in qua quidem visione gradus attenditur secundum quod aliqui aliis clarius Deum vident, qui est omnium rerum causa.* On blessedness as primarily an intellectual perfection, see 1a, 12, 1; 1a, 26, 1; 1a, 62, 1; 1a2ae, 3, 4. A typical example of this is Thomas's interpretation of I John 3:2: *'similes ei erimus', scilicet omnia scientes; sicut qui haberet librum ubi esset tota scientia, In ad Col.* 2, 1 (82).

[79] Cf. Héris, *Le Verbe incarné*, vol. II, p. 328.

Thomas holds that a similar perfection exists in Christ's soul in the sphere of the volitive life, though he does not discuss this as fully as the *scientia* of Christ.[80] Like other men Christ has free will, *liberum arbitrium*, but in a more perfect manner than they, since his will like that of the blessed has a firm and resolute inclination to good. His will is free from the vacillation between higher and lower desires that affects the wills of other men,[81] and through a perfect love for God attains in his soul to its supreme *perfectio*.[82]

In the preceding sections of the present chapter we have seen how Thomas defines this perfection of man's intellect and will through grace as an invisible sending of the Son and the Spirit to man. It is quite natural, therefore, that Thomas should speak of a *missio invisibilis* to Christ's human soul also. It occurred at the very moment of conception,[83] and through this perfect bestowal of the gifts of grace the human nature that was bound to the divine Word was raised to a plane above all other men and is nearer to God, *propinquius ad Deum*, than any other.[84] From first to last it is the work of divine love. As we saw earlier,[85] Thomas follows Aristotle in defining love as *velle alicui bonum*, and never before has God willed so great a good for anyone as that which he has bestowed on the human nature of Christ, which by the *gratia unionis* has received *ipsum esse personale Verbi*, and by *gratia habitualis* the fullest possible realisation of both natural and supernatural potentialities. The fact that this particular human nature is 'better' than any other is for Thomas a direct expression of the love which God has shown in Christ,[86] for *ex hoc sunt aliqua meliora, quod Deus eis maius bonum vult*.[87] Here, too, the

[80] Christ's *scientia* is dealt with at length in 18 articles (3a, questions 9–12), while the corresponding perfection of his will is noted only in passing. Here too the fundamental interest which Thomas has in the question of knowledge in theology is expressed quantitatively in his arrangement of the material.

[81] 3a, 18, 4.

[82] 3a, 7, 1: *necesse est ponere in Christo gratiam habitualem . . . propter nobilitatem eius animae, cuius operationes oportebat propinquissime attingere ad Deum per cognitionem et amorem. Ad quod necesse est elevari humanam naturam per gratiam;* see also *Compend. Theol.* 213.

[83] 1a, 43, 6, ad 3: *Ad Christum autem fuit facta invisibilis missio in principio suae conceptionis;* cf. 1a, 43, 7, ad 6.

[84] 3a, 26, 2, ad 1: *Ex qua quidem plenitudine (scil. gratiarum) habet ut sit super omnes homines constitutus, et propinquius ad Deum accedens.*

[85] See p. 105 above.

[86] 1a, 20, 4, ad 2: *naturam humanam assumptam a Dei Verbo in Persona Christi. . . Deus plus amat quam omnes angelos: et melior est, maxime ratione unionis.*

[87] 1a, 20, 4. The interpretation of John 3:16 which is given by Schwalm, *Le Christ*, p. 19, is that God's love for the world means his love for the human nature of

ultimate presupposition of the self-giving love which marks this divine activity is God's absolute transcendence and independence of the creature. The strong expressions which Thomas uses to convey the unchangeableness and transcendence of God even in the incarnation are intended to affirm the character of the event as pure grace. The incarnation can be seen to be an act of pure liberality, a love which does not 'seek its own', precisely because it cannot imply any gain or perfection on God's part. It is in this perspective of God's giving to men that we are to see also the perfection of Christ's human nature which we have just discussed, for in this giving a grace is given in such measure that, flowing from the soul of Christ, it is transferred to others, *quoddammodo transfunderetur in alios*,[88] and is communicated through the sacraments from Christ, the head of the church, to its members.[89] To say that God is *immutabilis* and independent of all that occurs in the creaturely sphere does not mean that he has no part in the incarnation. On the contrary, the incarnation is the work of God in the world from first to last. But this act of God follows the same causal scheme that applies, as we noted above, both to creation and to grace. Here, too, the love of God ultimately coincides with causality itself,[90] and the intensity of this love is expressed in a supremely perfect *effectus* in the sphere of creation. Consequently, the same rule that defines the causal relationship between God and the world applies also to the incarnation: *causa est in effectu per modum effectus*.[91] The divine being itself no more transcends or transgresses the limits appropriate to its nature in the incarnation than the perfection which was effected when human nature was bound to the divine Word in Christ's assumption of our flesh implies a transgression of the limits which are so appropriate to its place in the hierarchy of existence as human nature. The gift which is given must be conformed to the part that receives—it must be created, for *receptum est in recipiente per modum recipientis* (the

Christ which contains within itself all degrees within the hierarchy of existence. This is entirely in harmony with Thomas's own understanding.

---

[88] 3a, 7, 9.

[89] It is precisely on the basis of this overflowing fullness of grace that Thomas speaks of Christ as *caput Ecclesiae*, cf. 3a, 8, 5: *in anima Christi recepta est gratia secundum maximam eminentiam. Et ideo ex eminentia gratiae quam accepit, competit sibi quod gratia illa ad alios derivetur. Quod pertinet ad rationem capitis. Et ideo eadem est secundum essentiam gratia personalis qua anima Christi est iustificata, et gratia eius secundum quam est caput Ecclesiae iustificans alios.*

[90] Cf. p. 110f. above.   [91] See p. 161 and 188 above.

thing received is in the recipient after the mode of the recipient).[92]
Within the limits of what is possible for nature, however, grace—and
all that is implied by grace—has found its fullest expression in the
human nature of Christ.[93] Just as the seventh day of creation means
the final and perfect consummation of nature, so for Thomas the
incarnation means the *consummatio gratiae*.[94] And since the blessedness which God set before man as his supernatural end is precisely
gratia consummata,[95] the incarnation of Christ means that for the
first time in human history this goal is realised and its significance
shown in Christ, *in natura assumpta salutis humanae finem ostenderet
per gratiae et sapientiae perfectionem* (in the nature which he had
taken to himself he showed the end of man's salvation through the
perfection of grace and wisdom).[96] Grace did not first enter the
world with Christ. It was also given to godly men and women in the
old covenant,[97] though none of these attained a state of blessedness,
and only through Christ did they receive this *beatitudo*.[98] The
incarnation thus means the absolute perfection of human nature
through grace and therefore also both the original and perfect
attainment of man's supernatural end and a guarantee that just as
this end has been attained in one human nature, it may also be
attained in others.[99] In his infinite love God has here fulfilled all man's
potentialities since in Christ all man's potencies—both those given
by nature and those given supernaturally in the *potentia obedientiae*—
have been perfectly realised.[100]

---

[92] 3a, 11, 5; cf. *CG* IV, 55: *servata tamen proprietate utriusque naturae, ut nec
excellentiae divinae naturae aliquid deperiret, nec humana natura per exaltionem
aliquam extra terminos suae speciei traheretur;* 3a, 7, 11: *Anima autem Christi est
creatura quaedam, habens capacitatem finitam.* See also *Compend. Theol.* 215, where
Thomas uses the metaphor of Christ's human nature as a vessel whose capacity
to receive grace is determined by the *quantitas determinata* of the vessel.
[93] 3a, 7, 12: *gratia Christi pertingit usque ad summam mensuram gratiae.*
[94] 1a, 73, 1, ad 1.   [95] *De Ver.* 27, 2 ad 7.
[96] *Compend. Theol.* 226; cf. how Thomas speaks in 3a, 9, 2, ad 2 of Christ's
beatitudo: per quam anima eius in ultimo fine humanae naturae constitueretur.
[97] 1a, 43, 6, ad 1: *missio invisibilis est facta ad Patres veteris Testamenti.* See also
3a, 53, 3, ad 3; cf. ib. obi. 3.
[98] Cf. 3a, 52, 5.
[99] *CG* IV, 54: *Per hoc autem quod Deus humanam naturam sibi unire voluit in persona,
evidentissime hominibus demonstratur quod homo per intellectum Deo potest uniri,
ipsum immediate videndo. Fuit igitur convenientissimum quod Deus humanam naturam
assumeret ad spem hominis in beatitudinem sublevandam.*
[100] Cf. E. Mersch, *The Theology of the Mystical Body*, St Louis and London 1951,
p. 211: 'The Incarnation is the unparalleled work in which God goes to the limit
of His love and of man's capacity'.

Since grace is a perfecting of the entire nature to which it is given, the normal functions of Christ's human nature must also be perfectly ordered, and, indeed, Thomas can say that *in Christo huiusmodi operationes fuerunt magis humanae quam in aliis* (such activity was more human in Christ than in other men).[101] Since his soul was an *anima ordinata*, all the lower functions of his soul acted in perfect harmony with reason, as in man before the fall.[102] There is a difference, therefore, between the pain (*dolor sensibilis*), sorrow (*tristitia*), anguish (*agonia*) or fear (*timor*) which the Evangelists ascribe to Christ and the sufferings we ourselves endure, for in Christ's case they did not extend beyond that level of the soul which has the function of feeling. In all other men sorrow, fear, anguish and pain also arise in and affect the higher levels of the soul, the intellect and will. But in Christ the intellect and will are independent of what is experienced in the lower parts of the soul, where all *passiones* are at an inchoate stage, and are not therefore *passiones* in the proper sense, but only what Thomas calls *propassiones*.[103]

Thus on the purely natural plane also there is a stratification in the various distinctive functions of the soul which parallels the various kinds of supernatural *scientiae* just discussed. These psychological analyses, which seem so subtle and remote from the simple, biblical narratives, are implied in Thomas's phrase that since Christ is *perfectus homo*, his human nature must be perfect in every respect.[104] In

---

[101] 3a, 19, 2, ad 1.

[102] 3a, 19, 2: *in homine Iesu Christo nullus erat motus sensitivae partis qui non esset ordinatus a ratione.* On this basis Thomas is incapable of dealing adequately with the accounts of Christ's temptation, which becomes reduced to little more than the pretence of a struggle (cf. the commentary in P. Synave, *Vie de Jésus*, vol. II 1928, p. 412: 'Le Christ n'a point réellement subi la tentation'), the ultimate explanation of which is that *tentatus est, ut daret nobis exemplum, ut secundum similitudinem eius, tentationem sustineremus et omnia conaremur vincere, In ad Heb.* 4, 3 (237). See also 3a, 41, 1–4.

[103] A detailed statement of this relation is to be found in *De Ver.* 26, 8; 3a, 15, 4 and *Compend. Theol.* 232. On the concept of *propassio* see 3a, 15, 4: *passio perfecta intelligatur quando animo, idest rationi, dominatur; propassio autem, quando est inchoata in appetitu sensitivo, sed ulterius subi non se extendit.* Cf. also 3a, 15, 6, ad 1: *tristitia removetur a Christo secundum passionem perfectam: fuit tamen in eo initiata, secundum propassionem;* 3a, 15, 7, ad 1: *timor non fuit in Christo: sed solum secundum propassionem;* 3a, 18, 6, ad 3: *agonia non fuit in Christo quantum ad partem animae rationalem. . . Fuit tamen . . . quantum ad partem sensitivam.* See also Schwalm, *Le Christ*, p. 302ff.

[104] Cf. e.g. III *Sent.* 18, 3: *Christo attribuere debemus secundum animam, omnem perfectionem spiritualem quae sibi potest attribui; Compend. Theol.* 216: *nulla perfectio creaturis exhibita, animae Christi, quae est creaturarum excellentissima, deneganda est;* 3a, 19, 3: *omnis perfectio et nobilitas Christo est attribuenda.*

terms of the scheme of act and potency perfection is equivalent to the actual realising of all existing potencies, and since any form of development from lower to higher is inconceivable in Christ, since this implies imperfection, the specific qualities mentioned above must all therefore exist in Christ's nature from the very first moment of his conception, or, to use a common expression of Thomas, *in primo instanti suae conceptionis.*[105] According to Thomas, therefore, a distinction must be made between the human nature of Christ and that of other men. As *missio invisibilis* grace presupposes a being possessing reason and will, and the entire perfection of the faculties of the soul which is given by grace and which we have described above must be understood as the immediate consequence of the elevation of human nature implied by the union of this nature with one of the persons of the godhead. This perfection is coincident with this human nature itself as such. But for Thomas the necessary logical consequence of this is that at the very moment of its conception Christ's human nature must have possessed an *anima rationalis* which sets him apart from all other men.[106] But a soul of this kind cannot exist without a fully developed body with organs which function as in a creature fully formed, and so the implication of what Thomas has to say about the perfection of Christ's human nature is that the body associated with this nature must be perfect (*perfectum*) and fully formed (*formatum*) at the moment of conception (*in primo instantu conceptionis*), save in regard to size, for growth is a matter of biological necessity.[107]

Protestant theologians tend to reject ideas like these at first sight as extremely peculiar psychological and biological arguments, on the ground that they are essentially incomprehensible subtleties of

[105] See e.g. on blessedness, 1a2ae, 5, 7, ad 2; 3a, 34, 4; on free will, 3a, 34, 2–3; on the fullness of grace, *De Ver.* 29, 8; 3a, 7, 12; 3a, 34, 1; on knowledge, *In Joan.* 1, 8 (3); 3a, 12, 2.

[106] 3a, 33, 2: *oportuit quod in primo instanti conceptionis corpus Christi esset animatum anima rationali; Compend. Theol.* 218; *CG* IV, 44; 3a, 6, 4, ad 2. In Thomas's day it was believed that there was a gradual development in the foetus in which the preliminary and purely vegetative function of the soul was slowly replaced by an *anima sensitiva*, which in turn after about forty days of foetal development, when the body became *formatum*, was succeeded by an *anima rationalis* which included the other functions of the soul. See 1a, 76, 3, ad 3; 1a, 118, 2, ad 2 and also the commentary in Synave, *Vie de Jésus*, vol. I, p. 275f.

[107] *In Joan.* 1, 9 (9): *Christus enim in instanti suae conceptionis fuit perfectus Deus et perfectus homo, habens rationalem animam perfectam virtutibus, et corpus omnibus lineamentis distinctum, non tamen secundum quantitatem perfectam;* cf. *Compend. Theol.* 218; *CG* IV, 44; 3a, 6, 4, ad 1; 3a, 33, 1.

scholasticism, lacking any real religious significance. For some, for instance, the Christology of Thomas is marked by 'subtle and religiously unfruitful speculations about the psychic life of Christ, etc.',[108] while others simply view it as 'a conceptualised mythology of the worst type'.[109] But if we take what Thomas says in the context of the causal relationship between God and the world which he defines in his scheme of act and potency, we shall see that so far from being mere subtleties void of any genuine religious sense, his statements are rather a clear and logical consequence of a truly profound and suggestive concept: salvation as the perfection and elevation of what is human. The perfection of Christ's human nature is an expression of the fact that in a peculiar way this nature is the object of God's love, or—and for Thomas this is simply a different way of expressing the same thing—that the effect of the divine causality is more intense at this point than anywhere else in the created world. Nowhere does God's effect as *causa exemplaris* produce so perfect a result amongst men as in the soul of Christ, for no *anima rationalis* can be so perfectly assimilated to God's own eternal life within the godhead. In the soul of Christ the image of God in man has come to absolute perfection.

A close study of what Thomas means by the statement that Christ is *perfectus homo* would indicate, however, that his thinking—if followed consistently to the end—would be flatly contradictory of much of what the Bible says concerning Christ. To say, for instance, that Christ is the most perfect of all the blessed (*beati*) would properly imply also that his body was *impassibilis*, for blessedness means essentially the perfection of the whole man.[110] In and of itself the beatific vision of God as a *perfectio animae ex parte intellectus* (perfection of the soul on the part of the intellect)[111] is, to be sure, independent of the body, but the blessed state of the soul has as its normal consequence the glorification of the body, *ex beatitudine animae fit redundantia ad corpus* (from the blessedness of the soul

---

[108] Hj. Lindroth, *Katolsk och evangelisk kristendomssyn. En typologisk studie* (Uppsala universitets årsskrift 1933, Teol. 4), Uppsala 1933, p. 253, cf. ib. p. 97: 'But from the standpoint of religion these questions were quite profitless', and p. 161f.

[109] R. Seeberg, *Lehrbuch der Dogmengeschichte*, vol. III, 2nd and 3rd ed., Leipzig 1913, p. 379f.

[110] *In 1 ad Cor.* 15, 6 (988): *Cum ergo anima fuerit perfectissima, conservabit corpus omnino impassibile;* 1a2ae, 3, 3, ad 3: *in perfecta beatitudine perficitur totus homo.*

[111] 1a2ae, 4, 5, ad 1.

P

there is an overflow on to the body).[112] Even though the body does
not belong as such to the essence of blessedness, it belongs to its
bene esse.[113] In order to make Christ's sufferings and the circumstances of his death comprehensible and possible, Thomas is therefore forced to assume that a deviation from the normal state occurred
in Christ's human nature and by special divine intervention, miraculous in character, the normal process by which the body is glorified
did not take place in Christ. The restriction of *beatitudo* to his soul
made it possible for his body to become temporarily *passibilis*,
despite the perfect blessedness of his soul.[114] As we noted earlier,
Thomas holds that there is an absolute distinction in Christ between
divine and human, according to which each nature remains within
its own limits—there can be no conjoining of divine to human nor
addition of human properties to the divine. But in addition, Thomas
argues, there is an equally pronounced distinction in Christ's human
nature itself before the resurrection, not a distinction between body
and soul but between different levels of the soul. There is a 'barrier'
in the soul which prevents the pain and anguish suffered, for instance,
in the crucifixion, from reaching the *superior pars animae* and
destroying the unmingled joy which resides in the perfect blessedness
of the intellect and the will, while on the other hand this joy and
blessedness neither reduce nor remove the pain of suffering which
the soul experiences in its functions of sense.[115] The explanation
of this is that the various parts of the soul have different objects—the
pars inferior (sensuous will) has to do with physical functions and the
world of sense experience, while the *pars superior* (rational will)
contemplates God and the things of God in undisturbed contemplation.[116] According to the view of Thomas the sufferings of Christ

[112] 1a2ae, 4, 6: 3a, 14, 1, ad 2: *secundum naturalem habitudinem quae est inter
animam et corpus, ex gloriae animae redundat gloria ad corpus; De Ver.* 26, 8 ad 8.
[113] 1a2ae, 4, 5.
[114] 3a, 45, 2: *Quod enim a principio conceptionis Christi gloria animae non redundaret
ad corpus, ex quadam dispensatione divina factum est, ut in corpore passibili nostrae
redemptionis expleret mysteria;* cf. 3a, 14, 1, ad 2.
[115] 3a, 15, 5, ad 3: *virtute divinitatis Christi dispensative sic beatitudo in anima
continebatur quod non derivebatur ad corpus, ut eius passibilitas et mortalitas tolleretur.
Et, eadem ratione, delectatio contemplationis sic continebatur in mente quod non
derivebatur ad vires sensibiles, ut per hoc dolor sensibilis excluderetur;* see also III
Sent. 15, 2, 2, 1; *De Ver.* 26, 9; *Compend. Theol.* 232; 3a, 15, 6. Cf. Diekamp and
Jüssen, *Dogmatik*, vol. II, p. 304f. and the works cited and also the detailed
discussion in Synave, *Vie de Jésus*, vol. III, p. 216ff.
[116] *Compend. Theol.* 232: *Superior igitur ratio animae Christi, quae rebus aeternis
contemplandis et consulendis inhaeret, nihil habebat adversum aut repugnans, ex quo*

affected neither his divine nature, which is *impassibilis*,[117] nor even the superior part of his human nature: *superior pars animae perfecte fruebatur, Christo patiente* (the higher part of his soul enjoyed perfect bliss all the while he was suffering).[118] This division in Christ's nature also enables Thomas to explain why Christ's will was apparently not always the same as God's (Matthew 26:29). The words which Christ uttered in his struggle in Gethsemane had their origin in the *voluntas sensualitatis* (sensual will), which, in accordance with its nature, recoiled from death, while the *voluntas per modum rationis* (will modified by judgment) remained throughout his agony perfectly at one with God.[119] Thus Thomas repeatedly speaks of Christ as *simul comprehensor et viator*—he has attained the glory of heaven but remains a pilgrim on the earth, he has reached his appointed end but is still on the way to attaining it.[120] He is not, however, 'on the way' in the same manner as other men—for example, by virtue of the fact that he is *beatus* he does not have faith, since sight precludes faith.[121] He is *viator* only with respect to the lower functions of the soul and the body, which do not share in the beatification which is given by the act of God. These parts of his human nature are still in process of attaining their end, which is the *gloria corporis* and whatever else pertains to the glorification of the body. By the aid of grace, therefore, Christ can attain this end, while his soul, unlike the souls of other men, does not achieve beatification on the ground of preceding merit but is already perfectly beatified from the very moment of his

aliqua nocumenti passio in ea locum haberet: potentiae vero sensitivae, quarum objecta sunt res corporeae, habere poterant aliquod nocumentum ex corporis passione: unde sensibilis dolor in Christo fuit corpore patiente.

---

[117] An unusually expressive statement of this relation is found in 1a2ae, 102, 5, ad 6, where Thomas interprets Lev. 16:21ff., which speaks of the sending away of the goat in the wilderness, as a figure of *ipsa divinitas Christi, quae in solitudinem abiit, homine Christo patiente;* cf. also the interpretation of Lev. 14:53 in ib. ad 7.

[118] 3a, 46, 8.

[119] 3a, 18, 5.

[120] 3a, 15, 10: *Christus autem, ante passionem, secundum mentem plene videbat Deum: et sic habebat beatitudinem quantum ad id quod est proprium animae. Sed quantum ad alia deerat ei beatitudo: quia et anima eius erat passibilis, et corpus passibile et mortale. . . Et ideo simul erat comprehensor, inquantum habebat beatitudinem animae propriam: et simul viator, inquantum tendebat in beatitudinem secundum id quod ei de beatitudine deerat.* See also *De Ver.* 10, 11, ad 3; *De Ver.* 26, 10, ad 14 and ad 15; *De Ver.* 29, 6; III *Sent.* 18, 2; *Compend. Theol.* 231; 3a, 7, 8; 3a, 8, 4, ad 2; 3a, 11, 1, ad 2; 3a, 11, 2; 3a, 18, 5, ad 3.

[121] 3a, 7, 3.

conception.[122] This barrier between the higher and lower levels of his human nature, which is necessary in order to make possible his sufferings and his *meritum*, is briefly and temporarily removed at the transfiguration, and entirely taken away in the resurrection, *post resurrectionem ex anima gloria redundabit in corpus* (after the resurrection glory will overflow from the soul to the body).[123]

The incarnation is not known to us by way of reason. We have knowledge of the incarnation, as we have of the Trinity, through revelation. At these points rational argument simply breaks down. And yet it is possible for reason illuminated by faith to gain 'a certain understanding of the mystery'[124] and thus to explain the revealed content of faith. Clearly then, it is not revelation but a rationally attained knowledge of the character and potentialities of human nature that provides the point of departure in seeking to understand more fully what the incarnation means and also how our conceptualisation of it is to be determined. One could argue from this point of view with a certain justification that Christology is a special form of anthropology in general and of the doctrine of grace in

---

[122] 3a, 19, 3: *Unde nec gratiam, nec scientiam, nec beatitudinem animae, nec divinitatem meruit. . . Et ideo dicendum est quod Christus gloriam corporis, et ea quae pertinent ad exteriorem eius excellentiam . . . habuit per meritum.* Cf. III *Sent.* 18, 1–5; *De Ver.* 29, 6; Héris, *Le Verbe incarné*, vol. III, p. 342ff. On the concept of *meritum* in Thomas, which we do not have the opportunity of examining here more fully, see especially the exposition in 1a2ae, 114, 1–10. For an act to be meritorious, two things are necessary: it must proceed from free will and the infused grace of God. There is no opposition between these entities, for *gratia . . . facit nos libere operari* (1a2ae, 108, 1, ad 2; cf. 1a, 23, 5), since both are present in human nature, the former as a natural quality, the latter supernatural and perfecting the former (on this idea see especially Mulard, *La grâce*, p. 273f. and 299ff.). To use the terms commonly employed in the history of dogma, the same act is *meritum de congruo* if it proceeds from free will and *meritum de condigno* if it proceeds from grace (1a2ae, 114, 3). Both *liberum arbitrium* and *gratia* are found to their fullest extent in Christ, and this makes possible his *meritum*. Thus we should note that for Thomas the choice of an act which is unnatural, i.e. a sin, is not an expression of *libertas* but constitutes a *defectus libertatis* (1a, 62, 8, ad 3). Since Christ was incapable of sinning, it follows that he possessed freedom of the will to a higher degree than any other (cf. III *Sent.* 18, 2, ad 5; 3a, 18, 4). See also Garrigou-Lagrange, *De gratia*, p. 288ff. and Diekamp and Jüssen, *Dogmatik*, vol. II, p. 486ff.

[123] 3a, 11, 2; 3a, 54, 2: *anima Christi a principio suae conceptionis fuit gloriosa per fruitionem divinitatis perfectam. Est autem dispensative factum . . . ut ab anima gloria non redundaret in corpus, ad hoc quod mysterium nostrae redemptionis sua passione impleret. Et ideo, peracto hoc mysterio passionis et mortis Christi, anima Christi statim in corpus, in resurrectione resumptum, suam gloriam derivavit.* On the transfiguration of Christ as a momentary suspension of this barrier, see 3a, 45, 2.

[124] On the part played by reason in the theology of the incarnation, see A. Michel's article, 'Incarnation', in *DTC* 7:2, col. 1458f.

particular. These deductions from *ratio* are checked by truths of *revelatio* which act as a control to unrestrained speculation, and Thomas is therefore forced to hypothesise a psychological miracle which disrupts the normal sequence of events, in order to be able to speak of what is central to the New Testament message, viz. the sufferings and death of Christ. Since Thomas speaks of salvation primarily in terms of a perfection of human nature, his discussion of Christology differs markedly from what we find in the Gospels by concentrating in fact on this perfection which is found in Christ from the very moment of his conception—thus in the *Summa theologiae* he discusses the hypostatic union and its implications as well as Christ's *conceptio* itself in 176 articles (3a, q. 1–34), while he devotes only 64 articles (3a, q. 46–56) to his death and resurrection.[125] Thomas is, of course, aware of the difficulty presented by the statement of Paul that he was determined 'to know nothing except Jesus Christ and him crucified' (I Corinthians 2:2). In his commentary on the passage Thomas explains this to mean that Paul confined himself while amongst the Corinthians to preaching lesser truths, *inferiora*, and therefore acted *as if* he knew nothing except the cross of Christ.[126]

---

[125] Even more striking is what we find in the *Summa contra Gentiles*, where Thomas deals in general terms with the incarnation in Book IV, chapters 27–55, but simply does not discuss Christ's suffering and death at all, in spite of the stated intention of the whole work, which is to *veritatem quam fides Catholica profitetur, pro nostro modulo manifestare* (I, 2).

[126] See *In 1 ad Cor.* 2, 1 (75). The *infirmitates* which are associated with Christ's human nature cannot be a manifestation of any divine reality, Thomas holds, but must rather be understood as a concealment of God's nature: 3a, 14, 1, ad 4: *per huiusmodi infirmitates absconderetur eius divinitas, manifestabatur tamen humanitas.* Thus in the events of the crucifixion Thomas does not find the expression of his divinity in his sufferings on the cross, but in the miraculous events which took place around him: *In Joan.* 11, 5 (7): *Ubi notandum est, Christum verum Deum esse, et verum hominem: et ideo ubique fere in factis suis mixta leguntur humana divinis, et divina humanis: et si quandoque ponitur aliquid humanum de Christo, statim additur aliquid divinum. Nihil enim infirmius de Christo legimus quam ejus passionem; et tamen eo in cruce pendente, divina facta patent, quod sol obscuratur, petrae scinduntur, corpora sanctorum qui dormierant resurgunt.* We find a completely different interpretation of the relation between Christ's divinity and humanity in Luther, for whom the suffering on the cross represents 'the most concentrated revelation' (R. Bring, *Dualismen hos Luther*, Lund 1929, p. 150) of God's being, self-giving love. Luther conceives of God as most fully revealed precisely in what seems to be something utterly unlike God, *Deus revelatus in abscondito;* on this idea see Bring, *Dualismen*, p. 132ff. or E. Vogelsang, *Der angefochtene Christus bei Luther* (Arbeiten zur Kirchengeschichte 21), Berlin and Leipzig 1932, to cite only two examples from an abundance of works on Luther. The miracle of the incarnation does not consist primarily in a biological and psychical phenomenon produced by God and manifested in the human nature of Christ, but is rather that God himself encounters

But this cannot be the centre of sacred doctrine, for he had been entrusted with the task of imparting the knowledge of God, *Dei cognitionem tradere*, and according to Thomas the being of God is expressed more fully on the human plane in the perfect image which inheres in the glorious soul of Christ than in his *corpus passibile*.

To say that God sends his Son into the world means then, according to Thomas, that the eternal procession of the Son from the Father is accompanied by an *effectus temporalis*.[127] In our earlier discussion of the term *unio* we have already studied in some detail the effect of the transcendent divine cause in time from the standpoint of the change effected by the incarnation in the creaturely sphere. If now instead we attempt to indicate the nature of this change, we find that Thomas defines it also in terms that directly parallel his doctrine of grace. We come, therefore, to the final aspect of the divine causality in its relation to the incarnation.

In examining the concept of *missio invisibilis* we found that the idea of grace as an *elevatio* or raising up of human nature is one of the most characteristic features of Thomas's thought. He employs the same terminology also in speaking of God's presence in Christ, as we might well expect since he conceives of the incarnation also as grace. The incarnation took place apart from any prior merit from the side of man.[128] Since all grace by definition implies an elevation of what is human, the same must also be true of the unmerited gift given in the union of a human nature with one of the persons of the godhead and its coexistence with his *esse personale*. If we regard this union from the standpoint of what occurs in the creature, according to Thomas we shall speak of what happens as we speak of grace in general as an *elevatio humanae naturae*.[129]

To confine ourselves, however, to a discussion only of the hypostatic union and the perfection resulting from this union would

us precisely in the fact of Christ's humanity, in his insignificance, his willingness to serve, and his suffering on the cross. Luther does not find any difficulty in seeing in these human actions a direct expression of God's nature—on the contrary, it is precisely in the searching, self-sacrificing love which offers itself in the death of the cross that we see his nature.

---

[127] 1a, 43, 2, ad 3. Cf. p. 191 above.   [128] 3a, 2, 10, and 11.

[129] 3a, 2, 10: *Elevatur autem humana natura in Deum dupliciter. Uno modo, per operationem: qua scilicet sancti cognoscunt et amant Deum. Alio modo, per esse personale: qui quidem modus est singularis Christo, in quo humana natura assumpta est ad hoc quod sit personae Filii Dei.* Dondaine, *La Trinité*, vol. II, p. 424, is therefore incorrect when he states that elevation is a characteristic only of the *missio invisibilis*.

suggest in the last resort a misdirected preoccupation with the creaturely aspects of the *missio visibilis*. Nor is this all, for the incarnation involves a divine as well as a human element, both of which must be seen in their context if we are to have a true understanding of the incarnation. Thomas himself uses the term *assumptio*, which, since it unites both elements and quite clearly conveys his understanding of the incarnation, offers us as good a starting-point as any. The term expresses the whole event of the incarnation as such, *sicut in fieri*, and not only its effect.[130] Thomas explicitly states that the term is simply a different way of expressing what is meant when we speak of God's 'visible sending' of the Son into the world.[131]

It is of particular interest to note the etymology of the word which Thomas gives, always in the same form: *dicitur enim assumptio* QUASI AB ALIO AD SE SUMPTIO (assumption means a taking to oneself from another).[132] He means by this that to assume or take to oneself is to determine the end or object in the direction of which a particular movement occurs, and also that this movement is ultimately dependent upon and is caused by the active subject. 'Movement' is not, of course, to be understood here in the local or temporal sense of preceding or leading to the union of divinity and humanity in Christ, but rather in the metaphysical sense of the elevation that coincides in time with the conception of his human nature. The term *assumptio* signifies that from first to last the incarnation is a work of God and not a human achievement—*elevatio humanae naturae* is not an autonomous increase of man's natural powers but God's act of elevation. The term, however, allows Thomas at the same time to emphasise the divine action in the incarnation without in any way doing violence to the immutability of the divine being. In speaking of the incarnation Thomas prefers the term *assumptio* rather than *incarnatio*, which he uses less frequently and

[130] On the distinction between *unio* and *assumptio*, see 3a, 2, 8: *prima et principalis differentia inter unionem et assumptionem est quod unio importat ipsam relationem: assumptio autem actionem secundum quam dicitur aliquis assumens, vel passionem secundum quam dicitur aliquid assumptum. Ex hac autem differentia accipitur secundo alia differentia. Nam assumptio dicitur sicut in fieri: unio autem sicut in facto esse. . . . Ex eodem etiam sequitur tertia differentia . . . assumptio determinat terminum et a quo et ad quem, dicitur enim assumptio quasi ab alio ad se sumptio: unio autem nihil horum determinat;* see also III *Sent.* 5, 1, 1, 3.
[131] 3a, 7, 13: *persona Filii . . . secundum hoc dicitur 'missa esse in mundum' quod humanam naturam assumpsit; In ad Gal.* 4, 2 (202): *sua missio fuit assumptio carnis;* cf. also 1a, 43, 1.
[132] 3a, 2, 8; 3a, 3, 1: *dicitur enim assumere quasi ad se aliquid sumere;* 3a, 4, 2: *aliquid dicitur assumi ex eo quod ad aliquid sumitur.*

therefore generally with reservation, the explanation being simply that the former term does not suggest, as the latter does, that God was changed or transformed by becoming man.[133] By employing the term *assumptio*, that is to say, he subsumes the incarnation under the *ordo ad Deum* which defines in general the relation between God and the creature and in the light of which all of Thomas's theological statements are to be interpreted. Just as God is *principium* and *finis* of all that occurs in the created world, so also we may say that he is *principium* and *terminus* in the incarnation.[134] Here again we note the marked emphasis on the aspect of finality which, as we saw at the beginning of this chapter, is so strongly emphasised by Thomas in his interpretation of the general relationship between God and the creature.[135] It is characteristic of Thomas that he sees the act of God in the incarnation as 'a centripetal action, the Word drawing human nature to itself in order to unite personally with it,' to use the striking expression of M. T.-L. Penido.[136] Thus God's presence in Christ or his sending of the Son into the world does not imply any movement by God towards men; rather, this *actio* of God is fully and entirely expressed in a movement towards God on the part of the creature. For Thomas there is no question at all here of any 'descent' on the part of God—from a metaphysical standpoint such a thing would be inconceivable—but rather of an *elevatio* of the human element, or, to quote Penido once more: 'It would not be necessary to interpret this "new" mode of being to mean that God really began to exist in a man; in fact, the reverse is true, and far from God descending, it is the creature who ascends.'[137]

---

[133] Cf. 3a, 3, 2: *Et secundum etiam hunc modum dicitur natura incarnata; non quasi sit in carnem conversa; sed quia naturam carnis assumpsit;* cf. *In Joan.* 1, 7 (1), where Thomas asks why the Evangelist chose the expression *Verbum caro factum est* rather than the phrase which he himself constantly uses, *Verbum carnem assumpsit.*

[134] 3a, 3, 1: *in verbo assumptionis duo importantur, videlicet principium actus, et terminus: dicitur enim assumere quasi ad se aliquid sumere. Huius autem assumptionis persona est et principium et terminus;* cf. 1a, 2, prol., where Thomas states that the task of *sacra doctrina* is to give knowledge of God *secundum quod est principium rerum et finis earum.*

[135] Cf. p. 96ff. and 103 above.

[136] Penido, *Le rôle de l'analogie*, p. 407, though Penido mistakenly restricts the centripetal movement to the incarnation. In the relationship between God and the creature, however, God is primarily understood as *causa finalis*, see p. 101 above.

[137] Penido, *Le rôle de l'analogie*, p. 408. Cf. also C. von Schaezler, *Das Dogma von der Menschwerdung Gottes im Geiste des hl. Thomas*, Freiburg im Breisgau 1870, p. 82: 'seine Menschwerdung bewirkt keine Herabsetzung des Göttlichen, sondern vielmehr die *Erhebung* der menschlichen Natur', or the definition of the incarnation given by Michel in his article on the same subject in *DTC* 7:2, col. 1450: '*l'opération*

The fact that Thomas seems on occasion to reject the interpretation of the incarnation as an *ascensus* does not involve any contradiction. What he is rejecting is the heretical idea of the incarnation as the growth to perfection of a human nature that was in existence prior to the hypostatic union, until it comes to unite with the godhead.[138] As we have seen, the term *assumptio* wholly denies any such idea by attesting that from first to last the incarnation 'comes from God' and is totally a gift of grace. The fact that Thomas speaks at times of the incarnation as a descent, *descensus*, in the language of the New Testament itself, does not imply any departure from the above conclusion, as a study of the respective passages will at once disclose. The crucial point is not so much the appearance of a particular concept as the meaning attached to it. In order to explain what he means, Thomas, as we shall see, makes use not only of this concept of *assumptio*[139] but also of the term *esse novo modo* (to exist in a new way),[140] or just *esse per novum effectum in terris* (to exist on earth by means of a new effect), adding that *descensus* is simply to be understood *metaphorice*.[141] It is evident from this that when he speaks of a divine descent he does not mean more than is conveyed by the terms *missio visibilis* and *assumptio* themselves, viz. an *elevatio* of human nature.[142]

We began our discussion of Thomas's doctrine of the presence of God in Christ by examining his treatment of the biblical concept of the incarnation as God's sending of his Son into the world, and we have concluded our discussion by examining what he calls the *assumptio humanae naturae*, a phrase for which Thomas has a

par laquelle Dieu élève jusqu'à lui une nature humaine déterminée'. This idea of elevation which is so characteristic of Thomas's Christology is concisely expressed by M. Grabmann in his *Die Geschichte der katholischen Theologie seit dem Ausgang der Väterzeit*, Freiburg im Breisgau 1933, p. 80, when he attempts to summarise the contents of Part Three of the *Summa theologiae* in a couple of lines: 'pars III, inwiefern Gott selbst durch die Inkarnation und die Sakramente *uns sich nahebringt*' (italics ours).

---

[138] 3a, 33, 3, ad 3: *in mysterio incarnationis non consideratur ascensus, quasi alicuius praeexistentis proficientis usque ad unionis dignitatem: sicut posuit Photinus haereticus;* see also 3a, 34, 1, ad 1.
[139] See *In Joan.* 3, 2 (4); 13, 1 (1); *In ad Eph.* 4, 3 (209).
[140] *In ad Phil.* 2, 2 (57); 3a, 5, 2, ad 1.   [141] III *Sent.* 22, 3, 1, ad 2.
[142] Manteau-Bonamy, *Maternité*, boldly states that for Thomas the incarnation has the character of a divine descent (see especially p. 78 and 102f.), but on p. 65 he can actually say that '*cette descente divine est en réalité une montée et une exaltation de la créature en Dieu*'.

particular preference and which sums up well his understanding of the incarnation. Though we do not find the term used in this sense in the New Testament writings,[143] this is of no great significance for our discussion. The word 'incarnation' itself is not biblical, and the crucial question is the meaning attached to the term. The fact that he takes his starting-point in a rationally defined concept of cause based on a scheme of act and potency and in a rationally given knowledge of human nature obviously means that Thomas's definition of the incarnation raises considerable difficulties when he turns to interpret and relate some of the Christological statements of the New Testament that deal with the event of the cross. We have already seen how this is expressed indirectly by Thomas in the emphasis which he attached in his Christology to the actual moment of conception, and which purely in terms of proportion is quite different from what is contained in the Gospel accounts.[144] The difficulty becomes acute in view of the fact that Thomas regards salvation primarily as a perfection of human nature, and such a conception apparently prevents him from doing justice to various passages in the New Testament in which the meaning of the incarnation is expressed in such phrases as to 'descend from heaven,' to 'become poor', to 'empty himself', and to 'give himself for others'.[145] Though there is no question that for Thomas the incarnation is to be treated seriously as a quite tangible reality which from first to last manifests the love of God, it is also clear that his approach to such biblical concepts

[143] The corresponding terms ἀνάλημψις and ἀναλαμβάνειν are used in the New Testament only of the events of the last days of Jesus' earthly life and seem always to be connected with the ascension, cf. Luke 9:51; Mark 16:19; Acts 1:2, 11, 22; I Tim. 3:16. Cf. D. M. Baillie, *God was in Christ. An Essay on Incarnation and Atonement*, 2nd ed. London 1948, p. 17: ' "Assumption of human nature" is not a wholly satisfactory phrase as applied to the Incarnation, as indeed it hardly belongs to the world of the New Testament'.

[144] See p. 217 above.

[145] See e.g. John 3:13, 16; Rom. 8:32; II Cor. 8:9; Gal. 1:4; 2:20; Eph. 5:2; 5:25; Phil. 2:7ff. Of particular interest to us as a typical example of Thomas's line of thought is his interpretation of this last passage in his Commentary on the Epistle to the Philippians, see In ad Phil. 2, 2 (56–61): To say that Christ did not understand his equality with God as 'a thing to be grasped' means that he *cognoscit bene naturam suam*, and so he knew that this was not something that he possessed wrongfully but something that was his by nature. To say that he 'emptied' himself means that he *incepit esse novo modo in terris . . . assumendo naturam humanam*. *Exinanitio* does not therefore refer to anything on God's side but to the human nature which by that nature is *in potentia ad plenitudinem* in contrast to the divine nature, which is *satis plena*. The 'divine' self-emptying is therefore actually to be understood in terms of something opposite to it, viz. an enrichment of human nature, *mutata est in melius, quia impleta est gratia et veritate*.

as these precludes discussion of others of crucial importance. There is clearly an underlying tension at this point between *ratio* and *revelatio*, a tension of which Thomas himself was not wholly aware. In the following chapter we shall return to this critical problem which will also throw light on our discussion of the relation between reason and revelation.

With this we conclude our investigation into what Thomas means by God's presence in the world. God is in everything primarily by the very fact that a thing exists and is therefore utterly dependent on him. But he is also specially present in the righteous as the object of the will and intellect that have been brought to perfection in them by grace. Finally, he is also in Christ, in that the human nature of Christ has been raised to union with one of the persons of the godhead, and exists with his *esse*. Each of these three forms of presence, according to Thomas, is represented in Christ, for God is in Christ *per essentiam, praesentiam et potentiam, sicut in ceteris creaturis* (by essence, presence, and power, as in other creatures), and also *per gratiam gratum facientem, sicut in sanctis* (by sanctifying grace, as in the saints), and finally, though only in the case of Christ, *per unionem personalem* (by personal union).[146] It is clear that Thomas does not conceive of God as remote or static but as actively at work in the created world. But in all three types of divine presence which we have studied, this activity of God is expressed in the same basic scheme—the 'presence' of the transcendent cause in an effect wholly dependent on this cause. In each case this dependence is expressed in the assumption of a unilateral relation to the Creator that exists in a real sense only in the creature. The divine activity *within* the creature is not something above or beyond its own *actio* but in the last resort coincides with it. But this does not mean that man is autonomous or independent of God. Man himself *is* and acts—and therefore is accountable for his deeds—but both his *esse* and *operatio* issue at every moment from God and are immediately dependent upon him. They are gifts given to men by a gracious and benevolent God, though their fashion and form is determined by the nature of the recipient, for *receptum est in recipiente secundum modum recipientis*. The principle, *causa est in effectu per modum effectus*, is therefore applicable to every form of God's presence in the world. The 'receiving' nature can be transformed by a perfection given to it by God and thereby its own *actio* brought to resemble even more

[146] 3a, 2, 10, ad 2.

closely the activity within the godhead itself. But this resemblance to the transcendent activity of the godhead seen in the actions of the creature never becomes identical with it. The action of the creature continues to be determined by the limits given with its nature, just as God himself continues to be transcendent. This is true even of God's presence in Christ. Even in Christ God is present only insofar as the transcendent cause is in an effect which is conformed as closely as possible to it.[147] Thus here, too, 'presence' is ultimately reduced to the relationship of absolute dependence—that immediate dependence upon God on the part of all creation which is given expression in the unilateral real relation to God.

[147] Cf. Congar, *Christ, our Lady and the Church*, p. 53: 'It is not a question of God in Christ, but of the sacred Humanity of Jesus in as much as by its union with the divinity in the Person of the Word it is, in itself and as humanity, raised to an admirable dignity and filled with power and holiness'.

III

RATIO AND *SACRA DOCTRINA*

1

GRATIA SUPPONIT NATURAM

The task of theology, as Thomas understands it, is to show and interpret the meaning of the truth which has been given by revelation and is essential for salvation. This task of interpretation is the work of reason, illuminated by faith. We may briefly summarise the relationship which constitutes the presupposition and background of the whole of the present study as follows: In Chapter I we noted, first, the interpretation given by Thomas to revelation. We saw, too, how he understands this revelation to be transmitted to each new generation, and in particular we discussed the integral relationship which he finds between scripture and *sacra doctrina*. In this whole chapter the question of revelation was therefore central. In Chapter II we sought to understand the relationship between *ratio* and *revelatio*, and by turning to Thomas's own presentation of *sacra doctrina* we learned something about the nature of this relationship in his theology in general and particularly in key sections which bear on our study. Against the background of these two earlier chapters we now summarise our conclusions, and therefore *ratio* and the function which it fulfils in theology becomes of particular interest to us. Before going further, however, we consider it necessary to try to state what Thomas himself says about the role of reason within theology.

We may conveniently begin our discussion with Thomas's statement that the revelation contained and communicated to us in scripture also includes certain cognitive elements which lie within the scope of natural reason. These include what Thomas usually terms the *praeambula fidei*, for example, the knowledge of God and of created things which can be found even amongst the philosophers.[1] Most people, however, either because they lack the intellectual gifts or have insufficient time for study or simply are lazy, are incapable of attaining this knowledge of God on their own. A further fact to be reckoned with is the uncertainty caused by the conflicting opinions of

---

[1] *De Ver.* 14, 9, ad 8; *In De Trin.* 2, 3; 1a, 2, 2, ad 1.

227

philosophers whose arguments contain a mixture of truth and error which makes it impossible to find out what is really true without some additional help.[2] Though this knowledge is accessible to reason, it is also, however, necessary for salvation, and since it has reference to all men, it was necessary that it should be included in the revelation given to us, otherwise, of course, saving truth would have been granted only to those schooled in philosophy.[3] Thus within *sacra doctrina*, which expresses the content of revelation, there is a sphere that is directly accessible to reason and is specifically its own domain.

There are, however, revealed truths which lie beyond the grasp of even the most brilliant philosopher, inaccessible to all the efforts of reason, and these must therefore be received in faith by *all* men, however different their circumstances otherwise may be. Amongst these truths Thomas includes, for example, the Trinity, creation, the incarnation, and the sacraments. With regard to these, all Christians, as long as they are *in via*, are on the same level. In this sense Thomas has no place for the distinction quite frequently drawn in the history of theology between the great mass of the faithful who have only 'faith' and the enlightened who in addition have also 'understanding' of the content of faith.[4] Granted that the ignorant must accept in faith what to the philosopher is certain knowledge, just as the angels and the blessed in heaven now see and know what for us is attainable only through faith, yet it is impossible that the same truth can be the object both of faith and knowledge in the same person.[5] There is thus a sphere within *sacra doctrina* which transcends the competence of reason and in which proof ceases to be applicable, since we cannot prove what is incapable of proof, and to try to do so, as Thomas puts it, would be to expose oneself to the ridicule of unbelievers, who would quickly discover the shaky basis of any such line of argument.[6] Revelation is to be understood rather as a benefit added to rational knowledge which frees it from a great many possibilities of error, and above all from the source of all error,

---

[2] *De Ver.* 14, 10; *In De Trin.* 3, 1, ad 3; *CG* I, 4; 1a, 1, 1: 2a2ae, 2, 4.

[3] As is clear from *De Ver.* 14, 10 and *In De Trin.* 3, 1, Thomas derives his argument at this point from Moses Maimonides. Characteristically, however, Thomas deduces from this argument the universality of revelation—revelation is for all—while Maimonides concludes that metaphysical truths should not be imparted to the masses, who do not yet understand them.

[4] Cf. E. Gilson, *Reason and Revelation in the Middle Ages*, New York 1938, p. 74f.

[5] *De Ver.* 14, 9; *In ad Heb.* 11, 1 (560); 1a2ae, 67, 3; 2a2ae, 1, 5: *impossibile est quod ab eodem idem sit scitum et creditum.*

[6] *Contra Graecos, Armenos et Saracenos*, 2; *CG* I, 9; 1a, 1, 8; 1a, 46, 2.

the idea that reason is the measure of all that exists.[7] Faith takes up where reason leaves off and argument fails. Like the student before he comes to learn all that he needs to know, we must believe the word of the teacher—in our case, the word of God.[8] We shall attain to perfect knowledge only in the life eternal where faith gives way to sight,[9] but until then we must remain content with believing because of the weakness of our reason.[10]

Thomas thus draws a clear line of distinction between knowledge and faith. But this certainly does not mean that revelation fulfils its function only when it discloses what is known only by faith, for *all* sacred doctrine is simply an exposition and interpretation of the content of revelation. But by its very nature this revelation includes some truths that at least to certain men are accessible to reason and others that can only be attained through revelation. Thomas has no place for 'natural' theology, if by this is meant any speculation that would have precedence over revelation or exist independently of it and, as it were, go half-way before giving way to revelation.[11] Revelation is his starting-point and revelation alone is the *raison d'être* of his work as a theologian. Natural knowledge of God has a place in *sacra doctrina* because it is not simply a necessary pre-supposition of revelation but is also confirmed, renewed and corrected by revelation. In one sense, therefore, we may say that for Thomas revelation covers the whole field of *sacra doctrina*.

In making this distinction between *ratio* and *fides*, however, Thomas does not limit the operation of reason only to those truths which are capable of rational proof. Just as we might say that in one sense the whole of *sacra doctrina* is to be subsumed under *revelatio*, so we could also say that it is properly subsumed under *ratio*, for theology, as Thomas understands it, is the activity of reason illuminated by faith. The two are not to be regarded as separate spheres, independent of one another, and the relationship between them is best understood as a particular instance of or a

[7] *CG* I, 5.

[8] *In 1 ad Cor.* 15, 1 (896): *ibi incipit articulus fidei, ubi deficit ratio;* see also *De Ver.* 14, 10 or 2a2ae, 2, 3: *ad hoc quod homo perveniat ad perfectam visionem beatitudinis praeexigitur quod credat Deo tanquam discipulus magistro docenti.*

[9] 1a2ae, 67, 3.

[10] *De Ver.* 14, 10: *quaedam talia sunt, quod in hac vita de eis perfecta cognitio haberi non potest, quae totaliter vim humanae rationis excedunt: et ista oportet credere quamdiu in statu viae sumus; videbimus autem ea perfecte in statu patriae.* Cf. p. 27f. and 36f. above.

[11] Cf. p. 122f. and 154 above.

Q

parallel to the relation between nature and grace—SIC ENIM FIDES
PRAESUPPONIT COGNITIONEM NATURALEM, SICUT GRATIA NATURAM,
ET UT PERFECTIO PERFECTIBLE (for faith presupposes natural knowledge, just as grace does nature and all perfections that which they
perfect).[12] Faith does not disclaim the contribution made by reason,
but presupposes and perfects it. For Thomas, faith and revelation
alike are to be regarded as *actus intellectus*, and therefore there is no
opposition between them and natural reason. They simply perfect
the inherent intention of *ratio*, which is to acquire knowledge
and thereby to be made perfect, since both faith and reason have
fundamentally the same object in view, viz. truth itself.[13] Just as
grace is more than an external addition to nature, like a second
storey added to it, and is rather the *elevatio* of this nature to a higher
and more perfect life, so the knowledge that is revealed through faith
means more than an external addition to reason. The view which a
climber sees when he has followed a guide to a mountain top is no
less true and no less his simply because someone else brought him
there.[14] Nor is reason condemned by the *lumen fidei* to cease from
its proper activity, but on the contrary this is how its work is brought
to perfection, without in any way its ceasing to be human reason
with all the limitation this implies in regard to other existing rational
beings. It is from this basic view of the relationship between nature
and grace that we are to interpret Thomas's understanding of the
interplay between philosophy and revelation in *sacra doctrina*.

Since grace does not abolish or do away with nature, but presupposes and perfects it, it becomes not simply natural but inevitable
that *sacra doctrina* should include and make use of knowledge
attained by the philosophers.[15] In his commentary on the *De
Trinitate* of Boethius Thomas shows how this may be done in three
different ways.[16]

   1. *Ad demonstrandum ea quae sunt praeambula fidei . . . ut deum esse,*

[12] 1a, 2, 2, ad 1; cf. 1a, 1, 8, ad 2 and *De Ver*. 14, 10, ad 9.
[13] Cf. p. 20ff. above on revelation as a *cognitio*. Cf. also 1a, 79, 8: *Intelligere enim
est simpliciter veritatem intelligibilem apprehendere*, and 2a2ae, 4, 2: *Credere
autem est immediate actus intellectus: quia obiectum huius actus est verum, quod
proprie pertinet ad intellectum*. On the cognitive aspect of faith see also Skydsgaard,
Metafysik, p. 249ff. and p. 27f. and 36f. above.
[14] Gilson, *Thomisme*, p. 33.
[15] 1a, 1, 8, ad 2: *Cum enim gratia non tollat naturam, sed perficiat, oportet quod
naturalis ratio subserviat fidei*.
[16] *In De Trin*. 2, 3; on what follows cf. Congar, 'Theologie', in *DTC* 15:1, col.
382ff. and Grabmann, *Erkenntnis- und Einleitungslehre*, p. 178f.

deum esse unum et alia huiusmodi vel de deo vel de creaturis in philosophia probata, quae fides supponit (to demonstrate the presuppositions of faith . . . that God is, that he is one, and other statements of this kind about God or the creature which are proved in the philosophy assumed by faith).[17] In dealing with these questions, e.g. the existence of God, reason is on its own ground and can convince the sceptic with a rationally conclusive line of argument. On the other hand, however, this kind of argument has no place in that sphere to which only faith has access, and there is therefore a clear distinction at this point between Thomas and Anselm.[18] His use of philosophy is consequently limited to truths which are accessible to reason. Philosophical arguments which may be cited in favour of truths of faith are not to be regarded as proofs but at the most as *verisimilitudines* or *persuasiones*, which may be used to show that the content of faith is not contrary to reason but quite compatible with it.[19]

2. This brings us to what Thomas regards as the second function which philosophy has to fulfil in *sacra doctrina*—*ad notificandum per aliquas similitudines ea quae sunt fidei* (to demonstrate what belongs to faith by means of analogies). By way of illustration Thomas here refers to Augustine who in his *De trinitate* cites a great many analogies from philosophy *ad manifestandum trinitatem* (to throw light on the Trinity).[20] We have already seen in discussing his doctrine of the Trinity how frequently Thomas makes reference to philosophy. The knowledge of the functions of the human soul given by philosophy helps us to understand and gives substance to the dogmatic formulations which have been handed down to us.[21] That is to say, by starting with what we already know, we seek to understand what, as long as we are still *in via*, we must accept in faith.[22] Within the area of revealed truths accessible only to faith philosophy, which has so large a part to play in the theology of Thomas, fulfils this function.

3. Theology also makes use of philosophical arguments *ad resistendum his quae contra fidem dicuntur* (to resist attacks on faith).[23] The function which philosophy fulfils in defending the faith is related to

---

[17] *In De Trin.* 2, 3.   [18] Cf. Manser, *Thomismus*, p. 122ff.
[19] *In De Trin.* 2, 1, ad 5; *CG* I, 8–9; 2a2ae, 1, 5, ad 2; 2a2ae, 2, 10, ad 2.
[20] *In De Trin.* 2, 3.   [21] See p. 143ff. above.
[22] Cf. 1a, 1, 5, ad 2: *ex his quae per naturalem rationem (ex qua procedunt aliae scientiae) cognoscuntur, facilius manuducitur in ea quae sunt supra rationem, quae in hac scientia traduntur.*
[23] *In De Trin.* 2, 3.

the fact that, as Thomas maintains, there can be no opposition between rational and revealed knowledge. The latter may, indeed, transcend rational comprehension, but the opposition is merely apparent, as we see in the analogous case of the simpleton who thinks it utterly contrary to reason to believe the philosopher when he says that the sun is larger than the earth.[24]

Thomas nowhere suggests that reason has a distorted knowledge of God or that the natural knowledge of God is an inadequate knowledge. He is, of course, sceptical of philosophers, since they may err, even Aristotle,[25] but he nowhere expresses any hesitation about the use of reason itself as such, as if it could be used in theology only with extreme caution, though, of course, it must be used within its proper limits. The destructive effects of sin, according to Thomas, are not to be found primarily in the intellect but in the will.[26] Our earlier discussion of the meaning of revelation has already shown how this positive view of reason is also stressed by Thomas in his unwillingness to connect the need for revelation with any reduction or distortion of our knowledge of God that is due to sin,[27] and he explicitly says that human nature is *magis . . . corrupta per peccatum quantum ad appetitum boni, quam quantum ad cognitionem Veri* (more corrupted by sin in regard to the desire for good, than in regard to the knowledge of truth).[28] In his exposition of Paul's reference in I Corinthians 1 :18 to the 'word of the cross' as 'foolishness', Thomas offers a characteristic interpretation. He interprets Paul's statements by making use of the analogy of the simpleton and the philosopher, and holds that the gospel is 'foolish', not because there is any opposition between it and rational knowledge, but because men have a lack of knowledge, a *defectus sapientiae*, about these things.[29] As an intellectual function man's reason is in fact directed towards the truth, and faith, as it may be expressed, lies in the extension of this process, since the object of faith is nothing other than Truth itself, *veritas prima*.[30] God has given man both the first principles of thought and the articles of faith, and if at any point faith and reason were to come

[24] *De Ver.* 14, 10, ad 7.   [25] Cf. p. 123f. above.
[26] 1a2ae, 74, 1: *peccatum sit in voluntate sicut in subiecto.*
[27] See p. 34f. above.
[28] 1a2ae, 109, 2, ad 3; cf. also p. 34 above, footnote 73—Thomas has difficulties in defining unbelief as sin.
[29] *In 1 ad Cor.* 1, 3 (49): *id quod est in se bonum, non potest alicui stultum videri, nisi propter defectum sapientiae;* see also ib. (50) and (62) and also 2, 3 (114f.).
[30] *De Ver.* 14, 8: *per se obiectum fidei veritas prima est;* 2a2ae, 1, 1; cf. also p. 27ff, above.

into conflict, it would mean that God was the *auctor falsitatis*, which *a priori* is inconceivable.[31] But it follows from this that it is always possible in principle to prove on a purely philosophical basis, *ex principiis philosophiae*, that the arguments which are used against faith are not conclusive but may in fact be rejected as pure sophistry. When we use philosophy to contradict the substance of the faith we are no longer reasoning like philosophers, Thomas says, but are guilty of what he calls *abusus philosophiae*.[32] This apologetic use of philosophy in the service of theology is especially prominent in the *Summa contra gentiles*, as we might expect from the purpose of this work which is to convince unbelievers that none of the arguments which they bring against the Christian faith really stands up to closer examination.[33]

In addition to these three tasks listed by Thomas in his commentary on Boethius as the specific tasks fulfilled by philosophy within theology, there is a further task which we have already mentioned in our discussion of *sacra doctrina* as a *scientia*, viz. the systematic interpretation of the content of the premisses given in the *articuli fidei*.[34] Theology is to be distinguished from faith because it not only presupposes revelation but also seeks to attain a proper understanding of the consequences and implications of this revelation. The mere citation of 'authorities', whether these are found in scripture or the articles of faith, may indeed convince a man that what they say is true, but they do not give him any profound understanding of *how* this is so, *quo modo est verum quod dicitur*. Methodologically, therefore, the theological task cannot just mean solving the problems that are raised merely by quoting chapter and verse in scripture. If we do no more than this, says Thomas, we simply do not get beyond the given starting-point provided by the content of

[31] *In De Trin.* 2, 3: *impossibile est quod ea, quae per fidem traduntur nobis divinitus, sint contraria his quae sunt per naturam nobis indita. Oporteret enim alterum esse falsum; et cum utrumque sit nobis a deo, deus nobis esset auctor falsitatis, quod est impossibile;* cf. also *CG* I, 7 and 9 ; *Contra Graecos, Armenos et Saracenos,* 2.

[32] *In De Trin.* 2, 3: *Si quid autem in dictis philosophorum invenitur contrarium fidei, hoc non est philosophia, sed magis philosophiae abusus ex defectu rationis; CG* I, 7: *quaecumque argumenta contra fidei documenta ponantur, haec ex principiis primis naturae inditis per se notis non recte procedere. Unde nec demonstrationis vim habent, sed vel sunt rationes probabiles vel sophisticae;* see also ib. I, 9; 1a, 1, 8: *Cum enim fides infallibili innitatur, impossibile autem sit de vero demonstrari contrarium, manifestum est probationes, quae contra fidem inducuntur, non esse demonstrationes, sed solubilia argumenta.*

[33] In this connection see particularly the methodological discussion in *CG* I, 9.
[34] See p. 74ff. above and the references cited on these pages.

the faith. But the task of theology is in fact to go further and seek to understand and explain this content—Thomas thus gives clear expression to the scheme of *fides quaerens intellectum* formulated by Anselm and found in almost all the scholastic writers—and therefore theology must use a rational method analogous to that which is employed in other sciences.[35] Otherwise it would not be a *scientia*. The task of theology is therefore to explain by the aid of *ratio* what has been given by revelation.[36]

Thomas, however, is also anxious to avoid any misapplication of philosophy in *sacra doctrina*, for instance, the introduction of doctrines which are inherently inconsistent with revelation. Origen is one example of how philosophy has been so distorted.[37]Another error likewise rejected by Thomas is to allow philosophy to exceed its authority by defining the limits within which theology is to operate, when properly the very reverse should be the case. One example of this is to refuse to believe anything that cannot be validated by reason, or, for instance, to make the arrogant claim that by reason we can penetrate and comprehend all the mysteries of existence. To do this, Thomas says, is to subordinate theology to philosophy and to transpose the proper relationship between the two which, as Paul shows in II Corinthians 10:5, is that faith should be primary with philosophy at its service.[38] In *sacra doctrina* faith is both starting-

---

[35] *Quodl.* 4, 18: *Quaedam vero disputatio est magistralis in scholis non ad removendum errorem, sed ad instruendum auditores ut inducantur ad intellectum veritatis quam intendit: et tunc oportet rationibus inniti investigantibus veritatis radicem, et facientibus scire quomodo sit verum quod dicitur: alioquin si nullis auctoritatibus magister quaestionem determinet, certificabitur quidem auditor quod ita est; sed nihil scientiae vel intellectus acquiret, sed vacuus abscedet.* Cf. Gagnebet, *RT* 46 (1938), p. 253: 'La méthode propre à la théologie de saint Thomas ne sera donc pas une méthode d'autorité, mais elle sera une méthode rationelle, parce que, sans la raison, par l'autorité toute pure, il est impossible de conduire à l'intelligence, à la connaissance scientifique de la vérité enseignée par la foi'.

[36] Gagnebet, *RT* 46 (1938), p. 253: 'La théologie de saint Thomas semble donc s'être donné comme tâche propre de connaître les réalités révélées par nos procédés naturels de connaître'; Gilson, *Thomisme*, p. 22: 'Par la science de la parole de Dieu qu'il construit, le théologien ne fait qu'expliciter, à l'aide de la raison naturelle, le donné révélé'.

[37] Grabmann, *Erkenntnis- und Einleitungslehre*, p. 158, gives examples of what Thomas judged this distortion to be in Origen's theology.

[38] *In De Trin.* 2, 3: *Tamen utentes philosophia in sacra doctrina possunt dupliciter errare. Uno modo in hoc quod utantur his quae sunt contra fidem, quae non sunt philosophiae, sed corruptio vel abusus eius, sicut Origenes fecit. Alio modo, ut ea quae sunt fidei includantur sub metis philosophiae, ut scilicet si aliquis credere nolit nisi quod per philosophiam haberi potest, cum e converso philosophia sit ad metas fidei redigenda, secundum illud Apostoli 2 Cor. 10: 'In captivitatem redigentes omnem*

point and presupposition and it is grounded not on the teaching of the philosophers, so that *propter eam veritas fidei credatur* (on its account the truth of faith is believed), but on the truth revealed by God.[39] When a theologian makes use of philosophical arguments, he does so not because of the authority of the philosophers itself but because they have also found the truth at points where their teachings do not contradict the faith.[40] The *regula fidei* cannot therefore consist of the various manifestations of natural knowledge but only and solely of the *veritas divina*.[41]

Reason and the systems of knowledge which are dependent on reason exist, according to Thomas, to serve faith and accordingly have a subordinate and ancillary relationship to theology, *tanquam inferioribus et ancillis* (as subsidiary and ancillary),[42] because, quite simply, theology aims at a higher object than *cognitio philosophica*. While the latter cannot get beyond the knowledge of God which goes to make up the *felicitas viae* (blessedness of this present life), theology brings us to the infinitely higher and more perfect goal of the knowledge of God which will be given to us *in patria* (in heaven) and is already possessed in faith.[43] It is to be noted, however, that in

intellectum in obsequium Christi'; cf. ib. 2, 1: *Tripliciter tamen contingit in hoc peccare. Primo ex praesumptione qua scilicet aliquis sic ea scrutatur quasi ea perfecte comprehensurus . . . Secundo ex hoc quod in his quae sunt fidei ratio praecedit fidem, non fides rationem, dum scilicet aliquis hoc solum vult credere quod ratione potest invenire, cum debeat esse e converso. . . Tertio ultra modum suae capacitatis ad divinorum perscrutationem se ingerendo;* see also *In ad Col.* 2, 2 (92) and 1a, 1, 8, ad 2.

---

[39] *In De Trin.* 2, 3, ad 1: *doctrina philosophorum non sit utendum quasi principali, ut scilicet propter eam veritas fidei credatur; non tamen removetur, quin ea possint uti sacri doctores quasi secundaria;* cf. *CG* II, 38: faith is not *in vanis rationibus constituta* but *in solidissima Dei doctrina;* 2a2ae, 2, 10: *credere debet homo . . . non propter rationem humanam, sed propter auctoritatem divinam.* This point is particularly emphasised by Gardeil, *Le donné,* p. 201f.

[40] *In De Trin.* 2, 3, ad 8: *in quantum sacra doctrina utitur philosophicis documentis propter se, non recipit ea propter auctoritatem dicentium, sed propter rationem dictorum, unde quaedam bene dicta accipit et alia respuit;* 1a, 1, 8, ad 2: *Et inde est quod etiam auctoritatibus philosophorum sacra doctrina utitur, ubi per rationem naturalem veritatem cognoscere potuerunt; In 1 ad Cor.* 1, 3 (43): *Utitur autem sapientia verbi, qui suppositis verae fundamentis, si qua vera in doctrinis philosophorum inveniat, in obsequium fidei assumit.* [41] 2a2ae, 2, 6, ad 3.

[42] 1a, 1, 5, ad 2; see also *I Sent.* prol. 1, 1: *ista scientia imperat omnibus aliis scientiis tanquam principalis . . . ipsa utitur in obsequium sui omnibus aliis scientiis quasi vassallis; In De Trin.* 2, 3, ad 7: *omnes aliae scientiae sint huic quasi famulantes et praeambulae.*

[43] *I Sent.* prol. 1, 1: *Ita, cum finis totius philosophiae sit infra finem theologiae, et ordinatus ad ipsum, theologia debet omnibus aliis scientiis imperare et uti his quae in eis traduntur.*

Thomas's understanding this subordinate position of philosophical systems of knowledge does not in any way imply any encroachment on their freedom, as A. D. Sertillanges correctly observes: 'We must clearly affirm that they are free servants. . . . Within they are absolutely autonomous.'[44] In Thomas's interpretation Paul's words about taking every thought captive to obey Christ (II Corinthians 10:5) imply no idea of constraint, and the meaning is not that of taking captive but rather of 'freeing' for new and higher service. Faith gives reason a new and formerly unsuspected point of departure, but reason fulfils its function within theology in essentially the same way as it does in other systems of knowledge. There is no question, therefore, of a new logic or a new mode of thought,[45] and the only difference that faith makes as far as reason is concerned is to enable it to attain a fuller perfection than was possible for it apart from faith. A whole new range of action is thus opened up for reason, though no change in its natural structure or method of operation is involved. Theology is thus to be understood primarily not as the master of philosophy but as its liberator and perfecter.[46]

The fact that philosophy is to be used in theology in order to explain the meaning of revelation does not mean, however, that philosophy is only a department of *sacra doctrina*. The philosophical disciplines and above all metaphysics are essentially independent of all revelation.[47] Only in regard to truths which are related to or necessary for salvation does the question of cooperation between philosophy and theology arise—in every other area of truth philosophy has undisputed supremacy. A further indication of its autonomy is that it has a completely different point of departure from theology. While *sacra doctrina* starts with the revelation outlined in the articles of faith, philosophy takes its starting-point in the first principles and observed data of reason. It has no other light to guide it in its work

---

[44] Sertillanges, *Dieu*, vol. I, p. 329. Meyer, *Thomas von Aquin*, p. 54, expresses the relationship between theology and philosophy by saying that if the latter is to be defined as the handmaid of theology, she is 'eine solche, die der Herrin die Fackel voranträgt, damit diese nicht im Finistern herumtappt'.

[45] P. Wyser, *Theologie als Wissenschaft*, Salzburg 1938, p. 180: 'Nicht eine neue Logik ist es in der Tat, die uns der Glaube zu vermitteln hätte, sondern bloss neue, unmittelbare Prinzipien, deren Verständnis ebenso wie die Ausdeutung ihrer Virtualität Sache der menschlichen Vernunfttätigkeit ist' (quoted in Grabmann, *Erkenntnis- und Einleitungslehre*, p. 133).

[46] Cf. Skydsgaard, *Metafysik*, p. 189: '. . . Theology is not the master of philosophy but its liberator and perfecter'.

[47] On this point see especially Gilson, *Thomisme*, p. 35ff.

than the light which reason itself provides, 'which of itself recognises first principles and draws conclusions from them alone and combines them in logical relationships.'[48] Knowledge receives its content by abstraction from sense experience and philosophy gets its knowledge of God by starting from creation and moving from there to God. *Sacra doctrina*, on the other hand, is guided by the light which has been given in revelation, *lumen divinae revelationis*,[49] and therefore proceeds in a different direction from philosophy since it begins with God himself in order from this point to study creation in its relation to God, its *ordo ad Deum*.[50] As an imitation of God's own knowledge —he knows all things *seipsum cognoscens* (knowing himself)—the theological way is for Thomas the more perfect.[51] Both philosophy and theology thus speak of the same world[52] and the same causal relationship given in the *ordo ad Deum*, and the difference between their modes of operation could be expressed in this way: while philosophy starts with the processes of the created world and moves from here to their first cause—a typical example of this is Thomas's proofs for the existence of God—theology proceeds from the revealed knowledge of the first cause and its nature in order from this perspective to study its effects in creation. There is a difference of degree between the revealed knowledge that is given by faith and knowledge which has been attained through the exercise of reason, in that the former gives a higher, more perfect and quantitatively richer knowledge,[53] but the profoundest and most crucial distinction between the two is that each starts from a different point and approaches

---

[48] Manser, *Thomismus*, p. 133.
[49] 1a, 1, 1, ad 2. Cf. *In De Trin.* 1, 1: *Sic ergo sunt quaedam intelligibiles veritates, ad quas se extendit efficacia intellectus agentis, sicut principia quae naturaliter homo cognoscit et ea quae ab his deducuntur; et ad haec cognoscenda non requiritur nova lux intelligibilis, sed sufficit lumen naturaliter inditum. Quaedam vero sunt ad quae praedicta principia non se extendunt, sicut sunt ea quae sunt fidei, facultatem rationis excedentia, et futura contingentia et alia huismodi; et haec cognoscere mens humana non potest, nisi divinitus novo lumine illustretur superaddito lumini naturali.*
[50] Cf. p. 93ff. above.
[51] *CG* II, 4: *in doctrina philosophiae, quae creaturas secundum se considerat et ex eis in Dei cognitionem perducit, prima est consideratio de creaturis et ultima de Deo. In doctrina vero fidei, quae creaturas non nisi in ordine ad Deum considerat, primo est consideratio Dei et postmodum creaturarum. Et sic est perfectior: utpote Dei cognitioni similior, qui seipsum cognoscens alia intuetur.* Cf. Gilson, *Thomisme*, p. 35ff.
[52] 1a, 1, 1, ad 2: *Unde nihil prohibet de eisdem rebus, de quibus philosophicae disciplinae tractant secundum quod sunt cognoscibilia lumine naturalis rationis, et aliam scientiam tractare secundum quod cognoscuntur lumine divinae revelationis.*
[53] 2a2ae, 2, 3, ad 3; *invisibilia Dei altiori modo, quantum ad plura, percipit fides quam ratio naturalis ex creaturis in Deum procedens.*

its material in a distinctively different way, the approach in each instance being determined by the different starting-point and orientation—in the case of theology, the supernatural destiny, *salus hominus*, which God has set before men. Here, again, the distinction which Thomas holds to exist between theology and philosophy is essentially the same as that which exists between grace and nature. The theology which is propounded in *sacra doctrina* is to be distinguished from metaphysical speculation about God, *theologia quae pars philosophiae ponitur* (that theology which is ranked as a part of philosophy),[54] by reason of the fact that it proceeds from a knowledge which is derived not from nature or *ratio* as such, but from God, just as grace is not a development of the inherent possibilities of nature but comes from God. Anything that 'comes from God', however, accords with the structure that is distinctive of nature and *ratio* and signifies its perfection.

Philosophy does not derive its *raison d'être* from the fact of being used in the service of theology: within its own sphere it is autonomous and follows the laws which are given to it by reason. But precisely on this account it is a necessary presupposition and an integral part of Thomas's work as a theologian, in the same way as nature is the necessary presupposition of its perfection through grace. The philosophy of Thomas is found concretely only in that synthesis of *ratio* and *revelatio* which constitutes *sacra doctrina*, and if we isolate it from this context, we also lose the possibility of coming to a correct understanding of his whole way of looking at the problem. Nothing can be found in Thomas that corresponds to the inordinate preoccupation with his philosophy, at the expense of this theology, on the part of many of the neo-Thomist writers. It is significant that those who seek to delineate a 'Thomistic' *philosophy* have to find not only the bulk of their material but also their leading ideas from Thomas's theological writings, the *Summa contra gentiles* and the *Summa theologiae*.[55] The modern idea that philosophy, if it is to remain 'pure' philosophy, should be discussed quite apart from revelation and its theological implications is something quite alien to Thomas. He never expresses

---

[54] 1a, 1, 1, ad 2: *Unde theologia quae ad sacram doctrinam pertinet, differt secundum genus ab illa theologia quae pars philosophiae ponitur.*

[55] We should note in this connection that even the *Summa contra gentiles*, which is often but improperly called 'the philosophical *Summa*', is a theological work throughout, cf. *CG* I, 2: *propositum nostrae intentionis est veritatem quam fides Catholica profitetur, pro nostro modulo manifestare*, and particularly the concluding section of *CG* II, 4. See also Chenu, *Saint Thomas*, p. 292ff.

any fear that philosophy would be impaired by being included in an *ordo* in which the principal ideas had been determined by theology, on the contrary, indeed, he is well aware of the danger that a misuse of philosophy will produce a distortion in theology.[56] Thomas does not regard philosophy as an end in itself but simply as an indispensable aid in understanding and interpreting the revealed truth that is given in scripture. This explains the considerable unevenness in his philosophical discussions. He does not deal with philosophical questions from the standpoint of their theoretical interest but only to the extent that they are prompted by or can help to explain a question raised by theology. There can be little doubt that Thomas did not think of himself as a philosopher but primarily as a *theologian*, and as a philosopher only in order to fulfil this function more effectively. In his general approach he is not so much a philosopher as a theologian who propounds his theology in what he calls *sacra doctrina*.[57] It is a real question whether neo-Thomism, by detaching the philosophy of Thomas from its context, as it so frequently does, and seeking to preserve it as a *philosophia perennis*, valid in its main outlines for all ages, has not in fact abandoned Thomas's own intention. The most obvious characteristic of the writings of Thomas is not their timid attachment to the past but rather his radical and courageous willingness to face the new problems and questions of his age. He did not, therefore, simply follow the lines of traditional Augustinian theology but moved in a new direction of his own. In this pioneering work he took it as his primary function not to deal with philosophical problems as such but rather with the ever and equally new *theologia perennis* of biblical theology—that is to say, to translate revelation into contemporary terms—and in discharging this task he was willing

---

[56] Cf. p. 234f. above. Gilson, *Thomisme*, p. 17: 'le problème n'était pas pour lui: comment introduire du philosophique dans la théologie sans corrompre l'essence de la philosophie? C'était plutôt: comment introduire du philosophique dans une théologie sans corrompre l'essence de la théologie?'

[57] Sertillanges, 'L'être et la connaissance dans la philosophie de S. Thomas d'Aquin', in *Mélanges thomistes* (Bibliothèque thomiste 3), Paris 1934, p. 175: 'sa doctrine prise dans son ensemble n'est pas une philosophie, c'est une théologie qui utilise la philosophie comme *servante*. Saint Thomas ne s'intitule jamais philosophe; les *philosophi* lui paraissent gens du dehors; il est, lui, *Doctor catholicus, theologus*, fervent de la *Sacra Doctrina*'. See also Gilson, *Thomisme*, p. 12ff. As Gilson points out, p. 26, footnote 3, if we attempt to use elements in Thomas's thought to construct a philosophy which does not raise the question of God or introduce questions of theology, we do not produce a Thomistic philosophy but a *philosophia ad mentem Cartesii*. For a comparison between Thomas and Descartes on this point see also E. Gilson, *God and Philosophy*, New Haven 1941, p. 77ff.

to use philosophy and especially the renaissance of Aristotelianism to explain what revelation means.

The uniqueness of *sacra doctrina*, in contrast to philosophy, is that it is grounded in the disclosure that God has set before men a goal of salvation which far transcends the perfection of which they are capable as created beings. The fact that it is man's salvation, SALUS HOMINIS, that is at issue means that both the starting-point and subject-matter of theology are primarily determined by the REVELATIO which is to be found in the canonical scriptures. *Sacra doctrina* is the explanation of what prophets and apostles taught about salvation and the means and method of attaining it. Theology does not exist to serve the purposes of natural knowledge, but because the salvation of men depends on the existence of teaching of this kind.

The unity expressed in the synthesis of *revelatio* and *ratio* which constitutes *sacra doctrina* is also demonstrated in the fact that Thomas conceives of revelation itself primarily as a giving of knowledge about God. For this very reason revelation implies a perfecting of the intention which is present in the human intellect and compels it to pass from the effects of the divine causality in creation to the first cause itself. Thus Thomas can say that *fere totius philosophiae consideratio ad Dei cognitionem ordinetur* (almost all of philosophy is directed towards the knowledge of God).[58] Even though reason cannot fully attain or comprehend the revealed knowledge of God *in via* because of its lack of power, yet by the light of faith it gains a far deeper insight into truth than it could otherwise have attained, and thus it comes to understand in a certain measure, *quodammodo*, what otherwise would have remained far beyond its comprehension.[59] This higher truth cannot, of course, be validated by reference to the first natural principles, but this does not mean that reason operates at this point in a sphere of uncertainty. The new knowledge comes from the one who is the Truth itself, and this means that reason gets sure and certain guidance from faith and does not need to fear that it may be wrong. Both philosophy and theology, therefore, Thomas holds, give preparatory answers to what he regards as the central question concerning knowledge of God. Even theology is only preparatory—it can only imperfectly anticipate the final answer to the question which will be given in the *visio Dei* in heaven, where the

---

[58] *CG* I, 4.

[59] I *Sent.* prol. 1, 3, 3: *Sed tamen ratio manuducta per fidem excrescit in hoc ut ipsa credibilia plenius comprehendat, et tunc ipsa quodammodo intelligit.*

incompleteness of faith will be at an end and the divine revelation of the knowledge of God given in that fullness of measure which is the essence of salvation and at the same time man's final perfection as an intellectual being. Since everything in *sacra doctrina* is ultimately related to *knowledge*, the role of *ratio* in theology is both crucial and, in regard to the structure and content of the truths communicated in theology, dominant and determinative.[60] At the deepest level, this explains why one of the striking marks of Thomas's discussion of what revelation signifies is a 'spirit of quiet confidence in reason.'[61]

[60] An illuminating example of how this preoccupation with the question of knowledge is to be seen even in the details of Thomas's exegesis is found in 2a2ae, 2, 3, ad 2, where he deals with the concern expressed in obiectio 2 that it is dangerous for man to assent to matters which belong to the sphere of faith. The 'danger' is that to all appearances one may be in error about what is true or false, since it is not possible to refer matters of faith in the regular way to the first principles of reason. The answer is found by Thomas, somewhat surprisingly, in the statement of Paul in Rom. 8:1: *per lumen fidei divinitus infusum homini homo assentit his quae sunt fidei, non autem contrariis. Et ideo 'nihil' periculi vel 'damnationis inest his qui sunt in Christo Iesu', ab ipso illuminati per fidem.* The risk of faith is that it binds men to truths which cannot evidently be seen and the danger for faith is that it is defined wholly in terms of theoretical cognitive discussion. Paul's statement about freedom from the condemnation of the law and from the wrath of God is thereby reduced to a declaration that the Christian who is illuminated by faith does not need to be condemned for being mistaken about what is true or false!

[61] Chenu, *AHDLMA* 2 (1927), p. 34; cf. also p. 34 where the author speaks of 'ce "rationalisme" ', which 'gouverne toute la théologie, en en fixant la méthode et l'esprit'.

2

RATIO AND THE ORDO DISCIPLINAE

In the prologue of the *Summa theologiae* Thomas explains the procedure which he proposes to follow in his presentation of *sacra doctrina*. He begins by criticising the earlier forms of theological teaching mentioned above in the introductory survey,[1] and finds that none of them is suitable for his purpose. In an earlier period the teacher was required to start with the text on which he was to comment—it might be a book of the Bible or the sentences of Peter Lombard—and he was restricted to the content and arrangement of that particular text. In a disputation the discussion was similarly restricted by accidental circumstances and the narrow limits of the theme of the disputation. The disputation frequently also gave rise to a great many sterile questions which merely helped to confuse those who heard them and prevented them from forming any total picture of the faith which had passed down to them and which it was the purpose of teaching to provide. In the view of Thomas neither *lectio* nor *disputatio* was therefore suited to provide the systematic summary necessary. Neither of them imparted knowledge *secundum ordinem disciplinae* (according to a sound educational method)—the very task which Thomas was determined to fulfil.[2]

In the last resort, however, it is not pedagogical reasons which determine the form that Thomas adopts for his work. The *ordo disciplinae* which he himself follows is based also on the nature of the knowledge that is imparted, as may be seen from the comparison which Thomas makes between his own interpretation of this knowledge and the interpretation given in earlier theological writing. His

---

[1] See p. 6ff. above.

[2] 1a, prol.: *Consideravimus namque huius doctrinae novitios, in his quae a diversis conscripta sunt, plurimum impediri: partim quidem propter multiplicationem inutilium, quaestionum, articulorum et argumentorum; partim etiam quia ea quae sunt necessaria talibus ad sciendum, non traduntur secundum ordinem disciplinae, sed secundum quod requirebat librorum expositio, vel secundum quod se praebebat occasio disputandi; partim quidem quia eorundem frequens repetitio et fastidium et confusionem generabat in animis auditorum.*

own *Summa* was certainly not the first attempt to summarise the substance of revelation in a systematic manner. One possible approach would have been to recapitulate the redemptive history of the Bible from creation and the fall to the incarnation and last things, and make the *opera restaurationis* (works of restoration) the organising principle. This is the approach, for instance, of Hugh of St Victor,[3] but it is explicitly rejected by Thomas. He also rejects the distinction between *res* and *signa* which was first made by Augustine and taken up by Peter Lombard in particular.[4] He is no more sympathetic to a Christocentric arrangement of his material around the theme of *Christus totus, idest caput et membra* (the whole Christ, i.e. head and members).[5] All of these questions, Thomas insists, are discussed in *sacra doctrina* in their proper context, but, it should be noted, *secundum ordinem ad Deum* (in their relationship to God).[6] They do not, however, constitute the organising principle in a theological presentation. In *sacra doctrina* God alone is the *subjectum scientiae* (subject of this science), and everything else is properly understood only when it is discussed in its relationship to him: *Omnia autem pertractantur in sacra doctrina sub ratione Dei vel quia sunt ipse Deus: vel quia habent ordinem ad Deum, ut ad principium et finem* (Now all things are dealt with in holy teaching in terms of God, either because

---

[3] Hugh of St Victor, *De Sacramentis* I, prol. 2 (*MPL* 176, 183): *Materia divinarum Scripturarum omnium, sunt opera restaurationis humanae. . . Opus restaurationis est incarnatio Verbi cum omnibus sacramentis suis; sive iis quae praecesserunt ab initio saeculi, sive iis quae subsequuntur usque ad finem mundi.* Characteristically, Hugh here puts the incarnation into the centre of his exposition; cf. *De sacramentis, Hoc opere contenta* (*MPL* 176, 173): *Primus liber a principio mundi usque ad incarnationem Verbi narrationis seriem deducit. Secundus liber ab incarnatione Verbi usque ad finem et consummationem omnium ordine procedit.* The interpretation in Hugh has something of the character of redemptive history, see Seeberg, *Lehrbuch der Dogmengeschichte*, vol. III, p. 174ff.

[4] See Peter Lombard, I *Sent.* 1: *Veteris ac novae continentiam diligenti indagine etiam atque etiam considerantibus nobis; praevia Dei gratia, innotuit sacrae paginae tractatores circa res vel signa praecipue versari. Ut enim egregius doctor Augustinus ait in libro I De doctrina christiana, cap. II,* 'omnis doctrina vel rerum est vel signorum; sed res etiam per signa discuntur'.

[5] E. Mersch, 'L'objet de la théologie et le "Christus totus"', in *Recherches de science religieuse* (=*RSR*) 26 (1936), p. 129ff., has a careful historical introduction and presents a modern argument in favor of taking *totus Christus* as the organising principle of theology.

[6] 1a, 1, 7: *Quidam vero, attendentes ad ea quae in ista scientia tractantur, et non ad rationem secundum quam considerantur, assignaverunt aliter subiectum huius scientiae: vel res vel signa, vel opera reparationis; vel totum Christum, idest caput et membra. De omnibus enim istis tractactur in ista scientia, sed secundum ordinem ad Deum.*

they are God himself or because they are relative to him as their origin and end).[7] It is clear that the choice of the *ordo disciplinae* which Thomas follows in his work is not made simply for pedagogical reasons, but particularly because it is a true expression of the *ordo ad Deum* which it is the task of theology to describe. Hence the very arrangement which he adopts in discussing his theme may prove helpful when we seek to understand the basic structure of his thought, a point often made by students of Thomas.[8] This may also be true in regard to what we view as the central questions of his work, for the *Summa theologiae* seeks to speak of *ea quae ad sacram doctrinam pertinent* (the things held by Christian theology),[9] in other words of what God has revealed in order to make salvation possible for man.

We now turn, therefore, to a brief summary of the plan adopted by Thomas in the *Summa theologiae*. Part I, the first of the three parts, deals particularly with what Thomas calls the *subjectum* of theology by turning immediately after an introductory discussion of *sacra doctrina* to the question of *Deus ipse*. Theology is to be distinguished from philosophy, as Thomas understands it,[10] by the fact that theology begins with God and then goes on to study creation, whereas philosophy reverses the process. At this point, therefore, he deals with the proofs of God, the well-known 'five ways' (q. 2), and then goes on to speak of the nature and attributes of God (q. 3–11). Next, he considers the problems bound up with our knowledge of God (q. 12–13; he discusses here, for instance, analogical statements about God, q. 13, a. 5), and then examines the *operationes Dei* (q. 14–26). A discussion of the doctrine of the Trinity follows, concluding with the section on *missio* which we have already dealt with above (q. 27–43).[11] With this Thomas concludes the part of his study which deals with the nature of God and relations within the godhead and then goes on to speak of God's actions in the world, first creation itself (q. 44–46) and the distinction between animate and inanimate creation; then, after a section *de distinctione rerum in*

---

[7] 1a, 1, 7; cf. p. 93ff. above.

[8] Cf. A.-D. Sertillanges, *La béatitude*, 1936, p. 263: 'le plan de la Somme, qui à lui seul révèle le chef-d'oeuvre, est le meilleur commentaire de la Somme'; Chenu, *Saint Thomas*, p. 301: 'The plan of his *Summa* opens the way to his mind', cf. ib. p. 314: 'The doctrine of Saint Thomas is already recorded and revealed in the very plan of his *Summa*'. See also P. E. Persson, 'Le plan de la Somme théologique et le rapport "Ratio-Revelatio" ', in *Revue philosophique de Louvain* 56 (1958), p. 545–572, and G. Lafont, *Structures et méthode dans la Somme théologique de saint Thomas d'Aquin*, 1961.

[9] 1a, prol.   [10] See p. 236f. above.   [11] Cf. p. 178ff. and 191ff. above.

communi (on the plurality in general of things) and *de distinctione boni et mali* (the distinction between good and evil) (q. 47–49), he deals with creatures purely spiritual in themselves (q. 50–64), the material creation (q. 65–74) and, finally, with the *creatura composita ex corporali et spirituali* (creature composed of body and spirit), i.e. man (q. 75–102; questions relating to psychology or theories of knowledge are here discussed). The rest of this part of the *Summa* deals briefly with aspects of the relationship between God and the world under the general heading, *conservatio et gubernatio creaturarum* (preservation and government of the creatures), and also with the interrelationships between created things and their effect on one another (q. 103–119).

Part II of the *Summa* is by far the most comprehensive, containing, as it does, 303 *quaestiones* against the 119 found in Part I, and these are often of considerable length. It is obvious that Thomas attaches particular importance to this part of the *Summa*. For this reason he divides it into two halves, the first of which (*Prima secundae*) begins with a definition of what is meant by the end or *beatitudo* which God has set before man (q. 1–5). The remainder of this first half and also the second deal with human life seen in its relation to this divine purpose and also with the means by which man is brought to the supernatural goal of blessedness as well as the obstacles which prevent him from attaining it.[12] Accordingly all ethical questions are considered here. In the first half of Part II he deals with human acts, both those which are peculiar to man as a being endowed with will (q. 6–21) and the *passiones animae* which man has in common with inferior creatures (q. 22–48). Thomas then goes on to define the principles of human activity. First, he defines the *principia intrinsecae* (the sources of human action within the agent), by considering man's habits, *habitus* (q. 49–54) which may be expressed both as good habits, *virtutes* (q. 55–70) or as evil habits, *vitia* (q. 71–89; it is in this context that Thomas speaks of the nature of sin). He turns next to what he calls *principia extrinsecae* (the sources of human action without the agent), i.e. the principles of human activity which confront man from without, and by which God directly helps man to attain his end. These are more exactly defined as *lex* and *gratia* (q. 90–113). Lastly, he examines the meaning of merit (q. 114). The

---

[12] Cf. 1a2ae, 1, introd.: *primo considerandum occurrit de ultimo fine humanae vitae; et deinde de his per quae homo ad hunc finem pervenire potest, vel ab eo deviare: ex fine enim oportet accipere rationes eorum quae ordinantur ad finem.*

R

positive evaluation of law as a God-given aid parallel to grace is a characteristic feature of Thomas's thought: *Deus . . . nos instruit per legem, et iuvat per gratiam* (God . . . builds us up by law and supports us by grace).[13]

In the second half of Part II (*Secunda secundae*) Thomas turns from his study of human activity in general to a consideration of particular acts. He devotes by far the largest part of his discussion (q. 1–170) to those acts which pertain to all, excluding gifts of grace or states. Here he treats of the so-called theological virtues and the manifestations of human activity associated with them, *fides* (q. 1–16), *spes* (q. 17–22) and *caritas* (q. 23–46), after which other particular acts are related in some way or another to the four cardinal virtues of ancient philosophy, and these are thoroughly and exhaustively dealt with: *prudentia* (q. 47–56), *iustitia* (q. 57–122), *fortitudo* (q. 123–140) and *temperantia* (q. 141–170). Those obligations for which men are held accountable to God—*religio* (q. 81), *devotio* (q. 82), *oratio* (q. 83) and also *obedientia* (q. 104)—are treated as subdivisions of *iustitia*. Under *fortitudo* Thomas also discusses *martyrium* (q. 124), *patientia* (q. 136) and *perseverantia* (q. 137), and under *temperantia* virtues or vices such as *virginitas* (q. 152), *superbia* (q. 162; having defined pride in q. 163 as 'the sin of the first man,' Thomas goes on to speak in q. 164 of death as the punishment for sin), and *studiositas* (q. 166). The remainder of the second half of Part II deals with specific matters which pertain to all who have been endowed with different kinds of graces gratuitously given (q. 171–178; the meaning of prophecy is here discussed at some length, q. 171–175), or which are related to monastic life or to those who have particular functions within the church (q. 179–189).

In Part III (*Tertia pars*), the third and final part of the work, Thomas deals with Christology and the doctrine of the sacraments. Following an introductory discussion of the *convenientia incarnationis* (the fitness of the incarnation) (q. 1) there follows a lengthy treatment of the hypostatic union (q. 2–15, the greater part of which deals with the *perfectio* of Christ's human nature) and its implications, *haec quae consequuntur unionem*[14] (q. 16–26; here, for instance, Thomas considers the problems raised by the *communicatio idiomatum* and also Christ's relationship to the Father and to us as the

---

[13] 1a2ae, 90, introd.; cf. 1a2ae, 92, 1: *proprius effectus legis sit bonos facere eos quibus datur, vel simpliciter vel secundum quid.*
[14] 3a, 16, introd.

mediator Dei et hominum).[15] Thomas then goes on to discuss the work of Christ, *restat considerandum de his quae Filius Dei incarnatus in natura humana sibi unita fecit vel passus est* (it remains for us to consider what the incarnate Son of God did or suffered in the human nature which was united to him),[16] and deals initially with the conception, birth and baptism of Christ, viz. those things which relate to his coming into the world (q. 27–39). The largest part of this discussion is devoted to the conception of Christ (q. 27–34), and it is here that we find Thomas's Mariology, which he includes simply as a subordinate part of his Christological discussion and not in a separate section on its own. A section on the life of Christ (the temptation, teaching and miracles) (q. 40–45) is followed by a comparatively brief discussion of his sufferings and death[17] (q. 46–52), after which the Christological part is concluded with a survey of the resurrection, ascension, *sessio Christi ad dexteram Patris* (his sitting at the right hand of the Father) and the *potestas iudiciaria* (judiciary power) of Christ (q. 53–59). The section dealing with the sacraments, *quibus salutem consequimur* (by which we attain salvation),[18] follows immediately the Christological section.[19] After discussing the sacraments in general (q. 60–65), Thomas takes them up for discussion individually: baptism (q. 66–71), confirmation (q. 72) and the eucharist (q. 73–83), and penance (q. 84–90). The author's death brought the work to an end before his treatment of the sacrament of penance could be concluded. Of the uncompleted ending which Thomas projected for Part III of his *Summa* we know little more than

---

[15] 3a, 26, introd.   [16] 3a, 27, introd.
[17] On this point see p. 217 above.   [18] 3a, prol.
[19] This direct connection is related to what Thomas holds to be a profound structural identity of function between incarnation and sacrament. As the incarnation took place on account of sin, so also the sacraments are necessary for man only after the fall, see 3a, 61, 2. The sacraments convey to men the abundant grace which permeated Christ's human nature: 3a, 7, 9: *Sic enim recipiebat anima Christi gratiam ut ex ea quodammodo transfunderetur in alios.* Thomas regards this human nature as the *instrumentum divinitatis*, 3a, 7, 1, ad 3 and many parallels, and the same instrumental interpretation is central in his understanding of the sacraments, cf. 3a, 62, 5: *Principalis autem causa efficiens gratiae est ipse Deus, ad quem comparatur humanitas Christi sicut instrumentum coniunctum, sacramentum autem sicut instrumentum separatum. Et ideo oportet quod virtus salutifera derivetur a divinitate Christi per eius humanitatem in ipsa sacramenta.* On this instrumental causality, which is a characteristic aspect of Thomas's theology, but which we were unable to discuss within the available limits of the previous chapter, see E. Hugon, *La causalité instrumentale en théologie*, Paris 1907; T. Tschipke, *Die Menschheit Christi als Heilsorgan der Gottheit. Unter besonderer Berücksichtigung der Lehre des heiligen Thomas von Aquin*, Freiburg im Breisgau 1940.

we read in the prologue: *de fine immortalis vitae, ad quem per ipsum* (sc. *Christum) resurgendo pervenimus* (the end of immortal life which we attain by the resurrection).[20]

When we study this general survey of *sacra doctrina* as Thomas presents it, two things in particular strike us at once. First, nowhere does Thomas deal explicitly with the nature of *the church*. We search the *Summa* in vain for a question *de ecclesia*. This fact may well be a parallel here to what we found above[21] in our discussion of tradition. The church, like tradition, was for Thomas something in which we lived and by which he was sustained, a self-evident presupposition of his work as a theologian, and in itself it constituted no real theological problem.[22] Congar has perhaps got to the heart of Thomas's understanding of the church when he says that for Thomas the church in fact coincides with what he describes in Part II of the *Summa*, where his whole discussion centres on and is dominated by the idea of the return of humanity to God as its final end.[23]

The second immediately obvious characteristic of the design of the *Summa* has more direct relevance to our own problem, and it concerns the place which Thomas gives to *Christology* in the work as a whole. It does not occupy a central place but appears at first glance to have been added as an afterthought, particularly if we consider what precedes it in the *Summa*. Even before he begins to speak about Christ, Thomas has already established his interpretation of the nature of God and man. He has also declared his mind on the meaning of salvation and of other crucially important theological concepts such as sin, law, grace and faith. If Congar's theory about Thomas's conception of the church is correct, the theological structure of the church should also be clear in Thomas before he comes to speak of Christ. It is particularly striking that Thomas speaks at length of grace without at any point relating it to the incarnation and

---

[20] 3a, prol.   [21] Cf. p. 46f. and 69 above.

[22] In the history of theology after Augustine the problem seems to become acute at the time of the Reformation and with the division of the church created by the Reformation. Both Roman Catholics and Protestants then began to discuss the nature of the church with considerable vigour. See M. Grabmann, *Die Lehre des heiligen Thomas von Aquin von der Kirche als Gotteswerk. Ihre Stellung im thomistischen System und in der Geschichte der mittelalterlichen Theologie*, Regensburg 1903, p. 2ff.

[23] Y. M.-J. Congar, 'L'idée de l'Église chez saint Thomas d'Aquin', in *RSPT* 29 (1940), p. 39: 'L'Église, pour saint Thomas, c'est la II Pars, c'est tout l'ordre du retour vers Dieu, *motus creaturae rationalis in Deum*'.

the work of Christ, and it is at this point that even Roman Catholic theologians express serious reservations in regard to his presentation of *sacra doctrina*.[24] An indirect expression of the effect which this criticism has had even in Thomistic circles is to be seen in the re-arrangement of the dogmatic material found in a work to which we have already made reference, the *Katholische Dogmatik* by Diekamp and Jüssen. Where Thomas characteristically places his Christology at the conclusion of his work and discusses it in relation to his doctrine of the sacraments, Diekamp and Jüssen, in spite of their claim to be following 'the principles of St Thomas', rearrange the material completely and place the Christological part *before* 'Die Lehre von der Gnade'. Another respect in which this work differs from Thomas is that Mariology is not treated as a subordinate part of Christology but is placed in a separate section on its own between Christology and the doctrine of grace.[25] A similar dislocation is found in the article on 'Le thomisme' by Garrigou-Lagrange in the *Dictionnaire de théologie catholique*, where the section, 'L'Incarnation rédemptrice dans la synthèse thomiste,' appears at the centre of the essay and is followed by the doctrine of the sacraments and the doctrine of grace, without any explanation being offered for this clear departure from the 'Thomistic synthesis' which is to be found in Thomas himself.[26] The different disposition of the material which we find in Thomas is not, however, merely an arbitrary arrangement in which the essentials of his thought might just as easily be expressed in one scheme as in the other. It is no coincidence, as will appear more clearly in a moment, that Thomas puts Christology in a particular place in the *Summa*. Its relationship to the work as a whole is in fact a natural and necessary consequence of his basic approach. As Gilson

---

[24] See e.g. H. Rondet, 'Bulletin de théologie historique', in *RSR* 38 (1951), p. 138ff., especially p. 153ff. Cf. also Carré, *Le Christ*, p. 10f. and Chenu, *Saint Thomas*, p. 314.

[25] See Diekamp and Jüssen, *Dogmatik*, vol. II, p. 176ff., 354ff. and 419ff. The very placing of the Mariological section is a clear expression of an idea not found in Thomas but quite characteristic of modern Roman Catholic theology, Mary as *mediatrix omnium gratiarum*. The 'Christocentric' exposition of doctrine which we find in Diekamp is generally characteristic of recent Roman Catholic theology and represents a more or less conscious departure from Thomas. Typical examples of this are several works by Mersch, notably *Mystical Body* and M. Schmaus *Katholische Dogmatik*, vols. I–IV, 3rd ed. Munich 1940–1953; cf. Schmaus's statement in the preface to vol. II, p. IX: 'Die Theologie . . . muss daher christo-zentrisch sein. Ist sie es nicht, dann hört sie auf, christliche, übernaturliche Theologie zu sein'.

[26] R. Garrigou-Lagrange, 'Le thomisme' in *DTC* 15:1, col. 823ff.

correctly says, anyone who 'is ashamed of going so far misses the main point of Thomistic theology; he is ashamed of St Thomas Aquinas.'[27]

What, then, from a doctrinal standpoint is the organising principle in the *ordo disciplinae*, in accordance with which Thomas constructs his *Summa*? Writers on Thomas frequently raise the question, to be sure, but they tend to discuss it incidentally and without relating it to the central question of *ratio* and *revelatio*. Let us, however, examine the solutions offered in two works written recently.

In his *Toward Understanding Saint Thomas*, 1964, M.-D. Chenu considers the problem at some length in his analysis of the *Summa theologiae* and proposes a solution of considerable interest, the originality of which, however, lies not so much in his thesis itself as in its presuppositions. Chenu begins[28] with a suggestion made by Thomas in his early work, the *Commentary on the Sentences*, in regard to the division of the material: *consideratio huius doctrinae erit de rebus, secundum quod exeunt a Deo ut a principio, et secundum quod referuntur in ipsum ut in finem. Unde in prima parte determinat de rebus divinis secundum* EXITUM *a principio; in secunda secundum* REDITUM *in finem* (this doctrine will consider things as coming forth from God as from a principle, and as being brought back to God as to their end. Hence, in a first part it draws conclusions about divine things on the basis of a coming forth from a principle; in the second on the basis of a return to an end).[29] Chenu maintains that this

---

[27] E. Gilson, review of Chenu's *Introduction à l'étude de saint Thomas d'Aquin* in *BT* 8 (1951), p. 9.

[28] Chenu, *Saint Thomas*, p. 308ff.

[29] I *Sent.* 2, divisio textus. Thomas is well aware that this represents a departure from the plan of the passage on which he is commenting, for he goes on at once to say: *Aliter potest dividi secundum intentionem Magistri, quod in prima determinat de rebus, in secunda de signis;* on the basis on which Lombard makes his division, see p. 243 above, footnote 4. Another passage which is typical of Thomas's line of thought is I *Sent.* 14, 2, 2: *in exitu creaturarum a primo principio attenditur quaedam circulatio vel regiratio, eo quod omnia revertuntur sicut in finem in id a quo sicut principio prodierunt. Et ideo oportet ut per eadem quibus est exitus a principio, et reditus in finem attendatur.* Behind these terms frequently used in the *Commentary on the Sentences*, such as *exitus, reditus, circulatio*, etc., there lies ultimately the characteristic idea of later Greek philosophy that the world is in the process of an eternal cyclical movement and that all things come from and return to their origin. On this cyclical idea of Greek thought in comparison with the early Christian view of time, see O. Cullmann, *Christ and Time*, p. 51ff.; Nygren, *Agape and Eros*, p. 186ff. ('the Alexandrian world-scheme') and p. 581ff. (on Pseudo-Dionysius); H. de Lubac, *Catholicism: A Study of Dogma in Relation to the Corporate Destiny of Mankind*, New York 1958, p. 70f.

scheme of the *Commentary*, which is neo-Platonic in origin, also provides us with a key for understanding the arrangement of the *Summa theologiae*.[30] Part I thus corresponds to the *exitus* of the emanation and Part II to the *reditus* of the return by which the circle is completed, but Part III is added as 'the means willed by God', the means by which the *reditus* is in the end made possible.[31] Chenu suggests that the terms *principium* and *finis*, which occur with great frequency in the *Summa*[32] and are used by Thomas to express the principal aspect by which God is known in *sacra doctrina*, ultimately coincide with this scheme of *exitus* and *reditus* and are to be understood in terms of it.[33]

We withhold comment for the present on the solution proposed by Chenu until we have also considered the modification of his scheme proposed in the second work, A. Hayen's *Saint Thomas d'Aquin et la vie de l'Église*, 1952, which deals with the question in much greater detail. In his discussion of Chenu's argument Hayen draws attention to the fact that the words *exitus* and *reditus* are not to be found in any of the expressions which are used by Thomas in the prologues of the *Summa* and which are clearly crucial for understanding his arrangement. Nor do the words appear either in the *Compendium theologiae* or the *Summa contra gentiles*. Moreover, the term *circulatio* (or *regiratio*), which refers in the *Commentary on the Sentences* to the scheme of *exitus* and *reditus*, acquires a completely different meaning in Thomas's later writings.[34] According to Hayen this indicates that Thomas apparently abandoned the neo-Platonic

---

[30] The same idea recurs with direct reference to the *Summa* in Nygren, *Agape and Eros*, p. 189, footnote 1, and p. 613.
[31] Chenu, *Saint Thomas*, p. 310: '1) in the *Summa*, emanation and return unfold in two sections closely knit together in the unity of two reverse movements; the *Ia Pars* and the *IIa Pars* are related to one another as are *exitus* and *reditus*. 2) in the Summa, Incarnation, which is the centre of the economy, enters into the circuit of emanation and return only as a means willed by God; it is dealt with in a *III Pars*'; cf. also p. 304f.
[32] See e.g. 1a, 2, introd.: *principalis intentio huius sacrae doctrinae est Dei cognitionem tradere, et non solum secundum quod in se est, sed etiam secundum quod est principium rerum et finis earum, et specialiter rationalis creaturae;* cf. also 1a, 1, 7: *Omnia autem pertractantur in sacra doctrina sub ratione Dei vel quia sunt ipse Deus; vel quia habent ordinem ad Deum, ut ad principium et finem.*
[33] Chenu, *Saint Thomas*, p. 308.
[34] Hayen, *Saint Thomas et la vie de l'Église*, p. 80f.; cf. *De Pot.* 9, 9 and 2a2ae, 27, 4, ad 2, where the term *circulatio* is employed to explain the different functions of the intellect and will. Cf. the representative selections given in the articles 'Exitus' and 'Reditus' in Deferrari and Barry, *A Lexicon of St. Thomas Aquinas*, p. 396 and 951.

scheme when he produced his final summary of *sacra doctrina*, and therefore it cannot be correctly understood in terms of what is properly the emanationist scheme in which the movement from God comes back again to God. Hayen sees in this repudiation of emanationist terminology by Thomas—and in this he is certainly correct— an expression of the real distinction in theological methodology between the metaphysics of ancient philosophy and Thomas's own metaphysics of existence with its quite different orientation.[35] He therefore proposes a scheme quite different from that of Chenu to explain the relationship between Part I and Part II of the *Summa*. The scheme may be expressed in the following way: the material in Part I is to be interpreted primarily from the standpoint of 'God as efficient cause'—*esse*—and in Part II from the corresponding standpoint of God as final cause'—*operari*.[36] We shall return later to this proposed solution.

It is of particular interest to us to note here the general agreement which we find in both these writers when they come to explain why Thomas concluded his whole work with a discussion of Christology. Thomas holds that revealed knowledge of God is given to us in the canonical scriptures. But for the most part these scriptures are accounts of historical events that took place within the history of a particular people, and their centre is a concrete, historical fact—the Jesus of Nazareth of whom we read in the Gospels—and this fact in turn is the presupposition and substance of the apostolic teaching which is given in the other writings of the New Testament. It is quite clear that *time* and therefore *history* is an essential constituent of these writings and their contents. The mighty acts of God for the salvation of men of which they speak are a historical reality and will not cease until the last day.[37] Since this is the substance of the revela-

---

[35] Hayen, *Saint Thomas et la vie de l'Église*, p. 88: 'En abandonnant le langage néoplatonicien du commentaire sur les *Sentences* pour le remplacer par celui de la *Somme*, il métamorphose du dedans l'univers antique en consacrant le triomphe de la cause efficiente sur la cause finale. . . plus exactement encore, en substituant peu à peu à l'émanatisme grec, son propre "réalisme théologal" '; cf. also the quotation from Gilson given on p. 75 of Hayen's work.

[36] Hayen, *Saint Thomas et la vie de l'Église*, p. 89. This interpretation is also suggested in Chenu, *Saint Thomas*, p. 310f., but it does not in any way influence his discussion which is dominated by the *exitus-reditus* terminology. Essentially the same scheme (*Prima Pars*—'Dieu en tant qu'être', *Secunda Pars*—'Dieu en tant que fin') is also found in F. Cayré, 'Saint Augustin et l'esprit de la Somme théologique', in *L'année théologique augustinienne* (=*ATA*) 14 (1954), p. 12.

[37] Cf. O. C. Quick, *The Gospel of Divine Action*, London 1933, p. 42: 'Thus in Hebrew religion history was viewed as the story of the mighty acts of God, whereby

tion which Thomas expressly indicates that he desires to provide in his *sacra doctrina*, the history recorded in the Bible would afford a natural organising principle for his work.[38] As we saw above, however, Thomas explicitly rejects such an idea, though it had been adopted earlier by Hugh of St Victor in particular.[39] The explanation is undoubtedly that, unlike any theologian before him, Thomas attempted to make theology a 'science' in the Aristotelian sense.[40] We saw in Chapter I how Thomas could define *sacra doctrina* as a *scientia subalternata* (subordinate science) on the grounds that it had its origin in the higher knowledge possessed *realiter* by God and the blessed saints.[41] But in saying this, Thomas found himself confronted by a difficulty, for, as Chenu points out, 'if there is a discipline that the Aristotelian classification of the sciences excludes from its orbit, surely it is history!'[42] The opposition implied by such a statement, however, goes far beyond the mere fact that history is irreconcilable with the Aristotelian system of science. It is in fact a symptom of the essential opposition which exists between Greek and Hebrew (and therefore biblical) thought, and which is clearly summarised in the statement of O. C. Quick: 'For Plato salvation consists in the philosopher-saint's knowledge of eternal unchanging realities, while for the Jew it consists in the action of a living God.'[43] What Quick here says of Plato is largely true of Greek thought in general and especially of later Greek philosophy, which had an abiding influence

His purpose for the salvation of His servants and the destruction of His enemies is finally worked out'. On the primitive Christian thinking about time see Cullmann, *Christ and Time*, especially p. 37ff.

---

[38] De Lubac, *Catholicism*, p. 69: 'For if the salvation offered by God is in fact the salvation of the human race, since this human race lives and develops in time, any account of this salvation will naturally take a historical form'. De Lubac is referring particularly at this point to the early church in which this idea was perfectly natural, above all in Augustine, whose philosophy of history has been influential well into the modern period.

[39] See p. 243 above.

[40] See in this connection Chenu, *AHDLMA* 2 (1927), and cf. p. 78 above, footnote 30.

[41] See p. 76 above.   [42] Chenu, *Saint Thomas*, p. 303.

[43] Quick, *The Gospel of Divine Action*, p. 48; cf. I Cor. 1:22f. An important discussion on the essential difference between Jewish and Greek thought is also to be found in E. Billing, *De etiska tankarna i urkristendomen i deras samband med dess religiösa tro*, 2nd ed. Stockholm 1936; Hessen, *Platonismus und Prophetismus* (on Thomas see especially p. 158ff.); C. Tresmontant, *Essai sur la pensée hébraïque* (Lectio divina 12), Paris 1953; T. Boman, *Das hebräische Denken im Vergleich mit dem Griechischen*, 2nd ed. Göttingen 1954.

in the formulation of Christian theology within the sphere of Hellenism. For the Greek, the question of salvation was primarily a question of knowledge, but it is not possible to have true knowledge of what is transient in history, only of what is permanent and unchanging.[44] Thomas's starting-point is essentially the same: everything in salvation depends on revelation, but revelation is conceived as the giving of an otherwise inaccessible knowledge of God.[45] We can indeed, says Thomas, have a knowledge, *scientia, de rebus mobilibus* (of movable things), but only on the assumption that we are aware of the immovable order that is presupposed by all motion and change and know how to refer such motion and change to *aliquid immobile* (something immovable).[46] This is the problematical question which directly occasioned the writing of the *Summa theologiae*. And it is against this distinction between biblical and Greek thought that we are to see such an apparently trivial matter as the arrangement of the *Summa* (its *ordo disciplinae*), and the relationship between *scientia* and *historia* which is indicated by this arrangement directly illuminates the relationship between *ratio* and *revelatio* which lies behind this other and is analogous to it.

The systematic starting-point in constructing a *scientia*, Thomas holds, cannot be found in any contingent events in the world of time and history—these do indeed form the material with which theology has to operate, but it is a material that becomes intelligible only by reference to the *ordo* which connects the changeable to the unchangeable. The historical events recorded in the four Gospels, for instance, are not themselves revelation, and they give knowledge of God only when that of which they speak is included in and understood with reference to the *ordo* in which God is related to the world of his creation. This *ordo*, however, is not derived by Thomas from Hebrew thought but constructed from elements derived from Greek philosophy. These elements create the structure that forms the organising

---

[44] Cf. Söhngen, *Einheit*, p. 297: 'nach Aristoteles gilt: *Scientia non est singularium*, mit unseren Worten: Eigentliches Wissen im aristotelischen Begriffe, Beweiswissen gibt es nicht vom Faktischen, sondern nur von Ideellen!'

[45] See p. 20ff. above.

[46] Cf. 1a, 84, 1, ad 3: *omnis motus supponit aliquid immobile: cum enim transmutatio fit secundum qualitatem, remanet substantia immobilis; et cum transmutatur forma substantialis, remanet materia immobilis. Rerum etiam mutabilium sunt immobiles habitudines. . . . Et propter hoc nihil prohibet de rebus mobilibus immobilem scientiam habere.* See also 1a, 86, 3, which deals with the problem *Utrum intellectus sit cognoscivitus contingentium.* In this question the general rule applies: *intellectus noster directe non est cognoscitivus nisi universalium,* 1a, 86, 1.

framework of the first two parts of the *Summa*, in which Thomas outlines his conception of the relationship between God and the world. From the systematic standpoint, therefore, a clear distinction is to be made between Part II and Part III, and the significance of this distinction is indicated in a statement found in Chenu: 'The transition from the *IIa* to the *IIIa Pars* is a passage . . . from an account of the structures to the actual story of God's gifts'.[47] The incarnation and its consequences, viz. the sacraments—which are discussed in Part III—are concrete events in the sphere of time and creation, and therefore stand in opposition to the essentially timeless scheme in which Thomas understands the *ordo ad Deum* of things, and which constitutes the organising principle of the first two parts. This is one reason why they are introduced only after the structure of the scheme has already been outlined. The other and perhaps conclusive reason is that for Thomas these concrete events are intelligible only against the background of the abstract scheme which he has described.[48] Their true significance is seen only when they are included in the universally valid *ordo ad Deum* which has reference to every event. This being so, Christology, for example—if we are to be consistent—cannot be dealt with except in the context of Part III, for when we come to Part III the theological system is structurally complete and must be complete if we are to have a correct understanding of what is given in history, since only thus can it become the object of a *scientia*. Gilson summarises Thomas's solution of the problem of knowledge and history: 'Here as elsewhere, history presupposes natures from which it is not deduced, but in accordance with which it takes place'.[49] The scheme itself is essentially timeless, a pure abstract construction from which no historical event as such can be deduced, but in conformity with which every event takes place. It is also self-evident that this scheme is not simply formal, having no significance in regard to the meaning of what it describes, but we shall return to this problem in the last section of the present chapter. It is primarily the history recorded in the biblical writings which fills out the abstract scheme and gives it life and movement, but the function, direction and limits of this movement are already known in advance when the subject-matter is introduced and this

[47] Chenu, *Saint Thomas*, p. 315.
[48] Hayen, *Saint Thomas et la vie de l'Église*, p. 91: 'C'est dans la lumière, évidemment abstraite, des deux premières parties de la *Somme*, que l'histoire sainte nous révèle toute sa signification'.
[49] Gilson in *BT* 8 (1951), p. 9.

subject-matter is assumed to follow a previously determined sequence. Thus, as we see, the very *ordo disciplinae*, which forms the ground-plan of the *Summa*, is in the final resort a new variation of the theme which we found in the preceding section of the present chapter to be expressed in Thomas's own discussion of the problem of *ratio* and *revelatio*, and which could be summed up in the phrase, *gratia supponit naturam* (grace presupposes nature). Just as grace in Thomas is defined from the perspective of a view of nature as a whole, and in particular is seen in the extension of structural lines already found in nature, so we may rephrase Thomas's definition by stating that *revelatio supponit rationem* (revelation presupposes reason).

Though in general terms we have followed Chenu and Hayen for their insight into the nature of the problem which underlies and determines the arrangement of the *Summa*, it is still uncertain whether their interpretation is entirely correct, and so we propose to conclude with a fuller discussion of the question.

The lucid summary of the plan of the *Summa* which Thomas gives in Part I provides us with a natural starting-point. Having first explained the meaning of *sacra doctrina* he then turns to the discussion of its content. After stating that the *principalis intentio huius sacrae doctrinae* (fundamental aim of this holy teaching) is *Dei cognitionem tradere, . . . non solum secundum quod in se est, sed etiam secundum quod est principium rerum, et finis earum, et specialiter rationalis creaturae* (to make God known, not only as he is in himself, but also as the beginning and end of all things and of reasoning creatures especially), he then offers this summary statement of what the *Summa* will contain: *ad huius doctrinae expositionem intendentes, primo tractabimus* DE DEO (Part I); *secundo,* DE MOTU RATIONALIS CREATURAE IN DEUM (Part II); *tertio,* DE CHRISTO, QUI, SECUNDUM QUOD HOMO, VIA EST NOBIS TENDENDI IN DEUM (Part III) (we now intend to set forth this divine teaching by treating, first, of God, secondly, of the journey to God of reasoning creatures, thirdly, of Christ, who, as man, is our road to God).[50] We may observe—and here we refer to the hypo-thesis of Chenu—that Thomas himself makes no suggestion at all that Part I is to be understood as an *exitus*. Moreover, he does not summarise the contents of Part II in terms of the *reditus* of an emanationist scheme but rather in terms of *motus*, the concept which corresponds most closely to the idea of *causa finalis*. As we have already indicated, Hayen is at this point undoubtedly correct in his

[50] 1a, 2, introd.

criticism of the interesting solution proposed by Chenu. It is quite clear that in the *Summa theologiae* Thomas abandoned the emanationist division which had come from neo-Platonism and is to be found in his *Commentary on the Sentences*. In his study of the concept of analogy in Thomas, H. Lyttkens indicates that this movement away from emanationism can be found throughout Thomas's writings in other areas also. For example, neo-Platonic lines of thought which are found in his early writings are absent from the later writings in which he discusses the meaning of analogy.[51] There is the additional fact that in Part I, which Chenu holds to correspond to *exitus*, Thomas does not apparently attach much importance to the procession of the creature from God. The work begins with a general definition of God *secundum quod in se est* (as he is in himself) (q. 2–43), following which only one question deals with the *emanatio rerum a primo principio* (emanation of things from the first principle) (q. 45).[52] After this, Thomas continues to speak of created things—again in general terms—defining the relationship between them and God under the concept of *gubernatio* (q. 103).[53] The controlling and organising principle of the work is already indicated in the words which preface the first part of the *Summa*: Thomas proposes to speak of God not only as he is in himself in his eternal being but also as the PRINCIPIUM *rerum et* FINIS *earum* (beginning and end of all things).[54] What this means will be seen more clearly by reference to two points which we have already had occasion to examine: First, the key passage, occupying the whole of *quaestio* 43, which is discussed under the rubric, *de missione divinarum personarum* (the mission of the divine persons).[55] This provides the transition from the doctrine of the Trinity to the discussion of creation in its relation to God which occupies the remainder of the *Summa*. This question is therefore of the greatest importance to us in determining the meaning of this relationship. Out study of the term *missio* in its various aspects shows that *missio* expresses a definite causal relationship between God and the world. Second, the discussion of creation which follows is introduced by *quaestio* 44, which is also important from this

[51] Lyttkens, *Analogy*, p. 283, 345.
[52] We should not be misled here by Thomas's terminology. The meaning of *emanatio rerum* is to be understood from the previous description of the causal relation between God and the world.
[53] Cf. 1a, 103, introd.: *Postquam praemissum est de creatione rerum et distinctione earum, restat nunc tertio considerandum de rerum gubernatione.*
[54] 1a, 2, introd.; cf. p. 93ff. above.   [55] Cf. p. 244 above.

standpoint, since it defines this causal relationship more precisely as a relation to a transcendent *causa prima*, which is at one time both *causa efficiens*, *causa exemplaris*, and *causa finalis*.[56] The thesis which we propose to maintain against the solutions already discussed above is that it is precisely this causal *ordo ad Deum*, in the particular form in which it appears in Thomas, that constitutes the organising principle in the arrangement of the material of the *Summa*. It is this *ordo ad Deum* which also determines the *ordo disciplinae* in Thomas's *sacra doctrina*.

It might seem as if in fact we were adding nothing new to the suggested improvement on Chenu's scheme which Hayen proposes, and in which the division between *causa efficiens* and *causa finalis* is represented respectively by Part I and Part II of the *Summa*. It is necessary to point out, however, in objection to Hayen, that he does not do justice in his scheme to the important place which the idea of God as *causa exemplaris* undeniably occupies in Thomas's thought. We need do no more than refer to the analysis of the causal relation between God and the world which we have given in the previous chapter, and particularly to the distinctive idea of grace as an *assimilatio* to the divine archetype. We might also in this connection point to Thomas's own words in the prologue to the first half of Part II: *postquam praedictum est de exemplari, scilicet de Deo . . . restat ut consideremus de eius imagine, idest de homine* (now that we have treated of the exemplar, i.e., God . . . it remains for us to treat of his image, i.e., man), and the crucial importance which the term *imago Dei* here has in Thomas's anthropology.[57] It cannot reasonably be maintained, moreover, that whereas Part I of the *Summa* deals chiefly with the idea of God as *causa efficiens*, no discussion of *causa finalis* is given prior to Part II. This is contradicted both by the prefatory definition of God as *principium et* FINIS and by the part which final causality plays in important passages in this part of the *Summa*, e.g. in explicating the *missio* of the persons of the godhead or the important term *gubernatio*, for *gubernatio nihil aliud est quam directio gubernatorum in finem* (government is nothing but the directing of the things governed to the end).[58] Hayen correctly points to the crucial

---

[56] Cf. p. 96ff. above.   [57] Cf. p. 149 and 166f. above, 1a2ae Prol.

[58] 1a, 103, 3; cf. 1a, 103, 1: *ad divinam bonitatem pertinet ut, sicut produxit res in esse, ita etiam eas ad finem perducat. Quod est gubernare;* CG III, 64: *Ordinare autem actiones aliquarum rerum ad finem, est gubernare ipsa;* CG IV, 20: *Rerum gubernatio a Deo secundum quandam motionem esse intelligitur, secundum quod Deus omnia dirigit et movet in proprios fines.*

importance of the causal relation between God and the world in understanding Thomas's *ordo diciplinae*, but the schematisation which he proposes seems to us incomplete and indeed misleading.

The three parts of the *Summa* appear to correspond in a remarkable fashion to the three forms of God's presence in the world which we have examined in the previous chapter.[59] We find here a direct counterpart to the problem which, as we noted above, lies behind what seems at first sight the peculiar position given to Christology in the *Summa theologiae*. Thomas, that is, clearly indicates the relation between these two forms of presence, so that the general presence in creation is a presupposition of both the special presence in grace and the presence in Christ which recapitulates and includes the other two.[60] This presupposition is to be understood not in a temporal but a metaphysical and logical sense, since the two latter forms of presence have no meaning apart from the first, just as an understanding of God's presence in Christ presupposes what we already know about the other two forms of presence. Every new form of presence implies something that is essentially new, a *novus modus* or a new *effectus* of the divine causality, but the new is worked out in accordance with the structural lines which have already been laid out in the interpretation which Thomas offers of the indispensable general presence. In this way he builds the doctrine of grace, which forms the centre of Part II, on the foundation which he has already laid in Part I where he sets forth the relation between God and the world and the main outlines of his anthropology. And it is in the extension of these lines that Thomas sees what is essential in the new revealed truth which he elucidates in Part III, where he deals with God's presence in Christ.

---

[59] This relationship has been pointed out in particular by Y. M.-J. Congar, 'Le mystère du temple de Dieu et l'économie de sa présence dans le monde', in *ATA* 13 (1953), p. 2, footnote 1: 'Sans doute ne serait-il pas exagéré ou étranger à l'intention de S. Thomas de retrouver les trois modes ou degrés d'union à Dieu et de présence, respectivement dans les trois parties de la *Somme*: I, présence par la puissance créatrice, selon la similitude; II, présence par la grâce, selon l'union à Dieu comme objet connu, aimé et possédé; III, présence par l'union hypostatique, selon l'être. Ou encore: immanence générale de Dieu à sa création, immanence à sa créature raisonnable et libre, immanence singulière et suprême en Jésus-Christ'.

[60] I *Sent.* 37, 1, 2, ad 3: *illi tres modi (scil. per essentiam, praesentiam et potentiam) . . . omnem creaturam consequuntur, et praesupponuntur etiam in aliis modis. In quo enim est Deus per unionem, etiam est per gratiam; et in quo est per gratiam, est per essentiam, praesentiam et potentiam;* cf. III *Sent.* 4, 3, 2, 2, and 3a, 2, 10, ad 2. Cf. Gardeil, *La structure de l'âme*, vol. II, p. 61ff. and Morency, *L'union de grâce*, p. 64f.

In each of these manifestations of the divine presence we have seen that the structure is determined by the causal *ordo* which, according to Thomas, characterises the relation between God and the world.[61] The central theological concepts which we have so far discussed have shown that the determining factor in each instance is ultimately this causal relation, as indeed we might well expect, since Thomas himself tation which Thomas offers of the indispensable general presence. says that *sacra . . . doctrina propriissime determinat de Deo secundum quod est altissima causa* (holy teaching goes to God most personally as deepest origin and highest end).[62] We now see that the elements which, as we saw earlier in our present study, constitute the structure of this causal relation are reflected in a remarkable way in the plan of the *Summa theologiae* itself. Thus, in discussing the relationship between Thomas and neo-Platonism we could show how he characteristically bases causality on the metaphysics of existence by using one of his own statements, *esse absolute praeintelligitur causae* (to be is presupposed to being a cause).[63] There is a direct parallel to this in the fact that Thomas's discussion of the nature of the divine cause is immediately preceded by an inquiry into the existence of God.[64] Just as God's *esse* is presupposed by his *operari*, so too the *esse* of things is presupposed by their increase and motion: *movere praesupponit esse* (to change presupposes to be),[65] and therefore his discussion of the creature is prefaced by a study of the *emanatio totius esse ab ente universali* (the issuing of the whole of being from universal being),[66] which for Thomas is the meaning of creation. Moreover, for Thomas God is at one time both *causa efficiens*, *causa exemplaris*, and *causa finalis*, but as our earlier discussion of the causal relation between God and the world indicated, there is a definite order among these types of cause. Amongst those mentioned the final cause is primary, for, as Thomas puts it, *finis est causa causarum, quia est causa causalitatis in omnibus causis* (the final cause is the cause of causes, since it is the cause of causality in every cause).[67] In every causal relation *omne agens agit propter finem* (every agent acts for the sake of an end),

---

[61] Cf. p. 159ff., 180ff., 199ff., and 203ff. above.   [62] 1a, 1, 6; cf. p. 95 above.
[63] 1a, 13, 11, ad 2; cf. p. 133f. above.   [64] 1a, 2, 1–3.
[65] *In De causis*, 18; cf. *Compend. Theol.* 68: *Primus autem effectus Dei in rebus est ipsum esse, quod omnes alii effectus praesupponunt, et supra quod fundantur.*
[66] 1a, 45, 4, ad 1; 1a, 45, 5: *Producere autem esse absolute, non inquantum est hoc vel tale, pertinet ad rationem creationis.*
[67] *De principiis naturae;* cf. p. 100 above and the references given in footnotes 37 and 38.

and this must also be true of divine causality.[68] It is not essential to God's nature, eternally unchanging as it is, to cause anything outside himself, for he is *ipsum esse* and therefore in every way perfect even apart from the existence of the creature. But *when* God causes a thing—and both experience and revelation indicate that he does cause things, Thomas holds—what is caused can occur only with reference to God as its *summum bonum*, and therefore Thomas can say with regard to divine causality that *inter nomina significantia causalitatem divinam, prius ponitur bonum quam ens* (among epithets signifying divine causality 'good' may be found preceding 'existent').[69] The primary 'effect' of divine causality is the *esse* of the creature, but this effect is also in the last resort subsumed under the all-inclusive final aspect as the first step taken by the creature towards its end, since *principium autem executionis est primum eorum quae sunt ad finem* (the principle in execution is the first of the things which are ordained to the end).[70] This accounts for the 'centripetal' aspect which, as we have noted on several occasions earlier, is typical of Thomas's whole approach,[71] and is related to his characteristic view of salvation as an *elevatio* or raising up of human nature.[72]

This all-inclusive final aspect of the relation between God and the world is given clear expression by Thomas in his exposition in the *Summa theologiae*. This is true particularly of Part II which, in Thomas's own words, seeks to define the *motus rationalis creaturae in Deum* (journey to God of reasoning creatures)[73] and is prefaced by a study in depth of the *beatitudo* which is man's *ultimus finis* (ultimate end).[74] It is also clear, as the overwhelming amount of space allotted to Part II in particular indicates, that it is on this second part that the primary emphasis of the whole work is laid. But Part III, which speaks of Christ, who, in Thomas's own concise expression, *secundum quod homo*, VIA *est nobis tendendi in Deum* (as man, is our road to God),[75] also comes under this final perspective, viz. the movement towards God of the rational creation. This is more fully explained in the prologue to Part III, which speaks of Christ as the one who *viam veritatis nobis in seipso demonstravit, per quam ad beatitudinem immortalis vitae resurgendo pervenire possimus* (showed us in his own person the way of truth by which we may attain the blessedness of

[68] 1a, 44, 4; cf. p. 100ff. above. [69] 1a, 5, 2, ad 1; cf. p. 100. above.
[70] 1a2ae, 1, 4; cf. p. 112 above. [71] See p. 100ff., 169, 186ff., and 221 above.
[72] See p. 37ff., 172, and 218ff. above. [73] 1a, 2, introd.; cf. p. 256 above.
[74] 1a2ae, 1–5. [75] 1a, 2, introd.; cf. p. 256 above.

S

eternal life by rising again).[76] On the assumption that men are summoned to a particular end, they need to know the way if they are ever to attain it. In the first two parts of the *Summa* Thomas defines this end and the abstract structure of man's movement towards it, especially the help which God provides in the law and grace, and then in Part III he turns to show how this end was first attained in the particular case of Christ's human nature. Here, too, he speaks of the concrete means—the sacraments—which are essential for men since the fall if they are to come to their destined salvation, and which mediate the grace that was given in such abundant measure in Christ.[77] Thus he includes both the incarnation and the sacraments within the universal final perspective as the means given to men whereby they may attain their God-appointed goal.[78] The fact that the incarnation and the sacraments are thus included

[76] 3a, prol. On this idea of Christ's human nature as *via nobis tendendi in Deum*, an idea frequently found in Thomas, see *Compend. Theol.* 2; 2a2ae, 1, 8; 2a2ae, 2, 7; 3a, 9, 2; 3a, 14, 1, ad 4. See also *In Joan.* 14, 2 where Thomas, as he often does, makes a distinction within the testimony of Jesus to himself in John 14:6: '*Veritas et vita*': *et sic ipse simul est via, et terminus. Via quidem secundum humanitatem, terminus secundum divinitatem. Sic ergo secundum quod homo, dicit, 'Ego sum via'; secundum quod Deus, addit, 'Veritas et vita'.* Thomas teaches that the statement concerning Christ as the 'way' applies exclusively to his human nature, while he restricts 'the truth and the life' to his divine nature, for Christ as God is *veritas prima*. The object of salvation for men is the vision of divine truth, which in concrete terms means a perfection of man as an intellectual being, cf. *CG* IV, 42: *ultima autem salus hominis est ut secundum intellectivam partem perficiatur contemplatione Veritatis Primae.* As we saw above in our examination of the divine presence in Christ, Christ possesses in his divine nature a perfect realisation of this beatific knowledge, and the salvation of all other men consists in their becoming like him in this respect, each on his own plane: *similes ei erimus, scilicet omnia scientes, sicut qui haberet librum ubi esset tota scientia, In ad Col.* 2, 1 (82). [77] Cf. p. 209 above, footnote 89.
[78] This is made very clear in one of the first articles of Part III, where Thomas deals with the question of the necessity of the incarnation: 3a, 1, 2: *ad finem aliquem dicitur aliquid esse necessarium dupliciter: uno modo, sine quo aliquid esse non potest, sicut cibus est necessarius ad conservationem humanae vitae; alio modo, per quod melius et convenientius pervenitur ad finem, sicut equus necessarius est ad iter. Primo modo Deum incarnari non fuit necessarium ad reparationem humanae naturae: Deus enim per suam omnipotentem virtutem poterat humanam naturam multis aliis modis reparare. Secundo autem modo necessarium fuit Deum incarnari ad humanae naturae reparationem.* There is no question here of an unconditional necessity, but of the *necessitas ex suppositione*, which is related to the idea of *causa finalis:* there is a goal set before man, and the question concerns the means that are necessary to attain it (on the different types of *necessitas* found in Thomas, see Synave, *Vie de Jésus*, vol. III, p. 211f.). There are thus two possibilities: 1) *sine qua non*—a means which is absolutely necessary, just as food is necessary to sustain life; and 2) *propter melius* —the best means of realising and attaining a purpose. It is in this second sense, Thomas holds, that we may speak of the necessity of the incarnation—the incarnation is the best and from all points of view most fitting means, appointed by

in the causal context, which defines man's relation to God, makes them ultimately intelligible to us, and it is from this context that they are understood in Thomas's theology.[79]

Even the first part of the *Summa*, however, which deals primarily with God,[80] is ultimately to be subsumed under this final *ordo ad Deum*, as we see very clearly if we turn to the discussion of man's *ultimus finis* with which Thomas prefaces the first half of Part II. The *beatitudo* which constitutes man's final end is here defined by Thomas in two different ways. On the one hand he states that it is nothing less than God himself, and therefore it is *aliquid increatum* (something uncreated), but it is also, as he prefers to put it, a perfection within man himself, and therefore *aliquid creatum* (something created).[81] Behind these two related definitions lies a distinction which Thomas found in Aristotle and which helps to show what he understands by *finis: sicut Philosophus dicit in II Physic. et in V Metaphys.*, FINIS DUPLICITER DICITUR, SCILICET CUIUS, ET QUO: *idest ipsa res in qua ratio boni invenitur, et usus sive adeptio illius rei* (as the Philosopher says in *Phys.* 2 and *Metaphys.* 5, the end is twofold—the end *for which* and the end *by which*; i.e., the thing itself in which is found the reason for good, and the use or acquisition of the thing).[82] With the help of this distinction it is possible for Thomas to solve the problem of how God can be the final goal for *all* existing things at one time. As *finis cuius* or *ipsa res quae est finis*, God is the end of all things, but every creature attains to God as its *ultimus finis* on the plane appropriate to its particular nature by realising the degree of likeness to God given with this nature, and this assimilation to the transcendent cause is the *finis quo* or *adeptio rei* of the creature.

God, for attaining the goal of salvation, in the same way as the horse made it possible to travel with less difficulty on the rough medieval roads.

---

[79] Chenu, *Saint Thomas*, p. 315: 'Redemptive Incarnation is the very substance of the Christian economy; yet *the basic source of its intelligibleness is its characteristic of being a means*. To see it thus inserted within the ontological framework of grace is not to minimise its marvellous unfolding in time' (italics ours); cf. also Hayen, *Saint Thomas et la vie de l'Église*, p. 91 (see p. 255 above, footnote 48).

[80] 1a, 2, introd.: *primo tractabimus de Deo*; cf. p. 256 above.

[81] See e.g. 1a2ae, 3, 1: *Primo ergo modo, ultimus hominis finis est bonum increatum, scilicet Deus, qui solus sua infinita bonitate potest voluntatem hominis perfecte implere. Secundo autem modo, ultimus finis hominis est aliquid creatum in ipso existens, quod nihil est aliud quam adeptio vel fruitio finis ultimi.*

[82] 1a2ae, 1, 8; cf. 1a, 26, 3, ad 2: *finis est duplex, scilicet cuius et quo, ut Philosophus dicit, scilicet ipsa res, et usus rei: sicut avaro est finis pecunia, et acquisitio pecuniae. Creaturae igitur rationalis est quidem Deus finis ultimus ut res; beatitudo autem creata ut usus, vel magis fruitio, rei.*

By seeking to attain to the likeness of God every creature also realises its own immanent perfection.[83] The expression of this perfection in man is that he is endowed with reason and will, and therefore on his plane he attains his final end *cognoscendo et amando Deum* (by knowing and loving God).[84] The transcendent end, *finis exterius*, and the immanent perfection, *finis interius*,[85] constitute a unity in Thomas's understanding by reason of the fact that the former is regarded as the cause of the latter: *Si ergo beatitudo hominis consideretur quantum ad* CAUSAM VEL OBJECTUM, *sic est aliquid increatum: si autem consideretur quantum ad ipsam essentiam beatitudinis, sic est aliquid creatum* (If, therefore, we consider man's blessedness in its cause or object, then it is something uncreated; but if we consider it with regard to the very essence of blessedness, then it is something created).[86] When in Part I of the *Summa* Thomas speaks of the being of God as one and triune, he is simply indicating what man's *ultimus finis* is, viz. his transcendent end (his *finis cuius*). In Part II he begins to speak of the causal connection between this and man's immanent perfection (his *finis quo*).[87] Thomas also speaks of this

---

[83] 1a, 6, 1, ad 2: *omnia, appetendo proprias perfectiones, appetunt ipsum Deum, inquantum perfectiones omnium rerum sunt quaedam similitudines divini esse;* see also p. 101 above, and the references given there in footnotes 41 and 42.

[84] 1a2ae, 1, 8: *Si ergo loquamur de ultimo fine hominis quantum ad ipsam rem quae est finis, sic in ultimo fine hominis omnia alia conveniunt: quia Deus est ultimus finis hominis et omnium aliarum rerum.—Si autem loquamur de ultimo fine hominis quantum ad consecutionem finis, sic in hoc fine hominis non communicant creaturae irrationales. Nam homo et aliae rationales creaturae consequuntur ultimum finem cognoscendo et amando Deum: quod non competit aliis creaturis, quae adipiscuntur ultimum finem inquantum participant aliquam similitudinem Dei, secundum quod sunt, vel vivunt, vel etiam cognoscunt;* see also 1a2ae, 3, 8, ad 2. By taking his point of departure in the distinction between *finis cuius* and *finis quo*, Thomas is able to explain how there can be degrees of beatitude amongst the numbers of the blessed, even though all of them seek to attain to God: 1a2ae, 5, 2: *Quantum igitur ad ipsum bonum quod est beatitudinis obiectum et causa, non potest esse una beatitudo alia maior: quia non est nisi unum summum bonum, scilicet Deus, cuius fruitione homines sunt beati.—Sed quantum ad adeptionem huiusmodi boni vel fruitionem, potest aliquis alio esse beatior: quia quanto magis hoc bono fruitur, tanto beatior est.*

[85] Cf. IV Sent. 49, 1, 2, 1: *Ultimus finis cujuslibet rei habentis esse ab alio est duplex: unus exterius, secundum scilicet id quod est desideratae perfectionis principium; alius interius, scilicet ipsa sua perfectio, quam facit conjunctio ad principium.*

[86] 1a2ae, 3, 1; the same terminology is found in 1a2ae, 5, 2; and cf. the passage quoted in footnote 84 above.

[87] It is within this context of finality that we are to examine the theme of the prologue of the first half of Part II which we have given on p. 258 above. In this prologue Thomas gives clear expression to the causal relation which connects the discussion of the first half with the second, and even though he concentrates in the passage quoted on God as *causa exemplaris*, even this belongs to the sphere of finality; cf. the allusion made by Thomas to man's creation *ad imaginem Dei* in the

perfectio hominis as an *operatio*,[88] by which through his knowledge
and love of God man is conformed to the blessedness which God
eternally enjoys by knowing and loving himself,[89] and this perfect
operatio is anticipated in an imperfect way in the human acts which
are dealt with in the remainder of this part of the *Summa*, and especially the knowledge and love of God to which man *in via* is raised
through grace.[90] Finally, in Part III Thomas speaks of the actual
realisation of the immanent *ultimus finis hominis* as this is to be seen
in time and history in the human nature of Christ.

Thus the salvation and perfection of man—his *ultimus finis*—
occupy a central place in the theology of Thomas. The question of
salvation is a question about *knowledge of God*, and therefore theology
comes to take the form of a *scientia* analogous to other sciences which
communicate knowledge of existence, and for the same reason it is
God alone who is the *subjectum huius scientiae*.[91] He is the *principium
et finis* of all things, and we have seen how the causal relation between
God and the world expressed in this phrase ultimately determines
also the structure of the *ordo disciplinae* which we find in the arrangement of the *Summa theologiae*. It is this causal relation with its
characteristic aspect of finality which ultimately forms the organising
theological principle in Thomas's *sacra doctrina*. If we should try to

text immediately preceding the passage which we have quoted, and the references
which we have given on p. 169 to the connection between this phrase and final
causality.

---

[88] 1a2ae, 3, 2: *secundum quod beatitudo hominis est aliquid creatum in ipso existens
necesse est dicere quod beatitudo hominis sit operatio. Est enim beatitudo ultima
hominis perfectio. Unumquodque autem intantum perfectum est, inquantum est actu:
nam potentia sine actu imperfecta est. Oportet ergo beatitudinem in ultimo actu
hominis consistere. Manifestum est autem quod operatio est ultimus actus operantis.*

[89] Cf. *In Joan.* 14, 1 (3): *Perfectio quidem beatitudinis absoluta est solius Dei: quia
solus ipse tantum cognoscit se et amat quantum cognoscibilis est et amabilis;* 1a, 26, 2:
*Attribuenda ergo est Deo beatitudo secundum intellectum, sicut et aliis beatis, qui
per assimilationem ad beatitudinem ipsius, beati dicuntur.*

[90] On the relation between *gratia* and *beatitudo*, cf. *De Ver.* 27, 2, ad 7: *gratia . . .
est sicut dispositio quae est respectu gloriae, quae est gratia consummata; De Ver.*
27, 5, ad 6: *Sicut enim caritas viae non tollitur, sed in patria remanet augmentata . . .
ita gratia, cum nullum in sui ratione importet defectum, per sui augmentum fit gloria:
nec dicitur esse diversa perfectio naturae in statu viae et patriae quantum ad gratiam
propter diversam formam perficientem, sed propter diversam perfectionis mensuram;*
1a, 62, 3: *Manifestum est autem quod gratia gratum faciens hoc modo comparatur
ad beatitudinem, sicut ratio seminalis in natura ad effectum naturalem;* see also 1a,
93, 4 and 2a2ae, 24, 3, ad 2: *gratia et gloria ad idem genus referuntur: quia gratia
nihil est aliud quam quaedam inchoatio gloriae in nobis.*

[91] 1a, 1, 7; cf. p. 94 above.

express this principle in a single phrase—realising, of course, the dangers inherent in any such simplification—the term *gubernatio Dei*, which we have already mentioned once or twice, may well be as good as any. Thomas uses the term to summarise the whole relationship between God and the world which is given in the various forms of divine causality, and the *gubernatio* of which he speaks is exercised in the characteristic aspect of finality.[92] This idea of divine rule also draws together in a remarkable way two separate ideas each thoroughly typical of Thomas's theology—first, the fundamental biblical concept of God as directly active in every event in the created world (a concept which we examined in the previous chapter from the standpoint of the concept of presence), and second, the causal approach which determines the whole of this theological thought. The term thus expresses *in nuce* the expression of the problem which is characteristic of Thomas's theological synthesis as a whole, with its interplay between biblical and Greek elements of thought. The truth communicated by revelation becomes intelligible, Thomas holds, only from the standpoint of the causal *ordo ad Deum* in which God is seen as *principium et finis*, and in the last resort it is this *ordo* which gives it its meaning. But the causal order of existence of which Thomas writes is not known by revelation but by *ratio*; its elements are derived from Greek philosophy, and Thomas uses it in order to explain the meaning of revelation. In the following section we shall attempt to define briefly the nature of the problem which this involves in the relation between *ratio* and *revelatio* in Thomas's theology.

[92] Closer examination will reveal that the term *gubernatio* includes all essential aspects of the causal relation between God and the world. Both the divine conservation, *conservatio rerum*—which, as we saw on p. 116, is identical with the created relationship itself as such—(and in this we understand God principally as *causa efficiens*), and the divine *motio in finem* (in which we understand God principally as *causa finalis*) are subsumed under the term *gubernatio* as two separate *effectus* of the divine governance. Furthermore, both of these *effectus* together express the *assimilatio Dei* which in this causal relation indicates what takes place within creation (in which God is principally seen as *causa exemplaris*). Cf. e.g. the following passages: 1a, 103, 3: *gubernatio nihil aliud est quam directio gubernatorum ad finem* (see also the references given in footnote 58, p. 258); 1a, 103, 4: *potest considerari effectus gubernationis secundum ea quibus ad Dei assimilationem creatura perducitur. Et sic in generali sunt duo effectus gubernationis . . . scilicet conservatio rerum in bono, et motio earum ad bonum.* Hence those who are endowed with reason have a special place among all other created beings on the grounds that they are actuated not simply *Deo interius operante*, but also *per hoc quod ab eo inducuntur ad bonum et retrahuntur a malo per praecepta et prohibitones, praemia et poenas,* 1a, 103, 5, ad 2; cf. also in this connection the place which Thomas gives to the law and grace as actuating factors in man's movement towards his goal.

3

RATIO AND REVELATIO

As we saw in Chapter One, Thomas holds that there is a close connection between scripture and theology. The scriptures teach of the supernatural truth which is essential for salvation and has been given to prophets and apostles by the event of revelation. Thomas sees his own task as theologian to be that of interpreting and communicating to his own age the substance of this teaching. This is the function of *sacra doctrina*, and since *sacra doctrina* starts from the articles of faith as its first principles, it is clearly a science, *scientia*, like any other. As a science, it is superior to all others because it originates in and communicates knowledge of the higher truth that is inaccessible to reason, though by the same token it is inferior to them in the sense that it cannot provide clear proof with regard to some of its contents. As we saw from our earlier discussion, the rational structure of *sacra doctrina* is due to this necessity of having a theology that is scientific in character, though it is quite clear that Thomas himself does not regard this science as an end in itself. *Sacra doctrina* exists not simply to allow *ratio* to develop certain lines of thought, it is primarily a means of interpreting and unfolding the saving truth that is communicated in the canonical writings. Thus Thomas can simply use the terms *sacra scriptura* and *sacra doctrina* as synonyms.[1] It is important not to lose sight of this idea, which in Thomas's view is basic and fundamental, for it shows that in his theology the relation between *revelatio* and *ratio* is ultimately from the *material* standpoint a relation between concepts and motifs which are biblical in origin and those which are derived from Greek philosophy. The fact that Thomas himself clearly regards his theology as an exposition of holy scripture and insists that the Bible is the norm and starting-point of theology allows us to raise the question of how his *sacra doctrina* expresses the programmatic statements given in this passage. It is not possible here to examine Thomas's biblical exegesis in depth and contrast it with the work of more

[1] See p. 86f. above.

recent exegetes. Quite apart from the anachronism involved in such a contrast and the fact that the comparison would do less than justice to the material, any such undertaking lies beyond the scope of the present work which is primarily concerned not with Thomas's exegesis as such, but with the interplay between elements of thought derived from quite different sources. It is not possible for us here to raise or attempt to answer the question of the correct interpretation of scripture; our intention is rather to establish what are the determinative principles implicit in the interpretation of scripture in this particular instance and in writings which historically are of crucial significance for later theological developments. Our task will be to summarise the questions and conclusions which from the standpoint of what we would call the 'common ground' of biblical theology open up the possibility of reexamining the material on which we have already touched in earlier parts of the present work. Our assumption in this is that the proper task of exegesis is to subordinate itself to the passages exegeted, particularly when—as in the case in Thomas—these passages are stated to have a normative character. Moreover, as we have indicated in the previous chapter, the relation between *ratio* and *revelatio* in Thomas's theology is not in fact as positive or unequivocal as his own statements suggest. On the basis of these statements we can make the kind of general statement which we offered earlier in this chapter, *revelatio supponit rationem*, but our task now is to get behind this general definition and try to state what is means *in concreto* by studying Thomas's own methodological procedure. It is primarily in reference to *content* that we see what is in fact the *essential* relationship between reason and revelation and this is why we have dealt at such length in our previous discussion both with what Thomas says about revelation and its content and also with the central motifs of his theology. Against this background and by using the materials which we can extract from it, a fruitful discussion of our main question will be possible. In our first chapter we dealt with the problem of biblical theology. In the second we examined Thomas's interpretation of the biblical concept of God's immediate presence and activity in all that happens in the created world. It was primarily in this second chapter that we dealt with the arguments and conclusions which will not only shed light on this problem but also define the relation between *ratio* and *revelatio* in Thomas's *sacra doctrina* against this background.

If we turn first to the decisive part played by *revelatio* in the theology of Thomas, it is quite clear that in *sacra doctrina* revelation provides the subject-matter and hence also defines the task of theology. Without revelation there would not be any *sacra doctrina*, for theology does not arise of its own accord out of philosophical speculation. Philosophy may indeed by the processes of thought come to a knowledge of the revealed truths that are accessible to reason, but it could never gain any understanding, for instance, of the Trinity or the incarnation. When we accept such ideas by faith, however, reason begins to operate with a completely new sphere, of which it had previously no inkling. Revelation thus gives theology a content which goes far beyond the limits of philosophy.

This new content also determines the form of the exposition. One example of this is the theocentric orientation of the *Summa theologiae*[2] which takes its starting-point in the concept of God, while pure metaphysics proceeds from actual, existing things in order to move from them to the first principle. This means that theology does not simply communicate a knowledge *about* God, it also has to do with a knowledge which comes *from* God. We may also point here to the significance of the doctrine of the Trinity in Thomas's theology. Though often disregarded, it is nevertheless quite central. The same is also true both of general anthropology (man as the *imago Trinitatis*) and particularly of the doctrine of grace (the perfecting of the *imago Trinitatis* through the *missio invisibilis*).

The crucial importance of revelation in regard to the content of the *Summa* is also demonstrated by the fact that we do not find in Thomas any autonomous 'natural theology' that is independent of *revelatio*. The knowledge of God given on the plane of nature is subsumed under the principal ideas given by the revealed content of faith, and it is only in this context that Thomas speaks of natural knowledge to any extent, for faith means not only that something new has been given but also that the natural is brought to perfection.[3]

Revelation does indeed imply a *perfectio intellectus* and is seen to be the extension of reason's own quest for knowledge, but at the same time truths which lie beyond the grasp of reason constitute an essential part of the content of revealed knowledge. By itself, reason cannot say in advance what God will do for the salvation of men. It cannot even know that God has appointed this end for men, unless revelation first discloses it. Revelation alone, therefore,

---

[2] See p. 93ff. above.
[3] On this whole problem see Skydsgaard, *Metafysik*, p. 185ff.

determines the limits of theology. Any philosophical ideas or speculations, moreover, that may contradict the substance of revelation are repudiated by the revelation of the being and activity of God. Philosophical knowledge is thus *ad metas fidei redigenda* (to be kept within the bounds of faith),[4]—this is what Paul means, says Thomas, when he refers to every thought being taken captive to obey Christ.

Since in its essential aspects the content of revelation transcends the natural limits of human reason, reason must acknowledge its limitations within the structure of theology. In the dazzling illumination given by the light of faith the human intellect, on account of its *debilitas*, is like the night-owl in the bright light of the sun.[5] Even theology, therefore, cannot gain adequate knowledge of divine things. With respect to rational knowledge faith does indeed give an incomparably more perfect understanding by showing *plures et excellentiores effectus* (more and greater works) of the divine causality than reason by itself can attain, just as it communicates also a deeper understanding of God's own being (triunity), nevertheless God remains for ever beyond any attempt to resolve the mystery of his being. Even for the theologian who has received the light of faith God remains the great Unknown, *quasi ignotus*.[6] Thomas uses this expression in speaking of the knowledge of God in order to affirm his absolute sovereignty, transcendence and independence of man. Theology, when it treats of God, can no more go beyond the oscillation of analogical knowledge between likeness and unlikeness than can pure metaphysics. Nor can any theologian explain definitively the nature of God as it is in itself, and therefore it is impossible to define what God is.[7]

There is not any doubt that by affirming in different contexts the sovereignty and transcendence of God—as we have seen in our discussion in the previous chapter—Thomas has given expression to an essential aspect of the biblical idea of God. The biblical idea of

---

[4] *In De Trin.* 2, 3; the passage is cited in full on p. 234, footnote 38.

[5] 1a, 1, 5, ad 1; 1a, 64, 1, obi. 2; *In ad Rom.* 12, 2 (978).

[6] 1a, 12, 13, ad 1: *licet per revelationem gratiae in hac vita non cognoscamus de Deo quid est, et sic ei quasi ignoto coniungamur; tamen plenius ipsum cognoscimus, inquantum plures et excellentiores effectus eius nobis demonstrantur; et inquantum ei aliqua attribuimus ex revelatione divina, ad quae ratio naturalis non pertingit, ut Deum esse trinum et unum;* cf. also 1a, 1, 7, ad 1: *licet de Deo non possimus scire quid est, utimur tamen eius effectu, in hac doctrina, vel naturae vel gratiae. loco definitionis, ad ea quae de Deo in hac doctrina considerantur.*

[7] Cf. p. 137 above.

the living and active God who is continually at work in his creation
but at the same time Lord of this creation is clearly one of central
importance in Thomas's theology. God for Thomas is not a static
and remote first principle without knowledge of the world, but is
actively 'present' in all that happens in creation. Nothing exists or
takes place that is not in its innermost being continually dependent
on God for all that it receives. Just as the light of the sun lights up
the sky but is not created by it, so ultimately everything in the order
of nature and grace comes from God and is not created by man—
it is continually received, as Thomas puts it, it is given *ab alio*.[8]
Precisely because God is sovereign in his freedom and independence
of creation, his giving is always a free gift which at the same time
creates what it gives. God's love is different from man's in this
regard that he does not use it to his own advantage. He does not give
as men do, *intentione retributionis* (with the intention of recompense),[9]
in order to receive or get something for themselves. Within a metaphysic wholly grounded, it appears, on Greek philosophical ideas
Thomas in this way gives expression to the biblical idea that 'everything comes from God'. At the profoundest level, not only the fact
that man *is* but also what he *does* are directly dependent upon God,
immediate . . . a Deo. This does not in any way prevent us from saying
that from another point of view man's actions are wholly his own.
But his power of action is given by God and does not limit the divine
activity. On the contrary, it necessarily presupposes this activity, in
that man's nature with its freedom of will and activity is at every
moment dependent on the *conservatio* of the divine omnicausality.[10]
This is true also in regard to those actions which belong in particular
to the supernatural order, and which bring man to his final blessedness. The theological virtues such as faith and love, which proceed
from the qualitative improvement of human nature brought about by
grace, and which are new and more perfect than the other virtues, are
not merely a development of man's natural powers but come from
God *sola gratia*, apart from any human deserving. In other words,
they are *virtutes infusae*, not *virtutes acquisitae*, they are not something
man can attain through his own efforts, but a divine gift. And yet as
qualities inherent and habitual in the soul, they are at the same time

---

[8] Cf. p. 129f. above.
[9] 1a, 38, 2; see also the full discussion of the same idea in I *Sent.* 18, 1, 2 and 3.
Cf. also p. 105ff. and the references given in the footnotes.
[10] Cf. p. 98, 116 and 162 above.

an activity of man's own reason and will, bringing man himself to perfection. Thus Thomas holds that at one and the same time *everything* is the work of God *and* of man, not *partim a Deo* and *partim ab homine*, but TOTUS AB UTROQUE *secundum alium modum* (not partly by God and partly by man, but the whole from each, though in a different way respectively).[11] But it is God who has the initiative, and by this stress Thomas gives clear expression to the biblical idea of grace within the structure of the causal relationship.

Furthermore, in his theory of knowledge, which he derived in the main from Aristotelianism, concrete things—including man's bodily existence—are assumed as a necessary presupposition and starting-point for the acquisition of knowledge, and consequently matter has a far more positive significance in Thomas than it had in the earlier tradition deriving from Platonism. Our impression that Thomas's theology expresses essential aspects of the biblical idea of God relating both to grace and the fact of creation itself is confirmed by this and also the key passage to which we have referred in the previous section of the present chapter, where our discussion focussed on the idea of the *gubernatio Dei*, God's direct government of the world.[12]

This may also be the appropriate occasion to indicate a further aspect of the part played by biblical ideas in Thomas's synthesis. We refer to a phenomenon which can be found frequently in the history of Christian thought when biblical and Greek ideas are brought together and the latter used as a vehicle of expressing the former, viz. the fact that tendencies and contradictions which are present in Greek thought are accentuated in the encounter with the Christian faith and emerge from this encounter in a radically new form.[13] We can study this process in Thomas particularly in the

[11] *CG* III, 70: *Virtus autem inferioris agentis dependet a virtute superioris agentis, inquantum superius agens dat virtutem ipsam inferiori agenti per quam agit; vel conservat eam; aut etiam applicat eam ad agendum . . . ita non est inconveniens quod producatur idem effectus ab inferiori agente et Deo: ab utroque immediate, licet alio et alio modo. . . . Patet etiam quod non sic idem effectus causae naturali et divinae virtuti attribuitur quasi partim a Deo, et partim a naturali agente fiat, sed totus ab utroque secundum alium modum.*

[12] See p. 266 above.

[13] Bring in particular has drawn attention to this and shown how the relationship has been expressed in the Christology of the early church and Augustine's doctrine of grace, see e.g. 'Kristendomens gestaltvandlingar', in *Vid Åbodomens fot 1924–1949* (Lutherska litteraturstiftelsens svenska publikationer 5), Helsingfors 1949, p. 89, 96 and 102, or *Kristendomstolkningar. Studier till en månghundraårig idéhistoria*, Stockholm 1950, p. 238 and 248.

interpretation of the relation between God and the world which he provides in his metaphysics of existence. If the relation between the first principle and the world is in fact primarily understood in Greek thought in terms of the enormous difference of *degree* between absolute perfection and the many varying forms of lower degrees of perfection, Thomas goes even further than this, no doubt led in this direction by the biblical teaching itself, by holding that divine transcendence is constituted in particular by the radical difference in *kind* between the One who, quite independently of the world, is himself *ipsum esse*, and the whole of creation which has no existence in and of itself but receives its existence *ab alio*. Characteristically, however, Thomas does not consider that this radically new interpretation of the difference between God and the world implies that we can no longer speak of degrees of difference or must at least modify such statements—this latter way of thinking is clearly included in the former and regulated by it. Thomas thus incorporates the whole Aristotelian view of cause in its entirety into his interpretation of the relation between God and the world—and there can be no doubt that it is ultimately from Aristotle that he derives this characteristic emphasis on finality—but this causality is not primary and presupposes that God is *ipsum esse*. In a sense the meaning of causality itself is also changed when God is defined as the *causa efficiens* of the existence of things, but the difference here is that we do not understand it to be an essential part of God's being to cause anything 'outside' himself. God is in actual fact *causa prima* of all existence and as such includes within himself all the perfection which is reflected in created things, but it is not this that constitutes his transcendence. He is not primarily a 'higher' being but a 'different' being, a being beyond man's grasp, and therefore unlike Greek philosophy Thomas can never conceive of God as an integral part of the world. In spite of all their agreements in terminology, it is not possible to identify Thomas's God with the first principle of the philosophers. The God whom we encounter in his *sacra doctrina* is the Creator of whom the Bible speaks and who deals with his creation in grace and love.

These general remarks and our earlier observations will show that in Thomas's *sacra doctrina* revelation does not simply provide the matter of theology and in this sense determine its content, but is a determinative principle as well in metaphysical conceptualisation. This does not mean that in interpreting the relationship between

God and the world as he does Thomas would be in agreement with the thought-world of the Bible. As we saw in discussing the problematical question implicit in the *ordo disciplinae*, Thomas's theological methodology creates a tension or interplay between central motifs in the material which he presents for discussion and equally central and structurally determinative motifs in the interpretation of this material which we find in *sacra doctrina*. The implications of this will become clearer if we turn from *revelatio* and attempt to define the actual function of *ratio* in Thomas's synthesis.

When we pass from the programmatic statement of the relationship between scripture and theology, which we discussed in Chapter I, and begin to study the *Summa theologiae*, it seems at first surprising that quotations from scripture appear so infrequently in the discussion, in spite of the fact that, in comparison with the teaching of the philosophers and the 'doctors' of the church, these are stated by Thomas to be the only indispensably binding theological arguments.[14] Scriptural citations are frequently found in the *Summa* only in the counter-statement offered in an 'article' in rebuttal of previously listed 'objections' and prefaced by the words *sed contra*, or in the answers to these objections which come after the expository part. Furthermore, Thomas does not directly expound theology out of of the articles of the faith, which for him are summarised in the Apostles' Creed, and the omission is surprising, since he explicitly states that this summary of the content of scripture represents the 'first principles' of theology.

This latter point is bound up with Thomas's conception of theology as a 'science' for which purely scriptural statements alone are not enough. These express the content of faith and this content is the starting-point and presupposition of the work of the theologian, but the undeveloped form in which this content comes to us is left behind by the theologian, precisely because it is a *starting-point*, a *pre-*supposition, as he moves on to the task of theology in order to show the inner relation between the *auctoritates* of scriptural statements.[15] Granted that the weakness of the human intellect prevents us, as long as we are *in via*, from gaining adequate knowledge of the object of faith, yet it is possible to have a *scientia* of these very propositions

---

[14] See 1a, 1, 8, ad 2; cf. p. 66 above.
[15] See Chenu, *AHDLMA* 2 (1927), p. 58. Cf. also Bonaventure, I *Sent.*, Proœmium, 1, conclusio: *credibile transit in rationem intelligibilis* (Quaracchi ed., vol. I, p. 7).

included in an intelligible *ordo*, in a way which *quodammodo* anticipates this perfect knowledge.

The systematising work of the theologian presupposes that in the
material which he is to expound and interpret there is a centre or
central point of reference to which all statements can be referred.
This brings us to the question of the articles of the faith and the
function which they serve as a starting-point for theology. The
articles summarise the content of the faith, *fides quae creditur*. They
may therefore be called the *prima credibilia* (the primary things to be
believed),[16] but this term is usually reserved for what Thomas considers the very centre of this already concentrated summary and consequently for what is the centre of *sacra doctrina* as a whole. Just as
the first principles of philosophy can be reduced to the single proposition, *impossibile est simul affirmare et negare* (the same thing
cannot be affirmed and denied at the same time), so, analogously,
Thomas holds, *omnes articuli implicite continentur in aliquibus*
PRIMIS CREDIBILIBUS, *scilicet ut credatur Deus esse et providentiam
habere circa hominum salutem* (all the articles are contained implicitly
in certain primary matters of faith, such as God's existence and his
providence over the salvation of man). He refers here to Hebrews
11:6, and interprets this rather loose definition to mean more
precisely that *in esse enim divino includuntur omnia quae credimus in
Deo aeternaliter existere, in quibus nostra beatitudo consistit: in fide
autem providentiae includuntur omnia quae temporaliter a Deo dispen-
satur ad hominum salutem, quae sunt via in beatitudinem* (the existence
of God includes all that we believe to exist in God eternally, and in
these our blessedness consists; while belief in his providence includes
all those things which God dispenses in time for man's salvation, and
which are the way to that blessedness).[17] The *prima credibilia*, which
include the whole content of the Christian faith, are often defined
with reference partly to the *maiestas divinitatis* (majesty of the godhead) and partly to the *mysterium humanitatis Christi* (mystery of
Christ's humanity),[18] but they can also be defined as corresponding
to the Christological dogma itself: *tota fides christiana circa divinitatem et humanitatem Christi versatur* (the whole Christian faith is

---

[16] 2a2ae, 2, 5: *prima credibilia, quae sunt articuli fidei.*   [17] 2a2ae, 1, 7.

[18] 2a2ae, 1, 8: *prima distinctio credibilium est quod quaedam pertinent ad maiestatem
divinitatis; quaedam vero pertinent ad mysterium humanitatis Christi; Compend.
Theol. 2: Circa haec ergo duo tota fidei cognitio versatur: scilicet circa Divinitatem
Trinitatis, et humanitatem Christi;* see also *Compend. Theol.* 185; 1a, 32, 4; 2a2ae,
1, 6, ad 1; 2a2ae, 174, 6.

centred on the divinity and humanity of Christ).[19] Thomas holds that the whole content of scripture is subsumed under these two main points[20] to which even the articles of the Apostles' and Nicene Creeds may be reduced.[21] Here for Thomas is the very centre of the revealed content of faith.

In seeking to explain the theological basis of this double definition of the central content of the faith which we find over and over again in Thomas, we may refer to our discussion of the arrangement of the *Summa theologiae* in the previous section. What we now find corresponds directly to what we earlier saw to be the organising principle of the *ordo disciplinae*. If we try to see the reason for the division which he makes in these passages in which he speaks of these *prima credibilia*, we shall find the same line of thinking presented again and again. Since faith is an earthly anticipation of the beatific vision, both faith and *beatitudo* have ultimately the same object. The difference between them is determined not by their object but by man's situation—in the one case he is *in via*, while in the other he has already attained his end and sees what before he only believed. The central object of faith, therefore, is simply that by which man is beatified, *fidei obiectum per se est id per quod homo beatus efficitur* (the object of

---

[19] *In articulos fidei et sacramenta Ecclesiae.*—When we spoke on p. 248ff. of the secondary place which is given to Christology in Thomas's theology, this does not, of course, mean that Thomas in any way regards Christ and his work as unessential. On the contrary, from one point of view Christology is presupposed in the whole of his theological work, since revelation was fully given only with Christ. The fact that Thomas can summarise the whole content of the faith in a Christological formula, *divinitas et humanitas Christi*, confirms the Christological foundation. In one sense, then, the whole of his theology is simply Christology, and when Thomas speaks about God and man in Part I and Part II of the *Summa*, he is also by implication speaking of Christ, for Christ is God, and his human nature is not structurally different from that of other men. Thomas holds, moreover, that the meaning of this Christological formula is to be understood only by reference to a general statement about the laws which apply to every relation between uncreated and created, and therefore also to Christ's divinity and humanity. It is for this reason that he postpones any explicit discussion of Christology in the proper sense until Part III.

[20] 2a2ae, 1, 6, ad 1: . . . *et alia huiusmodi, quae narrantur in sacra Scriptura in ordine ad manifestionem divinae maiestatis vel incarnationis Christi;* cf. 2a2ae, 2, 5.

[21] Cf. Congar's article, 'Théologie', in *DTC* 15:1, col. 381: 'Ces articles du Symbole ne sont qu'une première explication . . . de deux *credibilia* absolument premiers et qui contiennent implicitement toute la substance de la foi chrétienne. . . Au delà des *articuli fidei* qui sont essentiellement les énoncés du Symbole, c'est à ces deux *credibilia* qui, étant révélés et faisant objet de notre foi directement, en raison de ce qu'ils sont et de leur contenu, sont comme un critère pour toute l'économie de la Révélation'; cf. also the same author in *BT* 5 (1938), p. 498, and Bernard, *La foi*, vol. I, p. 249.

faith is that by which a man is made blessed).[22] The substance of what is expressed in the two *prima credibilia* is ultimately brought into a unity in the 'common denominator' or this central idea of the supernatural end or *beatitudo* which God has set before man.[23]

Here we quite clearly have an expression of the same idea of final cause as we found in the *ordo disciplinae*. The focal point of Thomas's theology is the salvation and perfection of man, man's *ultimus finis*. The division of *prima credibilia* into the two parts of *divinitas* and *humanitas*, or into eternal and temporal, ultimately goes back to the same distinction between *finis cuius* and *finis quo* by which Thomas interprets the meaning of man's supernatural end, his *beatitudo*.[24] The object of the beatific vision, man's *finis cuius*, is God himself and his divine nature, and in the human nature of Christ we see this end realised in a particular individual. In Christ's human nature man's *finis quo* is demonstrated in an anticipatory and prefigurative way, but Christ's realisation of man's supernatural end in the created world implies that other men will also realise it. We may therefore speak of the human nature of Christ as the *via in beatitudinem*, the means which God has provided for man's return to God, and it is significant that we find this expression in the context of Thomas's definition of the *prima credibilia*.[25] We may also note in studying the arrangement of the *Summa* developments comparable to what we find in regard to the Christology of the creeds of the ancient church. In the double formula by which Thomas defines the centre of the Christian faith we find no specific emphasis on the work of Christ as a concrete, historical event, of which the central point is the narrative of the passion, though, of course, the passion is so prominent a feature both of the New Testament and of the Apostles' and Nicene Creeds,[26] and indeed forms the major part of the Christological section of these creeds. Thomas summarises the whole of this

[22] 2a2ae, 2, 5; cf. 2a2ae, 2, 7: *illud proprie et per se pertinet ad obiectum fidei per quod homo beatitudinem consequitur.*
[23] 2a2ae, 1, 8: *illa per se pertinent ad fidem quorum visione in vita aeterna perfruemur, et per quae ducemur in vitam aeternam. Duo autem nobis ibi videnda proponuntur: scilicet occultum divinitatis, cuius visio nos beatos facit; et mysterium humanitatis Christi. . . Et ideo prima distinctio credibilium est quod quaedam pertinent ad maiestatem divinitatis; quaedam vero pertinent ad mysterium humanitatis Christi,* cf. *Compend. Theol.* 2; 2a2ae, 2, 5; 2a2ae, 2, 7; *In 1 ad Thess.* 7, 1 (5): *in fide Trinitatis, et divinitatis et humanitatis Christi, quia in horum cognitione erit nostra beatitudo.*
[24] See p. 263 above. [25] See e.g. *Compend. Theol.* 2; 2a2ae, 1, 7; 2a2ae, 1, 8; 2a2ae, 2, 7.
[26] Cf. e.g. the *verb* forms which recur in the Nicene Creed: *descendit, incarnatus est, crucifixus est, sepultus est, resurrexit, ascendit, venturus est.* On the transition from this recapitulation of the Gospel account to a 'Bevorzugung von Seinskategorien',

T

material—including the whole of the third of the three articles of the ancient creed[27]—in the phrase *humanitas Christi*. This however, does not refer to the work of Christ, but to what he is, his metaphysical status. The explanation of this is simply that in Thomas's understanding the historic events associated with Christ become intelligible only when placed within a metaphysically determined causal scheme and subsumed under its characteristic aspect of finality, *motus rationalis creaturae in Deum*.

The causal scheme, which is so characteristic of Thomas's thought, is thus not simply something which he expresses at certain particular points in his theology or can be shown to be an organising principle in its external form. It is also a factor which in a crucial way determines his choice of formulae in defining what is central to the Christian faith, and is therefore the primary starting-point from which the whole of theology proceeds. The *ultimus finis hominis* is thus the ultimate and all-determining perspective, the *scopus*, from which Thomas reads and interprets the whole of the Bible. The revelation given in the scriptures provides us with information and a knowledge of this end and the means and possibilities of attaining it.

The ultimate explanation of the dominance of the idea of causality, which we have been able to establish at point after point in our present study, is to be found in Thomas's definition of theology as a form of wisdom, *sapientia*. He refers to the wise man as follows: *ad sapientem pertinet considerare causam altissimam* (it is the part of wisdom to consider the highest cause),[28] and therefore, he says, *sacra doctrina* is the highest form of the *sapientia . . . quod per studium habetur* (wisdom . . . to the extent that it can be gained by study),[29] since it *propriissime determinat de Deo secundum quod est*

which was characteristic of the later development of Christological doctrine, see W. Elert, 'Fragen um Chalkedon', in *Evangelisch-Lutherische Kirchenzeitung* 6 (1952), p. 232.

[27] Cf. p. 247 above, footnote 19, on the connection between Christ's human nature and the sacraments and also Thomas's interpretation of the *sanctorum communio* as referring to the *communio bonorum* on the part of the faithful which is manifested in the sacraments; see *In symbolum Apostolorum*, 10.

[28] 2a2ae, 45, 1.

[29] 1a, 1, 6, ad 3. Thomas is speaking here of a *sapientia acquisita*, attained through study, in distinction from the *sapientia infusa* which is a gift of the Spirit; on this distinction see also 2a2ae, 45, 1, ad 2 and 45, 2. Krebs, *Theologie und Wissenschaft*, p. 63, draws attention to the fact that Thomas's predecessors and contemporaries

altissima causa (goes most personally to God as deepest origin and highest end).[30] This causal interpretation is applicable, Thomas states, both in regard to what theology expresses, the cognitive part which is essentially accessible to reason, *quod est per creaturas cognoscibile* (which can be gathered about him from creatures), and also in regard to the cognitive part which is communicated *per revelationem* alone.[31] The man who applies himself to the study of the ultimate *finis* of existence, which is also its *principium*, possesses true wisdom and may be said to be 'wise'.[32] This is why the causal scheme is presupposed as soon as the theologian begins to deal with the cognitive content, and this content, whatever its source, thus follows the lines indicated by the causal scheme, and in the last resort derives its meaning from it. But this whole procedure ultimately presupposes that the theologian is endowed with *ratio et intellectus*, for in the view of Thomas it belongs to the intellectual function of the mind to COGNOSCERE PROPORTIONEM FINIS ET EIUS QUOD EST AD FINEM, ET UNUM ORDINARE IN ALTERUM (know the relation of end and means to end, and direct the one to the other).[33] As we saw earlier in regard to grace, Thomas's principle—*cognita sunt in cognoscente secundum modum cognoscentis*[34]—has immediate application to every form of knowledge. The corresponding principle which we find in the causal scheme—*causa est in effectu per modum effectus*—is simply a variation of what is stated in this basic principle. In other words, the interpretation of what is given in revelation is ultimately determined by a preconceived view of human nature and knowledge: 'the revealed gift . . . is subordinated to the laws of the structure of the human

used the term *sapientia* in order to express the affective and therefore the unscientific or extra-scientific character of theology, while in Thomas the same term is used to express the supreme perfection of science.

---

[30] 1a, 1, 6; see also I *Sent.* prol., 1, 3, 3, 2 and 3; II *Sent.* prol.; *CG* I, 1; *CG* II, 4; *In ad Phil.* 2, 1 (47).

[31] 1a, 1, 6: *Sacra autem doctrina propriissime determinat de Deo secundum quod est altissima causa: quia non solum quantum ad illud quod est per creaturas cognoscibile (quod philosophi cognoverunt, ut dicitur Rom. 1: 'quod notum est Dei, manifestum est illis'); sed etiam quantum ad id quod notum est sibi soli de seipso, et aliis per revelationem communicatum. Unde sacra doctrina maxime dicitur sapientia.*

[32] *CG.* I, 1: *nomen autem simpliciter sapientis illi soli reservatur cuius consideratio circa finem universi versatur, qui item est universitatis principium; unde secundum Philosophum, sapientis est causas altissimas considerare.*

[33] 1a, 18, 3; cf. 1a2ae, 102, 3: *Ad rectam autem ordinationem mentis in Deum pertinet quod omnia quae homo habet, recognoscat a Deo tanquam a primo principio, et ordinet in Deum tanquam in ultimum finem.*

[34] 2a2ae, 1, 2; cf. p. 188 above.

mind'.[35] Even though revelation implies the communication of a knowledge otherwise inaccessible to man, this does not mean that he could come to understand the content of faith in any other way, *alio modo*, than that by which every form of human knowledge is known, viz. by proceeding from created things.[36] Even though the way by which natural reason comes to the knowledge of God may be referred to as an ascent from created things to God, while the knowledge of God given by revelation moves, as it were, in Thomas's view, in an opposite direction, since it is not just a knowledge *about* but also a knowledge *from* God, yet there are not two separate ways but *eadem via est ascensus et descensus* (the way of descending is the same as the way of ascending).[37] In both cases, Thomas holds, a causal relation is ultimately involved, whether we begin methodologically with the cause—as in theology—in order to proceed from there to a study of its 'effects', or—as in philosophy—with the effects, in order to deduce from them the final cause. It is clear, however, that it is in this latter movement from effect to cause that the road is laid out that is then followed in both directions.[38] The all-inclusive causal scheme is determined by the structure appropriate to human reason and its mode of operation.

We have already given several examples of what this means concretely in terms of defining essential theological concepts or interpreting passages of scripture. Beyond providing a few additional illustrations we shall therefore be content simply to offer a brief résumé against the background of the argument so far presented in the present section.

It seems as though there may be at least one point at which our thesis concerning the essentially rational character of the structure of the relation between God and the world breaks down—viz. the metaphysics of existence. It may be appropriate, therefore, to discuss

[35] Gardeil, *La structure de l'âme*, p. XXIV.

[36] *In De Trin.* 6, 3: *quamvis per revelationem elevemur ad aliquid cognoscendum, quod alias esset nobis ignotum, non tamen ad hoc quod alio modo cognoscamus nisi per sensibilia. . . Et sic restat quod formae immateriales non sunt nobis notae cognitione quid est, sed solummodo cognitione an est, sive naturali ratione ex effectibus creaturarum sive etiam revelatione quae est per similitudines a sensibilibus sumptas.*

[37] *CG* IV, 1: *Quia vero naturalis ratio per creaturas in Dei cognitionem ascendit, fidei vero cognitio a Deo in nos e converso divina revelatione descendit; est autem eadem via ascensus et descensus.*

[38] Cf. Lyttkens, *Analogy*, p. 346. Lyttkens shows how Thomas's 'theological' way from God to things presupposes 'the road to God via creation'; and on p. 361 he refers to this as 'the main line of St. Thomas'.

this question once again in the present context. As we saw above, there is a difference between Thomas and the ancient philosophers at this point, since in Thomas *revelatio* or, more precisely, the biblical doctrine of creation, plays a determining part.[39] We may therefore establish first that what Thomas regards as the fundamental thesis of the metaphysics of existence—the definition of God as *ipsum esse*, in contrast to which the *esse* of all created things is seen as an *esse receptum*, or, to express it in a different way, that in God *esse* and *essentia* coincide, whereas in the case of things there is a real distinction—this fundamental thesis is not to be thought of as something in itself inaccessible to reason. Revelation is not absolutely necessary in order to know what is the relationship between God and the world. This knowledge we can gain from a study of the necessary dependence of existing things on a primary cause which does not derive its own existence *ab alio*. To be sure, we are speaking here of a knowledge given by revelation—just as revelation gives knowledge about much that is in principle accessible to reason—but it does not have to be revealed in order to be known. The statement made in Exodus 3:14[40] is not simply a proposition to be accepted on faith, but is rather a revealed confirmation of something which in principle can be attained by *ratio*. In the strict sense this truth has nothing to do with *fides*, but belongs rather to the *praeambula fidei*, the knowledge which is certainly necessary for salvation and is therefore revealed, but which is still within the scope of verifiable rational knowledge. The fundamental relation is in no way altered by the fact that the truth in question is difficult to attain and would hardly have been disclosed apart from revelation. Moreover, even if it could be said that from the standpoint of historic research the priority of the question of existence is determined by revelation, with regard to structure and therefore content the answer to the question is no less determined by *ratio*. We see this very clearly in the fact that Thomas regards the distinction between *esse* and *essentia* as a particular instance of the distinction which Aristotle had already made between act and potency, and includes it within this distinction. This represents a correction of an earlier metaphysic of essence, but the correction in no way destroys the conceptual structure which we find in the metaphysics of essence but rather fulfils the lines of thought developed within it. The new metaphysics differs in substance from

[39] See p. 139 above.
[40] Cf. e.g. the passage from *CG* I, 22, cited on p. 141.

the older in this respect that it conceives of God as the pure act of existence and every being as directly and utterly dependent upon him at every moment of its existence. From the historian's point of view it may be said that as a philosophical thesis this conception is based on the biblical doctrine of creation, but at the same time there is no essential relation between the two. This becomes clearer if we note in this connection that for Thomas the knowledge that the world has not always been in existence is given by *fides* and not by *ratio*. This truth lies beyond the sphere of reason, and is no more capable of being proved than the Trinity. Like the Trinity, too, it is made known only through revelation.[41] There may, indeed, be good grounds for holding such a truth and it may well be possible to connect it with the knowledge which is given to us by *ratio*, but it is not possible to adduce any compelling proof for it. The whole conceptual structure which we have referred to above as Thomas's metaphysics of existence is not altered in the slightest degree if we omit this truth, which is given only through revelation, and there is therefore no essential connection between the two. As we have seen,[42] the biblical concept of a temporal beginning is not in Thomas's view constitutive of the created relationship as such. The meaning of this relationship can be expressed clearly and univocally without using any such idea, since *creatio* expresses the essentially timeless causal relationship of dependence between things and God.[43]

It is above all, however, in the sphere of theological statements, to

---

[41] Cf. 1a, 46, 2: *quod mundum non semper fuisse, sola fide tenetur, et demonstrative probari non potest: sicut et supra de mysterio Trinitatis dictum est.*

[42] See p. 114ff. above.

[43] The relationship between God and the creature remains essentially the same if we reject the idea of one thing succeeding another which is inherent in the concept of time. Since the creational relationship is to be understood primarily as a causal relation, time is not a constitutive factor in the relation between God and the world; cf. Sertillanges, *La creation*, p. 251: 'La succession, et par suite le commencement, est accidentelle à la causalité'. Prenter is correct when, speaking of Thomas's interpretation of creation, he says in his *Thomismen*, p. 85: 'This stringent metaphysical "purification" of the idea of creation seems to have taken us far away from that of which we read in Genesis 1 and 2'. The whole problem is related to Thomas's interpretation of the meaning of divine perfection. In his understanding the category of time is wholly inappropriate to God, for it implies an imperfection with respect to God and therefore to eternity. We cannot therefore conceive of God as active *in* time. Seen as a divine act the act of creation is therefore eternal, and only its *effectus*, that which is created, can be said to be temporal, cf. p. 115f. above. This understanding clearly prevents Thomas from expressing the sense of the biblical writings, cf. Cullmann, *Christ and Time*, p. 63: 'Thus time and eternity share this time quality. Primitive Christianity knows nothing of a timeless God'.

which revelation alone gives access, that we may study how the rational starting-point determines the interpretation of traditional teaching.

Thus in his exposition of the *Trinity*, as we have already seen, Thomas begins by examining the functions of the human soul, *intelligere* and *velle*, and moves from here to what is admittedly only an analogical but nevertheless a real knowledge of the Son and Spirit as God's eternal *Verbum* and *Amor*.[44]

He defines the nature of *grace* in a similar way in terms of a pre-conceived view of the structure of the human soul. Grace perfects but also presupposes nature, the meaning of the perfection being determined by the definition of human nature given apart from *revelation*.[45]

In an analogous way Thomas also understands *salvation, salus*, primarily as a *perfectio rationalis creaturae* (the perfection of the rational creature),[46] or more precisely as a perfection of man's intellectual powers, *ultima autem salus hominis est ut secundum intellectivam partem perficiatur contemplatione Veritatis Primae* (the ultimate salvation of man is to be perfected in his intellective part by the contemplation of the original truth).[47] The synonymous term *blessedness* is therefore also defined as a *perfectio rationalis seu intellectualis naturae* (the perfection of a nature endowed with reason or intellect),[48] which is attained *cognoscendo et amando Deum*.[49]

Again, the meaning of *sin* is to be understood in the light of the fact that man is intended by nature to seek the good, *peccare nihil aliud est quam deficere a bono quod convenit alicui secundum suam naturam* (to sin is simply to fail in the good which belongs to any being according to its nature).[50] This is clearly stated by Thomas when he says that original sin implies a *deordinatio naturae* (disorder of nature).[51]

The *law*, which expresses the true *ordo* of nature, is accordingly understood by Thomas to be defined by man's *ratio*. Its commands are seen to be good by their correspondence to reason.[52] This is also

---

[44] See p. 143ff. above. [45] See p. 175 and 190 above.
[46] See especially 2a2ae, 2, 3, where *salus* and *perfectio* are used throughout as interchangeable terms. Cf. p. 36 above.
[47] *CG* IV, 42. [48] 1a, 62, 1; cf. especially also 1a, 26, 1.
[49] 1a2ae, 1, 8. [50] 1a2ae, 109, 2, ad 2.
[51] 3a, 86, 2, ad 1; see also the references cited on p. 175 above, footnote 50.
[52] 1a2ae, 98, 1: *ita etiam lex aliqua ostenditur esse bona ex eo quod consonat rationi;* cf. 1a2ae, 71, 2: *id quod est contra ordinem rationis, proprie est contra naturam hominis inquantum est homo; quod autem est secundum rationem, est secundum naturam hominis inquantum est homo.*

true in principle with regard to the revealed law which, like grace, is indeed *supra naturam* (above nature), but is not therefore in any way *contra naturam* (contrary to nature).[53] Thus it is ultimately reason which for Thomas constitutes the norm for what is good or bad.[54]

It is also the rational definition of *good* in particular which is of crucial importance in Thomas's theology. 'Goodness' is always understood as a synonym for *perfectio*, perfection in a metaphysical sense. As the sum of all perfection God is also therefore to be defined as *summum bonum*. As we have already seen, this means that we cannot attribute any imperfection to God, not even statements which we find applied to him in scripture.[55]

The consequence of this is a certain ambivalent tension between *ratio* and *revelatio* of which, as far as we can judge, Thomas himself was not aware, for it is evident that this particular definition of the nature of the divine goodness means that we can express particular biblical concepts and motifs only with the greatest difficulty.

[53] Thomas states that, like grace, the law which is given by God is necessary, not because natural law is distorted or wrong but because God has set a goal before man which is far beyond his natural capacities and the *lex naturalis*, which is congruous with nature, is incapable of bringing him to this goal, see 1a2ae, 91, 4.

[54] 1a2ae, 90, 1: *Regula autem et mensura humanorum actuum est ratio;* 1a2ae, 91, 2: *lumen rationis naturalis, quo discernimus quid sit bonum et malum;* 1a2ae, 94, 2: *omnia illa ad quae homo habet naturalem inclinationem, ratio naturaliter apprehendit ut bona, et per consequens ut opere prosequenda, et contraria eorum ut mala et vitanda. Secundum igitur ordinem inclinationum naturalium, est ordo praeceptorum legis naturae.*

[55] For example, statements which refer to God as 'coming near' us, or 'repenting', or being 'angry'—these, Thomas holds, can be applied to God only *metaphorice*, since it is inconceivable, if we accept Thomas's presuppositions, to hold that there is anything in the divine nature which corresponds to what these terms imply. Hence the term 'wrath' cannot *proprie* be used of God, while 'goodness' on the other hand presents no difficulties from the standpoint of his system, since it can be interpreted without difficulty as a synonym of perfection in an ontological sense, see p. 120f. above. Perhaps it is in this light that we are to understand why, as Mersch, *Mystical Body*, p. 249ff. and Rondet, *RSR* 38 (1951), p. 158, footnote 25, and others have pointed out, the concept of satisfaction in its Anselmic form comes to have less and less importance in the theology of Thomas and in the *Summa* is clearly subordinated to the idea of the instrumental and efficient causality of Christ's human nature. Rejecting the idea of God's anger at sin, Thomas adopts the idea of satisfaction, not for systematic doctrinal reasons but because it belongs to the traditional teaching. It is also significant that Thomas does not regard sin as an offence against God, and in this too he differs from Anselm. God in his transcendent perfection cannot be affected by sin; sin is something rather that does injury primarily to the sinner himself, cf. Mersch, *Mystical Body*, p. 253: 'God is offended, not in the way a man is wounded or impoverished by the crime of another, but in the way the absolutely Transcendent can be touched: by the violence done to his creature, by the injury the sinner does to himself'.

Since we see this especially in his doctrine of grace and Christology, we shall discuss one or two examples which are related to our earlier discussion of God's presence in the world. As we have already shown,[56] Thomas defines divine love in terms of self-love. When, however, we posit this love of God, because of his absolute onto-logical perfection this love is entirely free of any of the selfishness which always characterises human love. For the same reason when God's love extends to include the created world it is experienced as a gracious creation and gift which 'seeks not its own'. God does not gain anything either by creating or by his activity in grace and the incarnation—the only one who 'gains' anything is man, who comes to perfection through this activity of God. Thomas here expresses essential aspects of the New Testament concept of love. But at the same time this whole conception of love is determined by the fact that God's love, as he understands it, must be understood in the first place on the analogy of human love as a love for itself and its own perfection. The 'centripetal' aspect which we see in the divine love of the godhead itself[57] remains even when it reaches out to include the creature, and therefore comes to be the mark of its relationship to God at every point. This constitutes the structure of finality which, as we saw over and over again in our discussion above, characterises the creature's *ordo ad Deum*, for *ex hoc quod Deus seipso fruitur, alia in se dirigit* (by reason of God's enjoyment of himself, he directs other things towards himself).[58] But this is related in turn to the fact that Thomas takes as the starting-point of his discussion of love a philosophical anthropology which regards self-love as the basic form of all love.

However, this 'centripetal' interpretation of the divine activity in creation and redemption means that other motifs, which are essential for an understanding of the New Testament view of divine love, cannot, or can only with great difficulty, be expressed.

We found a typical example of this in the previous chapter, where we discussed at some length Thomas's interpretation of the 'sending' of the persons of the godhead into the world. If we compare the language of the Bible to what Thomas says concerning the *missio invisibilis*, we find something quite peculiar to Thomas. When the New Testament refers to the sending of the Spirit, it uses a term of movement *about the Spirit himself* which clearly has reference to a movement out towards men, as, for instance, when Jesus promises to

[56] See p. 105 and 109 above.   [57] Cf. p. 146 above.   [58] *De Ver.* 22, 1, ad 11.

send the Helper to his disciples after he has left them (John 15:26, 16:7). In Thomas, on the other hand, the term *missio* denotes something that takes place *in man* and the movement, as it were, is in the other direction, from man to God, so that what occurs in the *missio invisibilis* is properly speaking an elevation of human nature.[59] The same sequence is also found in the incarnation. Thomas interprets God's sending of his Son into the world essentially as an *elevatio humanae naturae*, and the term which he prefers to use to express this is *assumptio*.[60]

It should be noted, however, that it is not only the biblical passages which appear to speak of a 'movement' in a local sense that present difficulties for Thomas. Statements of this type occur in his scheme in some form or another; he still speaks of 'movement', though no longer in the sense of a movement by God to the creature, but rather of the *elevatio* of the creature to God. A much greater difficulty is presented by the purely qualitative definitions of the incarnation as God's 'giving of himself for others', and parallel expressions. These cannot be applied to God, since they contradict Thomas's definition of divine goodness.[61] God can have no other purpose for his activity than his own perfection.[62] To 'be poor' or to 'give himself for others' cannot therefore tell us anything of *God's* nature as it is expressed in the incarnation, but must refer to Christ's human nature.[63] But here, too, essentially the same difficulty arises, since what occurs in the union of the divine Word with human nature is an act of absolute

[59] See the whole discussion on this question on p. 183ff.

[60] Cf. p. 225ff. above. There is a direct parallel here to a point discussed earlier on p. 125ff. Thomas holds that biblical statements which in his view imply imperfection in God actually refer to something which takes place in the creature, and these are improperly applied to God. Another example where Thomas expresses this in a striking way is his interpretation of Rom. 8:26, where Paul says (in the Vulgate translation), *ipse Spiritus postulat pro nobis*. Thomas again interprets what is said of the Spirit as a statement about man's own *postulatio*, viz. that its ultimate source is God. See e.g. *In ad Rom.* 8, 5 (692–93): *Et ideo exponendum est 'postulat', id est postulantes nos facit. . . Facit autem Spiritus Sanctus nos postulare, inquantum in nobis recta desideria causat;* cf. ib. (694): *Deus . . . scit . . . 'quid desideret Spiritus', id est, quid desiderare nos faciat; CG* IV, 23: *hoc modo dicitur quod Spiritus Sanctus 'postulat', quia postulantes facit: facit enim amorem Dei in cordibus nostris, ex quo desideramus ipso frui, et desiderantes postulamus;* see also *In ad Gal.* 4, 3 (215).

[61] In his *Filosofi och motivforskning* Nygren compares Thomas and Luther in their interpretation of the nature of the love of God, and, as we might expect, it is the interpretation of the term *bonitas* which clearly distinguishes the two.

[62] Cf. *De Pot.* 3, 15, ad 14: *communicatio bonitatis non est ultimus finis, sed ipsa divina bonitas.*

[63] See e.g. Thomas's interpretation of Phil. 2:7ff. on p. 222, footnote 145.

perfection, and is therefore the opposite of any 'giving' or 'emptying' of himself. The difficulty which Thomas finds in expressing adequately certain passages of the New Testament in terms of his preconceived definition of goodness and perfection may be illustrated in various ways,[64] but we shall content ourselves with a single illuminating example. We refer to Thomas's exposition of passages such as II Corinthians 5:21, Galatians 3:13 and I Peter 2:24. Christ, who *debebat esse maxime a peccatoribus segregatus* (ought especially to be separated from sinners),[65] cannot be said to have been 'made sin'. The meaning must rather be, says Thomas, that he was smitten by the *poena peccati* (punishment for sin), i.e. suffering and death.[66] But these *defectus*, he argues, in themselves have nothing to do with sin, but are rather a consequence of man's nature as *ex contrariis compositum* (composed of contrary elements),[67] even though sin is a factor in redemption. Sin is inherently unnatural, a *deordinatio naturae* (disordering of nature),[68] and therefore Christ can no more

---

[64] Since as man Christ was *perfectus homo*, it is impossible, as Thomas understands it, so interpret the statement in Luke 2:52 that Jesus increased in wisdom and favour with God and man in its literal sense. He treats this text in exactly the same way as he treats other statements about God, see p. 120. The statement in Luke cannot, he holds, refer to anything that took place in Jesus himself, but rather to something that occurred in those around him who 'increased in wisdom' as a result of his teaching, see *Compend. Theol.* 216: *profectus sapientiae Christi dicatur non quo ipse fit sapientior, sed quo sapientia proficiebat in aliis, quia scilicet per ejus sapientiam magis ac magis instruebantur;* see also p. 205 above, footnote 68. When Jesus says (Mark 13:32) that the Son has no knowledge of the last day, this means, Thomas says,—and for the same reason—that though Christ was well aware of it, he chose not to reveal it to the disciples, see 3a, 10, 2, ad 1. Cf. the comment by Schwalm, *Le Christ*, p. 191: 'le Fils déclare ignorer ce jour parce qu'il ne veut pas nous l'indiquer. Ainsi nous disons, pour nous dérober à une question indiscrète, pour garder un secret qu'on nous a confié: Je n'en sais rien'. Cf. also, as we have shown on p. 217, how for Thomas the crucifixion cannot as such reveal but rather conceals the nature of God, or the difficulties which he finds in dealing with the temptation narratives, see p. 211, footnote 102.

[65] 3a, 4, 6, ad 3.

[66] Cf. 3a, 15, 1, ad 4; 3a, 46, 4, ad 3; *In symbolum Apostolorum* 4. On the other hand it is inconceivable to Thomas that Christ, who as man was *beatus*, could in any way have suffered condemnation. His suffering on the cross meant that he underwent the *poena sensus*. but it did not involve the *poena damni*, see 3a, 1, 4, obi. 2 and ad 2.

[67] See e.g. III *Sent.* 16, 1, 1; *In ad Heb.* 9, 5 (475); 1a2ae, 85, 6; 3a, 14, 3, ad 2; 3a, 14, 4. Since the soul is *incorruptibilis*, death for Thomas means simply the dissolution of the body and its separation from the soul.

[68] III *Sent.* 16, 1, 1, ad 2: *peccatum non inest homini ex aliquo principiorum naturalium, immo est contra naturam rationis. Unde non est simile de peccato et morte quae ex principio materiali consequitur;* 1a2ae, 94, 3, ad 2: *omnia peccata, inquantum sunt contra rationem, sunt etiam contra naturam;* see also the references given on p. 175, footnote 50.

have any sin of his own than he can appropriate or make his own the sin and guilt of *others*. But death is intrinsic to man's nature as such, for man, as Thomas defines him, is *animal rationale mortale* (a rational mortal animal)[69] and *mors in hominibus semper est naturalis* (death in man is always natural).[70] According to another line of thought which we find in Thomas, Christ is said to be 'made sin' or a 'curse' *non quia sit, sed quia opinantur homines ita esse* (not because he is, but because men think that he is).[71] There is consequently no reality corresponding to this language, but simply an *opinio hominum, et praecipue Iudaeorum, qui reputabant eum peccatorem* (opinion of men, and especially of the Jews, who reckoned him a sinner).[72] That Christ should have borne or appropriated our sin and guilt is clearly an idea which Thomas, because of his presuppositions, cannot express. It is ultimately an impossibility. He does hold that as man Christ submitted to the conditions of sin, but only to certain of these, viz. to those which are inherent in man's nature as such and do not contradict Thomas's interpretation of goodness and divine love. But as we have seen,[73] even these 'defects' might have been laid aside in principle, since Christ's human nature manifests the *finis supernaturalis* of blessedness, and they are contingent on a special intervention of God, miraculous in character.

It is also clear from this, however, that the *scopus* from which Thomas approaches the texts in question forces him to adopt an an interpretation which at essential points contradicts ideas expressed in these passages. It is clear, too, that in spite of his stated intention in this area, he is unable to express the meaning,[74] *sensus*, of these statements. Manifestly, the formal scriptural principle does not of itself guarantee a truly biblical theology. We can see this most clearly in his Christology, and it is significant in this connection that the criticism which is sometimes made of scholastic Christology in recent Roman Catholic thought has its origin in biblical theology.[75]

---

[69] 1a, 29, 4, ad 2; see also p. 175 above, footnote 52.
[70] *In Joan.* 10, 4 (5). If grace had not been given to man, death would therefore have been *a defectus naturalis* before the fall. Since sin meant that the gift of grace was lost, the death which had been latent was released. This death is also, therefore, though only accidentally, a *poena*, see 1a2ae, 85, 5 and III *Sent.* 16, 1, 1, ad 5.
[71] *In 2 ad Cor.* 5, 5 (201).   [72] *In ad Gal.* 3, 5 (148).
[73] See p. 213ff. above.   [74] See p. 83f. above.
[75] See especially K. Rahner, 'Current problems in Christology', in *Theological Investigations*, vol. I; *God, Christ, Mary and Grace*, Baltimore and London 1961, p. 149ff. Cf. Rahner's prefatory statement on p. 154: '*Biblical theology . . .* should be the source of dogmatic theology and so also of Christology', and his criticism

We find here a dialectical mode of thought which can be traced throughout Thomas's writings. On the one hand, the content of scripture is normative in the formulation of theology. It is so, however, not only in the sense that it is the basic material on which Thomas builds as a theologian and which he amplifies by interpretation[76]—*sacra doctrina* therefore deals with truths unknown to philosophy. As Thomas sets about his theological task, moreover, and tries to give expression to patterns of thought which are essential

of scholastic theology on p. 168: 'If anyone were to attempt to discover the Biblical foundation of scholastic Christology, he would reach the conclusion, which does not seem false or unjust, that it contrives to get along with a handful of texts from the Bible. Its predetermined goal is the dogma of Ephesus and Chalcedon and nothing more. The only texts from Scripture, whether they are sayings of Christ himself or appear in the teachings of the Apostles, in which it is interested are those which can be translated as directly as possible into the terms of classical metaphysical Christology'. For Rahner's criticism see e.g. p. 176: '*He* is not a man as *I* am a man. For I am a man in such a way that the I, the person itself, becomes human through my human-being; this is its own lot, it does not itself remain untouched. And that is just what one cannot say about the Logos of God, according to just this doctrine of faith', or p. 177, where Rahner quotes the statement, 'One of the most holy Trinity has suffered', and says, 'we are bound to speak like this and . . . the whole truth, the single unique truth of Christianity, is contained in it', while according to the scheme of scholastic Christology this means that God 'only made just *another* human reality weep and die, and thus himself remains the Holy One, serenely exalted above death'. Cf. the author's comment on the same page: 'When what is to be redeemed happens to the Redeemer, then it is itself redeemed. But does it really happen to him, when he remains untouched by the lot of what is to be redeemed?' On p. 184 the author raises the crucial question of whether we should not sketch the outlines of a theological anthropology from the starting-point of Christology rather than the other way around, and therefore 'conceive our human selves in terms of that Man who as such is God's presence for us, existent in the world'.

---

[76] The fact that the tension in Thomas's theology between *ratio* and *revelatio* is seen more clearly today in discussing the meaning of *salvation* rather than the *relation between the Creator and the creature* may well be bound up with the fact that the metaphysics of existence, which expresses this latter *relatio* and at the same time defines the basic view which Thomas holds of the relation between God and the world, may in one sense be regarded primarily as a union of Greek thought and elements drawn from the Old Testament. We get the impression that Thomas's view of Christianity has a greater affinity with Old Testament lines of thought than with New Testament ideas. We could therefore say that Thomas interprets salvation in terms of creation, or, rather, in terms of a particular view of the creational relationship—or, to put it in a different way, he interprets salvation in terms of the Old Testament rather than the New. The dominant importance which he assigns to the *law* in his interpretation of the Christian's relation to God also points in the same direction. Even the gospel itself is interpreted by Thomas in categories of the law (*lex nova, lex Evangelii,* see the whole of 1a2ae, 106–109), though 'law', as Thomas understands it, is something quite different from the Old Testament concept.

to scripture, his earlier metaphysical outlook becomes sharpened and cast into a new form as a consequence of his theological work. On the other hand, he discusses these biblical ideas in continuity with a metaphysics which is alien to the Bible, but he does so in such a way that he fails to express—or, at least, expresses with the greatest difficulty—other central thoughts and motifs of scripture since if these were really allowed to speak their own distinctive word, they would destroy the structure of thought which in the last resort gives Thomas's synthesis its unity and cohesion. We have just seen how the new metaphysical orientation, which produces the metaphysics of existence, is determined ultimately by the biblical conception of creation, and therefore Thomas has expressed the essential core of this concept—God's sovereign and active presence in the world—as he has also faithfully conveyed the meaning of the doctrine of grace—the outgiving love and the idea that everything comes from God—yet he is at variance with the biblical teachings which he seeks to express, for he interprets them ultimately in such a way that they come into conflict with other biblical concepts, particularly in the New Testament, and most obviously with the doctrine of the incarnation. He defines the nature of God in such a way that it becomes impossible for him to express in it terms of a self-giving or a being made man—any such ideas, Thomas holds, would disrupt and ultimately destroy the causal relation between God and man. Where such ideas do appear in scripture, Thomas is forced by his presuppositions to reformulate them,[77] for the causal relation itself assumes that there is an insuperable *diversitas* between divine and human—*hoc nomen 'causa' videtur importare diversitatem substantiae, et dependentiam alicuius ab altero* (this term 'cause' seems to mean diversity of substance and dependence of one on another).[78] God can be *in* humanity only as the absolutely transcendent cause is in its utterly dependent effect.

Thomas's theology is a synthesis which at every point is constituted by a profound interrelationship between *ratio* and *revelatio*. He makes

[77] This has very seldom been noted in works on Thomas, and then usually as a purely peripheral matter only, see e.g. Chenu, *Saint Thomas*, p. 241f. After stating that 'the discovery of Greek philosophy' implied for theology 'not only instrumentation of an admirable kind but a conception of nature, man, and reason', Chenu also suggests in passing that 'the engagement of reason will at times compromise the unadulterable freedom of the word of God'. See the same author's 'Vocabulaire biblique et vocabulaire théologique', in *Nouvelle revue théologique* 74 (1952), p. 1029ff.
[78] 1a, 33, 1, ad 1.

use of elements derived from Greek thought in order to give expression to biblical concepts and motifs, and his attempt to create a synthesis is expressed, as we have seen, in the correction which each brings to the other. The correction of Greek metaphysics is to be seen in his rejection of certain alternatives which appear in the Greek philosophical tradition and the development of certain of its propositions, but even the content of revelation is subject to correction at crucial points, since there is a danger that it could destroy the conceptual framework. The theology of Thomas represents a fusion of quite different elements, and while this makes it necessary to identify and distinguish its constituent parts, any attempt—in line with prevailing definitions of Greek or biblical and Hebraic lines of thought—to attach primary significance in his theology either to *ratio* or to *revelatio* would be misleading. The relation can best be explained by reference to two recent writers. We have already[79] quoted O. C. Quick's interpretation of the essential contrast between Greek and Hebrew thought, and this may help us also to understand the relationship of revelation and reason in Thomas. According to Quick, salvation for the Greek is obtained by gaining knowledge of an eternal and unchangeable reality, while salvation for the Jew is given through 'the action of a living God'. It is clear, therefore, that we cannot get to the heart of Thomas's thought simply by identifying his approach with one or other of these alternatives. It is characteristic of Thomas that these are not alternatives but are in fact a conceptual unity. Salvation is indeed given through knowledge of an eternal, unchangeable reality, viz. the knowledge of God, which is given by *revelatio*, but this knowledge does not in fact come through human study or effort, but is given rather through 'the action of a living God'. We find the same point expressed in another work by Anders Nygren, who sees two different conceptions of revelation within the Christian tradition—first, the *active* concept of *biblical realism* and second, the *intellectual* concept, this latter being, he holds, a legacy of Greek thought. The former concept is designated by Nygren 'dynamic', the latter 'static'.[80] This distinction does indeed express the essential contrast between biblical and Greek thought in general, but it is no more possible here than it is in the case of Quick

---

[79] See p. 253.
[80] See A. Nygren, 'Uppenbarelsen och Skriften', in *En bok om bibeln*, Lund 1947, p. 85ff. Cf. also the contrast which Boman, *Das hebräische Denken*, p. 18ff., makes between 'dynamisches und statisches Denken'.

simply to identify Thomas's idea of revelation with one or other of these alternatives. In a peculiar way his concept is at one time both *intellectual* and *dynamic*. For Thomas revelation is primarily a work of God, something which 'comes from God', and occurs in the world in a truly real way, but at the same time he conceives of this divine *actio* entirely in cognitive terms as a form of communicated knowledge. The theological synthesis which Thomas constructs is thoroughly dynamic, and on any reasonable view can hardly be termed 'static'. But this does not mean that this dynamic character is merely an adaptation of the biblical view any more than his characteristic theological concept of finality could in any way be said to conform to the movement of redemptive history in the Bible to an eschatological goal, even though it may be said that the former is in one sense an expression of the latter.[81]

All of this will show us that it is far too easy a solution of the problematical question before us simply to define the function exercised by reason in Thomas's synthesis by reference to the scheme of question and answer which is sometimes employed and in which the question is usually stated to have been raised by *ratio*, viz. by ancient philosophy, while the answer to this philosophical question is stated to be derived from the traditional Christian faith, viz. from *revelatio*.[82] It is only too obvious that one might just as well say that traditional Christian faith raises the problem which is to be answered by philosophy, and that it is therefore *ratio* that provides the answer to the question posed by *revelatio*.[83] To speak of Thomas's metaphysics of existence as the philosophical answer to the question raised by the biblical idea of creation would be an illustration of this. But what ultimately makes this simple solution inadequate is that in Thomas 'question' and 'answer' are both alike controlled by the synthesis, and therefore it is not possible to isolate *ratio* and *revelatio* by assigning them to different parts of the definition. In this particular

[81] When Congar, therefore, maintains (in his Letter of introduction to van Ackeren's *Sacra doctrina*, p. 16) that there is a conformity between Thomas's concept of finality and what is spoken of in modern theology as 'eschatology' and 'Heilsgeschichte', his arguments must be rejected as misleading and indeed concealing the very profound problem which the relation between biblical and Greek elements of thought in fact presents in Thomas's theology.

[82] See e.g. Nygren, *Agape and Eros*, p. 626f. or Johannesson, *Person och gemenskap*, p. 10.

[83] Cf. Gilson, *God and Philosophy*, p. 110: 'Coming after the Greeks, the Christian philosophers had asked themselves the question: How obtain from Greek metaphysics an answer to the problems raised by the Christian God'.

example, therefore, even though the question itself may be said to have its origin in revelation, it is so narrowly conceived that in the answer essential aspects of the biblical conception are simply not brought out, e.g. the temporal element. We discover a similar problem if we turn to the central theological question with which Thomas is concerned, viz. the question of the knowledge of God, and it is this cognitive aspect which we find throughout Thomas's theology. We find it expressed both in his definition of theology as a *scientia* and in his statement that the primary task of theological instruction is to *Dei cognitionem tradere*,[84] but it also means that revelation itself is to be regarded primarily as a communication of knowledge—*primo et principaliter consistit in cognitione* (first and chiefly consists in knowledge).[85] When Gardeil says that 'if supranatural life exists, it must begin with a question of information', and then goes on to say: 'this information . . . *is* revelation',[86] he is simply expressing this fundamental emphasis of Thomas. But even though it may be quite correct to maintain that the central theological question in Thomas is the *knowledge of God*, we might equally well maintain that it is *man's salvation* that is central. As we have seen, Thomas speaks of the central object of faith as *ultimus finis hominis*, and this is the axle around which his whole theological discussion revolves. We might say, therefore, that for Thomas ultimately the question of knowledge and the question of salvation constitute a unity. It is clear from this, however, that Thomas is not simply referring to *any* knowledge or to *any* salvation—he is speaking of *God*, who deals with men in accordance with the biblical revelation. For Thomas, then, the central theological question is not that of the quest of the self-sufficient man to attain his own perfection but rather the revelation provided by God and the absolute dependence on God of those who have received this illumination for their salvation. The central issue, in other words, is salvation by *grace*, and apart from revelation, the question of grace would never have been raised. This means that the question itself is already determined in its very formulation by *revelatio* in such a way that it cannot simply be identified with the view of salvation which is found in Greek philosophy, even though there are obvious affinities between the two. Our study has shown perhaps that the answer which Thomas provides to the questions raised by salvation is governed by his synthesis—theology does indeed deal with the salvation

---

[84] 1a, 2, introd.   [85] 2a2ae, 171, 1.
[86] Gardeil, *La structure de l'âme*, p. 327f.

U

of which the Bible speaks and which originates with God and is accomplished by him—and in this sense we may say that the answer is given in *revelatio*—but at the same time Thomas formulates the question in such a way that he interprets the content of revelation from the first by use of categories of Greek thought and so under. stands revelation as a description of man's *finis supernaturalis*.

If we are unable to establish such a correlation between *ratio* and *revelatio*, this is simply because we cannot trace Thomas's theology back to one or other of these components, but rather to an element already determined by the synthesis, viz. *fides*. As *fides quae creditur* (faith which is believed) faith is determined by its object, revelation, but at the same time as *fides qua creditur* (faith by which we believe) it is determined by the structure and cognitive purpose provided by reason, for Thomas speaks of faith as an *actus intellectus*. This faith, in which the lines from *ratio* and *revelatio* thus coincide, is the point from which theology begins, and therefore theology itself is also a synthesis in which the two basic components, interacting continually upon one another, combine to form a total unit.

Therefore, even though it does not seem possible to define Thomas's view of the Christian faith in terms of *ratio* alone, just as any differentiation among its component parts in terms of 'question' and 'answer' is ultimately misleading, it may be possible for us to indicate which function *within* the synthesis belongs to *ratio* and which to *revelatio*.

We may conveniently start from our earlier[87] conclusion that the relation between the two can be seen as a particular instance or variant of the general relation between nature and grace which Thomas assumes in his theology. Grace cannot be derived as such from nature, but presupposes and is primarily to be regarded as a perfection and elevation of nature. As we have shown above,[88] this means that the meaning of grace is ultimately dependent on what is already known about human nature. By analogy, the gift of grace that is revelation cannot be derived from human reason, for it cannot be brought about by any human effort. The content of revelation does not therefore coincide with *ratio* but is something new and unexpected from the standpoint of reason. Human reason cannot of itself come to an understanding of the truths which are communicated in revelation, for instance, that God is triune in his being or that he has called men to an end which infinitely transcends

[87] See p. 229f.   [88] See p. 175f., 190 and 283.

the *facultas naturae* (scope of nature), and that this end is in fact realised and made possible for man to attain through the assumption of human nature by the divine Word for the sake of man's salvation. Just as grace, on account of man's situation after the fall, is experienced as a *gratia sanans* (healing grace), so too the knowledge which us given by revelation does not simply mean a completion but also a correction of the content of the natural knowledge of God. It is then incorporated into theology as a basis, confirmed by revelation, on which the theologian may continue to build. But revelation does not imply any correction of the structure which characterises the work of *ratio*. Just as grace is defined as a perfection of nature and is to be understood in terms of nature, so the new knowledge given through revelation is regarded by Thomas as an extension of knowledge gained through reason and is presupposed to follow and fulfil the lines of thought which are found in natural knowledge. So if it can be said that in Thomas's synthesis revelation primarily determines *content*, it is *ratio* that provides the structure which determines his theology. By itself, reason cannot speak of *what* God is and what he will do for man's salvation, but when this is disclosed by revelation the presupposition is that the divine activity will operate according to a rational scheme, and therefore *how* God will act is ultimately determined by this presupposition. That the divine activity does operate according to nature is of crucial importance from the standpoint of theology, for the *meaning* of a statement or a concept is determined in a mode of thought through the lines by which this structure of thought as a whole is determined. Revelation keeps these lines from forming a closed circle and causes them, as it were, to remain 'open', since God, being sovereign and transcendent, will always in the end evade any attempt to explain his nature, and therefore cannot be included in the *ordo* of existence as a 'thing'. But this does not alter the actual structure of Thomas's scheme, which takes its starting-point in an *a priori* conception of human nature and its intrinsic striving for perfection that is independent of revelation. We have seen above how this prior assumption permeates and controls his interpretation of every major theological concept.

The decisive function which *ratio* fulfils in *sacra doctrina* has its direct counterpart in Thomas's own primary definition of the meaning of revelation, and at this point we may refer once more to the discussion of his concept of revelation with which our work began. For Thomas, revelation, like any other act of cognition, implies receptivity, the receiving of knowledge, *acceptio cognitorum*, but it also has an active aspect, the systematising, interpretation and evaluation of what is given, *iudicium de acceptis*, and of these two aspects it is the latter which he emphasises.[89] *Revelatio* sharpens the interpretative capacity of the natural light of reason by a *lumen infusum, ex quo intellectus roboratur ad iudicandum* (light shed on us which gives the understanding strength to judge).[90] There may be new *species* of knowledge given directly by God, but revelation is essentially the new *light* which is given in the form of a confirmation and sharpening of the intellect of those who receive the revelation. *Revelatio*, therefore, does not come *from ratio*, but is given *in and in accordance with ratio*, for revelation does not alter man's natural reason except by bringing what it contains to fuller perfection. So it is not only the new cognitive content given by revelation which receives its meaning from the rational starting-point, but ultimately also revelation itself.

If it is *revelatio* which primarily determines the content of *sacra doctrina* it is *ratio* which primarily determines its structure, and therefore it is *ratio* which gives unity to the whole system of ideas. The decisive part played by revelation in its own sphere is to be explained by the fact that it is man's *salvation* that is absolutely central in the structure of Thomas's thought—for salvation is first made possible through *revelatio*—while the crucial function fulfilled by *ratio* is dependent on the fact that the salvation of *man* is pivotal in Thomas, and he defines man *a priori* in terms of philosophical anthropology as an intellectual being who reaches his perfection by gaining knowledge. Therefore, the new question introduced by revelation regarding salvation is now, by inner necessity, equivalent to a search for *knowledge*. Unity is given to the whole system of ideas by *ratio* simply because both *sacra doctrina* and its components, *ratio* and *revelatio*, are all included in and correlated by the common denominator of knowledge. The cognitive aspect implied in taking *fides* as the starting-point is emphasised by the fact that Thomas regards theology as a *scientia*, and in this sense therefore a continuous line extends from natural knowledge, through the imperfect anticipation of the beatific vision in theology, to the *beatitudo* which is man's final end, and which at the one time represents the fullness of knowledge, man's own highest perfection as an intellectual being, and the absolute climax of revelation. The uniform interpretation of

---

[89] See also p. 22ff. above.   [90] *De Ver.* 12, 7.

reality determined by Thomas's choice of a rational starting-point and expressed in the concept of knowledge on every plane is the source ultimately not only of the difficulty which Thomas finds in expounding central passages of the Bible but also of the magnificent harmonic unity which characterises his theology.

ABBREVIATIONS

AHDLMA	=*Archives d'histoire doctrinale et littéraire du moyen âge*
ALKMA	=*Archiv für Literatur- und Kirchengeschichte des Mittelalters*
AT	=*L'année théologique*
ATA	=*L'année théologique augustinienne*
BGPM	=Beiträge zur Geschichte der Philosophie des Mittelalters
BT	=*Bulletin thomiste*
CAG	=Conférence Albert-le-Grand
DTC	=*Dictionnaire de théologie catholique*
EP	=Essais philosophiques
EPM	=Études de philosophie médiévale
ETL	=*Ephemerides theologicae lovanienses*
FFD	=*Festschrift Franz Dornseiff*
FJN	=*Festskrift til Jens Nørregaard*
MAP	=*Mélanges Auguste Pelzer*
MFC	=*Mélanges offerts au R. P. Ferdinand Cavallera*
MJM	=*Mélanges Joseph Maréchal*
ML-SP	=Museum lessianum, Section philosophique
ML-ST	=Museum lessianum, Section théologique
MPL	=*Patrologiae cursus completus . . . series latina*, ed. J. P. Migne
MT	=*Mélanges thomistes*
PL	=*Positions luthériennes*
RB	=*Revue biblique*
RSPT	=*Revue des sciences philosophiques et théologiques*
RSR	=*Recherches de science religieuse*
RT	=*Revue thomiste*
RUO	=*Revue de l'université d'Ottawa*
SE	=*Sciences ecclésiastiques*
STK	=*Svensk teologisk kvartalskrift*
WA	=Weimarer Ausgabe

BIBLIOGRAPHY

1. TEXTS

Thomas Aquinas

Summa theologiae . . . *cum textu ex recensione Leonina*, Turin and Rome, 1948.
Summa contra gentiles . . . *editio Leonina manualis*, Rome 1934.
Scriptum super libros sententiarum Magistri Petri Lombardi, vols. I–II ed. by R. P. Mandonnet, vols. III–IV ed. by M. F. Moos, Paris 1929–1947.
Quaestiones disputatae, vol. I, *De Veritate*, ed. by R. Spiazzi, Editio VIII revisa, Turin and Rome 1949
Expositio super librum Boethii de Trinitate, ed. by B. Decker, Leiden 1955
Le 'De ente et essentia' de S. Thomas d'Aquin. Texte établi d'après les manuscrits parisiens. Introduction, notes et études historiques par M.-D. Roland-Gosselin (Bibliothèque thomiste 8), Paris 1948
Super Epistolas S. Pauli lectura I–II, ed. by R. Cai, Editio VIII revisa, Turin and Rome 1953
Quotations from other writings of Thomas have been taken from the Parma ed., i.e. *S. Thomas opera omnia*, 25 vols. (Parma 1852–1873, new photolithographic ed. New York 1948–1950)

Bonaventura

Opera omnia . . . 10 vols. Edita studio et cura PP. Collegii a S. Bonaventura. Ad Claras Aquas (Quaracchi ed.) 1882–1902

Other scholastic writers

Patrologiae cursus completus . . . *series latina*, ed. by J. P. Migne, Paris 1844–1864

Martin Luther

D. Martin Luthers Werke. Kritische Gesamtausgabe (Weimarer Ausgabe), ed. K. Knaake and others, Weimar 1883–1963

299

2. STUDIES

Ackeren, G. F. van, *Sacra doctrina. The Subject of the First Question of the Summa Theologica of St. Thomas Aquinas*, Rome 1952

Aubert, R., *La théologie catholique au milieu du XXe siècle*, Tournai and Paris 1954

Aulén, G., *Den kristna gudsbilden genom seklerna och i nutiden. En konturteckning*, Stockholm 1927

——, 'Kristendom och idealism', in *Svensk teologisk kvartalskrift* 8 (1932), p. 3–40.

Backes, I., *Die Christologie des hl. Thomas von Aquin und die griechischen Kirchenväter* (Forschungen zur christlichen Literatur- und Dogmengeschichte 17:3/4), Paderborn 1931

Baillie, D. M., *God was in Christ. An Esssay on Incarnation and Atonement*, 2nd ed. London 1948

Baroni, V., *La contre-réforme devant la bible. La question biblique*, Lausanne 1943

Barth, K., *Die kirchliche Dogmatik* I: 1, 5th ed., Zollikon—Zürich 1947 (ET *Church Dogmatics*, vol. I, *The Doctrine of the Word of God*, part 1, 3rd impr. Edinburgh 1955)

Bartmann, B., *Lehrbuch der Dogmatik*, vols. I and II, 8th ed. Freiburg im Breisgau 1932

Bernard, R., see: Thomas Aquinas

Beumer, J., 'Das katholische Schriftprinzip in der theologischen Literatur der Scholastik bis zur Reformation', in *Scholastik* 16 (1941), p. 24–52

Billing, E., *De etiska tankarna i urkristendomen i deras samband med dess religiösa tro*, 2nd ed. Stockholm 1936

Bohlin, T., *Den korsfäste skaparen. Förhållandet skapelse-frälsning i Luthers teologi mot bakgrund av skolastiskt tänkande*, Stockholm 1952

Boman, T., *Das hebräische Denken im Vergleich mit dem Griechischen*, 2nd ed. Göttingen 1954 (ET *Hebrew thought compared with Greek*, London 1960)

Bonnefoy, J.-F., 'La théologie comme science et l'explication de la foi selon saint Thomas d'Aquin', in *Ephemerides theologicae lovanienses* 14 (1937), p. 421–446; and 15 (1938), p. 491–516

Bouillard, H., *Conversion et grâce chez S. Thomas d'Aquin. Étude historique* (Théologie 1), Paris 1944

Bourassa, F., 'Les missions divines et le surnaturel chez saint Thomas d'Aquin', in *Sciences ecclésiastiques* 1 (1948), p. 41–94

Bourke, V. J., *Thomistic Bibliography 1920–1940*, St. Louis 1945

Bring, R., *Dualismen hos Luther*, Lund 1929

——, *Teologi och religion*, Lund 1937

——, 'Kristendomens gestaltvandlingar', in *Vid Åbodomens fot 1924–1949* (Lutherska litteraturstiftelsens svenska publikationer 5), Helsingfors 1949, p. 87–111

——, *Kristendomstolkningar. Studier till en månghundraårig idéhistoria*, Stockholm 1950

Broglie, G. de, 'Note sur la primauté de l'argument d'Écriture en théologie', in L. Bouyer, *Du protestantisme à l'Église*, Paris 1954, p. 247–250 (ET—'Note . . . on the Primacy of the Argument from Scripture in Theology', in L. Bouyer, *The Spirit and Forms of Protestantism*, Maryland 1961, p. 230–234)

Carré, A.-M., *Le Christ de saint Thomas d'Aquin*, Paris 1944

Cayré, F., 'Saint Augustin et l'esprit de la Somme théologique', in *L'année théologique augustinienne* 14 (1954), p. 9–21

Chambat, L., *Présence et union. Les missions des personnes de la Sainte Trinité selon saint Thomas d'Aquin*, Abbaye S. Wandrille 1943

Chenu, M.-D., 'La théologie comme science au XIIIe siècle', in *Archives d'histoire doctrinale et littéraire du moyen âge* 2 (1927), p. 31–71

——, 'Évangélisme et théologie au XIIIe siècle', in *Mélanges offerts au R. P. Ferdinand Cavallera*, Toulouse 1948, p. 339–346

——, *Introduction á l'étude de saint Thomas d'Aquin* (Université de Montréal, Publications de l'institut d'études médiévales 11) Montreal—Paris 1950 (ET *Toward Understanding Saint Thomas*, Chicago 1964

——, 'Vocabulaire biblique et vocabulaire théologique', in *Nouvelle revue théologique* 74 (1952), p. 1029–1041

Chossat, M., 'Dieu (sa nature selon les scolastiques)', in *Dictionnaire de théologie catholique* 4:1, Paris 1911, col. 1152–1243

Codex iuris canonici Pii X Pontificis Maximi iussu digestus Benedicti Papae XV auctoritate promulgatus. Praefatione Emi Petri Card. Gasparri et indice analytico-alphabetico auctus, Rome 1951

Congar, Y. M.-J., review of works by J.-F. Bonnefoy and M. R. Gagnebet in *Bulletin thomiste* 5 (1938), p. 490–505

——, 'L'idée de l'Église chez saint Thomas d'Aquin', in *Revue des sciences philosophiques et théologiques* 29 (1940), p. 31–58

——, 'Theologie', in *Dictionnaire de théologie catholique* 15:1, Paris 1946, col. 341–502

——, Letter of Introduction in G. F. van Ackeren, *Sacra doctrina*, Rome 1952, p. 13–18

——, *Le Christ, Marie et L'Église*, Paris 1952 (ET *Christ, Our Lady and the Church*, London, New York and Toronto 1957)

——, 'Le mystère du temple de Dieu et l'économie de sa présence dans le monde', in *L'année théologique augustinienne* 13 (1953), p. 1–12

Cullmann, O., *Christus und die Zeit. Die urchristliche Zeit- und Geschichtsauffassung*, Zollikon—Zürich 1946 (ET *Christ and Time. The Primitive Christian Conception of Time and History*, London 1951 and Philadelphia 1950)

Deferrari, R. J., and Barry, M. I., *A Lexicon of St. Thomas Aquinas*, Baltimore 1948–49

Deneffe, A., *Der Traditionsbegriff* (Münsterische Beiträge zur Theologie 18), Münster in Westfalen 1931

Denifle, H., *Die Entstehung der Universitäten des Mittelalters bis 1400*, vol. I, Berlin 1885

——, 'Die Handschriften der Bibel-Correctorien des 13. Jahrhunderts', in *Archiv für Literatur- und Kirchengeschichte des Mittelalters* 4 (1888), p. 263–311, 471–601

——, 'Quel livre servait de base à l'enseignement des maîtres en théologie dans l'université de Paris?', in *Revue thomiste* 2 (1894), p. 149–161

Diekamp, F., *Katholische Dogmatik nach den Grundsätzen des heiligen Thomas*, vol. I, 10th and 11th eds., Münster in Westfalen 1949

Diekamp, F., and Jüssen, K., *Katholische Dogmatik nach den Grundsätzen des heiligen Thomas*, vols. II and III, 10th ed., Münster in Westfalen 1952–54

Dondaine, H.-F., see: Thomas Aquinas

Dorner, J. A., *Entwicklungsgeschichte der Lehre von der Person Christi von den ältesten Zeiten bis auf die Neueste*, vol. II, 1st and 2nd edition, Berlin 1853 (ET *History of the Development of the Doctrine of the Person of Christ*, Division Second, vol. I, Edinburgh 1865, vol. II, Edinburgh 1862)

Dubarle, A.-M., 'La signification du nom JHWH', in *Revue des sciences philosophiques et théologiques* 35 (1951), p. 3–21

Elert, W., 'Fragen um Chalkedon', in *Evangelisch-Lutherische Kirchenzeitung* 6 (1952), p. 231–234.

Felder, H., *Geschichte der wissenschaftlichen Studien im Franziskaner-orden bis um die Mitte des 13. Jahrhunderts*, Freiburg im Breisgau 1904

Festugière, A. M., 'La notion du péché présentée par St. Thomas, I, II, 71 et sa relation avec la morale aristotélicienne', in *The New Scholasticism* 5 (1931), p. 332–341

Finance, J. de, *Être et agir dans la philosophie de saint Thomas*, Paris 1943

——, 'La finalité de l'être et le sens de l'univers. Réflexions sur le principe "omne agens agit propter finem" ', in *Mélanges Joseph Maréchal*, vol. II (Museum lessianum, Section philosophique 32), Brussels and Paris 1950, p. 141–158

Forest, A., *La structure métaphysique du concret selon saint Thomas d'Aquin* (Études de philosophie médiévale 14), Paris 1931

Gagnebet, M. R., 'La nature de la théologie spéculative', in *Revue thomiste* 46 (1938), p. 1–39, 213–255, 645–674

Galtier, P., *L'habitation en nous des trois personnes. Le fait—la mode*, Paris 1928

Gardeil, A., *La structure de l'âme et l'expérience mystique*, vols. I and II, 2nd ed. Paris 1927

——, *Le donné révélé et la théologie*, 2nd ed. Juvisy 1932

Garrigou-Lagrange, R., *De revelatione per Ecclesiam catholicam proposita*, vols. I and II, 3rd ed. Rome 1929–31

——, 'Thomisme', in *Dictionnaire de théologie catholique* 15:1, Paris 1946, col. 823–1023

——, *De gratia. Commentarius in Summam theologicam S. Thomae I^{ae} II^{ae} q. 109–114*, Turin 1947 (ET *Grace. Commentary on the Summa Theologica of St. Thomas, I^{ae} II^{ae} q. 109–114*, St. Louis and London 1952)

——, *Dieu. Son existence et sa nature. Solution thomiste des antinomies agnostiques*, 4th ed. Paris 1923 (ET *God: His Existence and His Nature. A Thomistic Solution of Certain Agnostic Antinomies* (translated from the fifth French ed.), vols. I and II, St. Louis and London 1955)

Geenen, G., 'L'usage des "auctoritates" dans la doctrine du baptême chez S. Thomas d'Aquin', in *Ephemerides theologicae lovanienses* 15 (1938), p. 279–329

Geiger, L.-B., *La participation dans la philosophie de S. Thomas d'Aquin* (Bibliothèque thomiste 23), Paris 1942

——, *Le problème de l'amour chez saint Thomas d'Aquin* (Conférence Albert-le-Grand 1952), Montreal and Paris 1952

Ghellinck, J. de, 'Patristique et argument de tradition au bas moyen âge', in *Aus der Geisteswelt des Mittelalters* (Beiträge zur Geschichte der Philosophie des Mittelalters, Suppl. III:1), Münster in Westfalen 1935, p. 403–426

——, ' "Pagina" et "Sacra Pagina". Histoire d'un mot et transformation de l'objet primitivement désigné', in *Mélanges Auguste Pelzer* (Université de Louvain. Recueil de travaux d'histoire et de philologie, Sér. 3:26), Louvain 1947, p. 23–59

Gilson, E., *Le thomisme. Introduction au système de saint Thomas d'Aquin* (Études de philosophie médiévale 1), 2nd ed. Paris 1922

——, *The Philosophy of St. Thomas Aquinas* (authorised translation from the third revised and enlarged edition of *Le thomisme*), 2nd revised and enlarged ed. Cambridge and St Louis 1929

——, *Reason and Revelation in the Middle Ages*, New York 1938

——, *God and Philosophy*, New Haven 1941

——, 'Le christianisme et la tradition philosophique', in *Revue des sciences philosophiques et théologiques* 30 (1941–42), p. 249–66

——, *The Christian philosophy of St. Thomas Aquinas*, New York 1956

——, *Le thomisme. Introduction à la philosophie de saint Thomas d'Aquin* (Études de philosophie médiévale 1), 5th ed. Paris 1948

——, *L'esprit de la philosophie médiévale* (Études de philosophie médiévale 33), 2nd ed. Paris 1948 (ET *The Spirit of Mediaeval Philosophy* (Gifford Lectures 1931–1932), New York and London 1936)

——, *L'être et l'essence*, Paris 1948

——, *Being and Some Philosophers*, Toronto 1949

——, review of M.-D. Chenu, *Introduction à l'étude de saint Thomas d'Aquin*, Montreal and Paris 1950, in *Bulletin thomiste* 8 (1951), p. 5–10

Grabmann, M., *Die Lehre des heiligen Thomas von Aquin von der Kirche als Gotteswerk. Ihre Stellung im thomistischen System und in der Geschichte der mittelalterlichen Theologie*, Regensburg 1903

——, *Die Geschichte der scholastischen Methode*, vol. II, *Die scholastische Methode im 12. und beginnenden 13. Jahrhundert,* Freiburg im Breisgau 1911

——, *Die Idee des Lebens in der Theologie des hl. Thomas von Aquin,* Paderborn 1922

——, *Die Geschichte der katholischen Theologie seit dem Ausgang der Väterzeit,* Freiburg im Breisgau 1933

——, *Die theologische Erkenntnis- und Einleitungslehre des hl. Thomas von Aquin auf Grund seiner Schrift 'In Boethium de Trinitate'. Im Zusammenhang der Scholastik des 13. und beginnenden 14. Jahrhunderts dargestellt* (Thomistische Studien 4), Freiburg in der Schweiz 1948

——, *Die Werke des hl. Thomas von Aquin,* 3rd ed. Münster 1949

——, *Thomas Aquinas: his Personality and Thought,* New York 1928

Gredt, J., *Die aristotelisch-thomistische Philosophie,* vols. I and II Freiburg im Breisgau 1935

Grundmann, H., *Religiöse Bewegungen im Mittelalter* (Historische Studien 267), Berlin 1935

Guitton, J., *Le temps et l'éternite chez Plotin et saint Augustin,* Paris 1933

Hägglund, B., *Theologie und Philosophie bei Luther und in der occamistischen Tradition* (Lunds universitets årsskrift. N.F. Avd. 1. Bd 51. Nr 4), Lund 1955

——, *Teologins historia. En dogmhistorisk översikt,* Lund 1956

Harnack, A., *Lehrbuch der Dogmengeschichte,* vol. III, 4th ed. Tübingen 1910 (ET *History of Dogma,* New York 1958)

Hayen, A., *Saint Thomas d'Aquin et la vie de l'Église* (Essais philosophiques 6), Louvain and Paris 1952

Henle, R. J., *Saint Thomas and Platonism. A Study of the* Plato *and* Platonici *Texts in the Writings of Saint Thomas,* The Hague 1956

Héris, Ch.-V., see: Thomas Aquinas

Hessen, J., *Platonismus und Prophetismus. Die antike und biblische Geisteswelt in strukturvergleichender Betrachtung,* Munich 1939

——, *Thomas von Aquin und wir,* Munich 1955

Horváth, A. M., 'Das Subjekt der Wissenschaft', in *Divus Thomas* 24 (1946), p. 29–44

——, 'Das Subjekt der Summa Theologica', in *Divus Thomas* 24 (1946), p. 288–310

——, *Studien zum Gottesbegriff* (Thomistische Studien 6), Freiburg in der Schweiz 1954

Hugon, E., *La causalité instrumentale en théologie*, Paris 1907
——, *Le mystère de l'Incarnation*, 9th ed. Paris 1946
Hultgren, G., 'Begreppet "kristen filosofi" ', in *Svensk teologisk kvartalskrift* 13 (1937), p. 33–60

Johannesson, L., *Kunskap och verklighet. En studie i realistisk filosofi med särskild hänsyn till thomismens tolkning av realitets-problemet*, Stockholm 1944
Johannesson, R., *Person och gemenskap enligt romersk-katolsk och luthersk grundåskådning*, Stockholm 1947

Krebs, E., *Theologie und Wissenschaft nach der Lehre der Hoch-scholastik* (Beiträge zur Geschichte der Philosophie des Mittel-alters 11:3–4), Münster in Westfalen 1912
Krempel, A., *La doctrine de la relation chez saint Thomas. Exposé historique et systématique*, Paris 1952
Kropatschek, F., *Das Schriftprinzip der lutherischen Kirche*, vol. I, *Die Vorgeschichte. Das Erbe des Mittelalters*, Leipzig 1904
Kusch, H., 'Der Titel Gottes "Dominus" bei Augustinus und Thomas von Aquino', in *Festschrift Franz Dornseiff*, Leipzig 1953, p. 184–200

Lafont, G., *Structures et méthode dans la Somme théologique de saint Thomas d'Aquin* (Textes et études théologiques 12), Bruges 1961
Lais, H., *Die Gnadenlehre des heiligen Thomas in der Summa contra Gentiles und der Kommentar des Franziskus Sylvestris von Ferrara* (Münchener theologische Studien, Syst. Abt., Band 3), Munich 1951
Lang, A., *Die Loci theologici des Melchior Cano und die Methode des dogmatischen Beweises. Ein Beitrag zur theologischen Methodo-logie und ihrer Geschichte* (Münchener Studien zur historischen Theologie 6), Munich 1925
Legrand, J., *L'univers et l'homme dans la philosophie de saint Thomas*, vols. I and II (Museum lessianum, Section philosophique 27–28), Brussels and Paris 1946
Lemonnyer, A., 'Les apôtres comme docteurs de la foi d'après saint Thomas', in *Mélanges thomistes* (Bibliothèque thomiste 3), Paris 1934, p. 153–173
Lindroth, Hj., *Katolsk och evangelisk kristendomssyn. En typologisk*

studie (Uppsala universitets arsskrift 1933, Teol. 4), Uppsala 1933

Lubac, H. de, *Surnaturel. Études historiques* (Théologie 8), Paris 1946

——, 'Sur un vieux distique: la doctrine du "quadruple sens" ', in *Mélanges offerts au R. P. Ferdinand Cavallera*, Toulouse 1948, p. 347–366

——, *Catholicisme, les aspects sociaux du dogme*, 5th ed. Paris 1952 (ET *Catholicism: A Study of Dogma in Relation to the Corporate Destiny of Mankind*, New York 1958 and London 1950)

Lyttkens, H., *The Analogy between God and the World. An Investigation of its Background and Interpretation of its Use by Thomas of Aquino*, Uppsala 1952

Mandonnet, P., *Des écrits authentiques de saint Thomas d'Aquin*, 2nd ed. Fribourg 1910

——, 'Chronologie des questions disputées de saint Thomas d'Aquin', in *Revue thomiste* 23 (1918), p. 266–287, 341–371

——, 'Chronologie des écrits scripturaires de saint Thomas d'Aquin', in *Revue thomiste* 33 (1928), p. 27–45, 116–155, 211–245; 34 (1929), p. 53–69, 132–145, 489–519

Mandonnet, P., and Destrez, J., *Bibliographie thomiste* (Bibliothèque thomiste 1), Kain 1921

Manser, G. M., *Das Wesen des Thomismus* (Thomistische Studien 5), 3rd ed. Freiburg in der Schweiz 1949

Manteau-Bonamy, H.-M., *Maternité divine et Incarnation. Étude historique et doctrinale de saint Thomas à nos jours* (Bibliothèque thomiste 27), Paris 1949

Maritain, J., *Approaches to God*, New York 1954

Mascall, E. L., *He Who Is. A Study in Traditional Theism*, London, New York and Toronto 1943

——, *Christ, the Christian and the Church. A Study of the Incarnation and its Consequences*, London, New York and Toronto 1946

——, *Existence and Analogy. A Sequel to 'He Who Is'*, London, New York and Toronto 1949

Mersch, E., 'L'objet de la théologie et le "Christus totus" ', in *Recherches de science religieuse* 26 (1936), p. 129–157

——, *Morale et Corps Mystique*, vols. I and II (Museum lessianum, Section théologique 34, 37), 3rd ed. Brussels and Paris 1949

——, *La théologie du Corps Mystique*, vols. I and II (Museum

Lessianum, Section théologique 38–39) 2nd ed. Brussels and Paris 1946 (ET *The Theology of the Mystical Body*, St. Louis and London 1951)

Meyer, H., 'Thomas von Aquin als Interpret der aristotelischen Gotteslehre', in *Aus der Geisteswelt des Mittelalters* (Beiträge zur Geschichte der Philosophie des Mittelalters, Suppl. III:1), Münster in Westfalen 1935, p. 682–687

——, *Thomas von Aquin. Sein System und seine geistesgeschichtliche Stellung*, Bonn 1938

Michel, A., 'Hypostase', in *Dictionnaire de théologie catholique* 7:1, Paris 1922, col. 369–437

——, 'Incarnation', in *Dictionnaire de théologie catholique* 7:2, Paris 1923, col. 1445–1539

Morency, R., 'L'union du juste à Dieu par voie de connaissance et d'amour', in *Sciences ecclésiastiques* 2 (1949), p. 27–79

——, *L'union de grâce selon saint Thomas* (Studia collegii maximi immaculatae conceptionis 8), Montreal 1950

Mulard, R., see: Thomas Aquinas

Nicolas, M.-J., 'Bonum diffusivum sui', in *Revue thomiste* 63 (1955), p. 363–376

Nygren, A., *Filosofi och motivforskning*, Stockholm 1940

——, 'Uppenbarelsen och Skriften', in *En bok om bibeln*, Lund 1947, p. 85–95

——, *Den kristna kärlekstanken genom tiderna, Eros och agape*, vols. I and II, 3rd and 2nd eds. respectively, Stockholm 1947 (ET *Agape and Eros*, Part I, *A Study of the Christian Idea of Love*, Part II, *The History of the Christian Idea of Love*, London 1957)

Olsson, H., *Calvin och reformationens teologi*, vol. I (Lunds universitets årsskrift N.F. Avd. 1, Bd 40. Nr 1), Lund and Leipzig 1943

Ortigues, E., 'Écritures et traditions apostoliques au concile de Trente', in *Recherches de science religieuse* 36 (1949), p. 271–299

Patterson, R. L., *The Conception of God in the Philosophy of Aquinas*, London 1933

Peghaire, J., 'L'axiome "Bonum est diffusivum sui" dans le néo-platonisme et le thomisme', in *Revue de l'université d'Ottawa*, Section spéciale (1932), p. 5*–30*

Pegis, A. C., *Saint Thomas and the Greeks* (The Aquinas Lecture 1939), 2nd ed. Milwaukee 1943

Penido, M. T.-L., *Le role de l'analogie en théologie dogmatique* (Bibliothèque thomiste 15), Paris 1931

——, 'Gloses sur la procession d'amour dans la Trinité', in *Ephemerides theologicae lovanienses* 14 (1937), p. 33–68

——, 'A propos de la procession d'amour en Dieu', in *Ephemerides theologicae lovanienses* 15 (1938), p. 338–344

Persson, P. E., 'Quelques réflexions sur l'Écriture et la tradition chez Thomas d'Aquin', in *Positions luthériennes* 5 (1957), p. 105–116

——, 'Le plan de la Somme théologique et le rapport "Ratio–Revelatio"', in *Revue philosophique de Louvain* 56 (1958), p. 545–572

Ploeg, J. van der, 'The place of Holy Scripture in the theology of St. Thomas', in *The Thomist* 10 (1947), p. 398–422

Prado, N. del, 'La vérité fondamentale de la philosophie chrétienne selon saint Thomas', in *Revue thomiste* 18 (1910), p. 209–227, 340–360

Prenter, R., *Skabelse og genløsning*, vol. II, Copenhagen 1952

——, *Thomismen*, Copenhagen 1953

——, *Spiritus Creator, Studier i Luthers theologi*, 2nd edition, Copenhagen 1946 (ET *Spiritus Creator*, Philadelphia 1953)

Quick, O. C., *The Gospel of Divine Action*, London 1933

Rahner, K., 'Probleme der Christologie von heute' in *Schriften zur Theologie*, vol. I, Einsiedeln, Zürich and Cologne 1954, p. 169–222 (ET 'Current problems in Christology', in *Theological Investigations*, vol. I, *God, Christ, Mary and Grace*, Baltimore and London 1961, p. 149–200)

Rohner, A., *Das Schöpfungsproblem bei Moses Maimonides, Albertus Magnus und Thomas von Aquin. Ein Beitrag zur Geschichte des Schöpfungsproblems im Mittelalter* (Beiträge zur Geschichte der Philosophie des Mittelalters 11:5), Münster in Westfalen 1913

Roland-Gosselin, M.-D., *Le 'De ente et essentia' de S. Thomas d'Aquin. Texte établi d'après les manuscrits parisiens*. Introduction, notes et études historiques (Bibliothèque thomiste 8), Paris 1948

Rondet, H., 'Bulletin de théologie historique', in *Recherches de science religieuse* 38 (1951), p. 138–160

Roos, H., review of R. Johannesson, *Person och gemenskap enligt*

x

310   *Bibliography*

romersk-katolsk och luthersk grundåskådning, Stockholm 1947, in *Credo* 29 (1948), p. 109–116

Rougier, L., *La scolastique et le thomisme*, Paris 1925

Schaezler, C. von, *Das Dogma von der Menschwerdung Gottes im Geiste des hl. Thomas*, Freiburg im Breisgau 1870

Scheel, O., *Martin Luther. Vom Katholizismus zur Reformation*, vol. II, Tübingen 1917

Schmaus, M., *Katholische Dogmatik*, vols. I–IV, 3rd ed. Munich 1940–1953

Schmidt, K. D., *Studien zur Geschichte des Konzils von Trient*, Tübingen 1925

Schulemann, G., *Das Kausalprincip in der Philosophie des hl. Thomas von Aquino* (Beiträge zur Geschichte der Philosophie des Mittelalters 13:5), Münster in Westfalen 1915

Schwalm, M. B., *Le Christ d'après saint Thomas d'Aquin* (Leçons, notes et commentaires, recueillis et mis en ordre par le R. P. Menne), 8th ed. Paris 1910

Seeberg, R., 'Scholastik', in *Realencyklopädie für protestantische Theologie und Kirche* 17, Leipzig 1906, p. 705–732

——, *Lehrbuch der Dogmengeschichte*, vol. III, 2nd and 3rd ed. Leipzig 1913 (ET *Text-Book of the History of Doctrines*, complete in two vols., Grand Rapids 1964)

Seppelt, F. X., 'Der Kampf der Bettelorden an der Universität Paris in der Mitte des 13. Jahrhunderts', in *Kirchengeschichtliche Abhandlungen* 3, Breslau 1905, p. 199–241

Sertillanges, A.-D., 'L'être et la connaissance dans la philosophie de S. Thomas d'Aquin', in *Mélanges thomistes* (Bibliothèque thomiste 3), Paris 1934, p. 175–197

——, *L'idée de création et ses retentissements en philosophie*, Paris 1945

——, see also: Thomas Aquinas

Skydsgaard, K. E., *Metafysik og Tro. En dogmatisk Studie i nyere Thomisme*, Copenhagen 1937

——, 'La connaissance humaine d'après saint Thomas d'Aquin', in *Classica et mediaevalia* 2 (1939), p. 86–120

——, 'Idealisme og Realisme i Thomismens Gudserkendelse', in *Festskrift til Jens Nørregaard 1947*, Copenhagen 1947, p. 272–290

——, 'Schrift und Tradition. Bemerkungen zum Traditionsproblem in der neueren Theologie', in *Kerygma und Dogma* vol. I (1955), p. 161–179

——, 'Nythomisme', in *Nordisk teologisk uppslagsbok*, vol. II, Lund 1955, col. 1291–1294
——, 'La signification luthérienne du Credo', in *Positions luthériennes* 4 (1956), p. 10–29
Smalley, B., *The Study of the Bible in the Middle Ages*, Oxford 1941
Söderblom, N., *Naturlig teologi och religionshistoria. En historik och ett program*, Stockholm 1914
Söhngen, G., *Die Einheit in der Theologie*, Munich 1952
Spicq, C., *Esquisse d'une histoire de l'exégèse latine au moyen âge* (Bibliothèque thomiste 26), Paris 1944
——, 'Saint Thomas d'Aquin exégète', in *Dictionnaire de théologie catholique* 15:1, Paris 1946, col. 694–738
Steinbüchel, T., *Der Zweckgedanke in der Philosophie des Thomas von Aquino* (Beiträge zur Geschichte der Philosophie des Mittelalters 11:1), Münster in Westfalen 1912
Synave, P., 'La doctrine de saint Thomas d'Aquin sur le sens littéral des Écritures', in *Revue biblique* 35 (1926), p. 40–65
——, 'La révélation des vérités divines naturelles d'après saint Thomas d'Aquin', in *Mélanges Mandonnet*, vol. I (Bibliothèque thomiste 13), Paris 1930, p. 327–365
——, see also: Thomas Aquinas

Thomas Aquinas, *Summa theologiae*. Latin text and English translation, Introductions, Notes, Appendices and Glossaries, ed. by Thomas Gilby and others, 60 vols., New York and London 1964—
Bernard, R., *Le péché*, vol. II, 1931
——, *La foi*, vol. I, 1941
Dondaine, H.-F., *La Trinité* vol. I, 1943; vol. II, 2nd ed. 1950
Héris, Ch.-V., *Le Verbe incarné*, vol. I, 2nd ed. 1927; vol. II, 1927; vol. III, 2nd ed. 1954
Mulard, R., *La grâce*, 2nd ed. 1948
Sertillanges, A.-D., *Dieu*, vol. I, 1925; vol. II, 3rd ed. 1926; vol. III, 2nd ed. 1935
——, *La création*, 2nd ed. 1948
——, *La béatitude*, 1936
Synave, P., *Vie de Jésus*, vol. I, 2nd ed. 1947; vol. II, 1928; vol. III, 1931; vol. IV, 1932
Synave, P., and Benoit, P., *La prophétie*, 1947
Thomas d'Aquin, *Somme théologique*, Traduction française avec notes et appendices, Paris, Tournai and Rome 1925—

Thomas von Aquin, *Vollständige, ungekürtze deutsch-lateinische Ausgabe der Summa Theologica* (Die deutsche Thomas-Ausgabe), Salzburg 1933—
I. Gottes Dasein und Wesen, 1933
II. Gottes Leben. Sein Erkennen und Wollen, 1934
Tresmontant, C., *Essai sur la pensée hébraïque* (Lectio divina 12), Paris 1953 (ET *Study of Hebrew thought*, Paris 1960)
Tschipke, T., *Die Menschheit Christi als Heilsorgan der Gottheit. Unter besonderer Berücksichtigung der Lehre des heiligen Thomas von Aquin*, Freiburg im Breisgau 1940

Vanier, P., 'La relation trinitaire dans la Somme théologique de saint Thomas d'Aquin', in *Sciences ecclésiastiques* 1 (1948), p. 143–159
——, *Théologie trinitaire chez saint Thomas d'Aquin. Évolution du concept d'action notionelle* (Université de Montréal. Publications de l'institut d'études médiévales 13), Montreal and Paris 1953
Villard, A., *L'Incarnation d'après saint Thomas d'Aquin*, Paris 1908
Vogelsang, E., *Der angefochtene Christus bei Luther* (Arbeiten zur Kirchengeschichte 21), Berlin and Leipzig 1932
Vooght, P. de, *Les sources de la doctrine chrétienne d'après les théologiens du XIVᵉ siècle et du début du XVᵉ avec le texte integral des XII premières questions de la Summa inédite de Gérard de Bologne*, Paris 1954
Vugts, A., *La grâce d'union d'après S. Thomas d'Aquin*, Tilburg 1946

Walz, P. A., 'De genuino titulo "Summa theologiae" ', in *Angelicum* 18 (1941), p. 142–151
——, 'Écrits de saint Thomas', in *Dictionnaire de théologie catholique* 15:1, Paris 1946, col. 635–641
White, V., 'Le concept de la révélation chez saint Thomas', in *L'année théologique* 11 (1950), p. 1–17, 109–132
Wingren, G., 'Från Platon till Luther', review of R. Johannesson, *Person och gemenskap enligt romersk-katolsk och luthersk åskådning*, Stockholm 1947, in *Svensk teologisk kvartalskrift* 24 (1948), p. 44–58
Wyser, P., *Theologie als Wissenschaft*, Salzburg 1938
——, *Thomas von Aquin* (Bibliographische Einführungen in das Studium der Philosophie 13/14), Bern 1950
——, *Der Thomismus* (Bibliographische Einführungen in das Studium der Philosophie 15/16), Bern 1951

3. ENGLISH TRANSLATIONS OF WORKS CITED

Summa theologiae, Latin text and English translation, Introductions, Notes, Appendices and Glossaries, ed. Thomas Gilby et al., 60 vols., London and New York 1964—

Summa contra gentiles, ET *On the Truth of the Catholic Faith,* with and Introduction and Notes, by Anton C. Pegis et al., 5 vols., New York 1955–56

De veritate, ET *Truth,* by Robert W. Mulligan et al., 3 vols., Chicago 1952–54

Expositio super librum Boethii de Trinitate, ET of q. 1, *On Searching into God,* by V. White, Oxford 1947; qq. 5–6, *Division and Method of the Sciences,* by A. Maurer, Toronto 1953

Compendium theologiae ad fratrem Reginaldum socium suum carissimum, ET *Compendium of Theology,* by Cyril Vollert, St. Louis and London 1952

In symbolum Apostolorum expositio, ET in *The Three Greatest Prayers: Commentaries on the Our Father, the Hail Mary and the Apostles' Creed,* by Lawrence Shapcote et al., with Introduction by Thomas Gilby, Westminster, Maryland 1956

No translations into English of the other works by Thomas which are cited in this book are available, so far as is known. The translations of frequently recurring terms or of citations from Thomas which are provided in the text have been taken mainly from the English versions listed above, with occasional editing in the interest of consistency. Where no translation exists, an attempt has been made by the translator to provide one. Since the new translation of the *Summa theologiae* is at present incomplete, the older and somewhat wooden Dominican version, *The 'Summa Theologica' of St. Thomas Aquinas,* literally translated by the Fathers of the English Dominican Province (or rather, by Lawrence Shapcote), 2nd and revised ed., London and New York 1921(?)–32, has been used with discretion, but the new translation is to be preferred as further volumes become available.

INDEX

315